French Communism
in the Era of Stalin

Recent titles in Contributions in Political Science
Series Editor: Bernard K. Johnpoll

The Vice President as Policy Maker: Rockefeller in the Ford White House
Michael Turner

A Contemporary Crisis: Political Hostage-Taking and the Experience of
Western Europe
Clive C. Aston

Socialism of a Different Kind: Reshaping the Left in France
Bernard E. Brown

Aging and Public Policy: The Politics of Growing Old in America
Edited by William P. Browne and Laura Katz Olson

Influence, Change, and the Legislative Process
Janet Miller Grenzke

Coherent Variety: The Idea of Diversity in British and American Conservative Thought
Michael D. Clark

The Social and Political Thought of Michael Bakunin
Richard B. Saltman

Managing Crisis Cities: The New Black Leadership and
the Politics of Resource Allocation
Bette Woody

National Conventions in an Age of Party Reform
James W. Davis

International Dynamics of Technology
Ralph Sanders

Party Politics in Israel and the Occupied Territories
Gershon R. Kieval

The Strange Career of Marihuana: Politics and Ideology of Drug Control in America
Jerome L. Himmelstein

French Communism in the Era of Stalin

THE QUEST FOR UNITY AND INTEGRATION, 1945–1962

Irwin M. Wall

CONTRIBUTIONS IN POLITICAL SCIENCE, NUMBER 97

GP

GREENWOOD PRESS
Westport, Connecticut
London, England

Library of Congress Cataloging in Publication Data

Wall, Irwin M.
    French communism in the era of Stalin.

    (Contributions in political science, ISSN 0147-1066;
no. 97)
    Bibliography: p.
    Includes index.
    1. Communism—France—History—20th century.
2. Communism—Soviet Union—History—20th century.
3. Parti communiste français—History—20th century.
I. Title. II. Series.
HX264.W34   1983   335.43′0944   82-20970
ISBN 0-313-23662-3 (lib. bdg.)

Library of Congress Catalog Card Number: 82-20970
ISBN: 0-313-23662-3
ISSN: 0147-1066

First published in 1983

Greenwood Press
A division of Congressional Information Service, Inc.
88 Post Road West
Westport, Connecticut 06881

Printed in the United States of America

10 9 8 7 6 5 4 3 2 1

To our parents

CONTENTS

ACKNOWLEDGMENTS

Acknowledging the many persons who helped in the production of this book is one of the greatest pleasures of seeing it through to publication. Several scholars generously acceded to my requests for interviews and were helpful with research suggestions, including Domenique Desanti, Louis Bodin, Vilem Kahan, Annie Kriegel, Georges Lavau, and Branko Lazitch. Jean Elleinstein and Jean Marabini took a continuing interest in my work through its completion. Two persons in particular gave unstintingly of their time and shared freely their incomparable knowledge and personal documentary collections. I am privileged to regard David Douvette and Philippe Robrieux as my friends. Both further assisted me in arranging the invaluable interviews upon which many of my conclusions are based. I am grateful in addition to all the participants in the drama of French Stalinism who shared their memories and reflections with me; they are listed separately in the bibliography.

Thanks also go to the librarians and staffs of the Bibliothèque Nationale (in particular Paulette Perec); the Institut d'Histoire Sociale, Paris; Institut Maurice Thorez; Bibliothèque de la Fondation Nationale des Sciences Politiques; Institute for Social History, Amsterdam; Fondazioni Giangiacomo Feltrinelli, Milan (thanks there to Giuseppe Del Bo); the libraries of Columbia University; the Hoover Institution, Stanford (where Agnes Peterson and Helen Berman were particularly gracious); the University of California, Berkeley; and last but not least, the University of California, Riverside.

An equally imposing group of persons provided technical help with the manuscript. Rachela Melezin provided research assistance and translations from the Russian. John Phillips, Charles Wetherell, and the UCR Lab for Historical Research guided my brief excursion into quantification. Sarah Neiman expertly and relentlessly attacked my prose, teaching me to live in fear and admiration of her blue pencil. Pierre Aubéry, Martha Hildreth, Alice Kelikian, Jolyon Howorth, Teddy Uldricks, Armen Antonian, and J. Arch Getty read and commented upon portions of the manuscript. Connie Young and Susan Lasater typed and retyped the manuscript with infinite patience. I received financial help from the Hoover Institution, the National Endowment for the Humanities, and the Research Committee of the Academic Senate at the University of California,

Riverside. Finally, Sarah and Alexandra Wall made the ultimate sacrifice, surrendering claims on the time of husband and father to the world of scholarship.

As the informed reader will quickly discern, the interpretations presented herein, and the errors, could only have been my own.

ACRONYMS

CDL	Comité Départemental de la Liberation
CFLN	Comité Français de Liberation Nationale
CFTC	Confédération Française des Travailleurs Chrétiens
CGPF	Confédération Générale du Patronat Français
CGT	Confédération Générale du Travail
CNR	Conseil National de la Résistance
CPSU	Communist Party of the Soviet Union
CRS	Compagnies Républicaines de Securité
EDC	European Defense Community
EDF	Electricité de France
FEN	Fédération de l'Education Nationale
FFI	Forces Françaises de l'Intérieur
FGDS	Fédération de la Gauche Democrate et Socialiste
FLN	Front de Liberation Nationale
FN	Front National
FO	Force Ouvrière
FTPF	Francs-tireurs et Partisans Français
GPRF	Gouvernement Provisoire de la République Française
MRP	Mouvement Républicain Populaire
NATO	North Atlantic Treaty Organization
OAS	Organisation de l'Armée Secrète
OS	Organisation Speciale
PCA	Parti Communiste Algerien
PCF	Parti Communiste Français
PCI	Parti Communiste Italien
PS	Parti Socialiste
PTT	Poste, Télégraphe et Téléphone
RDA	Rassemblement Démocratique Africain
RPF	Rassemblement du Peuple Français
SFIO	Section Française de l'Internationale Ouvrière

SNCF   Société Nationale des Chemins-de-Fer Français
SNECMA   Société Nationale d'Etudes et de Construction de Moteurs d'Aviation
UJRF   Union de la Jeunesse Républicaine de France

French Communism
in the Era of Stalin

INTRODUCTION

Communist parties operate simultaneously within a national political context and an internationally structured movement. The international movement has traditionally preoccupied political scientists and historians. Only since the disintegration of the world Communist monolith began in 1956 have scholars begun to interpret Communist parties in terms of their national experiences.[1] Among non-ruling parties, the French Communists have received the most attention. The French left has continued to hold universal significance and importance in the eyes of international progressives. The existence, therefore, of a powerful Communist party in France, which historically has aspired to hegemony on the left, poses a problem of enduring interest. One of the two largest and most influential Communist parties in the Western world, the Parti communiste français (PCF) has been most consistently loyal to the strictures of proletarian internationalism and solicitous of the politics of the International Communist Movement. French Communist history, nevertheless, requires explanation in terms of French national traditions and experience. The vast disparities in strength among European Communist parties can only be understood in terms of the different barriers or aids to development offered by the varied cultures, traditions, and historical experiences they encountered. A greater affinity for Communism has appeared to exist, for example, in Catholic and Latin Europe than in the Teutonic and Anglo-Saxon North. Comparisons between Communist parties and the church have therefore become commonplace; the bureaucratic similarities and shared practices of the cult of saints and self-criticism come readily to mind. Yet the two largest non-ruling Communist parties in the industrialized world, the French and Italian, although both in Catholic countries, have differed strikingly from one another, pursued divergent strategies throughout much of their history, and frequently been at loggerheads. The French Communist party, even at the apogee of Stalinism, was first, foremost, and most fundamentally French.

This is not to deny the importance of the Soviet Union in PCF history. To the French Communists, the USSR was the Socialist ideal translated into historical experience. The protection of Soviet foreign-policy interests was a constant consideration in PCF attempts to influence the French government. The record of PCF achievement in French foreign affairs, however, is meager; it would not have been much different in the last sixty years if the PCF were tiny and insignificant, rather than a powerful political force. Indeed France might have been less attracted to the North Atlantic Treaty Organization (NATO) and friendlier to the USSR had it not been for the widely perceived domestic Communist threat and consequent anti-Communism that dominated the outlook of the French political elite. The PCF claimed that the German question made French and Russian interests identical in modern history irrespective of ideology, ever since the Tsarist regime had allied itself with the radical and atheist French republic in 1894. This view was valid for Frenchmen across the political spectrum. French leaders did not need the PCF to goad them into a foreign policy of détente or alliance with the USSR, and the same perception by a good part of the French electorate doubtless explains much of the PCF's support. Not only has the PCF been most thoroughly Stalinist in its nationalism, but it has always managed to defend its politics of friendship and solidarity with the USSR in terms of the national interest.

While the PCF has not been able to affect French foreign policy, its impact on internal French politics has been enormous. The PCF's cooperation enabled the Popular Front to come into existence. The Communists spearheaded the Resistance. They participated in the government from 1944 to 1947 when the major legislative infrastructure of the French welfare state was created. In 1947, however, the party was thrust into political isolation. The period from 1934 to 1947 demonstrated that the PCF could function as an integral part of the French political mainstream; the Cold War re-emphasized the party's differences. From a party of government, the PCF became a counter-society whose dominant characteristics were defined under the rubric of Stalinism. Slavish devotion to the USSR, the personality cult, purge trials, an absurd quest for socialist-realism in art, secrecy, and mass hysteria convinced non-Communists that the party could never again be integrated into French political life. The consequences were great. Deprived of their natural coalition partners, the French Socialists governed in alliance with the political right. Socialism declined. The Fourth Republic, lacking a stable consensus, collapsed in the face of a military insurrection in Algeria. France experienced a single short-lived experiment of government by the left in the next thirty-four years. The Fifth Republic, until 1981, remained a hypothetical democracy: it had never experienced an orderly transfer of political power between majority and opposition parties of the right and left. Only after the Socialist-Communist alliance had been broken, and the PCF reduced considerably in electoral support, were French voters willing in 1981 to give a majority to the Socialist candidate, François Mitterrand.

Revival of the left in France remained inhibited by the PCF's Stalinist legacy. The era of Cold War Communism, 1947–54, assumed overriding importance, beyond either the Popular Front or the Resistance, in subsequent attempts to rebuild a left-wing coalition capable of governing France. The image the PCF acquired was that of an insurrectionary monolith, disciplined, purposeful, and committed to the global strategy devised by its Soviet masters. A generation of political scientists and analysts has echoed this view. For the PCF's most eminent recent historian, Philippe Robrieux, Maurice Thorez, who ruled the party autocratically, was never anything more than an obedient functionary of Stalin.[2] The view offered here differs substantially from that interpretation. More victim than actor during the Cold War years, the PCF was a weak and internally divided party without a revolutionary strategy. Thorez, never more than first among equals in the Political Bureau, struggled against his colleagues and even his Soviet sponsors to implement what he perceived to be a Popular Front policy suitable to French national conditions. The internal reality of weakness and division lay hidden behind the monolithic exterior façade elaborately constructed by the rituals of Stalinism with its cult of personality and insistence on hierarchical, militarily centralized obedience.

Stalinism, as adapted to French national traditions, was a mechanism of bureaucratic control by means of which an elite drawn from working-class backgrounds tried to maintain itself in control of the labor movement. Mature Stalinism appeared designed to prevent the occurrence of specific bureaucratic developments in political parties as described by Robert Michels in his modern classic. Michels noted the tendency of Socialist parliamentarians to take precedence over party bureaucrats, the ability of middle-class bureaucrats to hold their places by a monopoly of ideological and organizational skills, and the dominance of intellectuals and Jews among working-class leadership positions. Stalinism laid down strict guidelines against these developments without, however, challenging the principle of oligarchy itself. A central place in the Stalinist lexicon was accorded to the prohibition against factionalism. Factionalism was endemic in the history of the left; it arose from internal differences over interpretation of ideology, disagreement about choices in political strategies, and the confusion of these with the personal ambitions of aspiring leaders. Factions almost always became personalized, and the history of the French left was cluttered with tendencies more or less organized in form and named for individual leaders: Broussistes, Allemanistes, Guesdistes, Trotskyistes and Pivertistes. Socialist parties institutionalized factionalism, giving organized tendencies representation on directing party committees. Communist parties drove factionalism underground, but they could not eliminate it. The hidden struggle between tendencies surfaced, in periods of crisis, as obscurely motivated sudden shifts in the party line, as one or another faction rose to dominance and implemented its policies. By common agreement, however, the myth of a monolith was presented to the outside world of "the adversary." A disciplined façade was perceived by Communist leaders as promoting an image of unity, determination and strength. Stalinist bureaucratic procedures of public humiliation through criticism and self-criticism meanwhile served to insure that sudden shifts in the line were meekly accepted by the rank and file. In the absence of public discussion or votes over divergent policy options those in disagreement saw no way to have their views one day prevail. The only choice of a PCF dissident was exit; hence in part the PCF's often noted inability to hold onto its members, and the existence of a block of ex-Communists in France whose numbers probably exceed those of the party itself.

The PCF was continually accused of trying to foment insurrection during the Cold War years, but there is no evidence it ever aspired to anything more than re-integration as part of a democratic coalition. An internal French policy of economic expansion in which the working class, the PCF and the trade union the Confédération Générale du Travail (CGT) functioned as equal partners, and a foreign policy independent of American hegemony, summed up the PCF's aspirations for France. Given the polarization and hysteria created by the Cold War, the Communists' sense of isolation in pursuit of these objectives was extreme. Constantly subject to harassment and persecution, their commitment became fanatical, zealous, foolhardy, and at times, heroic. The PCF emerged from the Stalinist era slowly, painfully, and with difficulty. Participants in the drama of Cold War Communism wrote about the period as the central experience of their lives. The psychological atmosphere in France was one of civil war if the daily reality was much less dramatic. The divisions created by the Stalinist era were lasting. Rebuilding a left-wing alliance in France began in 1962 and required years of negotiation. The legacy of mutual distrust between Communists and Socialists brought the enterprise to collapse in 1977. The PCF evolved significantly in ideology and political practice after the Stalinist era, but its commitment to its internal principles of bureaucratic organization remained a central point of contention between the party and its potential allies. Without slighting the importance of the epochal dramas of Popular Front and Resistance in the PCF past, one may still note that the Cold War years remained the decisive period of Communist history in terms of subsequent French politics. Even after the victory of the left in the presidential election of 1981, it remained to be seen whether the PCF could overcome its Stalinist legacy.

The present work, written in large part prior to the victory of the French left in the 1981 elections, may still be taken as an attempt to explain an apparent paradox consequent upon the Socialist triumph. The most Stalinist, least "Eurocommunist" of major West-European Communist parties is the one that has again had the opportunity to govern. The offer of Communist participation occurred well after the PCF had abandoned its Eurocommunist phase and, through its alleged sabotage of the 1978 elections, condemned the movement to an early death. The historic consistency of full-fledged Stalinism with Social-Democratic practice thus stands revealed: the ambition of the PCF for full integration into French political life without sacrifice of its working-class character or *ouvrierisme,* democratic-centralist principles of governance, and controversial ties to the remnant of a Russian-centered World Communist Movement, is again thrust to the center of French political life. The results of the 1981 elections, with their triptich of PCF participation, sectarianism, and decline, constitute a logical culmination of thirty-odd years of post-war Communist political practice. The outcome of the current experiment will provide rich material for future historians.

NOTES

1. Two studies of the recent history of the French left are notable for their interpretation of the PCF from an internally French political perspective: R. W. Johnson, *The Long March of the French Left* (New York, 1981) and George Ross, *Workers and Communists in France: From Popular Front to Eurocommunism* (Berkeley, Calif., 1982).

2. Philippe Robrieux, *Histoire intérieure du Parti communiste,* Vol. I, 1920–1945, Vol. II, 1945–1972, Vol. III, 1972–1981 (Paris, 1980–82). See also his *Maurice Thorez, Vie secrète et vie publique* (Paris, 1975). Robrieux's achievement is monumental, and subsequent researchers will remain permanently in his debt. The *Histoire intérieure* has limitations if one tries to read it as comprehensive party history, however. It does not always deal with critical questions of party line, nor does it examine the PCF as a functioning element of the French political system. My debt to Robrieux, as well as my strong differences with him, will be readily apparent to the reader.

1
THE HERITAGE,
1920–1945

The French Communist party was born in December 1920 at the Socialist party congress of Tours when an overwhelming majority of the delegates voted to join the Third (Communist) International. The result at Tours reflected disillusionment on the French left following the two-fold defeat in 1919 and 1920 of its traditional ideologies.[1] In November 1919 the reformist Socialist party or Section Française de l'Internationale Ouvrière (SFIO) suffered a resounding defeat at the polls. The election of a conservative and nationalist Chamber of Deputies demonstrated that the French electorate was prepared again to accept the same elites who had subjected the nation to the most devastating war in its history. The drift to the right in public opinion was matched by a radicalization of those still loyal to the left: the Socialists made a better electoral showing where their federations were more extreme in ideology. Bitter, protracted strikes occurred on May Days in 1919 and 1920, stemming from the disillusionment of trade-union elites, who expected recognition of their collaboration during the war years, and instead found themselves relegated to prewar positions of inferiority. The strikes met with determined opposition on the part of both business and government. The May 1920 strike was suppressed, and many railroad workers lost their jobs in the retribution that followed. The defeat was a severe blow to the Anarcho-syndicalist trade-union leadership, which appeared as impotent as its Jaurèssian Socialist counterpart in fulfilling post-war hopes for social and economic change.

The Socialist party underwent an internal transformation during the post-war years, membership growing from 35,793 in 1918 to 178,372 by the Congress of Tours in December 1920. Many of the new recruits were peasants, motivated by war-weariness and pacifism. The youth of the delegates at Tours and their lack of sophistication and total ignorance of Russian conditions, combined with the Russian success in the face of French reformism's failure, accounted for the ability of the French Section of the Communist International to carry off two-thirds of the SFIO's members in 1921.

The victory at Tours by supporters of the Russian revolution was conjunctural and accidental, as the leading historian of the period, Annie Kriegel, has noted. But if the reformists had instead captured a majority of delegates, a strong Communist party would have taken root in France nevertheless. Kriegel's argument that Bolshevism was "essentially" Russian in nature, and hence "grafted" onto the French social organism, is metaphysical rather than historical, and spawned a decade of misconceived debate among scholars about whether the party was really French. There was no such question in the minds of the historical actors directly involved. Bolshevism was championed in France by respected heirs of the Guesdist tradition including Marcel Cachin and L. O. Frossard. It successfully presented itself as successor to the Great Revolution and the Paris Commune. Bolshevism's debt to French sources impressed itself even on hostile critics like Léon Blum, who regarded it as a form of Blanquism. The delegates at Tours conducted their debates within the framework of a common inherited political vocabulary. Their differences reflected a basic disagreement within a common framework of discourse.[2] The new party had little in common as yet with Bolshevism. Its first tactical decision was to reject the December 1921 decision of the Communist International to impose a policy of united front with the Socialists. The French Section of the Communist International very early established a pattern of showing a greater degree of sectarianism than the Russians, a characteristic that was to reappear frequently in party history. Boris Souvarine complained in June 1922 of a complete absence of discipline in the French party, which lacked any sense of even the rudiments of Communism.[3] Souvarine was expelled in 1924 for Trotskyism. In 1923–24, according to Philippe Robrieux, the PCF remained an amalgam of French traditions. Among its leaders Louis Sellier was a Social-Democrat, Alfred Rosmer an Anarcho-syndicalist, Marcel Cachin a Guesdiste, and Albert Treint a pacifist.[4]

The centralization of the PCF's internal structure and subordination to Moscow began in 1924. Usually described as the "bolshevization" of the PCF, these processes might be more accurately labeled de-bolshevization, since they resulted in a purge of the PCF's "old Bolsheviks"—Souvarine, Loriot, Monatte, and Rosmer—and their replacement by a new generation of more pliant bureaucrats. From 1924 to 1926 the PCF underwent an initial process of reorganization that culminated in the development of a fully Stalinized party in the 1930's. The substitution of factory cells for residential sections was of limited success, however. The campaign to restructure the PCF was launched in August 1924 with an initial December target date for completion. But the deadline was postponed and then abandoned because Communist militants resisted the new system.[5] In March 1925 the party reported to the Comintern that 2500 cells had been created. By May 1926, of 3188 total cells, 1544 or 48.4 percent were functioning in factories. But industrial cells fell to 31 percent in 1927 and 25 percent in 1928. Despite repeated efforts the PCF was not able until the 1970's to organize more than 25 percent of its members in their working places.[6] Communists preferred organizing where they lived rather than where they were employed. The purpose of factory organization, moreover, became unclear once the party involved itself in trade-union work at the time of the Popular Front.

In 1925, following Josef Stalin and N.I. Bukharin's ouster of G.Y. Zinoviev and L.B. Kamenev, the PCF underwent a parallel shift to the more supple direction of Pierre Semard. At the January 1925 Congress of Clichy, two-thirds of the delegates present were young workers. But the congress still resounded with the clash of rival opinions. The PCF achieved a rough balance between the Leninist strictures of democracy and centralism. Semard's leadership, however, proved to be a short interlude. By 1927, Trotsky had been condemned and Bukharin's position seriously weakened. As Stalin embarked upon his program of collectivization and industrialization, he imposed the sectarian "class-against-class" policy upon the Comintern. The PCF resisted the new ultra-left Comintern tactics of 1927–28 as it had struggled against the turn to a united front in 1921–22. Bringing the French party to heel in the late 1920's and early 1930's was the Comintern's signal achievement. The result was the creation of a Stalinized party in France.

Stalinization involved the suppression of local initiative in party decision making, prohibition of "factionalism" in organization, and a facade of unity in governing organisms. The new organization involved the Russification of political vocabulary. The use of "cellule" for the smallest party units, and "rayon" for the next level of regional organization were both derived from the Russian. The most lasting effect of Stalinization was the proletarianization of the party leadership. The new generation of Communist leaders promoted in the late 1920's, Jacques Doriot, Henri Barbé, Pierre Celor, and Maurice Thorez, were all workers. The PCF assiduously set about insuring that the majority of its national and local candidates for office, as well as party functionaries, came from working-class backgrounds. A network of Communist schools was established, so that the party could recruit and train cadres from humble occupations. The PCF became an autonomous expression of working-class politics, an identity to which it has clung tenaciously ever since and from which a good many of its policies have derived.

It is doubtful that the PCF could accurately be described again, at any point in its history, as a "Leninist" party. Proletarianization, as practiced by the PCF, had a problematical relationship to Leninism. Leninism initially rationalized the existence of a disciplined revolutionary party made up of intellectuals and downwardly mobile persons or *déclassés* claiming to be the avante-garde of the working class. The Russian Bolsheviks spontaneously opened their ranks to politically conscious workers only during the revolutionary months of 1917. The PCF very early became a mass party led by bureaucrats recruited through a deliberate policy of selecting the most talented of the workers for special training and promotion. The PCF's historic leaders were self-taught intellectuals of humble origins of the kind described by Gramsci rather than Lenin; the PCF's bureaucrats later evolved into a "counter-society," or a virtually closed-in sub-culture.[7] It is not clear what relationship existed between the PCF's organization and its revolutionary aspirations. The French Communists borrowed their techniques from the Stalinist bureaucratic phase of the Russian experience of the 1920's, not from the revolutionary period. Stalinist bureaucratic techniques proved to be adaptable in France for specifically internal reasons. While they did nothing to help the PCF achieve revolution, they did effectively block meaningful integration of the party into French political life. The PCF's central goal has remained integration into French society while preserving the party's specific organizational characteristics and aspirations for substantive social change.

The PCF's simultaneous development of democratic centralism and proletarian-ization have long been recognized by scholars, but without recognition of the causal relationship between these characteristics. The functional relationships of the PCF's institutional habits cannot be understood by reference to Russian organizational models.[8] The development of democratic centralism was a function of the PCF's *ouvrierisme*. The need to insure that an elite drawn from the working class remained in control accounted for the practice of co-opting leaders rather than allowing their free selection. The practice of democratic centralism rapidly became the major difference between the PCF and the parent Socialist party, which continued to draw its elites from among bourgeois intellectuals, and allowed internal rivalries between different factions led by rival contenders for power.

Many of the characteristics associated with Stalinism in the PCF were a logical consequence of the party's *ouvrierisme*. The unschooled workers who came to leadership positions in the PCF looked for guidance to the USSR. The Russians obliged by providing advisers and policy directives which could be mechanically applied. By 1931 the maximum degree of obedience to Moscow was achieved with the leadership of Maurice Thorez and the influence of his Comintern mentor Eugen Fried, alias Clement. The personality cults of Stalin and Thorez later provided an additional means of shoring up the working-class elite. The cruder aspects of the cults reflected the lack of sophistication of the militants who practiced them. The vulgar Stalinism that passed for ideology in the PCF provided a pseudo-scientific justification for the elite's domination and conceptual tools easy to master and adequate to explain the world in which the party operated. The promotion of proletarian literature and socialist-realist art helped insure that workers would continue to dictate to intellectuals rather than the reverse.

What analysts have seen as ambiguity in the PCF's approach to the democratic process also stemmed from the party's *ouvrierisme* and democratic centralism. To exercise political influence the PCF had to win alliances and broaden its base of support beyond the traditional working class. When the party entered political coalitions, however, its mode of co-opting elites came into conflict with the values of the new social strata to which the party had to appeal. Democratic centralism was always under scrutiny and attack in the non-Communist press and public opinion. Given these contradictions, internal struggles invariably erupted within the party leadership, always carefully hidden to prevent non-Communist opinions and attitudes from weighing in the outcome. Indications of struggle could be gleaned from the PCF press, however, and the party oscillated back and forth in its line. The tendency to revert to sectarian "class-against-class" attitudes was always present; under normal conditions, however, Soviet interests were almost always best served by the PCF's adherence to a moderate line. While the Popular Front strategy clearly predominated after 1934, the party was always tempted back to a sectarian period of isolation during which the leadership of traditional working-class elites reasserted itself. During such periods the PCF characteristically refused to engage in the normal interchange of democratic politics and bitterly attacked the Socialists, who were the PCF's closest competitors for hegemony among its working-class base.

The classic formative periods of the PCF's alternative tactics were the "class-against-class" era, 1928–34, and the Popular Front, 1934–38. A currently fashionable interpretation of PCF history, encouraged by the party, attributes definitive importance to the 1934 shift to a Popular Front. Louis Bodin contends the real birth of the party was at the 1936 Congress of Villeurbanne.[9] While many of the PCF's dominant attitudes emerged in the Popular Front, the party remains incomprehensible without reference to the class-against-class years that preceded it. Thorez always related the two epochs, later arguing that a renewed class-against-class period was the necessary prerequisite to a revived Popular Front, and the current PCF leadership would appear, by its actions between the 1978 and 1981 elections, to endorse this view as well. The party leadership for the next thirty years was schooled during the class-against-class years. Maurice Thorez, Jacques Duclos, André Marty, François Billoux, Raymond Guyot, Etienne Fajon, Benoît Frachon, and Jeannette Vermeersch were all products of the "third period" of Comintern history, 1928–34. The Popular Front, by contrast, provided almost no new party leaders, although it gave rise to an explosion in membership.

The PCF proved recalcitrant to virtually every Soviet initiative until the leadership of the class-against-class period was finally installed. The party was slow to oppose French intervention in the Ruhr in 1923, and had no anti-colonial policy until pushed into action to protest French repression in Morocco in 1925.[10] The right-opposition, protesting the PCF's centralization in 1925, characterized the party as "20% Jaurèssism, 10% Marxism, 20% Leninism, 20% Trotskyism, and 30% Confusionism."[11] The class-against-class tactic was imposed on the PCF as part of the overall Comintern strategy in 1928.[12] When Pierre Semard, seconded by Doriot and Marcel Cachin, resisted the new tactics, which predictably cost the party heavily in the 1928 elections, militant Comintern officials allied themselves with a group in the party's youth organization who were rapidly promoted to the Political Bureau. Led by Henri Barbé and Pierre Celor, they included Thorez, Frachon, Billoux, and Guyot, all of whom were considered veterans of the anti-war struggle and proponents of the "bolshevization."[13] Thorez and Frachon were arrested in 1929, and the party was left under the control of Barbé and Celor, who became the instruments of the Comintern's policy of "Social Fascism."

Current PCF mythology claims that Barbé and Celor constituted a faction who led the party on a disastrous sectarian course until their activities were "unmasked" by Thorez in July 1931. Thorez later accused them of being police agents. During Barbé's and Celor's stewardship, party membership declined from an estimated 52,000 in 1928 to 30,000 in 1931; the real 1931 figure may have been as low as 18,000. The PCF was clearly in danger of becoming an impotent sect, and the Russians came to regret their wager on the French youth. There is no record of Maurice Thorez's opposition to such policies, however. Social Democracy, Thorez wrote, was the principal support of the bourgeoisie, which had assigned it the task of assuring the mass basis of bourgeois dictatorship.[14] Social-Democracy was more dangerous to the working-class cause than the liberal parties, an agent in the "fascisation" of the state; the party's task was "to liquidate Socialist influence over the masses." Thorez specified, moreover, that the entire Socialist party, not just its leadership, functioned as an instrument of the capitalists.

Thorez was counseled in the liquidation of the Barbé-Celor faction by Fried, who remained the Comintern agent in France until the war. Thorez's articles denouncing the Barbé-Celor leadership called for a cultural revolution in the PCF; slogans like "Pas de Mannequins" and "Les Boûches s'ouvrent," condemning silence and calling for free expression of opinions, became an ambiguous legacy for a Stalinized party. "Confessions" of factional activity were obtained in 1931 from Guyot and Billoux, and Barbé and Celor eliminated from the Political Bureau. The leaders were accused of indiscipline, sectarianism, and failure to carry out a policy of united front "at the base" with the Socialist workers. Very little punishment was administered to the group, however, perhaps because of Thorez's prior involvement with it and his belief, shared by Guyot and Billoux, that its policies had been in line with Comintern directives. The Barbé-Celor affair was also a power struggle among the PCF leadership. Thorez, backed by Duclos, Frachon, Marty, and the Russians, wrested control of the party from Barbé and Celor. As Secretary of the Political Bureau in 1931, and General Secretary after 1936, Thorez, through the cult of his personality, became the dominant figure among these men. But they enjoyed their own independent sources of power and remained on the Political Bureau like so many quasi-independent feudal barons. Frachon became the invaluable Tsar of the Communist trade unions and Duclos the master of parliamentary tactics and the confidant of the Russians. Marty became a high Comintern official and leader of the International Brigades in Spain. Billoux and Guyot, both of whom had been compromised in the Barbé-Celor affair, were allies and intimates of Thorez.

The role of Fried in the 1930's is now acknowledged by PCF writers. A cultivated East-European Jewish intellectual, he became an intimate friend and mentor to Thorez, whose ex-wife became his mistress. Maurice Thorez, Jr., revealed in the 1960's that he regarded Fried as his father, and quoted Thorez as having said that if the French knew all that Fried had done for them, they would raise a monument to him.[15] André Ferrat, who left the party in 1936, attributed to Fried the paternity of all the Communist decisions of the 1930's, from the policy of the "outstretched hand" to Catholics to the Front populaire. Duclos, on the other hand, said Fried never substituted himself for the party leadership, but offered only analysis and advice. There is no real contradiction here if one assumes Fried's advice was always taken. All Communists regarded close alignment of the PCF and the Comintern as normal in the 1930's.

The historical debate over whether the Popular Front policy in 1934 was a French or Russian initiative is a misleading one. The shift to a Popular Front was a total Comintern policy in the formulation of which the French party's experience played a critical part. Sentiment in favor of unity of action with the Socialists had continued to exist in the PCF and was openly championed by Jacques Doriot within the leadership.[16] Thorez held rigidly to the social-fascist line and refused to abandon the positions of bolshevism in order to fall back into what he termed the "social-democratic vomit." The initiative for a shift in the Comintern line, according to Soviet historians who have access to Comintern archives, came from the head of the International executive, Georgii Dimitrov, on April 7, 1934.[17] In preparation for the Seventh Comintern Congress, originally scheduled for the fall of 1934, Dimitrov called for an end to characterizations of the Socialists as "Social-Fascists," and "principal supporters of the bourgeoisie."[18] Social-Democrats, he argued, were not now the main danger, nor were all Socialist leaders traitors to the working class. On the contrary, recent events had demonstrated the need for a united front with the Socialist masses and their leadership against fascism.

The February 6, 1934, fascist riots in France, which almost resulted in an assault on the Chamber of Deputies, appear to have tipped the balance in favor of Dimitrov on the Comintern Executive. A spontaneous manifestation of unity between Socialist and Communist workers was clearly evident, moreover, in the anti-fascist demonstration of February 12 and the formation of local anti-fascist committees afterward. Doriot and Thorez were instructed to come to Moscow on April 21; Thorez responded immediately while Doriot declined. The Executive had intended a confrontation between the rival French factions.[19] On May 11, Thorez alone was received by Dimitrov, who told the French leader that the barriers to Socialist-Communist cooperation must come down and all attacks on reformist politicians cease. Thorez, however, resisted the new policy, which, although embraced by the Comintern leadership, was perhaps not yet favored by Stalin. The PCF continued bitter invective against the Socialist leaders through the first weeks of June. Further discussions in Moscow resulted in the dispatch of formal instructions to the French on June 11, in time for the new policy to be implemented at the PCF national conference at Ivry, June 23–26. Still, when Léon Blum offered the PCF a non-aggression pact on June 23, there was fear in Moscow that the French party would fail to accept. The PCF was still perceived as more sectarian than the Russians. Thorez did respond positively, however, signing a unity-of-action agreement with the French Socialists on July 27.

Doriot's exclusion from the PCF the day after Thorez announced the new policy toward the Socialists confused contemporaries but was normal Stalinist practice. The Soviets threw their support to Thorez because he had loyally applied the class-against-class policy in the face of adversity. Doriot had been undisciplined in prematurely advocating the shift to a Popular Front, and his future behavior was therefore regarded as unpredictable. Comintern suspicions were amply fulfilled when Doriot led his following at Saint-Denis on a political pilgrimage that finished on the extreme right of the political spectrum.[20]

Thorez and Fried preceded the Comintern in October by advocating the creation of a broader Popular Front including the Radicals. Soviet historians recognize the impulsion given by the French in this further shift in the Comintern line.[21] Within the Comintern Executive, Bela Kun and others still resisted the new tactics, temporarily prevailing upon Dimitrov and Manuilsky who defended Thorez and Fried. A message was conveyed to the French, through the Italian leader Palmiro Togliatti, to hold back the Popular Front initiative. Thorez and Fried went ahead anyway. The mass movement in favor of left-wing unity in France was the deciding factor.

The French Communists were now riding a wave of popular feeling sufficiently strong to convert a tactical shift into a lasting new orientation in party doctrine and strategy. Two aspects of the turn to a Popular Front proved definitive. The first was the appropriation of patriotic symbols. The PCF's "New Jacobin" image was a matter of psychological relief to party militants and a source of lasting attraction to the French masses. As party mythology tirelessly repeated thereafter, "Maurice Thorez returned to us the colors of France."[22] The second change was the adoption of a new attitude toward labor unrest and strikes. Prior to 1932 the PCF had interpreted strikes following Lenin's strictures against Economism, ignoring their wage-hour demands while seeking to use them politically. The Popular Front taught the PCF to appreciate the importance of workers' economic struggles. Communist trade unions sought to ascertain and articulate working-class grievances; the party translated them from economic into political terms.[23] The PCF assumed a functional role of mediator between the working class on the one hand and the political system on the other. By the great strikes of June 1936 the PCF actively sought to control and dissipate the movement as it participated in negotiations for an economic settlement acceptable to the workers.

The strategic turn of 1934 was a prerequisite for a successful implantation of the PCF on the local level. Communist strength, beyond the calculation of electoral totals and party membership, must be evaluated in terms of the infrastructure of power and control the party was able to construct in villages, communes, trade unions, or even housing projects of France.[24] The class-against-class strategy of the early 1930's hampered the penetration of the party; the Popular Front favored it. Party membership, as low as 20,000 in 1933, grew to 323,283 in December 1937. CGT membership grew from less than 1 to over 4 million. Thanks to the reunification of Communist unions into the parent CGT, the party was able to entrench itself solidly among the activist new recruits in the aftermath of the strike movement that greeted Léon Blum's exercise of power. In geographical terms, the PCF tended to grow in areas where it was already successfully established in the 1930's.[25] The Popular Front was more enthusiastically followed in Paris than elsewhere; the Paris region, which accounted for 28 percent of the Communist party in 1928, rose to 36 percent in 1936. By contrast, in 1945, when party membership was in the vicinity of 1 million, the Paris share had fallen to 17 percent. The Resistance and Liberation made the PCF a truly national party.

The Popular Front was also the occasion for the growing Communist subculture to internalize the values of French society at large. The PCF abandoned its quest for a specifically "proletarian" literature, and its writers joined the mainstream of French literary life. The evolution of Communist attitudes on social mores also shifted dramatically during the 1930's.[26] The PCF had advocated free love and sexual revolution; now it rejected notions of a new "proletarian sexuality." Love was properly heterosexual, the family became the bedrock of the social order, and *L'Humanité* advised female readers on fashion and coquetries while reporting the results of beauty contests. At the Congress of Villeurbanne in 1936, the PCF reversed its advocacy of abortion and opposed birth control. The PCF always considered itself feminist and consistently advocated equal pay for equal work. But it promoted few women to its directing organisms until the 1970's and was very slow to change its attitudes on such women's issues as contraception and abortion. It continued in the 1960's to regard homosexuality as a glaring example of bourgeois decadence.

Although the PCF embraced the Popular Front eagerly, it declined to participate in the Blum government of June 1936. Some historians have seen in this decision evidence of the party's struggle to preserve its "revolutionary potential."[27] The PCF did hope to differentiate itself from Blum and capitalize on whatever disillusionment the Socialists might create among the masses. But support without participation had been the usual Socialist tactic in the inter-war period, and the PCF remained conscious of the symbolic importance of the issue of nonparticipation in bourgeois governments in the history of the French left. Communist sources have claimed that Thorez actually favored participation in the Blum government but was overruled by the Political Bureau.[28] These accounts are unconfirmed; but the PCF announced it would accept an offer to enter the Chautemps government in June 1937 after Blum's fall. Thorez's stated intention in 1936 was to exercise a "ministry of the masses," by means of Popular Front committees organized throughout France. This tactic was not an attempt to create a "dual power," however, but was meant to bring pressure on the government to remain loyal to the Popular Front program. It has long been Communist dogma that parliament will do nothing in the absence of mass pressure. The PCF has always made a maximum effort to mobilize the masses by means of petitions, telegrams, letters, and delegations to elected officials, all in the hope of pressuring those in power. It was to do so again during the Liberation and in the era of the Common Program after 1972. The PCF criticized Blum for his non-intervention policy in Spain, turn toward economic conservatism, and failure to purge the French administration of "anti-Republican" elements. These criticisms were also shared by a majority of Blum's party, and were articulated at the Socialist Congress of Marseille after his fall.[29] They corresponded to the wishes of an influential group within the Radical party as well. The PCF's gains during the Popular Front stemmed from its loyalty to left-wing positions in the face of Blum's abandonment of them. With the exception of a single abstention over Spanish policy, the Communists remained loyal to Blum in the Chamber of Deputies, despite their criticisms.

The characteristic turn of the PCF policy in 1936 was not toward revolution, but the proposal to extend the Popular Front into a "Front français" encompassing all anti-fascist segments of French opinion including the right. Front populaire and Front français remained the two poles of the PCF's collaborationist modes. The former corresponded to domestic priorities when social reform appeared the paramount concern; the latter to considerations of foreign policy usually dictated by the security needs of the USSR. It was clearly the issue of Spain, superceding the Popular Front's concern with social reform, that prompted the Communist effort to create a Front français in August 1936. The Socialists reacted frigidly to the proposal, and the Communists quickly dropped it. But it remained an aspiration of PCF policy, and the party followed Blum loyally in his attempts to create a variant of a national anti-fascist coalition in 1938. The Communists similarly attempted to create a coalition with the Right, including even Gaullists, against the European Defense Community project in 1953–54. PCF policy caused a good deal of bewilderment among Socialists on that occasion as well, and observers again wondered whether the PCF was not looking to a new tactical alliance with the Gaullists on foreign policy issues when it broke with the Socialists in 1977. Front populaire and Front français remained alternative modes of PCF collaboration because the party was constrained to find different allies on domestic and foreign-policy issues.

The Popular Front brought a lasting shift in the PCF's attitude on colonial questions, integrating the party into the colonial consensus underlying French politics. It marked a permanent change in the PCF's opposition to military expenditure and defense and a cessation of anti-war activities. It marked the beginning of the PCF's "outstretched hand" policy toward Catholics, which the party has never abandoned. It gave the party an aura of legitimacy and respectability, making Maurice Thorez a national political personality of importance. But despite the PCF's participation in coalition politics, the Popular Front marked no corresponding moderation in terms of internal organization or the party's ties to the USSR. The PCF plunged deeply into the Stalinist universe, demonstrating the consonance of Stalinist internal practices and Social-Democratic policies. The PCF demanded the suppression of Trotskyists as agents of Hitler. It demonstrated complete solidarity with Stalin's show trials and purges, and lobbied actively for the Franco-Soviet alliance and a follow-up military convention. Finally, the French Communists eagerly promoted the cult of Stalin in France and aped it unashamedly in the increasing adulation that began to surround the name of Maurice Thorez. The PCF leader was given a prominent place at the Seventh Congress of the Comintern in July 1935, marking his increasingly important stature in the International Communist Movement as well as French politics. In 1937 *Fils du Peuple,* Thorez's alleged autobiography, appeared. Ghostwritten by Jean Freville with Comintern guidance, it rapidly became the major work of theoretical initiation for new party militants and was distributed in hundreds of thousands of copies.[30] Thorez was promoted by his party to the rank of original theorist, and successor of Marx, Engels, Lenin, and Stalin. Flattery and extravagant praise became the vulgar norm. Among other things, the almost completely Stalinized "party of Maurice Thorez" was born at the PCF Congress of Villeurbaine in January, 1936. Democratic centralism, loyal devotion to the USSR, the cult of Maurice Thorez, and Jacobin-nationalist rhetoric: these, and not any so-called revolutionary potential, were the hallmarks of originality in the PCF counter-society that took shape during the Popular Front.

Much of the PCF's spectacular gain in membership and electoral support during the Popular Front was lost in the 1939–41 period. Only the French government's suppression of the party after the Nazi-Soviet pact saved it from irreparable harm.[31] The PCF continued to support the French war effort until September 20, 1939, when Raymond Guyot brought word of the Comintern's changed attitude with regard to the war.[32] Owing to the suppression of *L'Humanité,* the PCF still had not publicized its position when the party was legally dissolved on September 26. Communist Deputies reorganized themselves into a Worker-Peasant Group immediately thereafter. The first overt party act in accordance with the new Comintern line was a letter to President of the Chamber Edouard Herriot on October 1 asking for the negotiation of an immediate peace. PCF deputies were repeatedly prevented thereafter from expressing their unpopular views. On November 30 their parliamentary immunity was lifted following a denunciation of the war by Florimond Bonte. On January 9, 1940, four mobilized Deputies were subjected to physical violence in the Chamber when they refused to salute French armed forces. On January 16, following a bold denunciation of the war by Etienne Fajon, Communist Deputies were legally deprived of their representative functions. On March 20 the Communist Deputies were tried for illegally reconstituting the PCF in the guise of the Worker-Peasant Group. Forty-four were sentenced to prison. The PCF machinery was smashed throughout France and thousands were arrested, providing the party with the opportunity to claim martyrdom. For Communist Deputy Fernand Grenier the "phoney war" from September 1939 to May 1940 was declared against Germany but fought against the USSR, the PCF, and the working class.[33] Charles Tillon notes that the French people had to chose only between different defeatisms in 1940, those of Edouard Daladier and Thorez.[34]

The new line bruised the sensibilities of many Communist militants who had taken the Popular Front shift as permanent and never imagined that the rhetoric of anti-fascism could be compromised. Communist historians today criticize the Comintern for forcing a pacifist line on the PCF, sacrificing its interests as a corollary to the strategic necessity of the Nazi-Soviet pact. The PCF characterized the war as the product of imperialist rivalry between the City of London and the Nazis. France had an absolute right to remain neutral. The French bourgeoisie, the Communists said, was seeking to restore the imperialist hegemony it had enjoyed in the aftermath of the signing of the Treaty of Versailles. The PCF repudiated its earlier support for the war as an error, extended its criticism to the whole of the Popular Front policy, and again accused the Socialists of stabbing the working class in the back.[35] The party claimed it was not advocating revolutionary defeatism and specifically repudiated the conversion of international into civil war, the slogan of Lenin in 1917. Communists only wanted peace. They hated Hitler and his anti-worker regime, but denied to the "men of Munich" the right to anti-Hitlerism, while fascist methods were imposed in France.

Twenty-one of a total of seventy-four Communist Deputies and Senators broke with the party after the Nazi-Soviet pact. So did a handful of intellectuals, among them the prominent Communist writer, Paul Nizan. Two defectors were especially prominent, Marcel Gitton, who as Secretary for Organization had responsibility for the party's plans for clandestine operations, and the Senator Jean Marie Clamamus. Gitton was subsequently denounced as a police agent and was executed by the party's Special Organization (OS) in September 1941. An attempt was made on the life of Clamamus after the war as well. The PCF regarded all those who defected in 1939 as traitors and marked several for physical liquidation. One of the defecting Deputies, Maurice Honel remained a secret party member acting on special assignment, presumably to infiltrate and report on the others.[36]

The trauma of the French defeat was the stimulus for the adoption of these extreme methods, the legacy of which remained with the party for a generation. The Communists did nothing, however, to contribute significantly to the fall of France. Maurice Thorez, at Comintern urging, left his army post on October 4, 1939, made his way to Brussels where he joined Duclos and Fried, and went on to Moscow, where he remained until 1944. But Thorez warned party members against following his example. Leninist principles frowned on desertion; a good Communist carried on the struggle among the masses and where circumstances placed him. There were some minor instances of sabotage in French military production in 1939, but they added up to very little and were vehemently denied by party sources.[37] Party propaganda probably harmed French army morale during the "phoney war," but the fighting spirit of the French was beyond repair anyway.

It has proved impossible for the party to deny the initiative to German occupation authorities in June 1940 to request permission for the legal publication of *L'Humanité*. The party now repudiates this action as the erroneous undertaking of some zealous Communists motivated by a deeply felt need to keep the party in liaison with the masses.[38] But similar initiatives were undertaken by Communists in other countries under German occupation, notably Norway, Denmark, and Belgium. The policy was probably ordered by Stalin through Duclos, who returned to Paris from Brussels on June 10 to see to its implementation.[39] It was fully consistent, moreover, with the line followed by the clandestine *L'Humanité*, which complained that the "war-mongering" press was permitted by the Germans while *L'Humanité*, which had advocated peace, was suppressed. *L'Humanité* also called for fraternization between Parisians and German soldiers.[40] Maurice Tréand, an assistant to Duclos, would never have approached the Germans without being directed to do so. Tréand and two other Communist emissaries were arrested by French police on June 20, just after their meeting with occupation authorities. All three were released a few days later at the request of the Germans. Tréand was ostracized by the party after the war when it became necessary to repudiate his act; he suffered in silence, receiving his reward as a loyal militant only when Thorez and Duclos brought flowers to his funeral in 1949.[41]

The controversial question of whether the PCF resisted before the German invasion of Russia on June 22, 1941, has no simple answer. Official PCF propaganda opposed the war until June 1941, but the Communists remained the only political force to oppose the Vichy regime as well. The party claimed two acts of resistance following the Battle of France. On June 6, Benoît Frachon allegedly proposed to Premier Paul Reynaud that arms be distributed to the masses for the defense of Paris. A popular appeal dated July 10 and signed by Thorez and Duclos indicted the Vichy plutocrats and proudly proclaimed that France would never be a nation of slaves. But the tract appeared much later than July 10 and opposed only the "band in power" while rejecting the subordination of France to British imperialism. The PCF categorically repudiated the call for resistance by de Gaulle. Of the German occupier, the Thorez-Duclos appeal said nothing.[42]

Individual Communists who carried out acts of resistance to the Germans before June 1941 were acting contrary to the line of the leadership. Paradoxically, by their acts of indiscipline these men saved the party's honor and had to be rewarded after the war. The result was the creation, from a Stalinist perspective, of an intolerable situation, which was only corrected with the purges of 1950–53. At least four independent centers of Communist-led resistance sprang up in opposition to the German occupation in 1940. In the Nord and Pas-de-Calais, a miner, Charles Debarge, carried out acts of sabotage against German military equipment and automobiles with Julien Hapiot and René Camphin.[43] Debarge and Hapiot did not survive the war; Camphin commited suicide under mysterious circumstances in 1954. The most prominent early resister in the Nord was Auguste Lecoeur, who played a leading role in the miners' strike from May 26 to June 10, 1941. It is not clear, however, whether that strike was primarily economic or patriotic in inspiration.[44] In Brittany, Auguste Havez established a band of resisters assisted by Robert Ballanger and Marcel Paul. A guerrilla band sprang up in the Limousin headed by the fiercely independent Georges Guingouin. Finally Charles Tillon issued calls to anti-German resistance on behalf of the party in Bordeaux.[45] All of these Resistance leaders were subsequently penalized by the party for their indiscipline. Havez, Guingouin, and Lecoeur were excluded in the 1950's and Tillon demoted. Guingouin became the center of one of the PCF's most obscure attempts at retribution in 1952. Ballanger was a victim of the purge of 1950, and Marcel Paul, a Minister after the war, was subsequently relegated to a marginal role as well.

The immediate reaction of the party leadership to these acts of indiscipline in 1940–41 remains shrouded in mystery. In the fall of 1940, the PCF created a special paramilitary arm known as the Organisation Speciale (OS). The ostensible purposes of the unit were the physical protection of party workers in the carrying out of illegal tasks such as the distribution of tracts, and collection and storage of arms. Duclos later insisted that the OS was a bonafide Resistance organization from its inception.[46] According to numerous sources, a primary aim of the OS, however, was the liquidation of "traitors." The complication stems from the party's definition of treason. Since the PCF was illegal, anyone dissenting from its line fell under suspicion as a possible source of betrayal. By this logic, those who carried out acts of resistance from 1940 to 1941, or who dissented from the party line, were possible targets for physical liquidation. The OS agents' murder of Marcel Gitton as a police spy, in September 1941, was accompanied by other such acts. The questions are which and how many.

Another well-documented case involved a young militant, Georges Deziré, executed as a Gestapo agent by OS personnel on March 17, 1942, while on a mission for the party leadership.[47] Deziré was apparently an inconvenient witness to another murder and a political suspect; Jacques Duclos admitted in 1952 that Deziré had been unjustly accused of being a police spy. Duclos rejected any leadership responsibility for Deziré's execution, however, placing the blame on unnamed zealous and undisciplined subordinates. A more notorious incident involved Gabriel Peri, a well-known Communist advocate of anti-fascism before the war in parliament and the press. Peri was a dissenter on the Nazi-Soviet pact, and authored an anti-German pamphlet in the spring of 1941. He was arrested on December 16, 1941, and shot by the Germans at Mont Valerian with a number of other PCF hostages. The party later claimed him as a martyr, but it appears that his whereabouts were given to the police at Duclos' orders.[48]

According to some knowledgeable sources, the OS had a list of Communist militants pre-selected for a similar fate. How many were actually executed remains obscure. The PCF also liquidated some Trotskyists. But local branches of the OS were also created and used for resistance work by Communist leaders dissenting from the party line. Charles Tillon's OS units in Bordeaux became the basis for the creation of the PCF's Resistance army, the Francs-tireurs-partisans (FTP) under his command. But French intelligence services attributed Tillon's OS the task of liquidating party members who had broken with the defeatist line. This might explain why Tillon was not interfered with, and instead brought directly into the PCF's clandestine troika leadership with Duclos and Frachon.[49] It has also been suggested that Frachon dissented from the PCF's pacifist line. Since he assured the only party contact with Tillon, Frachon could have covered Tillon's resistance acts on his own authority.[50] The OS units in Brittany created by Auguste Havez also carried out acts of resistance. Havez was informed of the party line and currency of the slogan "Thorez to power" in Paris; he refused to obey, observing if "Thorez took power in such conditions, it could only be as Gauleiter."[51] Guingouin created a guerrilla force in the Limousin, intercepted OS agents who were on a mission to kill him, and broke all relations with the party, only agreeing to resume contacts in late 1942.[52]

The saga of the OS is testimony to the trauma the PCF suffered as a result of the early war years. The availability of young, disciplined, and fanatical adherents who were willing to carry out the most repulsive acts for their party bears remarking, as does the will to resist shown by idealistic Communists who were unaware of the conflict between patriotic duty and the needs of the USSR. The PCF fought its own civil war in microcosm before the Germans invaded the USSR in June 1941. That act enabled the party to bind its wounds and emerge from the experience of the Resistance as the strongest party in France. But the PCF remained troubled by the necessity of rewarding those who had been right too early against the party and chastising those who had erred out of loyalty. This dilemma explains the inner conflict of the 1950's, and a good part of the mystery with which the PCF continues to surround itself to this day. Alone among French parties, the PCF is deeply concerned with its history, of which it disseminates an official version. The PCF uniquely bears the burden among French parties, therefore, of honestly evaluating its history before it can win full acceptance.

Following the German invasion of the USSR, a troika leadership directed the PCF's policies. Jacques Duclos took primary responsibility for internal organization, seconded by Auguste Lecoeur. Duclos also oversaw implementation of the party's political line and became a conduit for the famous Russian espionage network in France known as the "Red Orchestra." Charles Tillon directed the PCF's military arm, the FTP. Benoît Frachon exercised primary responsibility for the trade unions, the party's economic propaganda, and liaison with the masses.[53]

After the German invasion of Russia, the party sought to create a broad coalition of forces in opposition to the Germans under an umbrella organization known as Front National (FN). Tillon's FTP were nominally subordinate to the FN. The PCF's campaign of terror against the occupant was designed to galvanize internal resistance and create a de facto second front to relieve pressure on the Soviet Union. On July 18, 1941, a sixty-car train was derailed in the Paris region. On August 21, 1941, Communist Pierre Georges, known as Colonel Fabien, killed a German officer at metro station Barbès. From June to December 1941, Tillon's forces carried out 107 acts of sabotage, 41 bomb explosions, and 8 train derailments.[54] The Germans responded by taking hostages and shooting them en masse. The cycle of terrorism and counter-terrorism continued through 1942 at great cost to the PCF. Communist losses far outweighed damage inflicted on the Germans. But the PCF established its credentials as a candidate for leadership of the internal Resistance, attempting to monopolize control as it entered into negotiations with General Charles de Gaulle.

In 1943 the PCF downplayed its emphasis on military action in favor of trade-union organization and strikes against the Vichy regime. The shift was engineered by Frachon, who also insisted on direct appeals to the Socialists and a revival of Popular Front rhetoric as the only means of re-establishing party liaison with the working classes.[55] The PCF was also obliged to recognize the development of a non-Communist internal Resistance, with which it finally agreed to collaborate by entering the Conseil National de la Résistance (CNR) under Georges Bidault. The Communists played a waiting game between de Gaulle and General Giraud, while rallying behind the Algiers Comité Français de Liberation Nationale (CFLN), which they recognized as the provisional government of France. Party propaganda emphasized the necessity of an internal insurrection by French forces prior to any liberation of France from the outside by the allies, and the rapid development of a mass movement behind the Front National.[56] PCF contacts with the Socialists during 1943 were frequently interrupted and ultimately led nowhere; the Communists sought a wider national coalition, Front National remained dominant over Front populaire, although some tension existed between the two strategies and their advocates, Duclos and Frachon.

In October 1943 the PCF agreed to accept two cabinet-level posts in the CFLN offered by de Gaulle. Negotiations were long and arduous because of the party's insistence that it, not de Gaulle, choose the persons who were to exercise ministerial functions. The issue was not compromised until April 1944. De Gaulle personally chose Fernand Grenier as Minister of Aviation, but was forced to accept François Billoux as Minister of State after categorically rejecting Etienne Fajon. By insisting on Fajon or Billoux, two prominent defenders of the anti-war line of 1939–41, the PCF sought to win symbolic acceptance and integration into the political system. The PCF enthusiastically supported the conversion of the CFLN into a provisional government, the *Gouvernement Provisoire de la République Française* (GPRF) in March 1944, and the Communists were represented in the Consultive Assembly. They also campaigned for the bureaucratic posts of Secretaries-General in the Ministries of War, Justice, and Education, meeting with success in the latter two cases.

The PCF's major concern was to develop and control the popular Resistance organisms on the local and national levels: committees of liberation in municipalities, communes, and departments as well as the national umbrella organization, the CNR. The Communists also sought to fuse their military forces, the FTP, with the military organization of the Resistance, the Forces Françaises de l'Intérieur (FFI), in the hope that the latter would become the nucleus of the new French army. Finally the PCF supported local militias, the Milices Patriotiques, as an adjunct to all Departmental Liberation Committees (CDL) and a manpower reserve for the FTP. The party's obsessive concern with local organs of the Resistance has led to the suspicion, repeated by modern historians, that its aim was the creation of a dual power, which could have become the de facto administration of a revolutionary France given the unlikely occurrence of either a successful wartime putsch by the PCF or the export of the Soviet revolution to France by the victorious Red Army.[57] Neither of these scenarios was possible, the PCF well understood, with American troops overseeing the Liberation of France. The party did not seek to confer actual power on local Resistance committees, but rather to subordinate and discipline them to its own purposes.

Tension between the party's resisters and political leadership was evident in the final stages of the liberation of France. Duclos and the PCF regular organization were disturbed that a variety of Tillon's FTP activities, particularly "brigandage," might cast discredit on the party as a whole. Disagreements occurred over the numbers of men to be supplied by the party to the FTP, the FTP's demands that it be able to conscript Communist women for a variety of military-support tasks, and military tactics.[58] The culmination of the dispute was Tillon's call, on behalf of the FTP, for the Paris insurrection on August 10, 1944, a task that Duclos insisted more properly belonged to the party.

The legacy of the war, then, was an internal trauma for the PCF that could have proven fatal if the French bourgeoisie had not suppressed the party, and the party's eventual submersion into the Resistance, which laid the basis for a new Communist strength and popularity. The internal tensions created by the war between the leadership, compromised by its line of 1939–41, and the resisters, who became heroes by opposing that line, remained to work themselves out. A settling of accounts was delayed by the PCF's turning to another new experience, as a government party, after the war. By offering the prospect of a definitive integration into French national life, the years of government also promised to reward and strengthen a French national Communism that might have meaningfully differentiated itself from the USSR. But the experience in power ended in disillusionment, and the Cold War forced the party into a renewed sectarianism, endowing it with those characteristics that continue to define it today.

NOTES

1. The classic work here is Annie Kriegel, *Aux origines du communisme français 1914–1920* (Paris, 1964) 2 vols. See also Robert Wohl, *French Communism in the Making* (Stanford, California, 1966).

2. See Blum's speech at the Congress of Tours in Annie Kriegel, ed., *Le Congrès de Tours* (Paris, 1964), 101–36. Also Jean-Baptiste Marcellesi, *Le Congrès de Tours (Dec. 1920): Etudes sociolinguistiques* (Paris, 1971).

3. See the Archives Boris Souvarine in the Institute for Social History (Amsterdam), letter dated June 15, 1922.

4. Robrieux, *Histoire intérieure*, I, 169. Robrieux's first volume is the most detailed treatment available of the PCF in the 1920's.

5. See Jedermann (pseudonym), *La "Bolchevisation" du PCF 1923–1928* (Paris, 1971).

6. Curiously the PCF's membership drive in the 1970's was most successful at the work place, so that by 1978, 37 percent of total cells were in factories. Johnson, *The Long March of the French Left*, 178.

7. For the counter-society thesis see Annie Kriegel, *Les Communistes français* (Paris, 1968), and Ronald Tiersky, *French Communism, 1920–1972* (New York, 1974).

8. Pierre Gaborit, "Contribution a la théorie générale des partis politiques: L'exemple du PCF pendant la cinquième République." Thèse pour le doctorat en Science Politique, Université de Paris. Also Georges Lavau, *A quoi sert le Parti communiste français?* (Paris, 1981), 40–52.

9. Louis Bodin, "De Tours a Villeurbanne: Pour une lecture renouvelée de l'histoire du PCF," *Annales, Economies, Sociétés, Civilisations*, XXX, 2–3 (March-June 1975), 279–295.

10. Nicole Le Guennec, "Le PCF et la guerre du Rif," René Gallisot, "Question coloniale, question nationale," *Le Mouvement Social* 78 (January-March 1972).

11. Louis Bodin and Nicole Racine, *Le Parti communiste français entre les deux guerres* (Paris, 1972), 142–50.

12. See William Hoisington, "Class Against Class: The French Communist Party and the Comintern," *International Review of Social History,* XV (1970), Part I, 19–42.

13. On the famous "Barbé-Celor Affair" see Jacques Fauvet, *Histoire du Parti Communiste Français* (Paris, 1964), I, 92–96. J. P. Brunet, *L'Enfance du Parti communiste 1920–38* (Paris, 1972), and his article, "L'Achevement de la bolchevisation: le 'group' Barbé-Celor," *Revue d'Histoire Moderne et Contemporaine* (July-September 1969). Also Robrieux, *Histoire intérieure,* I, 349–58.

14. Maurice Thorez, *Oeuvres,* Livre deuxième, Tome deuxième, Juin 1931-Février 1932 (Paris, 1950), 199–215 and passim.

15. Maurice Thorez, Jr., in *Le Monde,* May 11–12, 1969. Cited in Brunet, *L'Enfance du PC.* See also Philippe Robrieux, *Maurice Thorez, vie secrète et vie publique* (Paris, 1975).

16. Daniel Brower, *The New Jacobins: The French Communist Party and the Popular Front* (Ithaca, N.Y., 1969).

17. B. M. Leibzon and K. K. Shirinia, *Povorot v politike Kominterna* (Moscow, 1975), 90–112. I am indebted to Rachela Melezin for the translation.

18. Dimitrov's proposals appeared as "Documents of G. M. Dimitrov for the VII Congress of the Communist International," *Voprosy Istorii KPCC,* VII (1965), 83–88. I am grateful to Villem Kahen for pointing this out. See also the article by John F. Santore, "The Comintern's United Front Initiative of May, 1934: French or Soviet Inspiration," *Canadian Journal of History,* XVI, 3 (December 1981), 405–23.

19. See Robrieux, *Histoire intérieure,* I, 454–58. Also, Branko Lazitch, "Informations fournies par Albert Vassart sur la politique du PCF entre 1934 et 1938," and the manuscript by Cilly Vassart, "Le Front populaire en France," Archives of the Hoover Institution, Stanford, California.

20. J. P. Brunet, "Reflexions sur la Scission Doriot, Fev.-Juin 1934," *Le Mouvement Social* 70 (January-March 1971), 43–63.

21. Leibzon and Shirinia, *Povorot.* . . . Also Giulio Ceretti, *A l'hombre des deux T: 40 ans avec Palmiro Togliatti et Maurice Thorez* (Paris, 1973), 159–62, and Aragon's verbal comments in the Robrieux Archive.

22. First argued by Louis Bodin in "Le PCF dans le Front populaire," *Esprit,* XXIV, 353 (October 1966), 436–39.

23. Bertrand Badie, *Stratégie de la Grève: pour une approche fonctionnaliste du PCF* (Paris, 1976).

24. For this thesis see the collection of essays put together by Jacques Girault, *Sur L'Implantation du PCF dans l'entre deux guerres* (Paris, 1977). Communist historians have offered the concept of "implantation" as a more meaningful way of understanding the PCF in relation to French society than offered by the traditional devices of electoral studies or analyses of the "counter-society." Girault and his followers fall back upon voluntarist explanations of the PCF's local successes, however, assuming there are no structural impediments to Communist expansion. If Communism fails to take hold, it is because local Communists were personally incapable of accomplishing their historic responsibilities. This unsatisfactory explanation is the necessary fruit of the ideological assumption that Communism is the natural ideology of the salaried working class, with which the peasantry and petty bourgeoisie must ally.

25. For the effects of the Popular Front on the trade-union movement the basic work

remains Antoine Prost, *La CGT a l'époque du Front populaire* (Paris, 1964). For PCF membership, Annie Kriegel "Le Parti Communiste sous la IIIᵉ République, Mouvement des effectifs et structures d'organisation," in *Le Pain et les Roses,* 175–233.

26. J. P. A. Bernard, *Le PCF et la question litteraire 1921–1939* (Grenoble, 1972). François Delpla, "Les Communistes français et la sexualité," *Le Mouvement Social,* 91 (April-June 1975).

27. For this argument see Annie Kriegel and Michelle Perrot, *Le Socialisme et le pouvoir* (Paris, 1966), and Ronald Tiersky, *French Communism.*

28. Repeated by Thorez in the latest edition of *Fils du Peuple* (Paris, 1970), and by Giulio Ceretti, *A l'hombre des deux T.*

29. Irwin Wall, "French Socialism and the Popular Front," *Journal of Contemporary History,* VI, 3 (1970), 1–20.

30. Early editions of *Fils du Peuple* contained an acronym, made up of the first letters of words in a particular passage, stating that Jean Freville was the author of the book. See Robrieux, *Maurice Thorez,* 207.

31. A. Tasca (Rossi), *Les Communistes français pendant la Drole de Guerre* (Paris, 1951). Germaine Willard, *De Munich a Vichy, la drole de guerre* (Paris, 1969).

32. The most comprehensive summary is in Stephane Courtois, *Le PCF dans la guerre* (Paris, 1980).

33. Fernand Grenier, *Journal de la Drole de Guerre* (Paris, 1969).

34. Charles Tillon, *On Chantait rouge* (Paris, 1977), 293.

35. A. Tasca (Rossi), *Les Cahiers du Bolchevisme pendant la campagne 1939–40* (Paris, 1951).

36. On Gitton's death see Courtois, 240. Also Alain Guerin, *La Résistance, chronique illustrée* (Paris, 1972), I, 328–29. Guerin had access to secret party sources for the information on Honel. The Clamamus case was recounted after the war in *La Dépêche de Paris,* November 7, 1946.

37. Tasca, *Drole de Guerre,* 207. Courtois, 102.

38. See the account in Guerin, I, 364, and the Preface to the glossy reissue by Editions Sociales of *L'Humanité clandestine* (Paris, 1975), I, 181. Also Duclos' preface to *Le Parti Communiste français dans la Résistance* (Paris, 1967), 73.

39. Auguste Lecoeur, *Le Partisan* (Paris, 1963), 142. *Le PCF et la Résistance, 1939–41* (Paris, 1968), 83–85. Tillon, *On chantait rouge.*

40. *L'Humanité clandestine,* Nos. 58, July 1, 1940; 59, July 4, 1940.

41. See Guerin, II, 188. Also Pierre Teruel-Mania, *De Lenine au panzer-communisme* (Paris, 1971), 27–30, and Robrieux, *Histoire intérieure,* 509–15. Also the article by Communist dissidents Guy Konopnicki and Michel Renard in *Le Monde,* June 28, 1980.

42. The *appel* of July 10 was an unnumbered issue of *L'Humanité*: No. 60 was dated July 7, 1940, and No. 61 was dated July 13, 1940. The issue of July 13, moreover, does not refer to the *appel,* but rather repeats the call for fraternization between Parisians and German soldiers. See *L'Humanité clandestine,* especially the commentary, 182. The text is also reprinted by Guerin, II, 190. The line "Never will a great people like ours become a nation of slaves," very often cited in party accounts, continues with the following words: "and if, despite the terror, this people, in the most varied forms, has been able to show its unwillingness to see France chained to the chariot of British imperialism, it will know how to signify also to the band presently in power, Its Will to Be Free."

43. Auguste Colpin, *L'Aurore se lève au pays noir* (Paris, 1966); Madeleine Riffaud, ed., *Les Carnets de Charles Debarge* (Paris, 1951).

44. Auguste Lecoeur, *Croix de guerre pour une grève* (Paris, 1978).

45. Guerin still claims the actions of these men on behalf of the party: II, 164, 202–10. Lecoeur insists on their opposition to the party line: *Le PCF et la Résistance 1939–41*.

46. Guerin, II, 275–88. Jacques Duclos, *Le PCF dans la Résistance*, 120–23.

47. This case was most extensively dealt with by Teruel-Mania, 31–35. An account may also be found in a French police report which found its way into the collection of the Hoover Institution, Stanford, entitled "Historique du Parti Communiste pendant le guerre 1939–1940," typescript. Lecoeur also refers to the Deziré case but claims it was not an example of a generalized procedure: *Le PCF et la Résistance*, 36. Robrieux, *Histoire intérieure* offers a full account of what can be confirmed of the PCF's liquidations, I, 542–44.

48. Teruel-Mania charges the PCF with having betrayed Peri, and his version is accepted by Courtois, 202. These accounts have been independently confirmed.

49. The allegation about Tillon appears in a short biography of him prepared in the *Renseignements Généraux*. A compilation of short biographies of all members of the Central Committee, translated into English, may be found in the U.S. National Archives, Record Group 226, entitled "Who's Who on Members of the Central Committee of the French Communist Party," Document #XL 21481. The Rumor of a "black list" of those to be executed for resisting the Nazi-Soviet pact appeared in *La Dépêche de Paris*, November 6 and 7, 1946.

50. The thesis of Frachon's differences with Duclos is developed by Courtois, 102 and *passim*.

51. On Havez see Roland Mareuil, *Les Contradictions du Parti Communiste*, (Paris, 1958). Also Lecoeur's organ, *La Nation Socialiste*, No. 4, January 1958.

52. On the Guingouin affair, Lecoeur, *Le PCF et la Résistance*, 36–38, and Chapter 7 following.

53. Courtois deals with organization during the war in detail. See also Tillon, *On chantait rouge*.

54. Courtois, 240. See also *Le PCF dans la Résistance*, and Guerin, Vols. 3 and 4.

55. Courtois, 314.

56. See Henri Michel, *Les Courants de pensée de la Résistance* (Paris, 1962), and Angelo Tasca (Rossi) *La guerre des papillons* (Paris, 1954).

57. Courtois and Michel argue that the PCF was ready and able to take power in 1944. Robrieux has endorsed this view in Volume II of the *Histoire intérieure* as well. For the counter-argument see the article by Jean Elleinstein in G. Willard et al., *De la guerre a la Liberation* (Paris, 1972), and Chapter 2 following.

58. The reports, which clearly emanated from the Vichy police, may be found in the Fondazione G. Feltrinelli, *Fonde Angelo Tasca*, Carton 160, Folder marked PCF, 1942–1944. The reality of the disputes with which they deal was confirmed by Tillon in a personal interview, May 29, 1978.

2
A PARTY OF GOVERNMENT, 1945–1947

The years in government were as important to subsequent Communist party history as the war period. France was devastated by the war. It had simultaneously to contribute to the ongoing struggle against the Germans until May 1945, rebuild a shattered economy, and launch new political institutions on a firm foundation. In contributing to these tasks, Communists had the opportunity to demonstrate that they could be pragmatic reformers, authoring legislation, administering complex ministries, and engaging in negotiation and compromise. Governmental responsiblities caused the PCF to put its internal disputes aside, and out of concern for its public image, reward and promote Communists who had disobeyed past directives. But cooperation in France's reconstruction worked to the party's advantage: membership and electoral support rose until 1947. Communist administration of crucial economic ministries permitted the party to preside over major innovations in social legislation: workers' committees in industry, the social security system, nationalizations, and new legislation governing the status of functionaries. Within the nationalized enterprises the Communist-controlled labor union, the CGT, achieved a level of power and influence from which it was only with great difficulty later dislodged.

Controversy surrounded the PCF role in the post-war period. Conservatives denounced what they saw as insidious infiltration of the state for the purpose of converting France into a version of the East-European people's democracies. Others argued that the Communists pursued a policy of loyal integration which, carried to completion, might have resulted in the creation of a pacific and authentically French Communism independent of the Russians. Ironically, each of these perceptions has its measure of truth. The Communists methodically sought to conquer as much of the bureaucratic machinery of the welfare state as possible in the hope of leading France to a more "advanced democracy." The ultimate aim was some approximation of the People's Democracies, but nobody believed this to be immediately attainable. As Communists wielded a greater measure of legitimate power in France, they found themselves obliged to moderate their goals, proclaim a French road to Socialism, and differentiate themselves from the USSR. These developments were later reversed by the Cold War.

There was no thought of a Communist attempt to seize power by violent insurrection at the moment of the Liberation.[1] In Moscow, Thorez told the Free

French delegate that "the Communists do not contemplate taking power, neither now, nor after the Liberation." In Paris, Duclos busied himself with securing Maurice Thorez's return to a party whose new influx of members were worshipping other idols.[2] Communists sought the fullest party participation in state institutions. Thorez asked that the Communist, Georges Marrane, be awarded the Prefecture of the Seine, a request that was echoed by *L'Humanité* during the Paris insurrection of August 1944. The liberation of France, the PCF said, must be the work of the French people. Departmental Committees of Liberation (in which some observers feared incipient soviets) were under the authority of the National Council of the Resistance (CNR), which took orders from the Provisional Government of General de Gaulle. Duclos recalled that "had we tried an operation of force we would have been abandoned by part of our adherents who came to us under the conditions of the struggle for liberation."[3] The party's Liberation propaganda put primary emphasis upon the need for France to restore her economy and make the maximum military effort against Germany: France must field an army of at least a million.

As a parallel theme the Communists demanded a purge in the state administration, said to be infiltrated by holdovers of the Vichy regime and "saboteurs" who worked for the trusts. A successful purge would have opened many positions which Communist cadres might aspire to fill. The darker side of the policy was the violent settling of accounts with those castigated as Vichyites and traitors, many of whom were renegades from the party's own ranks.[4] The demand for a purge was not part of an insurrectionary strategy, however. By mobilizing popular energies behind preparation of the "Estates General of the French Renaissance," which convened without effect in July 1945, the PCF meant to help the government's war policy and national reconstruction. Duclos was clear: "There is not, there cannot be, any duality [of power] between the Resistance and the Government, which bears exclusively the responsibility of power before the nation, while the organisms of the Resistance have the duty of mobilizing the popular masses in order to support the Government in its effort to apply its program of war and national renaissance."[5] France of 1944 was not Russia of 1917. The battle for productivity was the incarnation of the class struggle.

Stalin's policy was the same in 1944–47 as in 1939–41, but with the Americans in the role of the Germans. To quote Tillon, "no trouble in France."[6] The party accepted the dissolution of the patriotic militias, ordered in October 1944, after some angry protest. On the same day de Gaulle amnestied Thorez from the charge of desertion. De Gaulle, according to one account, sat in shocked silence a month later in Moscow, while Stalin cynically asked him whether he now intended to have Thorez shot.[7] The elimination of the militias, Duclos editorialized, deprived the trusts of any pretext for creating their own paramilitary forces and engaging in provocations against the working class.[8] Thorez was summing up the policy long in effect, not proclaiming a new one, when he made his dramatic plea at the January 21, 1945, meeting of the Central Committee for a single state, army and police.[9] Reports in French newspapers alluded to supposed internal resistance to such "opportunist" Communist policies from within the party. The rumors could have been responsible for Stalin's reported remark to de Gaulle's ambassador, General Catroux, in June 1945 that the French government should take strong measures against all internal obstructionists including, if necessary, those in the PCF. He, Stalin, would not interfere.[10]

The line of cleavage in the PCF in 1944–45 between its military and civilian branches continued to trouble the party. Communists who had resisted the Germans prior to 1941 fell under suspicion from comrades who had followed the Moscow line. The problem was aggravated because the party was constrained to claim all insurgent acts carried out before June 1941 as its own and promote and glorify their authors. Those who had been deported were also suspect; all were fully interrogated about their experiences in the camps and told to name collaborators and write personal memoirs. PCF militants were screened for their possible deviation from the party line in "moments dangereux," presumably August 1939. Communists must break with clandestine habits since the PCF was now "un grand parti légal."[11] Former maquis leaders deeply resented the regular party bureaucrats pushing the line of legality. Resistance leaders were the heroes of the new influx of PCF members, many of whom aspired to a model of insurrection based on the Yugoslav experience.[12] These issues were to surface in the purge of 1950.

There was no overt factional struggle in the PCF during the Liberation period. The Resistance leaders, however, were a clearly definable cohort, most of whom had become accustomed to making their own decisions during the party's forced wartime decentralization. They now had difficulty adjusting to reimposed discipline. Tillon contrasts the *Esprit FTP* with *Esprit du Parti*. Lecoeur talks of Communist Frenchmen as opposed to French Communists. For Tillon the *Esprit FTP* expressed itself in a generalized desire to merge with the national insurrection of all Frenchmen against the Germans and identify with the patriotic aspiration for democracy and social change. These two goals, for the party's wartime activists, summed up the Resistance.[13] The PCF's participation in power partially satisfied these aspirations. But FTP leaders looked to new popular organs of the Resistance as constituent elements of the new French social order, thus coming into conflict with the party line, which supported established institutions. The aspiration to merge with a broader national movement was widespread in Communist parties throughout the world after the war and became a cause for concern throughout the International Communist Movement. It precipitated Duclos' famous onslaught against "Browderism," the heresy named for Earl Browder's dissolution of the American party into a "Communist Political Association." Duclos' attack on Browder in April 1945 was meant as much for French Communist Resistance leaders as for the Americans.

Other differences existed among the party's historic figures on the Political Bureau and the Central Committee, reflecting the separation between Communists who spent the war years in Algiers (Marty, Billoux, Guyot, and Fajon), those resident in Moscow (Thorez, Vermeersch, and Ramette), and the Paris-based leadership of Duclos, Frachon, and Lecoeur. Maurice Agulhon attributes to the Algiers group a greater "pessimism" about the party's prospects from a policy of participation in government. Domenique Desanti more bluntly insisted they were advocates of a sectarian line, "class against class always." Tillon observed the party leadership restored to authority "the former 'class against class' cadres who had been controlled before the war by the Communist International." Among these he names Billoux, Guyot, Ramette, and Léon Mauvais.[14] Billoux and Guyot were sectarian stalwarts of the Barbé-Celor group in 1929–31, Marty was never comfortable outside the confines of the Communist counter-society, and Fajon was close to Marty.[15] In contrast, Duclos and Frachon were pragmatic and at ease dealing with the French establishment, and frequently advocated the more subtle, opportunist policies. Thorez, torn between the pragmatic statesman and the sectarian revolutionary, was the arbiter between these perspectives, but constantly drawn toward the left by Jeannette Vermeersch. In Laurent Casanova's observation, "The basis of Thorez's character was opportunism. He was, however, on guard against that, and this pushed him into taking more dogmatic positions in order to hide it because he was ashamed—basically he was more *Guesdiste* and oriented toward parliamentarism and the role of the statesman."[16]

De Gaulle tried to play upon the party's internal differences to his own advantage. In Billoux's terms, de Gaulle wanted to "discriminate" between Communists who had spent the war years in metropolitan France and those who had been abroad.[17] The General trusted Fernand Grenier, his Communist Minister of Aviation, whom he had gotten to know while Grenier had been PCF representative to the Free French in London, but despised the party-chosen representative in his government, François Billoux. Ironically, Grenier clashed violently with de Gaulle over the issue of whether supplies could be effectively dropped to the Vercors insurgents in June 1944. Billoux never gave the General any trouble. Grenier was eventually replaced as Minister of Aviation by Charles Tillon, head of the FTP. Duclos claimed that he pressed Tillon upon de Gaulle out of a perverse kind of amusement, enjoying the prospect of obliging the patriotic General to accept as collaborator a mutineer of the Black Sea. Tillon insisted that de Gaulle chose him because the two men had acts of disobedience in common in 1940: de Gaulle resisted the army's collaboration, while Tillon resisted the party's.[18] But de Gaulle wanted Tillon in his cabinet to insure that all lines of military authority came under the General's direct authority.

The differences remained muted during the Liberation but became important after the party returned to a period of enforced isolation, leading to the purge of former Resistance leaders in 1950, and playing a role in the struggle between opportunist and sectarian currents in the Political Bureau from 1952 to 1954. From 1944 to 1947 a broad consensus existed within the PCF in favor of participation in the government. Disappointment grew with the results of the experience in power, but it was exaggerated in the press. The realities of international politics and the heritage of the Resistance combined in the Liberation to create an enlarged and reinforced version of the Popular Front. With the USSR as an ally of France, loyalty to the Socialist homeland was once again consistent with French patriotism; the PCF returned to the Jacobin themes of the 1930's with a vengeance. The PCF had always defended the interests of France; the Communists incarnated the workers, the rising national class, against the decadent bourgeoisie of Munich, Vichy, and treason. The fusion of the working class and the national interest was the result of historical law; the national and the revolutionary idea were one. Stung by the reproaches of Léon Blum, who doubted the PCF's nationalism, Florimond Bonte wrote proudly that all members of the Communist party Central Committee, at least, "have their roots deep in the national soil."[19]

There was a frenetic, nervous quality to this propaganda, which may have stemmed from a party complex about the events of 1939–41. The deliberate exaggeration in the claim of 75,000 Communists who were allegedly shot, a figure higher than the total of all those killed in France by the Germans, was resented by the non-Communist Resistance, and the party knew it to be fictional. André Marty's private estimate was 15,000, which in proportion to the total number of Communist militants before the war was certainly distinguished enough.[20] The PCF engaged in a constant effort to win symbolic recognition of the party's national character. Following the October 1945 elections, de Gaulle announced that the PCF was ineligible for any of the key ministries with reverberations on foreign policy: Foreign Affairs, Defense, or the Interior. The party felt constrained to demand one of those posts in order to force recognition of its patriotism; it could have accepted the sacrifice of these ministries in the name of national unity, but not for de Gaulle's reasons, considered "injurious to our honor as Frenchmen." "Are there two categories of Frenchmen?" Duclos asked, "one good for getting killed and the other for governing?"[21] The crisis was settled on de Gaulle's terms. Charles Tillon accepted the post of Minister of Armaments but not Defense; Thorez became Minister of State without portfolio. For the moment these had to suffice as recognition of the PCF's national character, all "insinuations" regarding which, Duclos argued, had now been voided. But the issue continued to disturb the PCF, and the crisis erupted again a year later. The PCF then refused to back down until Billoux was granted the Ministry of Defense, but shorn of all but symbolic functions. In 1947, to accommodate the Communists, the Army, Navy, and Air Force were separated from the Defense Ministry; their secretaries reported directly to the Premier. But again it was the symbol, not the substance of power which was critical for the PCF. With Billoux as Minister of Defense, the Political Bureau saluted the end of the Communist "exclusion" from any particular ministry.[22] Three months later the Communists were excluded from all cabinet posts for the next thirty-four years.

For some, a historic opportunity was lost to integrate the Communists definitively into French national life in the post-war period. Many French leaders were prepared to believe in the PCF's patriotism, among them de Gaulle, who wanted Communist cooperation in securing labor peace, and Georges Bidault, who two years later showed vitriolic anti-Communist colors. Bidault told U.S. Ambassador Jefferson Caffery that Thorez's speech of January 1945, on the theme of one army, police, and government, was agreed upon with the cabinet before it was delivered. "I am working hard on Thorez," Bidault said "who is the best of the lot." "Can you count on them [the Communists] to put France first?" Caffery asked, to which Bidault replied that he did not know, but he was trying.[23]

Jules Moch insisted that he entered the Socialist-Communist unity negotiations in 1944 with sincere illusory hopes for success.[24] The negotiations were bound to founder, as in 1935–36, over the issues of defense of the USSR and democratic centralism. Neither was negotiable for the Communists, while both were anathema for the Socialists, even if Léon Blum did admit once that Stalin was a "genius." With the Comintern's formal ties dissolved and the PCF ostensibly free to make its decisions, Blum still perceived a psychic dependence on the USSR in the PCF's behavior, which he characterized as an emotion akin to love.[25] Why did the Communists persist in these unity efforts? Fajon explains the party greatly under-estimated the staying power of reformist ideology among French workers. Auguste Lecoeur says that the PCF pursued a deliberate policy of seeking to strengthen the Socialists as a buffer between itself and the rest of a suspicious society, even to the extent of having Communist militants clandestinely participate in the rebuilding of the SFIO after the war.[26] The secret apparatus or *section hors cadres* of the PCF was of legendary fame. Prominent Communist sympathizers like Pierre Cot, Emanuel d'Astier de la Vigerie, and Yves Farge probably held party cards in a clandestine apparatus headed by the Communist Prefect, Resister, and organizational specialist, Jean Chaintron. Communists sought to infiltrate Socialist parties throughout East Europe after the war. That they tried to influence the SFIO by means of the same tactic was hardly surprising. It was rather their lack of success in France that appeared unusual. No hidden Communist in the SFIO leadership emerged comparable to the Czech Fierlinger, and the heritage of anti-Communism in the SFIO insured that efforts to help it regain its prewar strength would backfire. The PCF enjoyed greater success finding collaborators among the Radicals. It lured Edouard Herriot into an honorary presidency of the Communist youth, rebaptized the Union de la Jeunesse Républicaine de France (UJRF). But the party tried to exclude the Christian-Democratic Mouvement Republicain Populaire (MRP) from its revived and rejuvenated Popular Front. The MRP offered many former advocates of Vichy a vehicle for re-entry into French political life under the Christian-Democratic umbrella. The PCF regularly denounced the MRP as a tool of the Vatican and the trusts.[27] But Communist efforts to drive a wedge between the MRP and the Socialists by means of a renewed emphasis on the anti-clerical issue failed.

The battle for production became a series of subsidiary efforts for higher productivity in the coal, steel, electricity, and textile industries. Raising productivity was the major means by which the PCF sought to demonstrate its mettle as a government party. The productivity effort was assimilated to the rhetoric of the class struggle. Communists charged that the trusts, the Vichy holdovers, and all the enemies of French democracy, were trying to sabotage the economic recovery effort. To the extent that productivity figures increased, their plans were defeated. According to *L'Humanité*, "To produce is today the highest form of duty to one's class. . . . we will win, against the trusts, the battle of production."[28] Higher production was the guarantee of a French foreign policy independent of the Anglo-Saxons. There was room for trade-union activity by workers to be sure, but pay increases must follow productivity rises, or else they were inflationary. The PCF accepted a version of the "bourgeois" wage-price spiral theory, the *cycle infernal* which became a staple of Socialist thought that the Communists later condemned. Said Monmousseau, "We must produce within the limits of human capacities, and make economic demands within the limits of national possibilities." *La Vie Ouvrière,* the CGT organ, celebrated the tenth anniversary of the Russian Stakhanovite movement in September 1945 and warned that strikes now were a weapon of reaction against the workers of the nation.[29] If strikes occurred, Frachon told the American embassy, Reactionaries and the trusts fomented them by means of paid provocateurs and Trotskyites. The unions were doing everything they could to prevent labor unrest.[30] Communist trade union publications unashamedly advocated bonuses for workers who demonstrated ways of increasing "norms of production." Thorez, in a famous speech at the coalfields at Wazières inveighed against worker laziness and absenteeism.

The message of productivity was concentrated on newly nationalized enterprises in which the PCF assumed a proprietary interest. The PCF was not against nationalization. But it was fearful of the electoral consequences of too radical an image and stressed that only the largest industries were ripe for takeover. Private property, "the fruit of labor and of savings," was sacred and would be better protected with state control of monopolies. Nationalization was not synonymous with socialism, however, as long as the state was not under working-class control. It was a democratic reform, whose targets were industries in which the prewar leadership, like Louis Renault, had collaborated with the Germans. The PCF demanded nationalization of the banks and did not hesitate to underline their cosmopolitan and predominately Protestant and Jewish character.[31] The Communists regarded peasant property rights as sacred and advocated the suppression of inheritance taxes.

The party flirted with demagoguery in its courting of the middle classes. It contributed to the defeat of Mendès-France's plan to forestall inflation by blocking all accounts and enforcing an exchange of banknotes in circulation. The latter measure was intended to tax illicitly garnered wartime cash profits stuffed in peasant mattresses. PCF advocacy of the peasants' interests on this issue raised questions among many militants. Peasant savings were going to be devalued in any case, if not by taxation, then by inflation, which defeat of the Mendès-France plan rendered inevitable. In tacitly advocating inflationary policies, the PCF found itself a circumstantial ally of the "neofascist party of the Vatican," the MRP. The PCF showed no hesitation in competing with the Christian Democrats in the rhetoric of economic liberalism. When Communist Ministers, after embarrassing delay, abolished the hated Vichy "Committees of Organization," they vaunted the newly created freedom of private enterprises from bureaucratic over-regulation and insisted that "Communists stood for the maximum of individual initiative."[32]

Similar concerns appeared in the PCF's ideas for the constitution of the Fourth Republic, the goals of which were widely misunderstood. By advocating a sovereign unicameral Assembly, to which the Government would be fully responsible, the PCF showed itself to be part of the consensus of all parties against the strong presidential regime that de Gaulle advocated. The PCF alone advocated a "no" vote on question two of de Gaulle's October 1945 referendum limiting the duration of the Constituent Assembly to seven months. But the party joined the Socialists against the MRP seven months later in advocating a "yes" vote on the constitutional draft the Assembly produced. Neither referendum was over substantive issues. Despite all the anti-Communist rhetoric about a "Marxist constitution," not even the MRP advocated a genuine upper house equivalent to the Senate of the Third Republic, which deliberately privileged rural areas and shared in the ability to hamper government action.[33] The Constitution adopted in November 1946 differed little from the one rejected in June. The only real change related to the French Empire, where the assimilationism of the first draft gave way to a restored colonial system, changed in name to the "French Union" but leaving the domination of the metropole untouched. On the colonial question, too, the PCF shared in a consensus of all the parties; blocking the presidential system of de Gaulle was considered more important than liberalizing the colonial regime.[34] Nobody perceived that these two issues would remain linked, paving the way for the regime's collapse in 1958. The PCF was unique among French parties in advocating the suppression of the prefectoral bureaucracy and the recall of elected officials by their constituents. Communist leaders knew that these proposals would find no support outside party ranks and advanced them for purely electoral reasons.

At the time of the municipal elections of May 1945 Charles Tillon, Minister of Aviation, and François Billoux, Minister of Health, were the only Communists in the cabinet. Both were regarded as "able and conscientious" in the performance of their duties and the cause of no particular problems.[35] De Gaulle allowed the party only two prefectures, held by Jean Chaintron in Limoges and Lucien Monjauvis in Lyon. Their administration was competent and unremarkable.[36] The municipal elections of 1945 showed PCF strength to have increased to roughly a quarter of the electorate since the inter-war period. While content to await the October national elections, the PCF demanded its new strength be translated into a greater share of government power. The elections demonstrated that the party was broadly based with an appeal in all regions and social classes. It had the highest total vote, and claimed the title of "the first party of France." The PCF was defeated on the second question of the constitutional referendum, however, which limited the Constituent Assembly's mandate to seven months. Consequently the party did not demand the position of head of the Government and rallied to de Gaulle.

A common understanding limited the Communists, other than Thorez who became Minister of State, to economic ministries. De Gaulle hoped to associate the working class with the effort of economic reconstruction. Charles Tillon, as Minister of Armaments, came into control of all state arsenals, to which aviation plants were now attached. His ministry was the largest single employer in France. François Billoux became Minister of the Economy with overall responsibility for prices. Two new faces, both trade-union militants as well as members of the Central Committee of the PCF, joined the cabinet. Ambroise Croizat, Secretary of the metalworkers, became Minister of Labor, and Marcel Paul, Secretary of the electrical workers, Minister of Industrial Production. But the crucial Ministry of Finance remained out of party control, and Billoux did not hold on to the Ministry of National Economy beyond January.

Communist ministers projected an image of competence, pragmatism, moderation, and accomplishment. Thorez, most in the limelight as Minister of State and then Vice-Premier, enjoyed the trappings of power. Uniformity of appreciation of Thorez's talents appears in the memoirs of those who worked with him. Auriol referred repeatedly to his wisdom and statesmanship. Daix and Tillon remarked that he knew how to perform as a statesman.[37] Most interesting is the agreement of two successive Socialist Ministers of the Interior, Edouard Depreux and Jules Moch.[38] Depreux wrote:

Thorez . . . had a clear mind, was efficient, had a sense of compromise, was not unhappy to be minister. . . . He distributed friendly handshakes to the most diverse colleagues, wanting to appear in every aspect a "man like the others."

Moch was even more laudatory:

Of the communists that I knew in the government, he was the one with the greatest sense of statesmanship. Once out of the mine . . . he educated himself and became a statesman. . . . I admit after having seen him at work in four governments, that I was struck by the clarity of his insights, his sometimes brutal frankness, and his sentiment of responsibility toward the country.

Tillon, former head of the FTP, was the most popular, but Labor Minister Croizat, soft-spoken, methodical, and capable, left the most lasting imprint on French society in the work he accomplished. The Communists cited Croizat's record to prove that humble workers could succeed in the highest posts. Marcel Paul, whose two first names reflected a background as an orphan, was a deportee, Resistance hero, and survivor of Auschwitz and Buchenwald. A loyal Stalinist, Paul gave the appearance of a gentle, humane, and quietly efficient man, a compulsive worker whose persuasiveness was increased by the concentration camp number prominently displayed on his forearm.[39]

A cabinet with Communist ministers functioned as cabinets always had: Communists demonstrated that they could perform in a manner that "bourgeois" politicians considered perfectly normal. The PCF ministers worked smoothly with high civil servants, valuing technical expertise over political obsequiousness. In appointments to their personal staffs, even in choosing among Communists, considerations of personal qualification prevailed, to the detriment, in this one special case, of the party's traditional *ouvrierisme*. A spirit of cooperation was also manifest in relations with cabinet colleagues.[40] When Depreux, whose Interior Ministry had authority over Algeria, disagreed with Thorez over the carving out of electoral circumscriptions there, both agreed to the arbitration of Premier Bidault, who ruled in favor of Thorez.[41]

Things were made easier by the Communists' support for Bidault's foreign policy, even though it differed from the USSR's. The PCF supported separation of the Rhineland from Germany after Stalin abandoned it in June 1946. Léon Blum, who opposed separation, noted he was in agreement with Stalin against the PCF and the Papacy against the MRP on the issue.[42] Even if the PCF adopted this position for tactical reasons, as many observers suspected, the incident demonstrated that the PCF's participation in government obliged it to pursue different policies from those of the USSR. In the long run such divergences were bound to become meaningful. Blum remarked that the party, on that occasion, showed its nationalism to be "solid, French, and authentic."

Some political problems acquired a new twist because of Communist participation. Tripartite governments displayed little teamwork. Ministers jealously guarded their autonomy with all the parties' propaganda focusing on the achievements of their own ministers. The masses knew, said Duclos, that whatever social reforms the government implemented were a consequence of the Communist ministers' presence. If any reforms had not been achieved, it was because Communists were there in insufficient numbers.[43] Compartmentalization was extreme. The Communists were frozen out of foreign policy decisions. Minister of Justice Teitgen told U.S. Ambassador Caffery that "in general we have our way in foreign policy but must pay for it by throwing a sop to the Communists here and there. . . ."[44] Communist ministers disclaimed responsibility for runaway prices, which were the fault of the MRP. The parties campaigned unashamedly against one another, highlighting the work of their own ministries while bitterly attacking their cabinet colleagues.

Democratic centralism was not particularly well suited to coalition government. Communist ministers remained disciplined party militants but could not share state secrets with their local party cells. They either ceased to attend meetings or created cells within their ministries.[45] Democratic centralism prohibited direct horizontal contacts by Communists, but Pierre Daix, who arranged all of Charles Tillon's trips around France, had carte blanche to facilitate local arrangements with Communist sections and federations across the country. Communist ministers did not resign their party or trade-union functions when they entered the cabinet. Marcel Paul continued as head of the electrical workers, and Ambroise Croizat remained secretary of the metalworkers. Maurice Thorez surrendered no authority over the party while serving as Minister of State. State secrets to which

Thorez and his cabinet colleagues were privy were certainly shared, one must assume, with Duclos, the party secretariat, selected members of the Political Bureau, and Moscow.[46]

There were five Communist ministers under de Gaulle (October 1945–January 1946), eight under his successor, Felix Gouin (January 1946–June 1946), and ten sharing power under Bidault, (June-November 1946). At its maximum, the Communist ministerial structure included:

Minister of State	Maurice Thorez
Minister of Armaments	Charles Tillon
Undersecretary	Georges Gosnat
Minister of Industrial Production	Marcel Paul
Undersecretary	Auguste Lecoeur
Minister of Reconstruction and Urbanism	François Billoux
Minister of Labor	Ambroise Croizat
Undersecretary	Marius Patinaud
Minister of Health	René Arthaud
Minister of War Veterans	Laurent Casanova

There was a certain makeshift quality to the Communist participation. Thorez had no portfolio and Tillon only the lesser half of the Ministry of Defense. Industrial Production and Reconstruction and Urbanism were new ministries, the first established under Vichy, the second born of the specific needs of the Liberation; neither was long to survive the Communist participation in power. Labor and Health had been on occasion joined to one another or to other ministries. When Ramadier dismissed the Communist ministers in May 1947, most did not need to be immediately replaced because their functions were easily assumed by others in the cabinet.

Yet the Communists enjoyed much more than only the semblance of power. Their cabinet posts afforded a unique opportunity to preside over the building of the modern French welfare state. Minister of Labor Croizat claimed credit for the many pay increases and benefits workers received during his period in office.[47] Most importantly, he was responsible for the establishment and initial operations of the new institutional structures of the liberation: the Workers' Committees of Enterprises and social security system. Neither was created by the Communists, and the PCF showed some ambiguity toward the "reformist" and "class collaborationist" implications of such reforms. Committees of Enterprises were first established by decree of Alexandre Parodi, de Gaulle's Minister of Labor, in February 1945. Although the CNR program spoke only vaguely of worker participation, the idea was part of the zeitgeist of the Liberation.

The Communists remained ambiguous about Parodi's work, crediting him with having launched the reform, but minimizing his role. In enterprises like the Berliot truck plant, they said, workers had acted on their own to seize control from the collaborationist direction. Alternatively, the Communists charged that Parodi's legislation was "Vichyiste" in spirit until reformed by Croizat in 1946.[48]

But Croizat had participated in drafting the initial legislation. It was at his insistence, moreover, that protection of trade-union prerogatives had been written into the law: Committees of Enterprises were forbidden to deal with economic issues such as wages and hours, and their powers were limited. Workers' self-management or *autogestion* was not a communist concern. The committees' role was primarily social, including the management of canteens, libraries, sporting clubs, and vacation camps for children. As a secondary task, committees were urged to make recommendations for the improvement of productivity.[49] Committee personnel were freely elected by all workers eighteen years of age and older by secret ballot. But special prerogatives were reserved for the trade unions to select candidates for committee posts, insuring that the reform would be kept under party control.

Once the "loi Croizat" had been implemented, extending Committees of Enterprises to all establishments over fifty workers, the reform was saluted in the Communist press as "an element of the new democracy" and "a landmark on the way to Socialism." Prior to the first elections, the committees were established by appointment of the Ministry of Labor, which gave a majority position to the "most representative" union, the CGT. The willingness of the French political establishment to tolerate this development is perhaps explained by the restricted role the Communists envisaged for the committees. At a National Conference in February 1946 Croizat defined as a principal task of the committees to assist management in achieving higher productivity. Under no conditions were they to be a substitute for established authority in the plants.[50] In the steel industry, Croizat noted approvingly, suggestions from committees saved the equivalent of 108,339 man-hours of work. In the second half of 1946, the party's view of the committees was expanded and a role created for them in the struggle to hold down prices. The committees enjoyed rights to financial information on the profitability of enterprises and could employ accountants. But a committee could only publicize price increases it thought illicit and complain to state authorities. Thorez allegedly came to look upon the committees as a constituent element of his "French road to Socialism" by early 1947. But the CGT defined them as "an instrument of the trade unions," leaving little room for maneuver.[51]

When the PCF returned to the opposition, the committees' Stakhanovite role was changed to one of "combat." Their extensive network of social concerns provided a convenient refuge for Communist militants fired by management for trade-union activities. Michel Collinet estimated that the 4,000 committees created in 1944–45 had expanded to close to 10,000 by the begining of 1947, although a percentage had only a paper existence.[52] These figures provide eloquent testimony to the enthusiasm with which the party was able to entrain the labor movement into an integrative role in the French economic system. But the "tournant" of 1947 brought decline in the committees' numbers and quality, and by 1953 only 7,000 were left in existence. Some of the largest committees became simply bastions of a beleaguered party, pillars of the Communist counter-society.

The establishment of the social security system offered Croizat another opportunity for the extension of Communist influence. The party's liberal interpretation of the reform stood in stark contrast to the very tight grip the CGT was initially able to establish over the system once established. The basic elements of the French social security plan were inherited from Parodi, but the major role in establishing it was Croizat's. The French plan fell between the ambitious British or Soviet "statist" plans and the modest American reform from which medicine had been excluded. The French system allowed for 80 to 100 percent reimbursement for medical expenses, free choice of physicians by patients, and the administration of a national system of 138 regional offices by the insured.[53] Croizat championed the French plan as "liberal medicine" and a "tolerant and flexible formula."[54] But the PCF and CGT successfully fought for a centralized structure including the family allowance program and unemployment insurance under its control. Croizat lost no time preparing for the July 1, 1946, inauguration date. As in the case of the Committees of Enterprises, elections were judged premature, and personnel to run the regional offices were chosen by the Ministry of Labor from the "most representative" union, the CGT. In January 1946 the union operated a training school for new administrators, and the CGT dominated a majority of newly established offices. Communist trade-union militant Henri Raynaud was elected the first president of the national federation of social security offices, serving in that position until 1949.

MRP politicians fought a rear-guard action to block or postpone initial operation of the system. *L'Aube,* the MRP organ, demanded immediate elections and complained of a Communist "power-grab." Leaders of the Confédération Française des Travailleurs Chrétiens (CFTC), the Christian trade union, accused Croizat of establishing "a veritable administrative dictatorship inspired by ideas far removed from reality."[55] The Communists asked the Socialists to join in defense against a "reactionary" threat to one of the major social conquests of the Liberation. In the National Assembly, Croizat argued that a delay in implementing the system was impossible; everything was ready and elections were only postponed to provide for "the education of the insured."[56] The Socialists backed Croizat's implementation of the social security system only after he promised to hold early elections, however.

Elections were finally set by Daniel Mayer during the one-month interlude of a homogeneous socialist government under Léon Blum (December 1946–January 1947).[57] But when they were finally held in April 1947, Croizat was again Minister of Labor, and CGT administrators campaigned as incumbents, defending their months of experience against the Catholic union's charges of "totalitarianization." The results permitted the CGT to consolidate its control, but the victory was less impressive than expected and revealed the Communist union's vulnerability. The CGT garnered 59.27 percent of the vote to 26.36 percent for the CFTC; in the separately administered family allowance system, the figures were 61.88 percent to 25 percent. In practical terms, these figures translated into CGT control of 109 of 134 regional offices and 101 of 111 family allowance offices. Communist control was pyramidal, analagous to a holding company: the PCF dominated the CGT, which dominated the social security system. Clearly, if non-Communists were to withdraw from the CGT and throw their support to the CFTC, Communists could be put in the minority. The stage was set for future power struggles in the system.

The much talked-of Communist "colonization" of the French social-political structure in the post-war period occurred largely within the confines of the new institutional framework of the welfare state. Where some saw a "trojan horse" technique aimed at the conquest of power, others saw democratic integration signifying the PCF's coming of age and maturity. The PCF attributed the greatest importance to educating cadres to occupy the many posts created by the new reforms.[58] The historical polemic over Communist integration as opposed to infiltration of the state is a sterile one: what mattered was the political climate in which integration occurred. Had France been weaker and geographically subject to Soviet domination, the fear of Communist infiltration might have been reasonable. On the other hand, had the French political class and its American allies been more accommodating, a shared sphere of Communist power within a democratic liberal-capitalist framework might have been achieved, and the PCF meaningfully integrated into French life.

Despite Croizat's effectiveness, Marcel Paul, at the Ministry of Industrial Production, became the focal point of most conservative attacks. Paul enjoyed greater visibility because of his Ministry's key role in managing critical shortages of coal and electricity. He took unusual initiatives in foreign affairs, vociferously demanding increased deliveries of coal from the Ruhr. He initiated a program for the manufacture of cheaply priced "articles of social utility" antagonizing business interests with the government competition. He pushed through the nationalization of electricity and placed Communists in key posts in the Electricité de France (EDF) and other enterprises under his control. Paul was personally vulnerable to attack because of a mysterious past at Buchenwald.

Paul ostentatiously attacked the shortages from the moment of his assumption of office, giving priority allocations of coal to homes with aged persons or children under six, closing down textiles and other non-priority industries several days a week to conserve fuel.[59] In the meantime, Paul announced, the heroic miners would do everything possible to meet the coal shortage, but the Germans must be forced to increase their deliveries from the Ruhr. The program creating articles of social utility was begun with a vast publicity campaign in May 1946. The Ministry allocated scarce raw materials by priority to small producers who agreed to meet standards of quality at fixed prices. Shirts, shoes, and textile products were made available, outside the black market, to merchants who "agreed to submit to necessary discipline."[60] Organizations of small businessmen were invited to constitute permanent committees to distribute the manufactured articles, which were specially marked "Production 1946, Renaissance Française." *L'Humanité* published lists of those cooperating and the Communist press urged consumers to patronize them. Parisians were said to have accepted the program with enthusiasm and "joy." Officially sponsored organizations of merchants with such neutral names as "Association Nationale de Repartition au Commerce" or "Fédération Nationale des Groupements d'Achat" were created to receive and control the allocation of goods. The Communists acted in defense of small property, "the fruit of labor and savings; our program is the struggle for the return of freedom of commerce."[61]

Critics were neither convinced nor amused. The party was assuming control of the production, retailing, marketing, advertising, and consumption of consumer goods, creating a Communist-controlled segment of the economy. According to the conservative press, the slogan was, "Belong to the PCF and you will have your goods."[62] In the midst of the election campaign for the second constituent assembly, the Christian-Democratic newspaper, *L'Aube,* claimed to have discovered a scandal in the distribution of scarce supplies by Paul's ministry. When bourgeois politicians accepted bribes, they did so for the money. But when Communists did so, they turned the money over to their party, *L'Aube* implied, which was much worse.

While Marcel Paul was diplomatically ill, Croizat admitted in the National Assembly to "some defects" in the Ministry of Industrial Production's operations. Bidault stepped in to see that the articles of social utility were distributed through normal commercial channels.[63] Paul defended himself against the charges. The associations of small merchants concerned, he said, were made up mostly of Jews and fellow concentration camp victims whom he was helping to restart in business. If Communists made some inroads in gaining support among the petty bourgeoisie, that was purely incidental.[64] There exists a considerable loyalty to the PCF in the families of many Parisian petty-bourgeois Jewish families to this day, among whom Marcel Paul remains an admired figure for his continued role at the head of the National Federation of Deportees. But Paul's most controversial role was in his administration of the nationalized enterprises.

Marcel Paul fought tenaciously for a centralized Electricité de France (EDF) including the distribution and production of electricity and gas, with the aim of bringing the newly created structure under CGT or Communist party control. Of eighteen statutory positions on the administrative council of the EDF, six were designated for worker representatives. Paul appointed five of the six from the "most representative union," the CGT. The remaining twelve seats were divided between representatives of the state and consumers; Paul filled these with Communists or "Progressives" in order to assure the party a majority. The new head of the enterprise, Pierre Simon, had no party identification but was acceptable to Paul and the Council.[65] Similarly, the inauguration of the administrative council of the nationalized coal industry, the Charbonnages de France occurred amid cries that Paul and Undersecretary Lecoeur had created a "party fief in the coal fields." Lecoeur openly welcomed the appearance of so many "comrades in struggle" on the first Council of Administration; of its eighteen members twelve were in the CGT, and ten clearly linked to the PCF.[66] Communist trade-union leader Victorin Duguet was duly elected first President of the enterprise. Nine out of eighteen members of the administrative council, the Communists proudly announced, had actually worked in the mines at some point in their careers.

The campaign against Paul's past in Buchenwald was designed to destroy his effectiveness in controlling the economy. The Germans left much of the administration of concentration camps to inmates, and Communists never hesitated to exercise such responsibilities as became available. Paul was in charge of French inmates at Buchenwald. The conservative press alleged that he chose who was to die, delivering "reactionaries and capitalists" to the Germans while saving Communists. Communist Kapos allegedly gave double rations of soup to their followers and inferior portions to everyone else on their block.[67] Prominent survivors of Buchenwald, some of them non-Communists, wrote public letters in defense of Paul's role. Marcel Bloch-Dassault claimed Paul's efforts saved his life. But the party was deeply disturbed by the attacks on Paul's administration of his Ministry and past; he was not included among Communist ministers in the Ramadier government formed in January 1947.

Charles Tillon's administration of the French armaments industry paralleled Marcel Paul's work in industrial production. Tillon had been a trade-union leader in Brittany before graduating to party functions. He was a pragmatist and activist, a man of independent ideas and initiative, who disdained theory and believed naively that Stalinism and the Russian revolution were the incarnation of the ideals of 1789 and French patriotism. As Minister of Armaments he functioned autonomously and independently, implementing a party line that appeared to him an organic expression of the imperative needs of France growing out of the Resistance and the Liberation. He was competent and imaginative, in Daix's estimation "a superb" minister.[68] Tillon sought to maximize productivity, while creating an arms industry that would enable France to pursue a foreign policy of national independence. He also tried to associate the working class in the national effort of reconstruction, appointing trade-union leaders to positions of authority in nationalized arsenals and forming Mixed Production Committees to augment output. Tillon did not, however, challenge established lines of authority in the factories, and within the plants the atmosphere was one of "Stakhanovism." For his party he was "the artisan of the Renaissance of French wings," father of both the Caravelle and the Concorde.[69]

He may have been that in spirit, but was less certainly so in fact. In the two post-war years, Tillon's plants produced 2000 airplanes and 3515 aviation motors.[70] But these inflated figures were achieved by producing models designed before or during the war, including German-style junker fighter planes for no apparent purpose. Tillon sponsored the production of a six-engine monster hydroplane, the Latécoère 631, designed to carry seventy-four passengers in conditions of unprecedented luxury, including private staterooms and cabins.[71] The plane was a fine example of the PCF's blind insistence on pursuing every possibility opened up by modern technology, paralleled today in the party's support of the Concorde. Several prototypes were manufactured, all plagued by technical problems. Some spectacular crashes occurred during test flights, which the party attributed to deliberate sabotage by the trusts, Americans, and opponents of nationalization. Jules Moch, who succeeded Tillon, claimed he found only obsolescent and unusable planes being produced.[72] The party regarded such charges as intended to justify a policy to purchase American airplanes, dictated by Marshall Plan aid. Communism remained a powerful influence in the nationalized aviation industry well into the 1950's, causing the French government to sponsor a new private industry and buy American aircraft.

Tillon used his ministry, as he had earlier run the FTP and was later to do with the Peace Movement, as an independent base for the implementation of his own policies. In January 1946 the Socialists proposed budget cuts in the French military, causing de Gaulle to resign. Duclos rallied to the Socialists' support, but Tillon was decidedly cool to the cuts and did not hesitate to reject them publicly.[73] Once the cuts were mandated, Tillon embarked on an ambitious program of reconversion of war industries to peace-time uses, in an effort to absorb a 40 percent reduction in the armaments budget. The initial dismantling of Tillon's work preceded the Communists' expulsion from the French Government in May 1947. Following the interlude of the homogeneous Socialist government in December 1946-January 1947, Tillon discovered from the newspapers that he was no longer Minister of Armaments, but had been included in Ramadier's government as Minister of Reconstruction and Urbanism in place of François Billoux.[74] Billoux had become Minister of Defense, and armaments were now subject to his jurisdiction. Logic dictated that Tillon become Defense Minister; Thorez had proposed him for the post in 1945. But Tillon's independent popularity made him as much an object of suspicion within his party as among conservative politicians. The PCF wished to demonstrate that a loyal party official like Billoux, who had not resisted the Germans before it was PCF policy to do so, could serve as Minister of Defense. At Reconstruction, Tillon barely had time to familiarize himself with the job before the Communist participation in power came to an end. The legacy of Tillon's tenure, like Marcel Paul's, fueled the social conflicts of the late 1940's.

François Billoux was known as an ideologue; yet when Tillon assumed the Ministry of Reconstruction and Urbanism, he found that it had been run on pragmatic lines. Billoux scorned urban theorists; his policy was to rebuild any usable structure to shelter France's 5 million inadequately housed persons in the shortest possible time.[75] Billoux sponsored legislation requiring the government to compensate all victims of war damages, the wealthiest receiving last priority. He had urban redevelopment projects submitted to local committees headed by Prefects and including Mayors, local entrepreneurs, union leaders, architects, and victims of war damages. He supported requisition rights for Mayors, which would have enabled them to expropriate almost any available structure for emergency housing. Billoux exercised tight control over his Ministry, insisting on vigilence against "sabotage," carrying out purges, and staffing his bureaucracy liberally with Communists, reportedly using party cells as a means of surveillance and control. He rejected all radical proposals for structural changes, sought to reassure and not frighten, and tried to appeal to non-proletarian elements of the population.

Maurice Thorez, as Minister of State, symbolized working-class collaboration in the task of economic reconstruction. Thorez also presided over creation of the statute of government workers or *fonctionnaires,* legislation which has remained in effect, with modifications, to this day. Thorez's statute gave French government workers the right to unionize and established a modern grievance machinery, including procedures regulating appointments, evaluations and promotions, and providing for sexual equality. Thorez supported the establishment of the Ecole Nationale d'Administration, initially intended to democratize recruitment.[76] The Thorez legislation was passed amid great publicity in the fall of 1946 just prior to the elections; it provides a fitting backdrop to Thorez's candidacy for Premier and famous interview with the *London Times.*

The PCF threw itself enthusiastically behind a "yes" vote in the referendum on the second constitutional draft of October 1946. On October 8, 1946, Thorez cited three reasons for the party's support of the Constitution: it was progressive and democratic, France needed permanent institutions immediately, and a strong government would facilitate a foreign policy of peace, security, and reparations.[77] On November 11, the PCF declared that having received 29.09 percent of the popular vote, it was "ready to assume all its responsibilities." The PCF was riding a crest of rising popularity, demonstrable both in votes and membership, which remained continuous so long as the party participated in power:

	Votes		Membership (PCF official figures)
October 1945	4,831,264	January 1945	387,098
June 1946	5,199,000	December 1946	775,352
November 1946	5,475,955	June 1947	895,130

PCF Congresses were ritualized massive demonstrations of unity, strength, and purpose. In November 1946, the PCF registered gains in all departments of France except twenty in the Center and South where it was already powerful. The PCF was progressing in regions traditionally hostile to it and broadening its social base. Its membership seemed to be within reach of becoming "a party counted in the millions." Marcel Cachin declared the PCF had become the largest party in France because it was "the most national, the most French, the most respectful of the historical traditions and the grandeur of the country."[78]

The party harbored no illusions when it proposed Thorez's candidacy for head of government on November 15. The aim was a "republican" and not a "Marxist" majority, Cogniot wrote, and he contrasted the widespread cooperation between Socialists and Communists in East Europe with the obstinate refusal to cooperate being shown by the French Socialists.[79] Thorez told Reuters that he wished to head a national, not a party government, and the *London Times* that there were other paths to Socialism than the one followed by the Russian Bolsheviks. France would chart its own way in conformity with its national traditions and genius. The PCF had moved far beyond the return to national and patriotic themes of the 1930's. On November 20, Thorez amplified his remarks for the American press club: the PCF was not an emanation from Moscow, he said, but had roots a century old in France.[80] The PCF was no more international than the trusts or the church; Communism could not be exported "like perfume." Thorez's government program was designed to reassure the middle classes: his aims were to defend the franc, balance the budget, and raise productivity. "France has voted for the PCF because it [the PCF] has shown itself to be a government party," Thorez said. The Communists had always been ardent defenders of democracy, and the People's Democracies demonstrated a transition to socialism without the dictatorship of the proletariat. Thorez repeated that "each country will pass to socialism in its own way."

Thorez received an impressive 261 votes in the National Assembly; Communist propaganda following the defeat was positive. Duclos said the large number of blank ballots cast showed clearly the necessary 310 votes were within the realm of possibility. Since the MRP had refused to support Thorez, the PCF blocked any MRP-headed government, making a Socialist-led government inevitable. The issue of a key ministry for the PCF was a sticking point, but the symbol, not the substance of power was the issue and Billoux accepted the restructured Ministry of Defense. The vote for Thorez as Premier and the Defense Ministry for Billoux had the same aim: to bestow symbolic respectability on a PCF that had, it thought, integrated successfully into the existing socio-political structure with its internal party structure intact. The new Thorez doctrine of a French way to socialism reflected the party's integration. Thorez's pronouncement was not, the party said, an incidental tactical comment, but a firm doctrinal commitment. In the following months, it was given wide publicity.[81] The French road to Socialism was the logical and necessary consequence of the Communist infrastructure that had been assiduously created and cultivated by the party's ministers in the preceding years. However much in line with momentary Soviet strategy, the doctrine of a French road to Socialism could only have been strengthened as Communist participation continued.

The PCF rallied to the support of a homogeneous government of Socialists headed by Léon Blum in December 1946, while the thorny conditions of its continued participation in the cabinet were hammered out. *L'Humanité* meanwhile threw its support to Blum's effort to hold the line on prices. The PCF gave its firmest support yet to the colonial consensus by endorsing Blum's handling of the exploding crisis in Vietnam. It was "perfectly reasonable" the party said, to postpone negotiations in Indochina "until peaceful law and order are re-established."[82] Observers continued to wonder whether the PCF's commitment to democratic processes could be trusted. But the party had little choice, in the absence of any revolutionary possibilities, but to follow a policy of legality. "We have enough confidence in the conquering virtue of our doctrine," Duclos said, "to be able to play the parliamentary game in the most correct manner."[83]

The PCF had ample opportunity in the post-war years to demonstrate its mastery of legal processes and parliamentary practices. But the immediate future obliged it to show its capacity for illegal action.

NOTES

1. Maurice Agulhon, "Les Communistes et la Liberation de la France," in Comité de la Deuxième Guerre Mondiale, *La Liberation de la France* (Paris, 1976), 70.

2. Maurice Baumont, Preface to *La Liberation de la France,* 41. Robrieux, *Histoire Intérieure du PCF* (Paris, 1981), II, 26.

3. *L'Humanité,* August 22, 1944. See Dominique Desanti in *Journal de la France,* 192 (February 19, 1973), 2707.

4. See Robrieux, *Histoire Intérieure,* II, 61–65, on the PCF's post-war liquidations, which included some former Central Committee members and Trotskyists, regarded as fascist agents of Hitler. Robrieux encompasses the demand for an administrative purge (*épuration*) within an overall PCF strategy of eventual insurrection, a view with which I disagree.

5. Speech before the Consultive Assembly, December 27, 1944, reprinted in *Cahiers du Communisme,* 3 (January 1945), 9.

6. Interview, May 29, 1978.

7. Gerard Jouve, "Témoignage, Le Retour de Maurice Thorez en France," *Le Monde,* November 28, 1969. Jouve says that de Gaulle himself did not circulate this story, which came instead from General Juin.

8. *Cahiers du Communisme,* 4 (February 1945), 4–7.

9. For the contrary view see Robrieux, II, 70–85, who argues the PCF effected a real turn in policy away from a strategy of dual power only after the Yalta conference in January 1945.

10. U.S. National Archives, Modern Military Branch, Record Group 226, Office of Strategic Services, report dated June 14, 1945.

11. Archives André Marty, Microfilm collection, Reel 8, "Les cadres decident de tout," dated February 20, 1945.

12. Pierre Daix, *J'ai cru au matin* (Paris, 1976), 161. Robrieux, *Histoire Intérieure,* II, 35.

13. Charles Tillon, *On chantait rouge* (Paris, 1977), 403. See also Paul-Marie de la Gorce, *L'après-guerre, 1944–1952: Naissance de la France moderne* (Paris, 1978).

14. Agulhon, "Les Communistes et la Liberation . . . ," Desanti, *Journal,* Tillon, *On chantait rouge,* 440.

15. Fajon has written of his association with Marty: *Ma vie s'appelle liberté* (Paris, 1976), 145.

16. Laurent Casanova interview in private archive of Philippe Robrieux. See the latter's *Maurice Thorez, vie secrète et vie publique* (Paris, 1975). Jolyon Howorth reviewed the literature on conflict within the PCF leadership in "The Dynamics of Disintegration: Inner Conflicts and Contradictions in the PCF's Handling of Left Unity and Foreign Affairs (1946–1947)," paper presented at the fourth International Colloquium of the Interuniversity Centre for European Studies, March 1981. Howorth concludes that the evidence is too contradictory to assert more than that leadership conflict existed.

17. François Billoux, *Quand nous étions ministres* (Paris, 1972), 51. Etienne Fajon, personal interview, April 10, 1978.

18. Jacques Duclos, *Memoires, 1945–1952: sur la brèche* (Paris, 1971), 50. Tillon, *On chantait rouge,* 440; personal interview, May 29, 1978. Robrieux thinks Tillon was made a minister to keep him from exercising party responsibilities. II, 26.

19. See Florimond Bonte, "A l'Echelle de la nation, response a l'auteur de 'A l'Echelle humaine,' " *Cahiers du Communisme,* 10 (August 1945), 39.

20. Marty Archive, Reel 8, memo of February 20, 1945, states that "15,000 of our best militants have been shot."

21. *L'Humanité,* November 16, 19, 20, 1945.

22. *Cahiers du Communisme,* 2 (February 1947), 159.

23. N.A. Diplomatic Branch, 851.00 B, dispatch dated February 5, 1945.

24. Jules Moch, *Une si longue vie* (Paris, 1976), 182.

25. Léon Blum, *Oeuvre* (Paris, 1958), July 18, 1945, 46.

26. Etienne Fajon, personal interview, April 10, 1978. Auguste Lecoeur, personal interview, July 10, 1978.

27. Waldeck Rochet, "Les origines et la politique du MRP," *Cahiers du Communisme,* 7 (July 1946), 547–57.

28. *L'Humanité,* January 17, 1946.

29. *La Vie Ouvrière,* September 6, September 20, 1945. George Ross, *Workers and Communists in France* (Berkeley, Calif., 1982) estimates that the PCF controlled twenty-one key CGT federations in 1946 to non-Communists' nine. The CGT swelled in size in 1945–46 to between 5 and 6 million. 26 and *passim.*

30. N.A. Diplomatic Branch, 851.00, dispatch dated February 19, 1946, by U.S. labor attaché.

31. Etienne Fajon, "Les communistes et la propriété," *Cahiers du Communisme,* 2 (December, 1944), 51–60, and by the same author, "Les communistes et les national-isations," 4 (February 1945), 30–39.

32. *France Nouvelle,* February 2, 1946, February 15, 1946.

33. De la Gorce, *L'Après-guerre,* 146–52.

34. Ibid. See also Bruce Marshall, *The French Colonial Myth and Constitution-Making under the Fourth Republic* (New Haven, Conn., 1973).

35. N.A., Military Branch, O.S.S. report dated January 27, 1945, from a source "high in the Interior Ministry."

36. See Chaintron's intervention in *La Liberation de la France,* 540.

37. *J'ai cru au matin,* 162. Tillon, *Nouvel Observateur* interview 1977, manuscript version in Robrieux archive.

38. Edouard Depreux, *Souvenirs d'un militant* (Paris, 1972), 279, Jules Moch, *Une si longue vie,* 206.

39. Personal interview, May 30, 1978.

40. Yves Roucaute, *Le PCF et les sommets de l'Etat, de 1945 à nos jours* (Paris, 1981), 113–67.

41. Depreux, *Souvenirs,* 226.

42. *Oeuvres de Léon Blum* (1945–47), 232.

43. "Notre Politique," *Cahiers du Communisme,* 3 (March, 1946), 194.

44. N.A., Diplomatic Branch 851.00, dispatch dated March 13, 1947.

45. Pierre Daix, personal interview, May 5, 1978.

46. So says Lecoeur, personal interview, July 10, 1978.

47. Tillon says of Croizat: "the continuation of our presence in the government determined our electoral following which depended on the action undertaken particularly

at the ministry of labor by Croizat and his team." *On chantait rouge,* 452. Croizat's contribution is recognized by Ross, *Workers and Communists,* 37, and Robrieux, *Histoire Intérieure,* II, 180.

48. *France Nouvelle,* February 13, 1947, called them "an element of the new democracy." For a denigration of Parodi's role see M. Dufriche, Les Comités d'Entreprise dans la démocratie française," *Cahiers du Communisme,* 3–4 (March-April 1947).

49. Michel Collinet, "L'Expérience française des Comités d'entreprise," unpublished typescript in Tasca archive, Fondazzione Feltrinelli (Milan), Carton 137. Dated October 15, 1953.

50. *L'Humanité,* February 23, 1946.

51. Robrieux alludes to this in his *Thorez,* 343–45. Collinet, "L'expérience . . ." stresses their limitations.

52. Collinet, Ibid.

53. Henri Galant, *Histoire politique de la Sécurité social française* (Paris, 1955), 1–13. See also Pierre Laroque, "Le plan français de Sécurité sociale." *Revue française du travail,* 1 (April 1946), 11–19.

54. *L'Humanité,* February 3–4, 1946.

55. *L'Aube,* July 7–8, July 9, 1946.

56. *L'Humanité,* July 7–8, July 10, 1946.

57. Galant, *Histoire politique,* 121. Daniel Mayer, personal interview, July 6, 1973.

58. Jean Bruhat, "La Formation des cadres syndicaux," *Revue française du travail,* 8 (November 1946), 646–54.

59. *L'Humanité,* December 5, 1945.

60. *L'Humanité,* May 3, 1946. See also Janet Flanner, *Paris Journal 1944–65* (New York, 1965), 56.

61. *L'Humanité,* May 21, 1946.

62. *L'Epoque,* October 26, 1946. *L'Aube,* October 17, 1946. The Socialist press also picked up these charges: *Le Populaire,* October 19, 1946.

63. *France Nouvelle,* October 12, 1946.

64. Personal interview, May 30, 1978.

65. This emerges even from the recent party apologia, René Gaudy, *Et la lumière fut nationalisée* (Paris, 1978), 136–37.

66. *Le Monde,* May 8, 1946. *L'Humanité,* September 1–2, 1946. For a complete and exaggerated account see Jean Rivero, *Le regime des nationalisations* (Paris, 1948), 25–48; Rene Gendarme, *L'expérience française de la nationalisation industrielle et ses enseignements économiques* (Paris, 1949), 112–26; Marcel Ventenat, *L'expérience des nationalisations* (Paris, 1947), 137–43.

67. *Paroles françaises* May 4, 18, 1946; August 27, 1946.

68. Daix, *J'ai cru au matin,* 162–75.

69. *L'Humanité,* April 21–22, 1946. Billoux, *Quand nous étions ministres,* 121–42. For criticism of Tillon see Gabriel Enkiri, *Militant de Base* (Paris, 1971), 51–53.

70. *L'Humanité,* November 1, 1946.

71. Tillon, *On chantait rouge,* 416. On the French "spruce goose" see *L'Humanité,* November 5, 1946.

72. *Une se longue vie,* 182–85.

73. *L'Humanité,* January 2, 1946.

74. Tillon, personal interview, May 29, 1978.

75. See François Pommerolle, "Etude de la gestion communiste du ministère de la

Réconstruction et de l'Urbanisme (January-November 1946)." Memoire de Maîtrise, University de Reims, 1968–69.

76. Robrieux, *Thorez*, 297–98, says it was "the most outstanding achievement of his life."

77. *L'Humanité,* October 8, 1946.

78. Ibid., November 13, 1946.

79. Ibid., November 15, 1946.

80. Ibid., November 16, 19, 20, 1946.

81. Guyot proclaimed the Thorez statement the "strategic guide" for PCF action: *Cahiers du Communisme,* 1 (January 1947).

82. *L'Humanité,* December 24, 1946.

83. Ibid., December 18, 1946.

3
THE TURNING POINT, 1947

The new year of 1947 opened in a climate of hope. Blum's homogeneous Socialist government appeared to have brought inflation under control. Vincent Auriol was elected to the Presidency with Communist support, Blum resigned, and a new tripartite government under Paul Ramadier took office, with Thorez as Minister of State and François Billoux as Minister of Defense. Few guessed in January that by the year's end tripartism would collapse, violent social conflict would explode, and France would firmly choose to side with the West in the emerging Cold War. Nor was it clear that the Communists would be consigned to a political ghetto from which they were not to emerge for thirty-four years. The conflicts of 1947 are most often explained in terms of international confrontation between the super-powers. Communists claim they were ousted from the French government in May as a direct consequence of American pressure. Non-Communists, pointing to the founding of a new International of Communist parties, the Cominform, and the "insurrectionary" strikes in France and Italy, argue that the PCF, acting under Soviet orders, sought only a pretext over which to leave the government, revert to a revolutionary line, and initiate a campaign of violence aimed at disruption of the Marshall Plan.

France was a Cold War battleground in the late 1940's but international dimensions of events have obscured their critical internal aspects. France's internal crisis involved political and social conflict of a classic kind. Violence occurred not because anyone tried to make a revolution, but because the stakes were high. In the political arena a struggle occurred over the rate of capital accumulation and the distribution of the costs of economic reconstruction. The Communists, once again in the opposition, turned their attention from questions of productivity to issues of working-class remuneration. In the social sphere, paradoxically, the issue became one of power: the extent of Communist influence in the nationalized industries, Committees of Enterprises, and the social security system. Entrenched Communist positions in these institutions were increasingly viewed as intolerable by the French political establishment.

From the Ramadier government's formation in late January, continued Communist participation appeared problematical. Disagreement was vehement over foreign policy, although the government fell on a domestic issue. On the Indochina question Ramadier stubbornly adhered to Blum's policy, enunciated in December

1946, that order must be restored prior to negotiations. The PCF was committed to the recognition of Ho Chi Minh's regime within the constitutional framework of the French Union. The party straddled the issue. Communist deputies abstained on the vote of war credits on March 18, while the party's cabinet ministers voted with the government. Minister of Defense François Billoux caused a sensation by refusing to rise while the National Assembly gave a moment of silent respect to French forces. In an attempt to patch up the dispute, Thorez was brought into a cabinet sub-committee to draw up instructions for the new High Commissioner in Indochina, Emile Bollaert.[1] In the interim, the National Assembly voted to lift the parliamentary immunity of Malgasay Deputies compromised in that island's insurrection. The Communists protested, claiming a violation of the constitution. But they were silent on the broader issue of a wave of repression by French forces on Madagascar, in which an estimated 80,000 perished. The party could not avoid the growing appearance that it condoned colonial repression.

Colonial peoples, Jacques Fauvet writes, were made to pay the cost of party policy in Germany.[2] If so, the colonies were sacrificed in vain, for the Communists could not achieve their ends across the Rhine. Foreign Minister Bidault returned from the April 1947 Moscow conference of the Four Powers having won Anglo-American recognition of French control of the Saar basin. But Molotov failed to endorse the French positions on internationalization of the Ruhr and reparations. The PCF complained that the Saar was a meager gain, secured at the price of a turn in French foreign policy toward the Anglo-Americans, but the Communist press neglected to comment on the Russian role in this turn of events.[3] Bidault was furious; Léon Blum confessed his consternation both at Molotov's refusal to condone the Saar arrangements and the PCF's angry charge, which he said slavishly followed the Soviet line.[4] But whatever the Soviet role, the party's suspicion of the accord on the Saar was confirmed; France got neither internationalization of the Ruhr, separation of the Rhineland, nor the reparations it demanded.

Participation in the government was becoming unpopular with many impatient party militants. Pierre Daix writes: "This government, with our participation, no longer had any *raison d'être*." Roger Pannequin insists the break with the Ramadier government was greeted with a sense of relief by the party's rank and file.[5] Among informed, non-Communist circles the party's Political Bureau was believed divided on continued participation in the government. The opposition was supposedly led by the "hardliners" under André Marty, Etienne Fajon, and Léon Mauvais, the Algiers group. According to President Auriol's information, Benoît Frachon threw the weight of the CGT behind the Marty-Fajon "block" at the Political Bureau meeting of April 17, 1947. No firm evidence existed of these reputed divisions, however, and the accounts were suspicious because of the absence of denial in the Communist press, indeed, the party's complicity in propagating the rumors. Maurice Thorez confided to Vincent Auriol that there were mutterings of "opportunism" against the leadership of the party in the Political Bureau, confirming reports Auriol was receiving independently from the French police.[6] According to one of these reports, Thorez and the Communist leadership had been outvoted at a meeting of the Central Committee.

If it was not an invention by French intelligence, Auriol's information could well have been leaked by the Communists, to encourage him to believe the party was divided. By threatening the government with a Communist party in opposition, led by the clan of "insurrectionaries" dedicated to fomenting labor unrest, Thorez emphasized his moderate reputation. Presumably his position against the hard-liners would be strengthened by concessions while the impression that the PCF functioned "democratically" like "bourgeois parties" was encouraged. The tactic was partially successful: Auriol believed the party divided, as did much of the non-Communist press. The American Ambassador, Jefferson Caffery, initially skeptical, was also convinced and dutifully reported the content of Auriol's reports to Washington.[7]

But the Socialists were in no mood to strengthen the hand of alleged moderates in the PCF. Ramadier rather sought to use the labor unrest to embarrass the Communists and make their continued participation in the government impossible. Ramadier imposed a freeze on wages and prices in an effort to prolong the respite from inflation achieved by Léon Blum. But the situation was inherently unstable. Workers received a 25 percent pay increase during 1946 as compared to 74 percent rise in retail prices.[8] The disparity led to a resurgence of strike activity: during the first trimester of 1947, 530,000 workdays were lost to the economy. Still a modest total, recent labor unrest appeared ominous viewed against the backdrop of a virtually strike-free economy in 1946, during which only 312,000 workdays had been lost in the twelve months.[9] Strikes by printers and bank employees accounted for more than half of the new activity; the Communists opposed both because they occurred among elite workers, where the party's influence was minimal. Consequently the Socialists encouraged the printers and bank employees in an attempt to outflank the Communists from the left.

Ramadier's wage-price experiment was meanwhile undermined by his reestablishment of free market conditions in the sale of meat; supplies disappeared from the shops and consumers blamed the government.[10] The Communists were hurt by their complicity in these policies, which contributed to their relative defeat in the social security elections of April 29. The CGT majority was eclipsed by the Catholic unions' (CFTC) 30 percent of the vote, far beyond their 10 percent organizational strength in the labor movement.[11] Membership in the CGT, moreover, was declining, and the social security elections occurred as the unions sought a response to the massive strike at Renault.

The Renault strike was another Socialist attempt to outflank the Communists from the left while retaining them as captives of a rigid wage policy. The strike was wildcat; early leadership came from a small nucleus of Trotskyists.[12] The Socialist press, unhampered by the constraints of democratic centralism, supported the strikers. The CGT, operating under the "transmission belt" theory of Leninism, could not take a different position from the Communist ministers.

Sentiment among Renault workers was always crucial for the party. If the CGT could not control the workers there, it would soon be overwhelmed by similar strikes throughout its industrial base, and the Communist party would never accept being outflanked on its left. There was no choice but to have the CGT champion the strike movement and assume its leadership.[13] On April 29, *L'Humanité* endorsed the "legitimate demands" of the workers. The CGT tried, however, to negotiate a rapid settlement, demanding a "productivity bonus" consistent with the government's policy of holding the line on salaries. The Communists wanted a return to work.

Thorez pleaded in the cabinet for a relaxation of the wage freeze policy. As a Marxist, he said, he could not in good conscience assent to the theory of the wage-price spiral; wages could be raised without incidence on prices, if profits were reduced.[14] Citing government statistics, Thorez argued that wages constituted a reduced portion of the national revenue than had been the case in 1938.[15] Reduced profits would mean lessened investment and a slower rate of growth for the economy as a whole; that Thorez left unsaid. But the debate was classic, consumption now versus accumulation for increased production later. The Communists argued that further deferral of mass consumption was impractical politically. The Socialists mindlessly eroded their political base by persisting in the longer view. Whatever the influence of the Americans or the infamous hand of Moscow, the May cabinet crisis unfolded according to the pattern of cabinet crises during the Third and Fourth Republics.

The Socialists changed the rules, however. The Communists expected the government to resign unless Ramadier retreated from his hard line on the wage question.[16] The CGT waited until the outcome of the cabinet crisis was clear before extending the strike movement. But since Ramadier's majority was large enough without the PCF, he simply published a decree in the *Journal Officiel* relieving the Communist ministers of their functions. No one was more surprised by this maneuver than the Socialist Premier's own party, but a hastily convened national council agreed, by a narrow majority, to authorize Socialist participation in the cabinet without the Communists. Thorez counted on a victory of the Guy Mollet faction, telling the PCF Political Bureau that a majority of the Socialist party's Directing Committee favored Ramadier's resignation.[17] Out-maneuvered, Thorez was still not bitter. He would have preferred to continue in the government, he told Auriol, but the pressures were just too much; "I am at the end of my rope."[18] Even though the government had survived its initial bout with labor unrest, Thorez reasoned, it would soon understand that it needed the cooperation of the workers. A few strikes in succession, Duclos said, would convince the Socialists to abandon their wage freeze and secure labor peace by inviting the Communists back in the government. It was only a matter of time. The PCF remained a responsible party of government, its departure from the cabinet was momentary. Those who talked of a general strike, were "imbeciles."[19]

The Renault strike was settled on May 10 with a modest pay increase of three francs per hour. Rid of the Communists, Ramadier showed greater readiness to compromise on the wage-freeze policy. The CGT followed by advocating generalized pay increases, thinly disguised as productivity bonuses, throughout Paris metallurgical industries. The crack in the government's resolve quickly widened; Citroen workers won a similar three-franc increase and other unions demanded the same.[20] On May 17 more metallurgical strikes occurred. Then the nation's millers walked out, their industry in the limelight because of a nationwide campaign, initiated by the government on May 15, to convince peasants to release grain stocks and alleviate a critical bread shortage. When gas and electricity workers threatened a stoppage on May 24, the government threatened to draft the workers and order them back to work. Saner heads prevailed, and both sides agreed to accept the mediation of *Conseiller d'Etat* Grunebaum-Ballin, but the social climate continued tense through June. A simultaneous walkout by Parisian bakers and railroad workers occurred; the latter strike threatened national economic paralysis.

Were these strikes orchestrated by the Communists? Social commentators and the government seemed to think so. Questioned in the National Assembly, Ramadier complained of "A kind of spiral movement of strikes . . . from one milieu to another . . . as if there were a clandestine orchestra conductor." Jules Moch, Minister of Transportation, alluded to "pernicious slogans" allegedly being spread by the CGT during the rail shutdown.[21] But Moch was duplicitous; he knew that the rail strike was based on genuine worker discontent and like the Renault strike, begun by Trotskyists. The CGT endorsed the workers' demands but did nothing to encourage the movement's spread.[22] Ramadier had himself to blame for much of the labor unrest. On May 23, one day before gas and electricity workers began their strike, he announced the government's decision to postpone until December a re-examination of the wage question, which had been promised for July. This was a fateful decision. PCF policy throughout the rest of 1947 remained focused on the December deadline, but the French working class was unwilling to wait.[23] The government meanwhile continued to appear hostile toward the workers throughout June. Ramadier grudgingly accepted the mediation terms of the electricity strike but threatened the further requisition of workers and restrictive strike legislation. For several days he stubbornly refused to negotiate with leaders of the railroad unions.

The PCF sought to project an image of moderation. Former Minister Marcel Paul, now again head of the electrical workers, rallied to mediation of the electricity strike. Paul insists today that the working class was on the defensive throughout 1947. The Communists joined with the government, despite long-standing differences in agricultural policy, in a solemn appeal to the peasantry to put their supplies on the market. The only "clandestine conductor" of the strikes, *L'Humanité* replied to Ramadier, was the workers' misery. During the rail strike the party repeatedly urged the government to negotiate a settlement. Thorez, acting according to the PCF press "as a great statesman," recalled the greater moments in Communist party history: the battle for productivity and June 1936 slogan: "We must know how to end a strike."[24] The CGT supported set-tlements in the rail and electricity strikes on June 13 and helped negotiate set-tlements in the troubled banks, department stores, and mines. On July 10 public employees presented wage demands; Duclos urged, in the name of badly needed order and calm in the country, that they accept the government's offer.

At the Party Congress of Strasbourg in July, the PCF vaunted its achievements in the cabinet, proclaimed itself a "government party," and repeated that the battle for production remained the new incarnation of the class struggle.[25] Thorez's "French road to socialism" was still on the agenda; the "dictatorship of the proletariat" need not apply to an advanced nation like France. Thorez took note of the Marshall Plan, rejected the idea of a Western bloc, but remained open to the idea of accepting American assistance on condition that French independence not be compromised. He projected the image of a youthful and dynamic party, claiming 819,155 members, of whom at least 500,000, according to Robrieux, were fully paid. Of 1200 delegates at Strasbourg, three-fourths were under age forty, and 200 were women, while a majority were workers.

In perhaps the most important passage of his speech, Thorez opened the prospect of career advancement for the PCF's socially promoted cadres in the structure of the state:[26]

The progress of democracy results in the placement of Communists in responsible positions in newly created economic, political, and administrative organisms. Consequently, the presence in all responsible party posts (and in positions occupied outside the party by Communists) of authentic cadres is a decisive question.

The phrase "decisive question" clearly denoted the issue upon which the PCF placed paramount importance. Trained, loyal, and competent Communist personnel were required to serve in the Committees of Enterprises, social security system, nationalized enterprises, price committees, municipalities, public services, and mass organizations. Participation in the government was only the surface issue; the French welfare state's infrastructure was all a potential sphere of Communist influence. But even as Thorez spoke, Communist-held offices were being challenged.

The Socialist offensive began during the short-lived Socialist government of Léon Blum in January. Daniel Mayer, Minister of Labor under Blum, set the date of elections in the social security system, which the Communist Minister of Labor, Ambroise Croizat, had repeatedly postponed. Mayer ordered proportional representation in the councils of social security disbursement offices, ensuring against monolithic control by the CGT.[27] Robert Lacoste, Blum's Minister of Industrial Production, meanwhile moved to limit CGT representation and strengthen the government's role on Councils of Administration of state-run economic enterprises. Lacoste later increased efforts to undo the Communist power structure in coal and electricity put in place by Paul and Lecoeur.[28] In June he dismissed three of Paul's appointees in the nationalized electric company and reduced the CGT's representation on the council of the coal industry from twelve to six. The Ramadier government, rid of the Communists as coalition partners, set to work purging them in all sectors of the government. The U.S. State Department noted in March 1947 that both the Army and the Interior Ministry were purging Communists from their ranks.[29]

Despite these menacing moves, the PCF campaigned through the summer of 1947 to get back into the government. In July the party appealed for unity of the left to defend the Republic and organized a mammoth July 14 demonstration under that theme. If the government would not act responsibly for labor peace, the PCF announced it would do so on its own. On July 17, the CGT and the Confédération Générale du Patronat Français (CGPF) began discussions on an interim wage settlement for the private sector of the economy. Labor and management agreed that, "The CGT does not challenge the authority of management, just as the CGPF does not challenge the exercise of syndical liberties."[30] The PCF Political Bureau heralded the accord as the way to achieve a renaissance of the French economy in a climate of tranquillity suited to the national interest. On August 1 Labor and Management agreed on an 11 percent pay increase and establishment of joint employee-worker committees to study ways of holding down prices and settling grievances.

The image of responsibility was designed to accomplish a victory in the October municipal elections and return to the government after a demonstration of the party's mass support. The elections would be a plebiscite on the work of the Ramadier government which, since the ousting of the PCF ministers in May, had been "sliding to the right" and projecting an image of disorder and powerlessness.[31] When Finance Minister Robert Schuman introduced a new austerity plan, *L'Humanité* promptly dubbed it a "plan of misery." Schuman's scheme called for a continued wage freeze and higher indirect taxes; some Socialist ministers, acutely aware of the growing labor unhappiness, fought the plan in the cabinet without success.[32] The government further refused to ratify the CGT-CGPF agreements, although it was unable to prevent their partial implementation in September.

Jacques Duclos made public a long list of Communist grievances against the Ramadier government in August, attacking price increases on postage, matches, tobacco, gasoline, and transportation. The PCF proposed instead a 77-billion-franc cut in military expenditures and a tax on corporate profits.[33] Duclos accused the government of hostility to the workers and insensitivity to the Gaullist threat and expressed suspicion of the Marshall Plan, which put German reconstruction before French. He denounced the Socialists' projected system of balloting in the forthcoming municipal elections as having a blatantly anti-Communist character. The Communists now condemned the ensemble of the Ramadier government's policies without reserve.

But Duclos still warned against any impatience, adventurism, or desire for confrontation in Communist ranks. Marius Patinaud denounced expressions of relief by some Communists following the break with Ramadier as a demonstration of irresponsibility which "fails to take into account the duties that go with the title of militant of the first (largest) party of France."[34] Duclos and Patinaud were clearly concerned with impatience among the rank and file with the PCF's moderate policies. Only a return of the PCF to the government, said Patinaud, could permit the extension of working-class conquests. The *fonctionnaires* needed Thorez to protect them; the workers and the aged missed former Labor Minister Croizat. Instead of the labor peace essential for the economy, workers had been constrained to adopt "former methods of struggle." With Communists in power strikes were unnecessary. The PCF was the party of the masses who wanted it in the government. The municipal elections, Duclos promised, would create a government in which the PCF shared responsibility proportionate to its electoral influence.

On September 20 Duclos and Fajon left for Warsaw to represent the PCF at the founding of the Cominform. In a Warsaw suburb, they listened to a scathing indictment of the policies of the French and Italian Communists from the Liberation through 1947. Togliatti had a sense of what awaited in Warsaw and according to Robrieux, advised Thorez not to attend. But if Thorez knew anything, he did not show it. The PCF, he repeated for Reuters the day of the delegation's departure, remained a party of government.[35] The hypothesis of the party's surprise at the turn of 1947 is further confirmed by the report Duclos read in Warsaw, which limited itself to a strong defense of the PCF's achievements while participating in the French government.

The conjuncture of the Warsaw conference of Communist parties and the violent strikes several weeks later endowed the PCF with the Jacobin insurrectionary image it retained for years afterward. The party was clearly too weak in 1947 to contemplate seizing power. But a historical consensus holds that the PCF sought to achieve political goals by violent confrontation. At a minimum, the Communists allegedly sought to disrupt the economy forcing cancellation of Marshall Plan aid. As a more ambitious goal, they supposedly hoped to force their return to a position of shared power.[36] Jules Moch, Minister of the Interior during the drama, insists the PCF was engaged in a rehearsal for an uprising, which would have been pushed to the limit in the event of a demonstrated weakness of public authority.[37]

Confusion continues to surround the founding conference of the Cominform. To what extent it represented an obligatory turn by Western Communist parties to a revolutionary line is unclear. Zhdanov's keynote speech divided the world into two camps, imperialist war-mongering versus socialist peace-loving nations. He bitterly attacked international Social-Democracy as the principal supporter of the imperialist bourgeoisie. But Stalin's emissary abstained from revolutionary rhetoric and stressed the need for peace.[38] Curiously, Duclos and Fajon, representing the PCF, were among the few persons present who finished out their careers within the orthodox Communist fold. Both downplayed the meeting's importance in their memoirs. Zhdanov died a year after the conference. The Yugoslavs Djilas and Kardelj, who acted as chief prosecutors of the French and Italians, were, with Tito, to be regarded as fascists within the same period of time. Other participants like Kostov, Slansky, and Gomulka, fell victim to purge trials in their countries, which most failed to survive. Why did Zhdanov permit the Yugoslavs to carry their indictment of the French to the point of reproach for failure to carry out an insurrection in 1944? Eugenio Reale, the Italian participant in the conference who later left the Italian Communist Party (PCI), portrayed Duclos as prostrate, humiliated, and having behaved "like a petty shopkeeper found guilty of fraud" in the face of Djilas' charges. But by denying that any insurrection was possible in 1944, Duclos was defending Stalin's position at the time. Fajon said Djilas made outrageous charges, to which Duclos responded firmly, putting the Yugoslav in his place. Duclos observed that "certain delegations" had decided to put the PCF on trial, with painful results.[39]

Duclos, on behalf of the PCF, pleaded guilty to opportunism, legalism, and parliamentary illusions and promised to go beyond parliamentary forms of action in the future. The Russians, however, did not lead in criticism of the French; Zhdanov offered the rather innocuous observation that the PCF, once ousted from the government, would have done better to drop the formula of a government party and call itself what it was, a party of opposition. Duclos, in his reply, accepted Zhdanov's criticism, but rejected Djilas' as having been "badly informed" in French affairs.[40] Fajon noted Zhdanov raised a purely "formal question" in any case, since an opposition party always intends to be a government party eventually. Thorez appeared initially to take the Cominform charges more seriously in his self-criticism speech of late October, promising to orient the party toward direct action. But according to Léo Figuères, Thorez was glad of Duclos' defense of French tactics in Warsaw and deeply hurt by the rejection of his "French road to socialism."[41] The creation of a new international organization of Communist parties meant the PCF would have more difficulty claiming its line was made in Paris. But it was not immediately evident what the conference meant for French politics.

With municipal elections pending, the PCF continued to refer to itself as a party of government, notwithstanding Zhdanov's criticism. Thorez made one important change in the formula. Instead of demanding simply a share of power, the Communists now insisted on "a government of democratic union in which the working class and its Communist party exercise, in the last analysis, a determining role."[42] It was a thoroughly ambiguous demand, ominous in tone; yet, in any coalition of the left, the PCF would be the strongest party both in membership and votes and might aspire to a determining role in the last analysis, whatever that meant in practice. This change in the PCF's slogan constituted the whole of its response to Zhdanov's criticism. *L'Humanité* called Thorez's speech historic. But evidence of a more substantive change in the PCF's line did not appear until a month later in reaction to French political developments, not Russian policy. In the strike movement of November the PCF found something more concrete to offer in response to the Russians' criticism.

The Communist press emphasized Zhdanov's message that the main responsibility of Communist parties was to defend the national independence of their countries against American imperialism.[43] The Marshall Plan must be combatted with vehemence. The disagreement with the Socialists was bitter; *L'Humanité* described Ramadier as "the Gauleiter of Truman." But despite the new invective the PCF continued to hope for a muncipal elections victory large enough to force the Socialists' return to a left-wing government. The PCF still stressed its states-man-like image and proposed to carry out only the most moderate and realistic programs. The Communist vote in the municipal elections held steady at 29 percent, far from the expected victory; the result showed some erosion in Communist support since the last local elections in 1946.[44] Instead of bringing a renewed period of Communist participation in power, the elections became a prelude to an assault on Communist positions through every level of French society.

The challenge began in the municipalities immediately after the elections, but quickly became entangled with working-class demands, and both issues dove-tailed in the dramatic November events in Marseille. Labor unrest was widespread in the fall, first manifested in the October 14 Parisian Metro workers' strike. The strike was not begun by the CGT, which announced its support two days later, but was caused by a dispute over reclassification of *fonctionnaires*.[45] Given the severity of recent price increases, workers also demanded a provisional indemnity to tide them over until the general re-examination of the wage question in December. The executive bureau of the CGT was scheduled to meet on November 12–13 to formulate its demands for presentation at the December negotiations. On October 18 Frachon announced he would propose at the November meeting that the CGT adopt as its negotiating position a raise in the minimum wage from the present 7000 francs per month to a new level of 11,000 francs. Frachon blamed governmental intransigeance for the continuation of the Metro strike, and endorsed the workers' demands for a provisional indemnity: "until then [December]," he said, "we must live." The Metro strike was settled within days on the workers' terms. CGT officials now suggested that the indemnity granted the subway workers be extended to other industries. Since price increases had averaged 26 percent since May, this was the only way, the union argued, further labor unrest could be prevented.[46]

But the government was not about to seek the CGT's help in forestalling labor unrest. During the Metro strike government negotiators by-passed the CGT and dealt directly with so-called autonomous unions, the nuclei of the anti-Communist Force Ouvrière (FO) which broke off from the Communist-controlled CGT in December.[47] By encouraging a split in the French labor movement, the government threatened the whole structure of social and political power acquired by the Communist party since the war. As a united labor federation the CGT routinely received from 60 to 70 percent of the vote in plant committees and social security offices. If 20 percent or more of the CGT vote could be lured away, the Communists' dominant position would be broken around the nation.

The Communists reserved their greatest expressions of indignation, however, for Socialist behavior in the aftermath of the municipal elections, in which

Gaullists and Communists had emerged as the two largest political forces in France. Around the country Socialists abandoned coalitions with the Communists, often resulting not only in the defeat of Communist mayors, but the election of Gaullists. The PCF regarded de Gaulle's "Rally of the French people" as fascist, and considered itself the "rampart of the Republic" in France's cities. In Marseille, Communists held sixteen of the necessary nineteen-vote majority on the City Council, but three crucial Socialist swing votes went to Gaston Deferre, permitting the election of the Gaullist, Carlini, as mayor. The same process occurred in eight municipalities in Paris' Red Belt and Le Havre. Throughout France, the U.S. Embassy noted with approval, a solid anti-Communist barrage had been created in French cities. The Communists lost control of 842 cities, 34 percent of those they had previously held, while losing only 3 percent of the popular vote. The PCF lost all seven of the largest cities in which Communist mayors had held office: Marseille, Saint-Etienne, Toulon, Reims, Limoges, Nantes, and Nîmes.[48] The Communists were incensed by the Socialists' reversal of alliances and could find only one word for it—treason.

The Socialist "betrayal" played an important role in Thorez's taking to heart the Cominform criticism of his policies. The PCF's internal bulletin, *La Vie du Parti,* equated the Cominform conference and the municipal elections as the two "key events" of the recent period.[49] Only after the delivery of the City Hall of Marseille to the Gaullists did the party begin regularly to repeat Thorez's earlier call for a government with the PCF in a preponderant role. The heart of the new Communist policy turn was the characterization of the Socialists as the "principal support of the bourgeoisie" and "leaders of the way to fascism," which appeared a return to the "class-against-class" rhetoric of the inter-war years. But from the PCF's perspective, the Socialists had earned these epithets.

On October 30, Thorez delivered his *mea culpa* speech on behalf of the Central Committee, accusing it of opportunism and vacillation in its policies.[50] The PCF had misinterpreted as a mundane ministerial crisis in May what had in fact been a U.S.-orchestrated ejection of Communists from governments of all the shortly-to-be "Marshallized" countries of Western Europe. The party had failed to recognize the new international situation and the treasonous policies of the right-wing socialists. Mesmerized by the idea of an entente with the Socialist leaders, the Communist leadership had repeated the errors of the Popular Front, failing to extend its political alliance to the local level, in party parlance, "at the base." In its vain hopes of returning to power, the party failed to oppose the Algerian statute of September 1947 and acted without sufficient vigor on other issues as well. Thorez offered a single, clear-cut remedy: the party must be oriented toward direct mass action, and align itself forcefully with working-class economic demands. To deal with the revived fascist danger, committees of republican defense, spearheaded by the Communists, must be formed throughout France.

In the new rhetoric of "unity from below" and direct mass action, observers saw evidence of a new PCF turn to class war and revolution. But those terms were absent from the Communist leader's rhetoric. Thorez had simply clarified the terms of the PCF's demand for a government with itself in a preponderant role. The PCF wanted to change both foreign and internal French policy. To do so it needed a coalition with the Socialists, clearly impossible under their present leadership. Hence the double tactic of leveling invective against the Socialist leadership while making overtures to their rank and file. When mass pressure from below forced a change in the Socialist leaders' attitudes, as occurred in 1934, cooperation with the PCF would again be possible. There was no better way to accomplish unity from below than with the theme of republican defense. By accenting the Gaullist danger, the PCF hoped to overcome its threatened isolation and pave the way for a renewed period of "no enemies on the left." Thorez was not offering a recipe for revolution. He still hoped to achieve a new Popular Front, the only policy he ever understood to be possible.

In aligning the party with working-class economic demands, Thorez recognized the damage done by the policy of productivity and Stakhanovism followed since the war. This was hardly a turn to a revolutionary policy either. The CGT returned to its functional role as mediator between French working-class demands and the political system. The Communists would not again sacrifice the economic well-being of the workers in a vain pursuit of political acceptance.

The active CGT role in the formulation of workers' demands was one of the principal differences between the November-December strike movement and the labor unrest that had preceded it. The outbreak of the strikes still had a large element of spontaneity, however, because the CGT was unable to influence the government's policies. On November 12 the CGT bureau adopted Frachon's demand for an 11,000-franc minimum monthly wage as its negotiating position in the reopening of the salary question in December. The union leaders further demanded a 25 percent across-the-board salary increase and a trimestrial revision of salaries based on raises in the price index.[51] The CGT did introduce a new twist in its procedures. Open meetings of workers were to be held within factories to approve these demands, thereby giving unorganized workers a direct voice in the determination of union policy. Vehemently protested by the non-Communist component of the CGT, Force Ouvrière, this unprecedented tactic became one of the main issues in the upcoming union movement split. Since the percentage of Communists was much higher among organized workers, Force Ouvrière's opposition to including the non-organized in the decision-making process can only be interpreted as evidence of the generalized combative mood of French labor.[52] The CGT Bureau was to reconvene on December 19 to decide what action to take following its consultation with workers, in the event the government proved unresponsive. No strike activity was planned in the interim. The Communist majority in the CGT bureau went on to condemn the Marshall Plan and demand the formation of a government of democratic union. To see the strikes in terms of these political goals, as hysterical politicians insisted on doing, is seriously to miss their meaning.

The workers' demands were defensive, aimed at catching up their purchasing power eroded by inflation. Purchasing power of mine workers, for example, had reached its lowest point since the German occupation.[53] In early November Jules Moch, Minister of National Economy, decreed yet another round of price increases. At his urging, the Ramadier government removed the government subvention from the coal industry, permitting prices to rise from 1350 to 2160 francs per ton.[54] Coal, as the basic fuel, affected the price of virtually everything else in the economy. Transport costs rose 25 percent on November 14, electricity and gas prices 45 percent. On November 8 *L'Humanité* foresaw further price increases likely on 473 different consumer items. These increases, coming just as the huge labor federation was in the process of formulating its demands, could only have been expected to exacerbate worker unrest. Moch knew as well that in singling out the coal industry, he was attacking a bastion of Communist power. The CGT was still powerful in the administration of the mines, and the PCF had supported continued government subsidies to the coal industry in September. Underlying the government's policy was a desire to increase productivity in the mines through the introduction of imported, modern, U.S.-made labor-saving machinery, available through Marshall Plan aid.[55] The Communists charged that raising French prices to world levels would result in the inundation of France with American coal and the ruin of the industry. On November 10 Victorin Duguet, the Communist President of the Council of Administration of the Charbonnages de France, resigned in protest against the government's alleged "sabotage" of the heroic work of industrial reconstruction carried on by the miners since the Liberation. Duguet angrily charged Robert Lacoste with systematically purging the the mines.[56] Lacoste responded by firing the government representative on the administrative council of the Charbonnages, the Communist André Delfosse, on November 14, ostensibly because Delfosse was out of sympathy with government pricing policy for the industry.

Delfosse's dismissal directly triggered the miners' walkout.[57] On November 15, not yet having had time to react, *L'Humanité* was still talking about the December 19 deadline, at which time the CGT would offer wage proposals based on the results of its unprecedented consultation and experimentation with direct syndical democracy. The Communists did not expect any strikes before December, if then. But over the weekend five pits were struck, and the union clearly had been obliged to follow along because "the workers were unwilling to wait" for their pay increase. By November 18, 130,000 miners already were out and the strikes spread to the Paris metallurgical industries. *L'Humanité* now announced that "the strength and authority of the CGT had been affirmed anew in this generalized action," precisely what it would not have said had the Communist union been leading the strikes rather than responding to events beyond its control.[58] The CGT quickly adapted to a leadership role, demanding a 25 percent indemnity and an end to the government's "assault on nationalizations," or threat to the Communist entrenched positions in the industry.

While the strikes were in their infancy, the nation's eyes were still riveted on the city of Marseille where the Socialist-condoned Gaullist seizure of the municipality had borne its first fruit. French historians have begun to interpret the Marseille events from a revisionist perspective, providing a key to understanding the November-December crisis.[59] One of the first acts of the Council was to raise tramway fares, precipitating a Communist demonstration of protest. Police arrested four demonstrators, one of them a Deputy. In the ensuing disorders, a Communist militant was shot causing massive protest walkouts in the city. When the four Communist demonstrators were arraigned at the Palais de Justice, an angry crowd stormed the building and forced their release. A fistfight broke out between Communist and Gaullist members of the City Council, while the crowds forced their way into the Hôtel de Ville and imprisoned the mayor in his office. Later the same day, angry bands of Communist youths attacked the city's night clubs, broke windows, and pillaged "symbols of luxury amid widespread want."

Given what government officials interpreted as an insurrectionary climate in the city, interest focused on the behavior of two companies of security police, the Compagnies Républicaines de Securité (CRS), who had failed to contain the crowds. These companies were officered by many Communists who had moved into police work after their Resistance experience in the armed militia and FTP. There was an unsual sense of camaraderie in these CRS units, which had not interfered with competent police work until the events in question. The Socialists charged Communist officers sided with the demonstrators, refusing to block their access to the Palais de Justice and the Hôtel de Ville on November 14. President Vincent Auriol angrily demanded the companies in be dissolved, which Interior Minister Depreux did on November 18, accusing the units of putting party above duty and being accomplices of the rioters.[60] The Communist press reported only that the CRS units had refrained from beating up workers. Communist deputy Raoul Calas, however, claimed the charge of CRS solidarity with demonstrators as a badge of honor during a filibuster on anti-sabotage legislation early in December. The CRS companies, Calas said, were like the heroic seventeenth regiment of guards during the 1907 Midi wine growers' insurrection, who rather than become accomplices in repression, fraternized with the protestors. Calas was censured and forcibly removed from the hall by indignant Deputies.[61]

Only 221 CRS men were on duty against an angry 15,000 demonstrators; they could not have held the crowd even with the strongest desire to do so. They received no authorization to use weapons or tear gas, and the crowd was never given the necessary summation to disperse. Whether the Socialists set a trap or simply used the incidents as a pretext for the dissolution of the CRS companies, the incidents fit within the context of a Socialist offensive against Communist-held positions:[62]

The presence, from that time forward judged to be dangerous, of Communist militants in positions of active responsibility, the "necessity" to eliminate them, and as a consequence the closure of the historical period opened by the Liberation, closure which was to give to the Fourth Republic its most lasting imprint.

It is ironic, writes René Gallisot, that the Socialists, who had successfully integrated into the state apparatus, should have been so obsessed with much more modest Communist efforts to do the same. The Prague coup still lay in the future. Yet for Auriol, Communism meant seizure of power by the technique of the Trojan horse, and with the egotistical Jules Moch shortly to take over the Ministry of the Interior, the situation was not far from civil war. Maurice Agulhon argues that PCF motives were benign: "It is certain that the PCF carried out a policy of very active integration into the machinery of State, [but] finally in a loyal manner, without any plan of subversion." René Gallisot, however, remains on firmer ground, judging the Communists by their acts and capabilities: "Their weight leaves far behind the accusations of conquest of power by means of the street, the affabulations of conspiracy, and the over-enlarged shadow of the Soviet phantom."[63] The PCF was far too weak to contemplate a coup but was desperately defending its positions gained during the Liberation era.

Ramadier resigned on November 20, leaving an expanding situation of labor unrest that was centered around a strike axis from the troubled coalfields of the Nord, through Paris, to the besieged city of Marseille. Each industrial center now had over 100,000 strikers. As a parting blow, Ramadier and Depreux fired the two remaining Communist prefects, Jean Chaintron and Lucien Monjauvis, both of whom had held office since the Liberation. In its call for resolution of the cabinet crisis, the PCF said Ramadier was resigning in "shame and dishonor." The only alternative, the party said, was a government of order and efficacy, a united government of Communists, Socialists, and Catholics, peasants, artisans, shopkeepers, and functionaries, in which the PCF exercised a determining role.[64]

By November 23–24, 1 million workers were striking. The movement at its crest approached 3 million, significantly larger than the Popular Front strikes eleven years earlier. There was little parallel between the two movements—the aging figure of Léon Blum, stepping forward again to offer, not conciliation as in the earlier crisis, but a declaration of war on both Communism and Gaullism, pointed up the differences. Blum was defeated because some deputies took offense at the nasty things he said about the Gaullists. It was the austere, monkish MRP leader, Robert Schuman, who instead succeeded in forming the government. With the coldly intelligent and efficient Jules Moch as Minister of Interior, the government's attitude toward the strikers was one of no nonsense. Bidault, again the foreign minister, insisted that no concessions be granted the strikers until order was restored, the same policy he followed in Indochina.[65] Several MRP leaders demanded a "political show of force" before meeting any strikers' demands. Moch was ready to give the workers an indemnity of 1500 francs, but only to deprive the strikers of any "legitimate" economic motives of discontent and lay bare the supposed political character of the movement. Daniel Mayer, Minister of Labor, remained in touch with CGT leader Benoît Frachon throughout the crisis, and argued in vain for greater comprehension of the legitimate basis of the workers' discontent. In his first circular to Prefects, Moch announced that the government would consider the strike movement as insurrectionary and act accordingly.[66]

On November 30, Schuman offered a 1500-franc cost-of-living increase to non-strikers payable after June 1948. The CGT rejected it, holding out for retroactive application of the raise and guarantees of future periodic revision of salaries based on the price index. On November 28, a special strike committee was formed with Frachon and René Arrachard, leader of the Construction Workers' Union, at its head. Virtually all the major industrial labor federations, and several organizations of government workers, were included, most but not all Communist-controlled.[67] Formation of a strike committee was a time-honored CGT tactic aimed at diminishing its own role and creating a more or less believable façade of unity; neither FO nor the CFTC would join although Jouhaux initially endorsed the strike demands. The government called up troops, introduced new anti-strike legislation, and increased the penalties for sabotage. It also tried to guarantee access to work for non-strikers. The Communists were outraged. A party tract denounced the proposed legislation as fascist inspired, and Communist Deputies filibustered to stop the legislation. Raoul Calas now proudly claimed that the CRS companies had fraternized with the Marseille protestors. Thorez, curiously just returned from a trip to the USSR, arrived in time to join in a parliamentary rendition of the song of the glorious seventeenth regiment. Outside of the political rhetoric the workers showed moderation. The strike committee promised the labor unrest would cease immediately upon the acceptance of its formulated demands, which were aimed only at guaranteeing the purchasing power of the workers.[68]

From December 1 through 9 the CGT actively sought to generalize the strike movement in an attempt to bring it under control and negotiate a settlement. Events clearly escalated out of control, however. On December 3 the Paris-Lille express was derailed, resulting in seventeen deaths. An investigation revealed that several meters of rail were deliberately unbolted. Many charged the Communists with sabotage. Neither terrorism nor sabotage was publicly condoned by the party, which placed the blame on "reactionary Gaullist provocation." The Union of Railroad Workers denounced the incident, and *L'Humanité* claimed it had clear proof of Gaullist complicity, but responsibility for the derailment still remains cloudy. Although Moch accused the Communists, the government made no arrests and charged nobody with the crime, while scores of workers were arrested for petty infractions during the strikes. Charles Tillon, who attended all the Political Bureau's meetings during the crisis, still believes the derailment to be a government provocation. Roger Pannequin claims to have carried out an independent investigation which ruled out any unauthorized action by party or trade union militants. The ready availability of derailing equipment in the vicinity, he says, points to the likelihood of government or railway officials' involvement.[69] Auguste Lecoeur, however, charged Pannequin and his Resistance associate René Camphin with responsibility for the sabotage, carried out without party authorization in the belief that the train was carrying CRS reinforcements. Thorez, according to Lecoeur, was so furious when he learned of the sabotage, that he resolved to end Pannequin's party career.[70] The only certainty appears to be the PCF leadership's non-involvement.

The sabotage contributed to the climate of hysteria that gripped both sides in the final days of the strikes. By December 2 the strike had completely paralyzed seven French departments.[71] Acts of sabotage occurred frequently. Coal miners in the Nord took control of the industry's truck park and dispatched militants to pits in which a return to work threatened. Roads were controlled by strikers in the coal regions while pickets stood guard over struck telephone, railroad, and electrical centers around the country. Moch used army engineers in the Paris electrical power plants to forestall an interruption of power in the capital. Believing an insurrectionary condition to exist, he appointed regional super-prefects authorized in emergencies to rule by martial law. Moch used troops to enforce right-to-work provisions of the emergency legislation and developed plans to abandon the capital to the Communists if necessary, the government retreating to Brittany to fight back from a guerrilla base.[72]

The strikes were unusually violent; workers fought pitched battles with the CRS to defend their pits. But the strikers observed legal procedures of their own while resisting the government. They disarmed and captured police agents, but always released their captives, retaining only a few of them for interrogation.[73] Communist behavior at the height of the strikes caused fear, and despite the camouflage of a National Strike Committee it was known that the PCF Political Bureau secretly met during the strikes and made all the crucial decisions.[74] The ad hoc worker assemblies formed by the CGT raised the specter of soviets. The PCF called upon its militants to form other local groups during the height of the crisis. In Marseille, local neighborhood committees were reported controlling the streets at various times during the crisis. The internal bulletin, *La Vie du Parti,* called on the committees to obtain the release of those arrested, "punish" attackers of PCF elected officials during the imbroglio at the City Hall, and administer "lessons" to night clubs overflowing with goods the masses lacked.[75] Neighborhood committees were also formed in the PCF bastion north of Paris, Saint-Denis. The party reactivated committees to control prices (in operation since 1946), organized groups to defend the interests of renters, taxpayers, and peasants, and formed associations to protect enterprises threatened by U.S. competition, specifically in the automobile, aviation, and movie industries.[76] U.S. Ambassador Caffery warned of "embryonic soviets" taking shape throughout France, and Secretary of State Marshall was sufficiently impressed to forward a resume from Washington to all U.S. European diplomatic posts.[77]

But the vast majority of committees either existed only on paper or were perfunctory at best; in many cases they were simply re-baptized local Communist cells. Only the committees to protect the aviation industry and French cinema won the cooperation of many non-Communists and continued to operate after the strike movement was over. The rest rapidly expired.

Angelo Tasca saw two central Communist goals during the strikes: to avenge the party's ouster from the cities and demonstrate that it could prevent any stabilization of the French economy attempted without its cooperation. Periodic salary adjustment based on prices was the only issue on which the CGT refused to compromise. That was not a recipe for the sabotage of economic recovery, as the party's opponents insisted. The PCF was forcing the French government to chose between working-class collaboration in the task of economic recovery and American aid; hence the injection of the Marshall Plan into strike rhetoric. But the same choice was clearly being imposed on the French by the Americans. As early as June 27, the U.S. Embassy reported that the possibility of the Communists returning to the government was believed in France to diminish the prospects for American aid: "In the negative sense we should do nothing to discourage this belief," Caffery wrote, although the situation was judged "not susceptible of treatment by U.S. government action." Caffery constructed a scenario according to which the PCF, by fomenting disorder, brought de Gaulle to power and then paralyzed him by means of a general strike. But Caffery's critical comment was financial: "I need hardly add that hope of American financial and moral support . . . will continue to constitute probably the most important force in strengthening the will to resist among all non-Communist Frenchmen, whatever their political persuasion."[78]

The PCF feared repression in the days following the train derailment as much as the government feared a coup. President Auriol's informants reported that the Soviet ambassador criticized the Strike Committee on December 3 for failing to create a "dual power." But the party only further moderated its position, and Auriol received another report according to which Thorez took the party to task for its *gauchisme* or leftist adventurism during the strikes.[79] French intelligence services were notoriously unworthy of credence. Auriol would have done better to look at the party's acts. The PCF repeatedly denied the strikes were political. Georges Cogniot pointed to the commercial employees' strike, which was headed by a member of the Directing Committee of the Socialist party. Thorez emphasized that wherever satisfaction was won, a return to work occurred peacefully and normally. The Strike Committee formally noted all negotiated returns to work with approval. In an effort to get negotiations off dead center, Frachon made a personal appeal to President Auriol. In classic manner Croizat blamed the prolongation of the strike on government intransigeance.[80]

In the end the PCF was defeated not because it failed to wreck the Marshall Plan, which was never a real issue, but because it failed to get the 25 percent salary increase, 11,000 franc minimum, or periodic salary revision according to prices. The government's five-point settlement offer of December 8 had only two points of substance as far as the CGT was concerned: the 1500-franc indemnity, which had been offered earlier, and a 22 percent increase in the family allowance allocation. The combined effect of these aspects of the strike settlement provided a significant, immediate increase in working-class purchasing power and a costly blow to the government's austerity policies. However, while there was no sanction for striking, there was no payment for strike days either, and many workers were prosecuted for acts growing out of the police confrontation. The government also promised a vague price-salary relationship to be monitored by the Economic Council.

In the absence of any more concrete achievements than these, Frachon's call for a return to work stressed consolidation and regrouping for further struggles and praised the magnificient demonstration of working-class combativeness and courage during the strikes. He also took heart later in the newly gained experience of youthful cadres who emerged to assume on-the-spot leadership.[81] In effect, the CGT continued to perform a functional role in the strikes, which constituted a moment in the PCF's mediation of its sometimes conflicting, often complementary relationship with the French working class on the one hand, and the political system on the other. The return to work occurred for very practical reasons: some unions had exhausted their means of resistance, and FO's call for a return to work was heeded by some Communist workers who simply could no longer hold out. International affairs were not a consideration insofar as rank-and-file workers were concerned. It is notable in the historiography of the confrontation that the politicization of the strikers, whose ultimate aim was higher wages, is normally assumed, while the government, representative of all employers and the victor in the struggle, has its own political motivations go virtually ignored. If, as Domenique Desanti speculates, the PCF was demonstrating its mettle to the Cominform, were the Socialists not demonstrating theirs to Washington?[82] Roger Quilliot, in exculpating the Socialists from responsibility in the drama, noted a majority of the rest of the French National Assembly wished to bring the PCF to its knees during the crisis.[83] On balance the 1947 events seem a demonstration of Pierre Fougeyrollas' observation that anti-Communism, not Communism, was the most divisive force in French life. The events of 1948 further seemed to bear that out.

NOTES

1. Vincent Auriol, *Journal du Septennat, 1947* (Paris, 1970), I, 160.

2. Jacques Fauvet, *Histoire du Parti Communiste Français* (Paris, 1965), II, 196.

3. *L'Humanité,* April 26, 1947.

4. Léon Blum, *Oeuvres 1945–47* (Paris, 1958), 383.

5. Pierre Daix, *J'ai cru au matin* (Paris, 1976), 179. Roger Pannequin, *Les années sans suite,* II, *Adieu camarades* (Paris, 1977), 78.

6. Auriol, *Journal,* I, March 1947.

7. U.S. National Archives. Diplomatic Branch, Decimal File 1945–49, 851.00B, Memos of March 31 and April 26, 1947.

8. On the economics of the period see Roger Nathan and Paul DeLouvrier, *Politique économique de la France III, Après-guerre* (Paris, 1957–58), 135 and *passim.*

9. *Revue Française du Travail,* 15–16 (June-July 1947).

10. Edouard Depreux, *Souvenirs d'un Militant* (Paris, 1972), 267. N.A. 851.00 Dispatch No. 339 dated January 31, 1947.

11. Henri Gallant, *Histoire politique de la securité sociale* (Paris, 1953), 125.

12. See P. Fallachon, "Les grèves de la Regie Renault en 1947," *Le Mouvement Social* (October–December 1972).

13. George Ross appears to imply that the CGT sided with the strikers, then putting Communist ministers on the horns of an uncomfortable dilemma. There is no evidence, however, of any lack of coordination between PCF and CGT policies during the strikes. See *Workers and Communists in France* (Berkeley, Calif., 1981), 45–47. The Socialist Minister of the Interior during the Renault strike was Edouard Depreux, not Jules Moch.

14. Auriol, *Journal,* I, 205–7.

15. *L'Année Politique, 1947,* 20, showed labor at 45 percent of the national revenue as opposed to 48 percent in 1938.

16. *L'Humanité,* May 4–5, 1947.

17. Philippe Robrieux, *Histoire Intérieure du PCF* (Paris, 1981), II, 193.

18. Auriol has Thorez literally in tears. *Journal,* I, 210.

19. André Barjonet, *La CGT* (Paris, 1968), 49. *L'Humanité,* May 8, 1947.

20. *L'Année Politique, 1947,* May-June.

21. *L'Humanité,* June 4, 8–9, 1947.

22. Moch reveals this in his Memoirs, *Une si longue vie* (Paris, 1976), 249.

23. *L'Humanité,* May 23, 1947. A point overlooked by Ross and Robrieux in their brief accounts of the pivotal year, 1947.

24. Ibid., May 15, 28, June 10, July 11, 1947. Also personal interview with Marcel Paul, May 29, 1978.

25. Parti Communiste Français, *Rapports du Comité Centrale pour le xiᵉ Congres à Strasbourg* (Strasbourg, June 1947). See also Robrieux, *Histoire Intérieure,* II, 201–8.

26. *Rapports,* Strasbourg, 338.

27. Daniel Mayer, personal interview, June 6, 1973. Gallant, 121.

28. Marcel Ventenat, *L'Expérience des nationalisations* (Paris, 1947), 142–43. See also Rene Gendarme, *L'Expérience française de la nationalisation industrielle et ses enseignements économiques* (Nancy, 1949), 118 and passim. A good account of the anti-Communist purge in the nationalized coal industry is in Darryl Holter, "Miners Against the State: French Miners and the Nationalization of Coal Mining, 1944–1949" (Ph.D. Thesis, University of Wisconsin, 1980).

29. Philippe Bernert, *Roger Wybot et la bataille pour la D.S.T.* (Paris, 1975), 167. N.A., 800.00B, Memo from Douglas [MacArthur] to Woodruff Wallner, March 26, 1947, labeled "personal and top secret."

30. *L'Humanité,* July 17, 1947.

31. See Duclos' editorial, "Notre Politique," *Cahiers du Communisme,* 24, 8 (August 1947), 691–708. Also, *L'Humanité,* September 1, 1947.

32. Auriol, *Journal,* June 17, 24, 317.

33. Duclos, "Notre Politique."

34. Marius Patinaud, "Un parti qui doit compter par millions," *Cahiers du Communisme,* 24, 8 (August 1947), 727–39.

35. *L'Humanité,* September 21, 1947. Robrieux, *Histoire Intérieure,* II, 225.

36. Ronald Tiersky, *French Communism 1920–72* (New York, 1974), 173–74. Ross thinks the party saw a demonstration of its strength, coupled with government weakness, as discouraging American aid. *Workers and Communists,* 51.

37. Moch, *Une si longue vie,* 282.

38. The best account is by Lilly Marcou, *Le Kominform* (Paris, 1977), 42–45 and passim. See also the invaluable Eugenio Reale, *Avec Jacques Duclos, Au banc des accusés*

a la réunion constitutive du Kominform a Szklarska Poreba, 22–27 September, 1947 (Paris, 1958).

39. Etienne Fajon, *Ma vie s'appelle liberté* (Paris, 1976), 210–11; Jacques Duclos, *Memoires 1945–1952* (Paris, 1971), 218–20. On the Congress see also Adam Ulam, *Titoism and the Cominform* (Cambridge, Mass., 1975) and Vladimir Dedijer, *Tito Speaks* (London, 1953).

40. Robrieux, *Histoire Intérieure*, II, 234.

41. Léo Figuères, *Jeunesse Militante* (Paris, 1971), 190.

42. *L'Humanité*, October 3, 1947.

43. Ibid., October 5–6, 1947.

44. The best analysis of the municipal elections of 1947 is in the U.S. National Archives, Diplomatic Branch, Decimal File 800.00, Report No. 9935, dated November 24, 1947.

45. Georges Lefranc, *Le Mouvement syndical de la Liberation aux évènements de Mai–Juin, 1968* (Paris, 1969), 51–53.

46. *L'Humanité*, October 18, October 23, 1947.

47. On the scission of Force Ouvrière see Lefranc, *Le Mouvement syndical*, Alain Bergounioux, "La scission syndicale dans les PTT en 1946," *Le Mouvement Social*, 92 (July-September 1975), 1–15, and Darryl Holter, "Miners Against the State."

48. *L'Humanité*, October 25–27, 1947. See also note 44 above.

49. *La Vie du Parti*, No. 1, November 1947.

50. Maurice Thorez, "Le Combat pour la République et pour l'independance nationale," *Cahiers du Communisme*, 24, 11 (November 1947), 1099–23.

51. *L'Humanité*, November 13, 1947.

52. Noted by Lefranc, *Le Mouvement syndical*, 57.

53. Holter, "Miners Against the State," 277.

54. *L'Humanité* announced the coal price increase on November 4, 1947. See Moch's *Une si longue vie* for a defense of his policies.

55. See the analysis in Holter, "Miners Against the State," 253–66.

56. *L'Humanité*, November 11, 1947.

57. Holter, "Miners Against the State," 351.

58. *L'Humanité*, November 15, 16, 17, 18, 1947. Also *Revue française du Travail*, 1–3 (1948), 96. Ross says "Events broke before the CGT had fully implemented its mobilization plans." *Workers and Communists*, 55.

59. Maurice Agulhon, *CRS à Marseille* (Paris, 1970). See in particular the exchange in *Le Mouvement Social* 92 (July-September 1975): René Gallisot, "L'Illusion républicaine: socialistes et communistes en 1947. Reflexion sur 'CRS à Marseille' et le 'journal' de Vincent Auriol" and M. Agulhon and F. Barrat, "Au dossier des 'CRS à Marseille'." Robrieux, *Histoire Intérieure*, II, admits that the "climate of the period explains Marseille, the hypothesis of a PCF role being unnecessary." 238.

60. Auriol, *Journal*, I, 1947, 550–56.

61. *L'Humanité*, November 15, 1947, December 2, 1947. See also Raoul Calas, *Souvenirs d'un condamné à mort* (Paris, 1976), 156.

62. Agulhon, *CRS à Marseille*, 246. Quoted by Gallisot, "L'Illusion républicaine."

63. Agulhon, "Au dossier," 89. Gallisot, "L'Illusion républicaine," 67.

64. *L'Humanité*, November 20, 21, 1947.

65. Auriol, *Journal*, I, 1947, 556–60.

66. Moch, *Une si longue vie*, 273.

67. For a list see Lefranc, *Le Mouvement syndical*, 57.

68. *L'Humanité,* November 29, December 2, 1947.

69. Tillon, interview, May 29, 1978. Roger Pannequin, personal interview, May 2, 1978.

70. Auguste Lecoeur, personal interview, July 12, 1978. Robrieux accepts Lecoeur's version in the *Histoire Intérieure,* II, 253.

71. See Georgette Elgey, *La République des illusions* (Paris, 1966), 352–61.

72. Moch, *Une si longue vie.*

73. Pannequin, *Adieu Camarades,* 90.

74. Tillon, interview, May 29, 1978.

75. *La Vie du Parti,* No. 2, December 1947.

76. See the very fine unpublished analysis of the strikes by Angelo Tasca in the *Fonde Angelo Tasca,* Fondazione Feltrinelli, Milan, Carton 162, manuscript entitled "La Crise de Nov.–Dec. 1947."

77. N.A. Decimal File 851.00B, memo of Jefferson Caffery dated January 27, 1948; memo of Secretary Marshall dated January 29, 1948, summarizing Caffery analysis and sent to all European posts.

78. Ibid., 851.00, dispatch dated June 27, 1947; File 851.00B, dispatch dated October 17, 1947.

79. Auriol, *Journal,* I, 583, also Moch, *Une se longue vie,* 282. Auriol did not comment on the contradictory reports.

80. *L'Humanité,* December 4, 5, 1947.

81. B. Frachon "Une étape de la lutte des classes en France: Les Grandes Grèves de November-December, 1947." *Cahiers du Communisme,* 25, 1 (January 1948), 5–33.

82. Domenique Desanti, *Les Staliniens* (Paris, 1975), 89.

83. Roger Quilliot, *La SFIO et l'Exercise du Pouvoir* (Paris, 1972), 279.

4
REPRISE,
1948

The immediate aftermaths of both world wars offer striking parallels in the history of the French Communist party and the working class. Both wars opened new possibilities of participation in reconstruction and the elaboration of a new social order. Both post-war crises ended in bitter left-wing disillusionment. After World War I French leftists transferred their revolutionary aspirations to the Bolshevik tide that promised to bring salvation from the East. The PCF relived this experience after World War II. Communist hopes of achieving a lasting integration into the French socio-political order by legal, parliamentary means were dashed with the humiliating ouster of the party from the cabinet by Ramadier in May 1947. The CGT's attempt to defend its social positions and demonstrate its indispensibility in the task of economic construction by a new militance in the strike movement of November-December, met with brutal, ignominious, defeat. In response, the PCF was again motivated to reverse directions and draw renewed sustenance from intensified solidarity with the USSR and the International Communist Movement.

But despite its defeats, in 1948 the PCF appeared reluctant to accept its isolated status as simply the French section of the International Communist Movement. To be sure, the PCF was drawn into the vortex of Cominform affairs by its solidarity with the Czech coup, eager endorsement of the excommunication of Yugoslavia, and acceptance of the cruder aspects of the Stalin cult. Stalin's bizarre behavior in 1948—his two major initiatives were, in medieval style, to lay siege to a city (Berlin) and excommunicate a heretic (Tito)—reflected negatively on the image of Western Communist parties.[1] The PCF nevertheless tried to defend its remaining *positions acquises* in the French economy, renewed its offer of working-class collaboration in economic reconstruction, and offered an alternative to bitter strikes and violent conflict. The year 1948 was dominated by many of the same problems that characterized the second half of 1947. Only after the renewed bitter, costly, and prolonged strikes in the coalfields in October–November 1948, did dialogue become impossible and confrontation total. In the terrible replay of the 1947 strikes the party once again presented starvation wages and working-class representation in the administration of the mines as the issues. The government, on the other hand, charged the party with subversion carried out under Cominform orders to bring about a Czech-style coup in France. Following the 1948 strikes it became possible to speak of the PCF's total immersion in the International Communist Movement as a lobby for Soviet interests in France.

The Czech coup of February 1948 traumatized the French political elite. The reaction of the PCF was conditioned by the experience of its rejection from the French government the previous May. Czech reactionaries, backed by American imperialists, tried to oust the Communists from the government and secure a strategic corridor for Washington to separate the People's Democracies from one another.[2] But unlike France the Czech party exercised a preponderant role in a democratic coalition, in proportion to its real strength among the electorate, causing the bourgeoisie to resort to illegal measures in an attempt to unseat it. Their maneuvers had been defeated by mass action, a useful object-lesson for the PCF. The Czech masses, *L'Humanité* noted, formed popular action committees allowing for new forms of political action beyond the boundaries of traditional electoral politics.[3] The PCF was not advocating the establishment of Soviets in France. Thorez did hope that a similar manifestation of organized mass pressure would bring the party back to a position of shared power.

The PCF enthusiastically supported the Cominform expulsion of the Yugoslavs, but as in the case of Czechoslovakia, for its own reasons. The Yugoslavs delivered the indictment of the French and Italian parties at the founding conference of the Cominform, going far beyond the Russians in their criticism. The Yugoslavs enjoyed great prestige in the French party, particularly among veterans of the Resistance already under suspicion for the advocacy of a broader national movement encompassing the PCF. Not unintentionally, the Political Bureau selected Charles Tillon, former leader of the FTP during the Resistance, to deliver the first major assault on Tito. According to Robrieux, the PCF's Organizational Bureau began an investigation of the past of all party resistance veterans in an effort to uncover possible links to the Yugoslavs. The machinery was in motion leading to the purge of former Resisters in 1950.[4] As a consequence the Russians now became very solicitous of the French and Italians' bruised sensibilities. The Cominform organ, *For a Lasting Peace, For a People's Democracy* praised the two parties for their corrective action after the Warsaw conference, and congratulated them on a valuable contribution to the continuing practice of Marxism-Leninism. *L'Humanité* in turn praised the Soviet initiative against the Yugoslavs as "proof of the clairvoyance of the party of Lenin and Stalin," noting that the Yugoslavs, who had "abused their rights of criticism" in regard to other Communist parties, rejected fraternal criticism themselves.[5]

The PCF had a greater stake in the Yugoslav case than mere revenge. Among the catalogue of Tito's sins was the accusation of a "Bukharinite" policy in the countryside, a coddling of the capitalist peasantry providing the social basis of a revived petty-bourgeois nationalism. At the same time the Yugoslavs were accused of "adventurism" in their agrarian policy by rushing pell-mell into collectivization before the way was prepared. The French presented their agrarian policies as avoiding the double Yugoslav errors of opportunism and sectarianism.

Waldeck Rochet, the PCF agrarian expert, denied the Cominform resolution implied an attack on small peasant holdings and reaffirmed the French Communists' commitment to the protection of peasant property.[6] The PCF advocated freedom of choice for farmers, precisely what the Yugoslavs denied their peasants.

The excommunication of Tito led to an intensification of the Stalin cult in France. On July 12, Thorez announced the term "Stalinist" was not an insult but rather a badge of honor which Communists must make every effort to deserve fully.[7] The Yugoslavs' cardinal sin was anti-Sovietism. The PCF resolved to fight any tendency to underestimate the role of the USSR, fortress of the world proletariat, rampart of peace and democracy, and liberator of France. The Central Committee reaffirmed its affection and confidence in Stalin, the "educator, guide, and sure and clairvoyant friend to all the downtrodden of the world." Fajon reminded the Yugoslavs that attitudes toward the USSR had been the touchstone and defining characteristic of all Communist parties for thirty years. The Communist party of the Soviet Union held a privileged position in the International Movement because it had been the first to "give to Marxist-Leninist doctrine the sanction of life experience."[8]

Such rhetoric magnified and increased the growing gap between Communists and other Frenchmen. It was a much greater obstacle to understanding than, for example, the Berlin blockade, an affair in which the Socialists expressed comprehension for Soviet policies and felt drawn by the Americans into a German policy that was against their own best interests.[9] The Stalin cult in France has a variety of explanations, none of them satisfactory, but also a peculiarly French flavor. The insensitive commitment of the PCF to its most extreme and repulsive characteristics compromised a continuing thrust of party policy, which was to unite with Frenchmen of all beliefs and social categories in the pursuit of common interests.

The contradictory aspect of PCF policy was apparent in the Peace Movement, the principal means by which the PCF hoped to escape its impending isolation. Anti-Communists quickly labeled it a lobby for Soviet interests. Thorez invited this interpretation and shocked French nationalist opinion by announcing on September 30, 1948, that the people of France would never wage war against the USSR. Togliatti made a similar statement in Italy. Both declarations were orchestrated by the Russians in a crude attempt to discourage a policy of preemptive war in the West. The party insisted that Thorez's statement, and the implication that the PCF would collaborate in the unlikely event of a Soviet invasion of France, were within the tradition of the Second International. Socialists in the past, including Jaurès, had tried to restrain potential warmakers by threatening them with the specter of a general strike. The statements were also made in the conviction that a Russian alliance remained the essential linchpin of any sane French foreign policy.[10]

Although the August 1948 congress of intellectuals in Wroclaw, Poland, marked the birth of the Soviet-sponsored Peace Movement, an independent French initiative was announced as early as March 1, when *L'Humanité* noted the formation of "Combattants de la Liberté," a new organization of former members of the French Resistance. Its aim was to recapture the climate of the Liberation, support the goals of national independence, and "reanimate the flame of the French resistance." The founders included Charles Tillon, Yves Farge, and Emmanuel d'Astier de la Vigerie, a combination of Communists and "Progressives," whose party membership was in doubt, but all of whom shared a distinctive past in the Resistance.[11] Tillon claims he started the new organization independently of PCF leadership to provide an alternative to the party's growing isolation and means of recapturing national unity, dissipated and disillusioned since the Liberation. Tillon's initiative was welcomed by the Soviet ambassador Bogomolov, who helped Tillon to win the Political Bureau's support for the initial existence of two separate Peace organizations in France. Responsibility for the French section of the Cominform-orchestrated Wroclaw organization went to Laurent Casanova.[12] Casanova's organization did not take on the character of a mass movement until 1949, while the first national convocation of Tillon's Combattants de la liberté et la paix gathered 12,000 persons in Paris in November 1948.

From the perspective of the PCF's participation in the International Communist Movement, the Czech affair, Yugoslavia, and the Peace Movement were the critical issues of 1948. They were not the major concerns in the party's daily struggle for power and influence in French society and politics, where the PCF saw itself on the defensive against a Socialist-led assault aimed at dislodging it from established positions in the state bureaucracy and economy. The new year began with the National Assembly's exclusion of the PCF from the vice-presidency formerly held by Jacques Duclos. Marcel Cachin, as the Assembly's oldest member, led a delegation to President Auriol to ask presidential intervention against a "flagrant violation of the constitution," but Auriol declined. *L'Humanité* insinuated that the maneuver was carried out on American orders, and the PCF's Political Bureau issued a ringing denunciation.[13] The protests did not prevent Jules Moch from dismissing PCF mayors in the eleventh and twentieth arrondissements of Paris a few days later. Similar moves were undertaken to limit Communist participation in the Council of the Republic (upper house) and exclude the party from membership in parliamentary committees. The campaign culminated in the 1951 elections with the adoption of a new electoral system reducing Communist parliamentary representation by one-third.

The nationalized enterprises remained the last stronghold of Communist power. The 1947 strikes consecrated the removal of Communists from the summit of the state industries; at the base, in the coal mines, CGT stewards remained in place. The CGT won a major victory in the elections of worker-delegates in the northern mines, receiving 82 percent of the vote and 98 percent of the delegate seats, 278 delegates out of a total of 286; Force Ouvriere received a bare 14 percent. On April 4, *L'Humanité* complained that the directors of all the nationalized aviation plants had all been replaced—a "chase after subversives" at the orders of Wall Street was under way. The issue was posed dramatically when

Thorez, at the invitation of the Committee of Enterprise of Nord Aviation, entered the factory to address the workers and was accused in the National Assembly of trespassing. Thorez defended his rights as a Deputy facing his constituents and charged that workers who invited him were subject to reprisal on the part of management.[14]

In defense of the party's industrial positions Communist propaganda resorted to angry tones of outraged nationalism. The Socialists were liquidators of French industries in the interest of the Americans, inviting corrupting influences from across the Atlantic. The PCF defended French technological achievement and fostered pride in national accomplishment, workmanship, and genius. The Blum-Byrnes accord of June 1946 opened the French market to American films as a condition of a loan. The PCF bemoaned the resulting "agony of French cinema" which had "so much contributed to the spread [*rayonnement*] of French art and thought in the world." France was now inundated instead by American tales of gangsterism and eroticism, "poison darts that corrupt the minds of French youth," perverse images of so-called Western civilization.[15] The PCF-sponsored committees for the defense of the French cinema brought together writers, actors, and directors, as well as cinema technicians and workers, to lobby for protective legislation.

In a more positive vein, the PCF exalted French creative ability and technological proficiency. France had once taught aviation to the world, and a healthy industry was the prerequisite for national independence. Under Communist Minister of Armaments Charles Tillon, France had excellent models and prototypes in all fields; since the influx of Marshall Plan aid, the government bought American planes and liquidated French productive capacity. The Languedoc 161 model on the Paris-London route was the fastest and safest aircraft available, better than anything produced by the Americans. The Laté 631 Hydroplane with its six engines, seventy-three-ton and seventy-two-passenger capacity was the most comfortable large transport in the world, a tribute to the superiority of French technicians. When one of the prototypes crashed, leaving nineteen persons dead, *L'Humanité* discovered it had been sabotaged by the enemies of French industry, its gas tank filled with water.[16] The French built the best dams; the dam at Genissat, second largest in Europe after Dnieprostroi, was a masterpiece of technique and labor, and the achievement of Communist Minister of Industry Marcel Paul. "The French construct solidly, not like those American dams which collapse with the first trickle of water." *L'Humanité* accused the government of suffocating the French *haute couture* industry in the interest of U.S.-made ready-to-wear goods of inferior quality, and ran a series of articles on the plight of French seamstresses.[17]

The PCF continued to do battle against Lacoste's efforts to bring non-Communist personnel into the nationalized enterprises. *L'Humanité* denounced the elimination of a Marcel Paul appointee as head of the Electricité de France and waged a daily campaign against the new nominee for that post, eventually forcing his withdrawal.[18] Four Tillon appointees were dismissed as leaders of the nationalized aviation plants, prelude to a major confrontation over government plans to reorganize and streamline operations at the SNECMA aviation-motor plant in June. The party accused René Mayer, Schuman's Finance Minister, of seeking to liquidate and destroy the industry. Aviation workers held a news conference to show the plant was viable and produced "the best aviation engine in the world." Deficits were due to the government's failure to pay for its orders, and reductions in personnel were unjustified. The PCF's Political Bureau denounced planned retrenchments at SNECMA, while the unions offered their program for the health of the industry: the government should pay its bills on time, fund prototypes under a separate budget, and stop buying abroad what was produced and available in France. Tillon charged René Mayer with personal interest in American aircraft industries; French prototypes were subject to deliberate production delays to give U.S. producers an opportunity to catch up and forge ahead. Thorez warned that nationalization was becoming simply a "modified form of capitalist exploitation" in the hands of the Socialists. PCF legislation to "save SNECMA" by maintaining its size, scale of production, and statute was defeated in the National Assembly by a vote of 410–182, the Communists standing alone. Marty expressed the PCF's defiance: "Know that despite you our factories will continue to produce."[19]

Confrontation was similarly building in the coal mines well before Lacoste's September 18 decrees on the reorganization of that industry, which led directly to the brutal strike of October. On April 5, 1948, Director General Guillaume of the Charbonnages de France resigned, citing the dominance of "political factors" in the administration of the mines inhibiting satisfactory economic results. The government's new appointee, Etienne Audibert, promptly denounced a "crisis of authority" in the mines, and promised the restoration of power to administrators and cadres whose positions had been undermined by the bureaucratic procedures introduced during the Liberation. Quasi-anarchy and "incessant perturbations" were the rule under Communist influence and absenteeism was endemic. The mines must be depoliticized and their swollen numbers of personnel reduced.[20]

In fact absenteeism was up and workers were fleeing the mines in droves in 1948 in part because the Communists no longer dominated the administration and the CGT's productivity drive was over. Coal miners held a special place in international proletarian mythology whatever the political expression of existing class consciousness, as demonstrated in the American film *Harlan County*. French miners thought of themselves alternatively as supermen or "Tarzans" of the proletariat. Their fierce pride was reinforced by Communist propaganda attributing to them the key role in national reconstruction after the Liberation. The party assiduously cultivated the myth of the "patriotic" miners' strike of May–June 1941, which occurred a month before the Nazi invasion of the USSR.[21] Auguste Lecoeur's rapid rise in party ranks was in part a reflection of his role in the strike. A personality cult developed around Lecoeur, who came to be thought of as the heir apparent of Thorez. The fact that both of these men had been miners was not incidental to their leadership positions. Every incident in the mines, and there were many during 1948, became a PCF drama. Following the accident at Courières on April 19, which killed twelve, Thorez rushed to the scene to comfort the bereaved. Lecoeur, in the National Assembly, meanwhile interpellated the government on the lack of adequate safety measures in the mines, and demanded the extension of worker-delegates' authority over security procedures. Victorin Duguet, former CGT president of the coalfields in the Nord, warned the government it must honor its miners out of "national necessity."[22]

The government intended to centralize and modernize administration of the mines, however. On September 18, 1948, Robert Lacoste issued decrees intended to restore the disciplinary powers of management by simplifying grievance procedures and eliminating the necessity of going through worker-management committees for minor infractions of discipline.[23] As a part of the drive against absenteeism, the decrees stripped the workers of control over the administration of accident compensation, made five unexplained absences equivalent to resignation, and cut surface personnel 10 percent. The decrees were denounced by the miners' union, which demanded their immediate annulment. Lacoste's decrees provoked the 1948 strike in the same way the removal of Delfosse sparked the strike of 1947.

Although workers' control in the mines was the central issue of the Lacoste decrees, wages remained central to the events of 1948 as well. The November–December strikes of the previous year had not gained the workers' principal economic demand, the automatic revision of salaries in accord with the price index. But the strikes had been followed by an immediate, measurable improvement in the wage-price relationship: workers had been granted a 1500-franc indemnity and a 22 percent increase in family allowances. These gains, as the government intended and the Communists feared, were rapidly eroded during 1948 by inflation.

Early in 1948 the PCF first focused its attention on the plight of the middle classes. The Schuman government introduced a new austerity plan including exceptional taxes that fell most heavily on peasants and small businessmen. Among the tax increases was a recall and reconversion of all five-thousand-franc notes, allegedly the major component of illicit savings stuffed in peasant mattresses. Holders of these notes faced substantial new tax burdens and the possibility of obligatory loans upon their redemption. The Communists denounced the conversion as punitive and harmful to peasant savings, and Marcel Cachin called on the party to capitalize on the "mass anger" the Schuman measures had caused. French small businesses were threatened with bankruptcy in the interest of U.S. corporations; French agriculture was ruined to pave the way for imports of American wheat.[24] Conscious of the centenary, the PCF resolved to avoid the errors of the 1848 revolution, when the imposition of a forty-five centime tax on peasants by the Republican government isolated the working class and led to its defeat. Alliance between the workers and the lower middle classes was a fundamental Marxist principle. The PCF organized committees for the defense of artisans and small businessmen and succeeded in attracting 8000 to a mass meeting of protest at the Salle Wagram. The party called upon Paris' small businessmen to close their shops simultaneously for one afternoon.[25]

The sudden concern for the middle classes suggests that the PCF considered the wage-price ratio achieved immediately after the 1947 strikes to be the best attainable; defense of the middle classes monopolized PCF propaganda for the first half-year, and the CGT did nothing to extend a stike in the coalfields in March. The salary question did not again arise until June 1948 when the Socialists in the government became alarmed by the erosion of workers' purchasing power. Thorez was explicit about the political purposes of courting the middle classes. The workers needed a majority to come to power, for the Communists "were not Blanquists." There was no question of a seizure of power in France by a party acting on behalf of a minority of the population, and the working class was not in the majority by itself. The workers had nothing to fear from the normal functioning of the democratic system, Thorez said. It was the bourgeoisie who could be counted upon to violate the democratic process whenever democracy threatened their interests, as had been exemplified by the ousting of Communists from the municipalities the previous September. The PCF program of Gennevilliers, published with much fanfare in April 1948, was significant because of its moderate economic proposals and concern for the middle classes. Party propagandists hailed its clear, constructive, and practical solutions to French problems. Here finally was the serious perspective behind the PCF's demand for a government of democratic union in which the working class and the Communist party would play a determining role.[26]

The Gennevilliers program was not likely to win middle-class support by advocating an end to the Vietnam war and the participation of France in the "peace efforts" of the Soviet bloc. But the program's domestic planks demonstrated the PCF's aspiration for integration with and participation in the normal coalition political process. The "defense" of salaries and "consolidation" of the social gains of the Liberation were combined with a fiscal program designed to reassure the propertied: stabilization of the franc, a balanced budget, reduced military expenses, progressive taxation, and the protection of property rights.[27] The only extensions of social reform proposed were increased housing and youth training. The rest of the program concerned lay education, army reform, the suppression of fascism, and the punishment of traitors. Thorez accompanied his party's adoption of the program with a plea for all Communists to struggle against "the great evil of sectarianism." The middle classes were not the "enemies of socialism" just as Socialist workers were not a "reactionary mass;" both could be won over to Communist positions.[28] As for Catholics, nothing had changed since 1936: "Our policy is that of the outstretched hand." These groups remained largely deaf to Thorez's pleas, perhaps because they never read beyond the ritual beginnings of his speeches, where the "continued progress of the socialist camp" and the "aggravation of contradictions in the imperialist camp" were summarized.

The wage issue resurfaced in the Communist press in May but possibly had been discussed in the party earlier. Auriol's police reports spoke of tension between Thorez, who was trying to restrain labor agitation during the spring, and Frachon, who wanted "direct action." Thorez, according to Auriol, criticized Frachon's impatience, counseled legal action and "playing the parliamentary game," and remarked that "the idea of an insurrectional *élan* carrying the PCF to power is a dangerous idea."[29] Frachon reportedly eschewed any idea of "disobedience" but pleaded the need for the CGT to have a policy different than the party. Could Auriol again have been fed these reports by the PCF? The intelligence may have played a role at the June 16, 1948, cabinet meeting, where Daniel Mayer warned that prices must be held or salaries raised, lest an explosion of labor unrest result.[30] Workers meanwhile provided confirmation of Mayer's warning. The Michelin tire works in Clermont-Ferrand were occupied in early June. Moch's police evacuated the plant quickly after declaring a state of siege, using tear gas, and administering a few beatings. Moch showed American Ambassador Caffery an array of improvised weapons that police had confiscated from the Michelin workers and admitted that prices must be held down to prevent a recurrence. They were not. On August 19 Caffery reported the French labor situation "on the brink of a precipice."[31] Non-Communist labor leaders "dare not oppose the demands of the rank and file . . . even were Communist demagoguery not present to fan the flames."

Caffery was clearly aware of what was going on within the French cabinet. Schuman fell in July. Auriol, as had remained the practice, held the obligatory consultation with Thorez on the 20th. Once again Auriol was told that the dispute over military expenditure, which had toppled the government, was not the real issue—instability would continue, Thorez said, as long as the Communists remained estranged from their rightful place in the majority. Auriol asked Thorez if there was anyone to whom the PCF was especially opposed. Thorez replied that "No head of government appearing to have carried special responsibilities, or [posing] as a returning war hero, [is] acceptable." Auriol, smiling at the reference to de Gaulle, said: "Listen, we have spoken for a long time in parables, I hear and I understand." But the Communists were not much happier with Auriol's choice of André Marie. Marie's new government featured both Léon Blum and Paul Reynaud as key figures. Reynaud, as Finance Minister, surrounded himself with classic symbols of the prewar right, Maurice Petsche and Joseph Laniel, both of whom became mainstays of Fourth Republic cabinets and Auriol feared correctly would produce "a disastrous effect on the popular masses."[32] True to form *L'Humanité* denounced Reynaud as the prewar "gravedigger" of France, the symbol of a government "that once before led us to catastrophe," while François Billoux blamed Léon Blum for all the mistakes made in France from 1936 to 1940.[33]

The PCF might have been expressing its disappointed hopes to participate in the government. Significantly, the party used the cabinet crisis to bury quietly its demand for a government in which the PCF would have a "determining role," and offered the Gennevilliers program as the answer to France's problems. A government of "democratic union" became the PCF's aim, and the party orchestrated telegrams, petitions, and delegations from workers to the Elysée to support it. *L'Humanité* noted the anniversary of the unity-of-action pact between Socialists and Communists in 1934 and the Franco-Soviet alliance of 1935, which if continued would have prevented Munich and the war.[34] There was a certain naiveté in the PCF's attitude: only days before, Thorez had announced his pride in being known as a Stalinist. The party perceived no contradiction between its Stalinism and desire to re-enter the government, as it again made clear two months later.

Despite the ill fate of Marie's government, the debates within the cabinet are of interest. They reveal not only that the French political class, as Pierre Nora writes, was unafraid of the Communists, but also total insensitivity to working-class demands that the burden of economic reconstruction be equitably shared. French conservatives were indifferent, moreover, to the major concern of their Socialist coalition partners: how to win the workers away from the Communists.[35] In the cabinet Reynaud was frank; prices would not go down and the workers must be made to understand that they must work, or catastrophe would result. Daniel Mayer's concern remained PCF influence: "If you say prices will not go down, you throw the working class into the arms of the Communist party." Reynaud, however, flatly rejected the idea that real wages could be raised back to the levels of January 1948:[36]

Pflimlin: "Prices will go up."

Reynaud: "Fine, the French will consume less."

D. Mayer: "Last January we created a split between the legitimate demands of the workers and the Communist party. This operation will rejoin them."

Reynaud: "We have to lower the living standard of the French."

Blum: "Once I had blood [of workers] on my hands, I don't want to relive that."

D. Mayer: "You stay with your figures, but Moch will be obliged to have recourse to the CRS, and the Premier will have to sign decrees of mobilization."

Jules Moch claimed he "knew in advance" of alleged Communist plans for a confrontation in the autumn. But everyone in the cabinet was aware that a massive confrontation with the workers was building. Some welcomed it; others followed along reluctantly for lack of an alternative.[37] But the PCF did not stop trying to offer one. Marie fell on August 28. The PCF declared that no stable majority was possible without the Communists and called for "a government of democratic union," asking only a role proportionate to its electoral strength. Thorez told Auriol the Communists would work with anyone, as long as the government was committed to progress, democracy, and peace. On August 30, Carrel wrote, rather curiously, that the real issue facing France was the preservation of national sovereignty: old notions of left and right on the political spectrum no longer had any meaning.[38] Even Jules Moch noted a moderation of the PCF's attitude and that the PCF had dropped its demand for a "determining role," but he was not drawn any closer to the PCF as a consequence.

As the crisis dragged on, the PCF reportedly approached Ramadier to discuss reviving the pre-May 1947 coalition and announced that a government of "democratic union" would welcome foreign aid from the United States, so long as any accompanying agreements implying the "subjection" of France were revised.[39] The party proposed a bilateral pact between France and the United States to replace existing international agreements and revived the theme of Thorez's London *Times* interview of November 19, 1946, according to which there were "other paths to Socialism than that of the Russians." Thorez's famous declaration did not otherwise appear in party literature between the founding of the Cominform in September 1947 and 1956 and had been implicitly repudiated by the Russians following the exclusion of the Yugoslavs from the Cominform in July.[40]

The PCF's overtures were in vain. While Thorez was announcing his willingness to accept American aid, Auriol was entrusting the formation of a cabinet to Henri Queuille, a Third Republic politician whose new government looked very much like its predecessor. The Communist reaction was bitter. The best qualified to Marshallize France, *L'Humanité* said, were those who had Hitlerized it; the "saviors" of France were denied a role in the government accorded instead to its gravediggers.[41] Everyone now seemed to understand that confrontation was imminent. Queuille's government immediately announced price rises on the basic commodities, including transportation, tobacco, postage, gas, coal, and electricity. The predictable reaction occurred on September 16: the CGT demanded an immediate across-the-board monthly salary increase of 3000 francs to a new minimum of 14,300. On September 24, the government announced pay increases of 15 percent which the union, citing a cost-of-living increase of 36 percent, found sadly insufficient. In the meantime Lacoste issued his decrees on the mines, injecting the question of governance of the nationalized coalfields into the wage dispute. The miners' union bitterly denounced the decrees as a violation of their statute and an assault on the principle of nationalization and demanded they be rescinded by October 1. A strike vote was announced for September 29: 88.5 percent of those voting, 60 percent of all eligible workers, declared for a walkout, which began on October 4.[42] The strike began amid unity and enthusiasm. *L'Humanité* said the issues were restoration of the wage-price equilibrium achieved in December 1947, safety, and the "reconquest of nationalization."[43] The union declared it would assure the necessary maintenance in the mines to prevent flooding, but only if the government refrained from bringing in either the police or strikebreakers.

Thorez and Moch both consciously decided to politicize the labor unrest. On September 30, immediately following the strike vote, Thorez announced that French workers would never make war on the USSR. Moch announced he intercepted secret orders from Zhdanov to the PCF instructing it to sabotage the Marshall Plan by fomenting labor unrest and discouraging U.S. aid.[44] On November 16 in the National Assembly, Moch also "revealed" the presumed secrets of the PCF's financing from the USSR, and accused the party of seeking to create a Prague-like situation leading to a People's Democracy in France. Moch never produced the secret Zhdanov orders which August Lecoeur denounced as "a gross falsification."[45]

The miners hoped for a broader strike movement, but the government granted substantial pay increases to other workers, securing their return to work and isolating the coal strike. Striking steel workers, for example, returned to work on October 14 with a 26 percent pay increase. Frachon warned the CGT congress that "one does not make a general strike as easily as one would like," and Ambroise Croizat deplored the government's refusal to grant the miners what it gave the steel workers. The miners repeated their warning against the use of police, but Moch had long since decided the issue. On October 18, CRS forces began the methodical takeover of the coalfields in St. Etienne. Maintenance was suspended the next day. On October 24 Moch's troops descended on the northern mines, workers defending their flooding pits in pitched battles against tanks and half-tracks. The miners succeeded in restoring their picket lines and ejecting troops from a few areas, but soon succumbed to military power and occupation. The mines were restored to the full authority of management; procedures involving joint worker-supervisor decision making were eliminated. By November 1, *L'Humanité* admitted that 50 percent of the pits were in CRS hands. Moch's victory bulletins included daily announcements of how much coal was being brought to the surface by returning workers in the "liberated" pits.[46]

It is not clear why the party permitted the strike, which was effectively broken by the end of October, to continue for another month. The unions called for a return to work on November 29, after the government voted a 25 percent increase in miners' pensions, but the costs of continuing were enormous. Not least was a permanent legacy of distrust between workers who had returned to work early and those who held out to the end.[47] The government suspended family allowance payments to strikers on November 11. The unions and the PCF responded with a pathetic effort to send striking miners' children to be boarded by sympathetic families all over France. Workers who went to these extremes remained understandably resentful of those who buckled under financial pressure and returned to work. The sectarian class-against-class policy adopted by the party thus became an objective reality among the working-class rank and file. The official Communist party history, published in 1964, condemned the prolongation of the strikes, blaming it on a "sectarian minority." Lecoeur was held responsible following his dispute with the party in 1954, but he blamed local Resistance leaders in the Nord who were trying to avenge the party's failure to make a revolution at the Liberation.[48] The party leadership, according to Lecoeur, although not in sympathy with the extremists, was reluctant to intervene for fear of again being criticized by the Russians.

The November 16 Assembly debate marked a high point of Socialist-Communist invective. Whatever the subsequent differences between the two parties in terms of policy, the memory of a rhetoric of mutual hostility was to make their future cooperation problematic. Blum, before the debate, declared his sympathy for a working class that was misled by a fanatical caste, acting in the interest of a foreign power, toward ends that were "abused and perverted . . . [the workers were] led by madmen or criminals toward pernicious and senseless undertakings."[49] Moch charged that France had been faced with a genuine insurrectional movement. The strikers had acted "savagely"; troops moved with "perfect precision" in carrying out their 1041 arrests, 300 of whom had already been convicted. Moch charged that "Communists at the base believed in the revolutionary nature of the struggle; at the level of the cells they expected to return to the government, at the higher levels they hoped for destruction of the Marshall Plan, at the summit they were practicing insurrectionary techniques and forming revolutionary cadres in preparation for a French people's democracy." Their goal had not been achieved because unlike Czechoslovakia, France did not have a Communist Minister of the Interior.[50]

Replying for the PCF, Lecoeur accused the government of fomenting anti-Communist hysteria to avoid discussion of the major issues. The Lacoste decrees that began the strikes, he noted, were ignored in Moch's speech. Lacoste rose to defend the decrees. They were essential to deal with slowdowns in the mines, cut costs, and restore discipline. Lecoeur admitted the need to improve operations in the mines. The workers, however, wanted their representatives to share in reforms; by transferring accident insurance funds from worker self-administration to management, the government had only insured that absenteeism would become more likely.[51] In concluding the debate, Premier Queuille made it clear that administrators in the nationalized coal industry who had solidarized with the strikers would be replaced. The government completed the purge in the mines begun the previous year. According to the official report of the Charbonnages, six of the eighteen-member administrative council were dismissed at the end of 1948. None remained from the CGT. Most of the some 3000 miners who were arrested during the strikes were never permitted to return to their jobs.[52] At the beginning of 1949, President Audibert reported that recent "fortunate" modifications of the miners' statute had finally permitted an initial, cautious "affirmation of authority" in the mines and consequently an increase in productivity.[53] In effect, the miners were not to be heard from again for fifteen years, during which French energy policy shifted heavily from coal to oil.[54]

Newspaper readers were not aware of these issues, which were eclipsed in the press by Moch and Duclos' debate over PCF finances. There was little of substance to their argument. East-European unions, who enjoyed access to their governments' monies, contributed generously to the CGT's strike fund in a display of international proletarian solidarity. Moch revealed aspects of the operations of the Soviet-owned Banque Commercial de l'Europe du Nord, in which the PCF deposited all its cash flow. The PCF's finances, hopelessly entangled with the totality of Soviet commercial dealings in France, remain a lively subject for polemicists and a basic part of the party's mystery.[55] The PCF's wealth has continued to grow since Moch's revelations. The party, like the Catholic church, has extensive property holdings and operates business enterprises within the legal framework of the capitalist system. Duclos' presentation of the party's budget took into account only political operations per se. These were financed by dues and the salaries of legislators and appeared to present a credible picture. French conservatives were scandalized that the PCF and *L'Humanité* carried on their financial dealings in a Soviet-owned bank. But they were not bothered by American subsidies to the Socialist newspaper *Le Populaire* and the non-Communist labor union Force Ouvrière. Moch and Duclos were playing to the audience. In terms of public opinion, Duclos might have got the better of the argument by requesting a parliamentary investigation into the financing of all political parties. The government refused.[56]

Thorez drew the lessons of the miners' strike on November 17. The government refused satisfaction to the miners, he said, because it wished to re-establish management authority in the mines. Operations were to be based on constraint, rather than the confident collaboration between engineers and miners established in the period of the Liberation. But talk of a general strike was irresponsible, an excuse for inaction. Communists were realists, they knew that "it is necessary to struggle for each day's bread." The Socialists' policy of fear was treasonous to the workers' cause and the PCF had a duty to expose it: "If they [the Socialist Leaders] were honest they would recognize that they had been mistaken, that they had fooled themselves and misled the workers." There was sufficient ambiguity in Thorez's formulation to leave room for a later reconciliation with the Socialists, should that prove possible. But for now, direct action alone could insure the working class "the determining part which belongs to it in all the levels of leadership of the political and economic life of the nation."[57]

Having failed to defend workers' living standards or block its isolation from the nation's political life (manipulation of elections for the Council of the Republic gave the PCF only 18 of 200 seats), Thorez looked to the successes of the Socialist camp for solace in the face of defeat. The USSR was performing economic miracles, and socialist revolution was spreading to China. The USSR urgently needed peace, while the Marshall Plan was designed to drag France into an anti-Soviet war. Peace was sure to be fatal to the capitalist class in the long run, Thorez said. By struggling for peace, in conjunction with all the world's oppressed peoples, the PCF could strike a decisive blow at imperialism. Hence the importance of Thorez's recent declaration that the workers of France would never make war against the USSR.

While the French miners were returning to work, overcome by terror and hunger and seething with hatred, according to Etienne Fajon, Charles Tillon's Assises Nationales pour la paix et la liberté gathered 12,000 delegates in Paris and announced the creation of local councils for peace and liberty throughout the country. Social conflict was quickly de-emphasized as the Communists threw themselves into the Peace Movement, deemed one of the most important characteristics of the existing political scene.[58] The movement offered nation-wide possibilities for meaningful political and social action. Some Communists resisted, objecting to "bourgeois impurities" in the Peace Movement. These comrades were missing the point. The PCF took up the cry of "la sale guerre," the dirty war in Indochina, a borrowed term now found fully justified as a description of the ugly reality in Indochina consequent upon French policy there.[59]

The struggle for an end to the Vietnam war and the generalized effort in favor of peace offered a needed sense of purpose to the defeated and isolated French Communists. Its domestic options foreclosed, the party returned to the USSR and the International Communist Movement for a sense of mission and hope of victory. The Socialists compromised their party in a reactionary government intent on pursuing anti-worker policies, while the Communists concerned themselves with Moscow. Where, then, was the authentic voice of the French left? American observers lamented the French government failure to use its defeat of the coal strikes for propaganda advantage. The government gave the impression of engaging in a showdown with the miners, not with the Communists. As a result, workers felt that without the PCF they would be left alone at the mercy of a selfish bourgeoisie. It is curious to read in an American diplomatic dispatch that only the creation of a new and authentic Socialist party could break the Communist hold on the workers.[60] More than thirty years later, despite numerous attempts to create such a party, the Communist hold on a major part of the French working class remained unbroken.

NOTES

1. William McCagg, *Stalin Embattled* (Detroit, Mich., 1978).

2. *Cahiers du Communisme*, Duclos editorial 4 (April 1948), 341.

3. *L'Humanité*, February 24, 28, 1948.

4. Philippe Robrieux, *Histoire Intérieure du Parti Communiste* (Paris, 1981), II, 259–60.

5. *For a Lasting Peace, For a People's Democracy*, June 15, 1948. *L'Humanité*, July 2, 9, 1949.

6. Waldeck Rochet, *Cahiers du Communisme*, 8 (August 1948), 771–81.

7. *L'Humanité*, July 13, 1948. See also Lilly Marcou, *Le Kominform* (Paris, 1977), 146.

8. *Cahiers du Communisme*, 8 (August 1948), 763–64, 9 (September 1948), 914–28.

9. On this issue see Paul-Marie de la Gorce, *L'Après-guerre* (Paris, 1978), 340–41; also Vincent Auriol, *Journal du septennat*, II, 1948, (Paris, 1974), 320.

10. *Cahiers du Communisme*, 12 (December 1948), 1323–35.

11. *L'Humanité*, March 12, 1948. See also Marshall Shulman, *Stalin's Foreign Policy Reappraised* (New York, 1965), 89.

12. Charles Tillon, personal interview, May 29, 1978. Corentin Borveau, personal interview, April 7, 1978. Borveau, who was not a Communist, became secretary of the Peace Movement in Paris and a career official within it.

13. See the issues of *L'Humanité*, January 14–17, 1948.

14. Ibid., February 18, 1948, June 23, 1948.

15. Ibid., January 3, March 19, April 20, 1948.

16. Ibid., January 11–12, 21, February 24, 1948.

17. Ibid., March 4, 1948.

18. Ibid., April 1, 2, 6, 1948.

19. Ibid., June 1, 3, 4, 8, 13–14, 20–21, 25, 1948.

20. Etienne Audibert, *Tribulations et perspectives des Charbonnages français* (1949). Darryl Holter, "Miners Against the State" (University of Wisconsin, 1980), 400–12.

21. Domenique Desanti, *Les Staliniens* (Paris, 1975), 125. See also Auguste Lecoeur, *Croix de guerre pour une grève* (Paris, 1978); also *Le Partisan* (Paris, 1963), 173. The party has continued to mythologize this strike: see Auguste Colpin, *L'Aurore se lève au pays noir* (Paris, 1966).

22. *L'Humanité*, April 20, 21, June 3, 1948. Ironically accidents increased during the Communist productivity drive. Holter, "Miners Against the State," 409–12.

23. Jean Rivero, *Le Régime des Nationalisations* (Paris, 1948), see Appendix No 736. Holter, 412–14.

24. *L'Humanité*, January 31, February 2, 1948. *Cahiers du Communisme*, 3 (March 1948).

25. *L'Humanité*, March 25, 26, 1948.

26. Ibid., January 22, 1948, April 16, 1948.

27. See the text in *Cahiers du Communisme*, 5 (May 1948).

28. *L'Humanité*, April 15, 1948.

29. Ibid., May 24, 1948. Vincent Auriol, *Journal du Septennat*, II, 1948, 184–85.

30. Auriol, *Journal*, II, 1948, 271–72.

31. U.S. National Archives (N.A.), Diplomatic Branch, Decimal File 800.00, dispatches dated June 27, 1948, and August 19, 1948. It is most important to keep this background in mind before concluding, as George Ross does, that the PCF was conducting a "war against the government" and using worker discontent to achieve political ends "behind the workers' backs." See *Workers and Communists in France* (Berkeley, Calif., 1981), 55–58.

32. Auriol, *Journal*, I, 325–35.

33. *L'Humanité*, July 26, 28, 1948.

34. Ibid., July 21, July 27, 1948.

35. Nora's comment is in the Preface to Auriol, *Journal*, II.

36. Ibid., 353, 372–78.

37. Jules Moch, *Une si longue vie* (Paris, 1976), 327.

38. *L'Humanité*, August 28, 30, 1948.

39. N.A. Decimal File 800.00, dispatch of September 10, 1948. See also *L'Humanité*, September 8, 1948.

40. *Cahiers du Communisme*, 9 (September 1948), 929–44. Lilly Marcou, *Le Kominform* (Paris, 1977), 152.

41. *L'Humanité*, September 9, 11, 1948.

42. Ibid., September 16, 24, 29, October 4, 5, 1948. Holter, "Miners," 420.

43. *L'Humanité*, October 4, 1948.

44. Jules Moch, *Une si longue vie* (Paris, 1976), 338–39. *L'Humanité*, October 14, 16, 1948.

45. *Journal Official de la République Française* (J.O.), Assemblée Nationale, Débats, November 16, 1948.

46. Ibid., November 1, 1948. Holter, "Miners," 420–41.

47. See Pierre Durand, *Vingt ans: chronique, 1945–65* (Paris, 1965), 75.

48. Lecoeur, *Autocritique attendue* (Paris, 1955); *Le PCF Continuité dans le Changement* (Paris, 1977), 150. *Histoire du PCF, Manuel* (Paris, 1964), 519.

49. *Oeuvre de Léon Blum, 1947–50* (Paris, 1963), 235.

50. J.O., November 16, 1948.

51. Ibid.

52. Curiously, on January 13, 1982 *L'Humanité* was still complaining that the Mitterrand government's amnesty policy had yet to be extended to miners dismissed in 1948!

53. Charbonnages de France *Rapports de Gestion* (1948).

54. Ross, *Workers and Communists,* Holter, *Miners Against the State.*

55. See Jean Montaldo, *Les Finances du PCF* (Paris, 1977).

56. J.O., November 16, 1948. Both Moch and Duclos had their speeches published as pamphlets in the propaganda war.

57. *L'Humanité,* November 17, 1948.

58. Ibid., November 29, 1948.

59. Ibid., December 14, 16, 28, 1948.

60. N.A. Decimal File 800.00, dispatch dated December 22, 1948.

5
STALINISM AND THE PCF, 1949–1951

The defeats of 1947–48 threw the PCF back into a closer reliance upon the USSR than at any previous point in party history. The Communists embraced the Peace Movement in a desperate hope to escape political isolation while furthering Soviet foreign policy objectives. But the PCF's isolation was dramatized by the Kravchenko affair; ostensibly a libel suit by Kravchenko against the Communist literary weekly, *Les Lettres Françaises*, which branded his anti-Soviet book a fabrication, the trial saw to it that the line between Communism and anti-Communism in France was clearly drawn. The peace struggle required the subordination of the party's other activities to a series of signature campaigns protesting the U.S. alliance and culminating in the Stockholm appeal, which sought to outlaw the atomic bomb. The party's frenzied efforts obscured a grave internal crisis that erupted at the Twelfth Congress in 1950. What seemed a promotion of youthful cadres to the PCF's Central Committee become a massive purge of former members of the French Resistance, critics of the party's collaborationist policies in 1940–41, and veterans of the Spanish civil war, suspected of advocating a French brand of "national communism" or Titoism.

The period from 1949 to 1951 witnessed the beginning of a power struggle within the PCF leadership between what may be termed Stalinist and Sovietized factions. Maurice Thorez remained, in his own terms, the "best Stalinist in France." Thorez governed the PCF by successfully adapting the Russian leader's techniques of rule to French circumstances. Stalinism in a non-ruling party may be defined as a series of devices designed to accomplish internal bureaucratic control on behalf of an elite drawn from working-class backgrounds. Thorez used Stalinist methods to consolidate his personal power and lead the party according to his conception of Communism; Stalinism, for Thorez, paradoxically, could be a means of independent action. Jacques Duclos represented Soviet interests in France, monitored Thorez's policies from Moscow's perspective, and tried to prevent Thorez from charting an independent course within the International Communist Movement. The 1950 purge of former resisters from the party leadership removed men loyal to Thorez, weakening his control of the party although his personal position remained unassailable. The Thorez-Duclos struggle involved differing perceptions of correct PCF strategy. Thorez saw the party in a class-against-class mode, which, from the perspective of past experience, he construed as a necessary preparatory period for the creation of a new Popular Front for internal reform, détente, and alliance with the USSR. Duclos, reflecting Moscow's pessimism about the prospects for political change in France, pursued the broadest possible coalition with any Frenchmen who would collaborate with the PCF in the achievement of a few basic Soviet foreign-policy objectives. Thorez's illness and removal from the scene at the end of 1951 opened the way for Duclos' Soviet-influenced stewardship and one of the most tortured and confused periods the PCF ever experienced.

The Kravchenko affair sealed the PCF's isolation. To dramatize his internationalism, Thorez rose to its challenge, declaring, on February 21, 1949, that in the event of a Soviet invasion of France the French people would greet the Red Army as liberators. French politicians were scandalized; some remarked that Thorez had posed his candidacy as successor to Pierre Laval. The Ministry of Justice threatened to prosecute Thorez for inciting the army to disobedience. But for French Communists, patriotism was not involved in Thorez's comments. The remark had been in the pacifist tradition of the working class, an addition to the Stuttgart anti-war resolution of the Second International in 1907. Thorez meant that a Franco-Soviet military alliance, feared by the right for ideological reasons, was a historic necessity for France: a Soviet invasion was inconceivable except in response to a U.S.-provoked war of imperialist aggression.[1] "Whoever says he is anti-Soviet," said André Wurmser at the Kravchenko trial's opening, "indicates in the same words that he is also anti-French."[2] Conservatives hoped to expose the absurdity of this claim through the Kravchenko trial.

Kravchenko chose France as his battleground with deliberation: "In France I was in the midst of a political battlefield, in which blows for and against Communism could be dealt with real effect . . . where the CP constituted a present political power which might . . . grow in strength or decline."[3] Unlike the American party the PCF was a worthy target for exposure as an agency of the Soviet dictatorship. The suit charged the French Communist literary weekly, *Les Lettres Françaises,* with slander for the contents of a November 1948 review of Kravchenko's book, *I Chose Freedom.* The reviewers alleged the book was a tissue of lies written by American intelligence services. The existence of Soviet labor camps and the historical events of forced collectivization and purges in the USSR became the central issues of the trial. To prove his claims, the Russian defector combed the displaced persons camps in Germany, which he found full of Soviet refugees only too willing to testify. The PCF weekly stood its ground on the party's nationalism and Resistance record, while denouncing Kravchenko as an anti-Soviet traitor and his witnesses as Nazi collaborators.

Several aspects of the trial worked to the PCF's advantage. Kravchenko's uncontrolled outbursts gave the case an aura of farce. Under cross-examination he appeared unfamiliar with his sources and was unable to produce a Russian version of his manuscript until late in the trial. Defense witnesses charged the book was originally written in English as vulgar propaganda aimed at denouncing liberals "soft on Communism."[4] Communist lawyer Joe Nordmann caused a sensation by revealing the pseudonym under which, allegedly for purposes of self-protection, the Russian émigré travelled to France. From that point on PCF propaganda focused on "Agent Paul Kedrine" of American intelligence services.[5] The Soviets obliged the PCF by sending witnesses who had known Kravchenko: they described him as a debauched adventurer and traitor. When a purported Russian version of *I Chose Freedom* was finally produced, PCF experts denounced it as a fraud, converted into English as an "anti-liberal instrument for internal American use."[6]

The PCF was nevertheless hurt by the trial. One of the alleged authors of the incriminating review, said to be an American journalist named Sim Thomas, clearly never existed. Friendly non-Communist witnesses, willing to characterize Kravchenko as a traitor, dissociated themselves from cruder aspects of PCF propaganda. Catholic author Louis Martin-Chauffier repudiated Communist attacks on Paul Nizan; British Laborite Zilliacus rejected Cominform denunciations of Ernest Bevin and warned that Western provocation would result in a further tightening of the Soviet "police-state apparatus." Not all fellow-travellers, apparently, were to be trusted. Communist Fernand Grenier, who did not speak Russian, reported he had seen no disturbances during the collectivization of agriculture in the USSR and described a purge as a simple question-and-answer session. Soviet witnesses at the trial were afraid to discuss many subjects. Finally, plaintiff efforts to characterize Thorez's 1939 departure from the front as desertion stung the defense. Witness André-Remy Morgnet noted that Kravchenko defected to the U.S., an ally of Russia in 1944, but Thorez deserted to the USSR, an ally of Germany in October 1939. Thorez was, therefore, a collaborator, Morgnet argued.[7]

The trial record contained more than enough material for another volume of *Gulag Archipelago,* but that was hardly the point. Domenique Desanti easily disbelieved all of Kravchenko's witnesses except for Margrete Buber-Neumann, the widow of German Communist leader Heinz Neumann, who, recalled to Moscow after fighting in Spain, disappeared in Stalin's purges.[8] Margrete Buber-Neumann, after a period in a Soviet labor camp, was turned over to the Nazis in 1940 with several other German political prisoners, a few of them Jews. Her comparison of Nazi and Soviet camps was especially damaging to the defense, as was the description of Stalin handing over German Jewish Communists to Hitler. PCF lawyers charged Heinz Neumann had been an advocate of the discredited social-fascist line in Germany, a Trotskyist, and an agent of the Nazis, but these claims had little effect.[9] Communist ideologue Joanny Berlioz told Desanti that Neumann had been manipulated by the Trotskyists; Neumann's case was a personal tragedy, which must not be construed as affecting the worldwide cause of Communism. Desanti was momentarily satisfied, but her doubts resurfaced later during the anti-Tito trials ultimately leading to her break with the party.

The court found *Les Lettres Françaises* guilty on three counts of defamation. Communists charged it was a class judgment, an act of hostility by the court against the USSR.[10] The Kravchenko trial attracted widespread publicity, widened the gap between Communists and other Frenchmen, and symbolized eloquently the PCF's absolute isolation. The PCF's ghetto was now intellectual as well as political and social. As the Fourth Republic found a period of relative stability, the PCF willingly entered a tunnel from which there appeared no way to emerge. Communists must not only identify with and defend the USSR, but apparently emulate the Russians as well. The party's isolation became painfully apparent when the 25 percent PCF vote in the March cantonal elections translated into a mere 2 percent of available seats.[11] Only 35 PCF incumbents were returned to local offices as opposed to 184 who held seats since 1947. The Gaullist RPF with fewer votes than the PCF attained 350 seats; the anti-Communist barrage of the October 1947 municipal elections was intact. The PCF denounced the election results as a swindle. At the April party conference, Léon Mauvais rejected suggestions that Thorez's declaration regarding a hypothetical Soviet invasion of France had been responsible for the defeat.[12] But the PCF needed a way to escape its ghetto, or its membership and electoral support might decline with its political influence.

Communists turned to the Peace Movement as a last hope for a national audience outside party ranks, the only means to escape isolation fully consistent with the aims of Soviet foreign policy. But the Peace Movement meant Front national, alliance with anyone; Thorez yearned for Front populaire, the only real tactic he understood to be possible. Thorez's calculated revival of the "class-against-class" rhetoric of the 1928–34 period; his republication of his early 1930's writings and venomous attacks on the Socialists were meant as a prelude to a new Popular Front: it was impossible to revive that period's rhetoric without reference to what had happened afterward. The "class-against-class" period no longer meant a policy alternative *sui generis*. The Popular Front was a "fundamental element of [Communist] policy," the correct application of Marxist-Leninist principles on the necessary alliance of the working and middle classes. The PCF would always struggle to preserve the liberties provided by bourgeois democracy.[13] In November 1949 Thorez clarified the PCF's demand for a government of "democratic union," which did not mean a rehash of the 1945–47 governments. No unity was possible with politicians like Schuman, Mayer, and Moch. But if a Popular Front remained out of reach, the Socialists alone were to blame. Mass action at the base was required to force a change in policy at the summit. The political relationships in parliament could be modified if a mass current toward unity was created from below, as in 1934–35.[14]

At the Montreuil April 1949 PCF party conference, Thorez defined the principal danger facing the PCF as "sectarian narrowness," a disdainful attitude toward those who disagree. Rancor and internal division remained rife in the party and the working class as a legacy of the 1947–48 strikes. Those resentments needed to be overcome.[15] Party officials denounced sectarianism as the "principal party failing"; Socialist workers were too often denounced as "reactionaries" in party ranks.[16] Many party officials offered self-criticism: in the Seine there was too much "gauchisme," in the Vendée too much anticlericalism. So it went, in a seemingly never-ending litany of self-flagellation, designed to avoid the spirit of "self-satisfaction" in the party.

Communist historical writing has attributed two principal doctrinal achievements to Thorez: first the Popular Front, which was said to have been his initiative and ultimately adopted by the Comintern, and second the proclamation as early as 1949 that war was not inevitable.[17] Thorez was obliged to launch the Peace Movement despite his preference for a Popular Front. On February 7, 1949, Thorez signalled the coming immersion of his party in the peace effort: the "decisive question of the hour," he said, "is the question of peace."[18] The United States and its allies intended to wage war on the USSR, but they could be stopped. The necessary strength among the people to prevent war existed in the capitalist countries. It needed only to be mobilized. Two dangers had to be avoided, Thorez said: failure to realize the imminent danger of war and the contrary conclusion that war was inevitable. The one was opportunist and the other sectarian, but both were really excuses for inaction. The duty of all good Communists was to unite with everyone who wanted peace, whatever their individual political opinions. The principal danger to peace stemmed from the Atlantic Pact, which was an anti-Soviet plan of U.S. domination and aggression, contrary to the United Nations charter and the interests of peoples everywhere. Thorez's declaration that the French would welcome the Red Army as liberators was meant to alert French leaders that if they engaged in an anti-Soviet war, their troops would not follow.

An open letter to President Truman was announced by the French National Peace Council on February 28, beginning the first of a series of signature campaigns that consumed PCF energies almost totally in the next three years. The American President was informed that France was prohibited by its constitution from engaging in aggressive war. The Atlantic Pact was invalid; its provisions were not legally binding on the French people. Millions signed the Truman letter: a crucial step was taken toward conversion of the PCF into a peace lobby. On July 2, 1949, Laurent Casanova announced that the Peace Movement had already borne its first fruits: the USSR had been sufficiently strengthened to lift the Berlin blocade.[19] This success provided encouragement for more energetic measures. On July 22 the Political Bureau called for intensified efforts against the ratification of the NATO pact: two weeks later, the Peace Movement called demonstrations against the arrival of General Bradley in Paris and the introduction of nuclear weapons to France. Police responded with some beatings and arrests. Meanwhile *L'Humanité* reported on July 9 that dock workers in Dunkirk had interrupted the loading of a ship with military cargo bound for Vietnam.[20] The campaign against "the filthy war" in Vietnam received a new vigor and impulse.

In September 1949 the PCF introduced a "peace ballot to preserve France from becoming a field of the dead or battleground of nuclear war." The declaration opposed German rearmament, the Vietnam war, nuclear weapons, and a swollen military budget and called upon the French to achieve national unity. On September 8 *L'Humanité* called for the most complete party action in this newest peace effort; a *journée nationale* (national day) for peace was declared for November, and caravans of peace were organized throughout France to descend on Paris for that occasion. Millions of signatures were collected for the Peace Ballot, indicating that a mass basis of sympathy existed for more direct forms of action. Ending the Vietnam war became the PCF's "task of honor."[21] In 1925 Communists had blocked the embarcation of troops and interrupted train schedules. They could do no less now. The party called for further action by dock workers to block arms shipments bound for Indochina, citing as successful examples work stoppages that had occurred at Dunkirk, Marseille, and Algiers.

The Cominform picked up on the PCF's campaign in November, extending it to all American shipments to countries covered by the American Mutual Defense Assistance Pact.[22] But despite widespread publicity the work stoppages and protests largely remained symbolic. They were restricted to port cities where Communists controlled the unions and limited in duration to a maximum of twenty-four hours. Some actions lasted no more than fifteen minutes. Moreover, they were in no sense construed by the party as illegal. On the contrary, on January 28, 1950, the PCF Political Bureau declared its continued support of strikes for "precise political objectives," a legal right enshrined in the French constitution.[23] American military authorities regarded the effort as no more than a nuisance and redirected military shipments through Cherbourg, where the unions were not under Communist control.[24] The French government responded predictably on March 8 with an anti-sabotage law. Communists attacked the law viciously in the National Assembly; yet such legislation may have been an expected or even intended result of the direct-action campaign. Within days a young sailor, Henri Martin, was arrested for distributing anti-war leaflets. The government's prosecution of Martin allowed an immediate shift in PCF efforts to a campaign for his liberation in the name of civil liberties. Actions against military shipments abruptly ceased as the party turned its efforts to a campaign that it found much more congenial.[25]

The Stockholm signature appeal against the atomic bomb was announced by the Peace Movement in December 1949. By spring 1950 it consumed a totality of the PCF's energies as militants embarked on a national effort to reach every household in France personally. Stockholm was the best known of the Peace Movement's campaigns and by far the most successful. The Political Bureau dutifully labeled it the "decisive task of the hour" to which "all Communists must commit themselves with all their heart and intelligence." Every signature was said to be a refusal to go to war. Peace, not workers' wages, was "the idea that grips the masses, transforming itself into a material force." The CGT executive bureau chided trade unionists for the slow pace of their efforts to collect signatures. On June 2 the World Peace Council asked for an intensified effort to convince people to sign.[26] Fourteen million signatures were ultimately claimed in France, the highest total of any non-Communist country. Combined with the propaganda effort on behalf of Henri Martin's civil liberties, the Stockholm appeal succeeded in winning the PCF its largest national following during the period of its political and social isolation and ostracism. Yet the seeming conversion of Communism to a lobby for peace and freedom coincided with the PCF's deepest plunge into the excesses of Stalinization: the apogee of the personality cults of Stalin and Thorez and the purge of former Resistance leaders at the Twelfth Party Congress of Gennevilliers in April 1950.

Stalinism as a system of political control in non-ruling Communist parties meant something quite different from the immediate interests and concerns of the USSR. The Comintern and the Cominform were means by which a political culture that originated in Russia was transmitted into France.[27] Stalinism owed its success in France to a particular historical conjuncture. As bolshevism was aided by French working-class defeats after World War I, Stalinism took hold after the brutal banishment of the PCF from participation in French political and social structures after World War II. Yet neither bolshevism nor Stalinism could have flourished without striking a responsive chord in French historical tradition. Bolshevism resembled Blanquism; French advocates of the Russian revolution convinced disillusioned workers that the Soviet state was the fulfillment of the tradition of Babeuf and the Paris Commune.[28] After World War II the PCF continuously returned to these themes, stressing the contribution of Blanquism to Leninism and the importance of French utopian socialism to Marxism, and incurring the wrath of Soviet ideologists by doing so. André Marty was excluded with the charge of Blanquism, while Roger Garaudy had to do self-criticism for failing to recognize the unique features of Marx's ideological breakthrough.[29] Russian Stalinism involved Great Russian nationalism; French Stalinism meant French chauvinism and jingoism, which at times irritated Moscow. The issue rose again in the 1960's in Garaudy's debates with Althusser and remains a staple of French Communist political culture today.

Garaudy was also the architect of the PCF's dialogue with Catholism and illustrated how elements of Catholic tradition were secularized in PCF practice, just as Stalin appropriated aspects of Russian orthodoxy. Icons and relics were evident in the cults of Stalin and Thorez; the regular practice of self-criticism played upon the youthful habituation of party militants to confession. Blanchette Gillet, leader of the PCF young women's auxiliary, became aware the party was an unconscious substitute for her strict Catholic upbringing when during a visit to the USSR she observed Soviet children decorating a portrait of Stalin with a garland of flowers, as she had done in her youth with portraits of the saints.[30] Intellectuals who left the Communist party repeatedly compared themselves to defrocked priests. Comparisons of the party to a church, once only common in anti-Communist literature, are now indulged in by Communist historians.[31]

The proletarian cult and chauvinism dovetailed in the notion of the French working class as the national class par excellence. Proletarian internationalism and attachment to the USSR were justified in terms of French nationalism; internationalism was not allowed to function to the detriment of the national myth.[32] Stalin was the leader of the Red Army and the architect of French liberation. A Russian alliance was a permanent aspect of French foreign policy which reappeared "at every turning point of history," an objective historical reality based on three German invasions of France from 1871 to 1945. France resisted the Germans in World War I because it had Russian help; it was defeated in 1940 because that help was denied. French nationalism reinforced the PCF's devotion to the USSR and proletarian internationalism. The PCF was the eldest son of the International Communist Movement. As home of the original revolutionary tradition, Paris would lay claim to primacy in the International Communist Movement once the PCF came to power. French industrial, technological, and cultural development were far beyond Russia's.[33] These ambitions provided a motive for the PCF's opposition to "polycentrism," as advocated by the Italian Communists and explained its unfriendly reaction to other Communist heresies such as the Yugoslav and Chinese. The PCF scorned heresy from an imperialist motive as well as a smug sense of superiority. As the eldest son of the movement, the PCF meant to inherit the patrimony.

Isaac Aviv noted the PCF's centralism internalized French unitary and centralist tradition. The French workers' community was consolidated on the basis of the same Jacobin-centralizing values prevalent among the bourgeoisie. Democratic centralism maintained the *ouvrieriste* or working-class character of the PCF leadership by institutionalizing a virtual system of affirmative action in favor of the socially disadvantaged.[34] Although Duclos, Thorez, and Frachon had not practiced their worker occupations for decades, their working-class origins and status as self-made bureaucrats and intellectuals remained the basis of their prestige. The PCF elite feared free debate because a de facto premium would be placed on oratorical skills much more common among bourgeois intellectuals than the working-class graduates of the party's schools. Communist leaders equated their worker hegemony over the PCF subculture with its continued voter appeal and success. A significant portion of the PCF electorate remains loyal because the PCF remains visibly identifiable as "the party of the working class."

Intellectual Stalinism, which took the virulent form of Zhdanovian socialist realism after World War II, was the consequence of *ouvrierisme,* sociologically determined. Its captivating simplicity of socialist realism appealed to the self-taught intellectual. Clearly delineated ideological criteria explained away the insecurity, misunderstanding, and hostility that abstract art and music engendered in a mass audience.[35] Zhdanovism was the means by which the PCF's self-taught "organic" intellectuals browbeat and brought to heel their bourgeois counterparts. Party intellectuals justified socialist realism by claiming they were in the tradition of Stendhal and Zola. PCF writers gladly accepted the accolades, guaranteed publication and translations in the USSR, and prizes offered by the counter-society. Stalinism corresponded to a felt need in a period in which all was either black or white, true or false, good or evil. Louis Aragon admittedly embraced socialist realism as an alternative to the apolitical, abstract, and rhetorical art of a new generation that escaped him.[36] Thorez was a more sophisticated critic than his cohorts in the Political Bureau. The socialist-realist craze reached a cruder level than ever before in his absence, reflecting its use in a power struggle by Duclos, Lecoeur, and others. But whatever its political uses, the Zhdanovian phenomenon was twisted to fit French purposes.

Stephen Cohen defined Russian Stalinism as not simply nationalism, bureaucratization, the absence of democracy, censorship, or police repression, but excess and extremism in each of these.[37] Cohen's definition highlights Stalinism's universal characteristics which the PCF shared. Even police repression occurred in PCF history, as the cases of the OS and post-war purges indicate. To be sure, the PCF never conducted civil war against peasants or forced industrialization. Whether it would have done so given the chance remains speculative. But the PCF indulged in a fascist-like chauvinism, and the Thorez cult resembled the deification of a despot. Cohen's categories do not exhaust the Stalinist phenomenon. Stalinism involved a universal mechanism of bureaucratic control found in subcultures or movements which demand full commitment, submission, and psychological dependence from their membership. In milder forms, its procedures may exist in any bureaucratic environment involving hierarchy, aspirations for promotion, secret personnel procedures, and the inculcation of corporate loyalty. In Albert O. Hirschman's terms the PCF was a loyalty-stimulating organization which repressed dissidence and exacted a high price for exit. The characteristics of personality cult, psychological "brainwashing," public humiliation, and self-criticism sessions may be observed in cults like Jonestown or the Moonies. These cults offer to their members as an important side effect a sense of discipline, purpose, and community.

Stalinist loyalty demanded continued striving after the impossible. A devoted Communist must be "in the line," apply policies and directives assiduously, but also anticipate changes before they occurred, act creatively and originally within a narrowly defined set of guidelines, and perform beyond what was expected. The line must be internalized as part of one's character and outlook.[38] The pressure was relentless. The line could never be questioned once "freely" decided upon and was always correct. If it did not result in the anticipated success, it was not properly applied. People submitted to the peculiar psychological universe of Stalinism with loyalty hard to fathom even for today's Communists. For Jean Chaintron, Resistance leader and former Prefect, being ill thought of or accused of failure by the leadership was intolerable, worse than a death sentence. Chaintron was both sentenced to death by Vichy and victim of a party purge; he could compare experiences. Advancement and responsibility in the PCF were dependent on a "politics of authenticity," conformity between one's innermost thoughts and outward behavior.[39] If the Stalinist system was diabolical, it was because one was never allowed to know how one failed to please; an attitude, a gesture, or a pattern of behavior might be at issue. If a superior gave a simple warning, the fault might be corrected. No warnings were ever given.

However enthusiastic or "creative and original" in applying the line, the good Stalinist also had to avoid any action that deviated either to the left or the right: "sectarianism" or "opportunism." Constant warnings against these twin evils rendered the implementation of policy a continuous balancing act. One had to attack the Socialists, but extend a fraternal hand to one's brother socialist worker; be resolutely lay and anticlerical, but open to one's Catholic neighbor; despise reaction, but cooperate with the right to defend French or national independence. Continuously in pursuit of the "correct" middle ground, it was in the nature of Stalinism never to find it. Stalinist militants were habituated to receiving contradictory directives and hence insensitive to genuine conflict among the leadership. French Stalinism evolved into a rationalization for immobility.

Capping the system was Thorez's personality cult which he promoted to consolidate his authority and make it impregnable. In February 1949 *Cahiers du Communisme* published a photo of Thorez with a caption describing him as the incarnation of the French working class and Leninism. The second edition of Thorez's autobiography, *Fils du Peuple,* appeared to reviews calling it "the book of the working class," the workers' guide and educator of a new type of man. From a mining family, Thorez spent the war period working on his uncle's farm. The man who ended the petty-bourgeois domination of the French workers' movement thus also embodied the peasantry. From 1934 through 1949 he led the French Communists in the pursuit of a single aim: unity. Thorez showed the way to good fellowship with the Socialists and offered an outstretched hand to Catholics. He was the best French Marxist of the contemporary era and a loyal disciple of Stalin. *Fils du Peuple* enriched Marxist-Leninist theory by French example and provided guidelines to achieve working-class unity. In December 1949 *Cahiers du Communisme* devoted a special issue to Stalin's seventieth birthday. The Soviet example loosened the floodgates in France. In his "homage to Stalin," Thorez rationalized the personality cult, observing that Marxists never underestimated the role of leadership. In April 1950 the party began publication of Thorez's collected works in celebration of his fiftieth birthday.[40] For the most part his 1930's journalistic efforts, militants were told they could find therein a prodigious wealth of insight, each article an original contribution to understanding the class struggle in France. Communist intellectuals paid homage to Thorez the economist, historian, and literary critic, who recaptured for the workers the progressive aspects of French tradition. Humble militants showed their devotion by presenting gifts in honor of Thorez's fiftieth birthday. Every cell gave at least one, and a special exhibition was organized for their display in Thorez's home municipality of Ivry.[41]

Almost never spontaneous, the cult of Thorez became an essential element of the Stalinist phenomenon in France. It infused charisma into an increasingly bureaucratic and lifeless party mechanism. It nationalized Stalinism by stressing Thorez's 1936 resumption of Jacobin rhetoric. It strengthened the redefinition of class as ethnicity in PCF propaganda. Thorez was the exemplary French worker and the native son of the French people. He embodied the working class as a national class. He showed the way to happiness. These conceptions strengthened Thorez's position and made his presence indispensable even if his control of party policies were challenged. The cult also isolated Thorez from the administration of daily party affairs and increased his distance from his collaborators with whom, except for his wife Jeannette Vermeersch, he was never close. It made obligatory a ritualized life-style that constricted his movements and imprisoned him. Yet it provided a solid enough power base so that Thorez could, if the occasion demanded, assert his independence from the Russians. Jacques Duclos, not Thorez, had primary responsibility for the execution of Moscow's will in France and implementation of the Cominform line. Duclos was a French Stalinist, Thorez a Stalinist Frenchman. The sectarian thrust of Thorez's policies against the more opportunistic line of Duclos obscured for observers that Thorez's, not Duclos', was the more authentically French line. The irony of the PCF's history is that it has often been, even during Stalin's lifetime, more Stalinist than the Russians. The PCF's native brand of Stalinism was the source of its limited independence. By being more Stalinist, the PCF became more French.

With the conclusion of the Stockholm campaign, Thorez began to chart an independent political line. Tension quickly developed between the two party strategies of Front national and Front populaire. The Peace Movement required unity with any politicians while the class-against-class tactic was aimed at the Socialists. The Socialists, because of their pacifist sentiments, were more receptive to appeals from the Peace Movement than other politicians, but direct attacks on them, dictated by the class-against-class line, repelled them from cooperation with the Communists. By mid–1950 neither cooperation toward peace nor steps toward unity were being achieved. Duclos began to make conciliatory advances to the existing Socialist leadership while Thorez maintained and even intensified his steady barrage of propaganda against them. Internal rivalry between Thorez and Duclos and their competing strategies troubled the PCF for the next five years and underlay the dramatic purge of 1950.

The first sign of the coming crisis occurred early in 1950 when Auguste Lecoeur was promoted to the post of Secretary for Organization, replacing Léon Mauvais. Mauvais had held the ill-fated post since November 1944. His predecessor, Marcel Gitton, was executed in 1941 as a police spy, and Lecoeur's successor, Marcel Servin, was disgraced in 1961. Mauvais received no warning; Thorez casually suggested at lunch that Mauvais return to trade-union work, which had been his forte before the war. Mauvais was barely able to suppress his tears.[42] In itself his removal needs no special explanation. Party membership had continuously declined since 1947 and would continue to do so through the 1950's. Lecoeur's promotion was extraordinarily rapid; he joined on the Secretariat the party's historic leaders Thorez, Duclos, and André Marty. Lecoeur's advancement also threatened Thorez's grasp on the party.

Lecoeur's promotion left Thorez isolated. Thorez's dislike of André Marty was of long standing, although Marty was a loner and not a threat to Thorez's power; Marty's disgrace in 1952 was regretted by nobody. Duclos was in no real sense Thorez's inferior. Duclos' responsibilities on behalf of Moscow extended to other West-European Communist parties and underground activities in France, in the past including espionage.[43] Duclos had unparalleled skills as a parliamentary orator, political strategist, and propagandist. During the war he ran the party as he was shortly to do again after Thorez fell ill. As fourth and last member of the Secretariat, Auguste Lecoeur was Duclos' creature. Duclos had made Lecoeur the party's second-in-command during the war; Thorez and Lecoeur had no admiration for one another. The two clashed violently in 1946 over party policy in the coal mines, with Thorez publicly reprimanding Lecoeur on that occasion. Yet Lecoeur's rise in the party was in no way impeded; his sponsorship by Duclos could have been the only reason.[44] Lecoeur also had difficulties with Jeannette Vermeersch, sharing her contempt with Tillon and Marty. In his subsequent writings, Lecoeur claimed he warned Thorez of the dangerous consequences of her influence.[45] In September 1950 Lecoeur criticized Vermeersch publicly and demanded she do self-criticism. Vermeersch admitted to Lecoeur's charges of insufficient peace activity by women Communists and weaknesses in the Communist women's organization.[46] Vermeersch had been promoted to the Political Bureau upon the insistence of Thorez.

Lecoeur's promotion was a prelude to the purge of resisters at the Congress of Gennevilliers in April 1950. The Resistance figures had become a continuous irritant to Duclos and the Soviets. Of necessity they showed independence and initiative in their conduct of the party's military operations during the war, coming into conflict with Duclos' stewardship of the civilian branch. After the war, they supported a merger of the PCF with a national movement in favor of social change, a domestic variant of Browderism, national Communism, or Titoism. Resistance leaders basked in popular glory while the party needed their national visibility during its participation in government. They were disillusioned with the party's return to isolation after 1947. Led by Tillon, they created a new coalition in the French Peace Movement, but the Russians quickly internationalized it to their own purposes. Within the Peace Movement, Resistance leaders found themselves accused of creating another independent power base to circumvent or oppose the party.

The resisters in the PCF did not form a group or faction. They remained unaware that any action was in preparation against them, did not communicate with one another (which would have violated the canons of democratic centralism), and even after the Congress, did not immediately perceive the meaning of what had occurred. Duclos masked the purge as a rejuvenation of personnel, promoting younger prominent Resistance figures to replace those purged: Jean Pronteau, Malleret-Joinville, and Maurice Kriegel-Valrimont joined the Central Committee in 1950.[47] The new men had joined the party and assumed prominent Resistance roles after the German invasion of the USSR, however, and they too fell victim to purges in a later period. The PCF seemed allergic to all the Resistance leaders who tried to remain active in its midst.

The 1950 purge victims were distinguished by their: (1) participation in the International Brigades; (2) opposition to the Nazi-Soviet pact; (3) involvement in the OS; (4) opposition to the party's pacifist line from 1939 and acts of resistance during that period; (5) involvement with or close knowledge of Duclos' dealings with German occupation authorities; (6) generally distinguished careers in the Resistance; and (7) particular intimacy with Thorez. Thorez sought to surround himself with Resistance heroes after the war to efface his own departure from French lines in 1939. Several joined Thorez's personal cabinet and became trusted collaborators; he had no reason to want them eliminated. The purge appeared orchestrated by Duclos with the backing of the Russians, who were rooting out Titoists and national Communist heretics at the time throughout Europe. A distinguished Resistance record was the single characteristic most victims had in common, but there were particular circumstances at play in almost all cases as is apparent from table 1.

Of the twenty-nine members of the Central Committee who were not re-elected at the Party Congress of Gennevilliers in April 1950, twenty-three had prominent roles in the Resistance.[48] Many of the same people were actively engaged in the International Brigades and the OS. Most worthy of note were Jean Chaintron, Marc Dupuy, Marcel Prenant, and Alain Signor. Chaintron was a veteran of the Spanish civil war, a key figure in the OS, and a leader of the Resistance in the Southern zone. Following the war he was Prefect at Limoges, then became Thorez's personal aide. Once an organizer of the Algerian Communist party, condemned to death during the war by Vichy authorities, Chaintron's most recent tasks had been to organize the special birthday celebrations of Stalin and Thorez in 1949 and 1950. Marc Dupuy, on the Central Committee since 1932, pursued a career in the Railroad Workers' union and served on the Political Bureau. Arrested by Vichy authorities on June 13, 1940, he escaped in August to become active in armed Resistance in the Southern zone. He first fought against "traitors" (indicating involvement in secret tasks of the OS) and then against the "invaders." Marcel Prenant, a Professor of Biology at the Sorbonne, was Chief of Staff of the FTP under Tillon. Prenant, for whom Thorez appeared to have a particular affection, was attacked by the party leadership in February and April 1949 for his refusal to accept fully Soviet claims for the biological theories of T. D. Lysenko. Alain Signor enjoyed a Resistance record almost the equal of Prenant's. Signor escaped from Vichy prisons to lead insurrectionary forces against the Germans in Brittany, where he was a regional party secretary. He was active in Resistance activities before the German invasion of the USSR, and later became a Central Committee delegate to Southern Resistance forces.

Other important purge victims included Auguste Havez and Robert Ballanger, both prominent in the Brittany Resistance. Havez opposed the Nazi-Soviet pact, participated in the creation of the OS, and struggled against the collaborationist line. Former Minister Marcel Paul, also active in the Breton Resistance, was not eliminated from the Central Committee but suffered some humiliation, and his career went into eclipse. Jean Chaumeil was an early organizer of the OS and argued against the policy of approaching the Germans to request the legal appearance of *L'Humanité* in 1940. He remained close to the party leadership throughout the Resistance period, fulfilling a variety of tasks. Mounette Dutilleul was secretary to Maurice Tréand and participated in the delegation to the Germans

Table 1
Schematic Table of PCF Purge Victims, 1950–1954

Name	International Brigades	Dissenting Role 1939–1941	O.S.	Resistance Role	Collaborator of Thorez	Other
Jean Chaintron	X		X	X	X	
Marc Dupuy			X	X		
Marcel Prenant				X	X	X (Lysenko case)
Alain Signor		X		X		
Julian Airoldi				X		
Raymond Bossus				X		
Henri Gourdeaux				X		
Lucien Labrousse				X		
Louis Lallemand				X		
René Lamps		X?		X		X (Catelas affair)
Georges Beyer				X	X	X (Tillon affair)
Robert Ballanger		X		X		
Auguste Havez		X	X	X	X	
Jean Chaumeil		X	X	X		
Mounette Dutilleul			X	X		X (Tréand assist.)
André Leroy		X	X			
François Vittori	X			X		
Albert Carn				X		
Robert Marchadier				X		
Joseph Pruja				X	X	
André Denis		X?		X		X (Guingouin affair)
Jean Lejeune				X		X (Tillon affair)
Later victims:						
Marcel Paul		X	X	X	X	
René Camphin		X	X	X		X (Lecoeur affair)
Roger Pannequin			X	X		X (Lecoeur affair)
Georges Guingouin		X	X	X		
Charles Tillon	X	X	X	X		
André Marty	X					
Arthur Ramette (BP)					X	
Auguste Lecoeur	X	X	X	X		

that requested the legal appearance of *L'Humanité*. She then worked for Frachon and Duclos on questions of personnel and cadres from 1940 to 1943, sharing responsibility in that capacity for the actions of the OS against "traitors." François Vittori was a veteran of the International brigades and leader of the Corsican Resistance, who owed his party advancement to André Marty. Several victims were involved in some of the party's "affairs" or associated with prominent dissenters later purged like Marty, Tillon, and Guingouin.

The limits of Thorez's power during the purges were demonstrated by subsequent revelations. Marcel Prenant, earlier attacked over the Lysenko affair, tried to resign from the Central Committee, only to have Thorez reject his resignation. "One does not resign from the Central Committee," Prenant was told. Prenant expected not to be re-elected at Gennevilliers but learned to his surprise that his name was included among new members. Ideologue Annie Besse, however, attacked Prenant as did, curiously, Jeannette Vermeersch as well. Yet Thorez was perplexed at this turn of events. Duclos rose to ask for "indulgence" on behalf of Prenant, but Prenant rejected any special consideration, and his removal was then voted unanimously. Prenant interpreted the little drama ultimately as being orchestrated by Duclos and Thorez against himself. But Thorez confided to Georges Cogniot he was opposed to the elimination of Prenant, but could do nothing about it.[49]

Few observers noted the striking similarity in the careers of the victims at the time, notwithstanding the East-European show trials and the hounding of Titoists there. Alone among the victims, Jean Chaintron expressed publicly his regret that the leadership had not thought better of his merits. He was rudely reprimanded by Thorez and reminded that a sovereign party congress was simply declining to re-elect him. The myth of party democracy must be upheld.[50] Auguste Havez later protested his removal in retaliation for which, he said, he was attacked physically and his car sabotaged. Roger Pannequin, ironically, observed to Jeannette Vermeersch just before the Congress that he was pleased to see so many Resistance leaders active in party affairs.[51] Her reply: they must not be permitted to think they could be right against the party. For Pannequin all the Stalinist deformation of thought was implicit in Vermeersch's reply: disagreement with the party's errors was more serious than the errors themselves. Lecoeur, in reply to the same observation, told Pannequin gruffly that the war was over. Prenant, Chaintron, and Havez were closest to Thorez, who was obliged to be their harshest critic, falling victim to the Stalinist tactic of extracting denunciations from those closest to the accused. Arthur Ramette, a longtime close associate of Thorez in the Nord, lost his seat on the Political Bureau at Gennevilliers as well. Thorez thus suffered another blow. Thorez's fiftieth birthday celebration, Pannequin wrote, was designed to make him swallow his political defeat more easily.

On September 7, 1950, in a lead editorial, Jean Kanapa denounced press reports of dissensions within the PCF leadership as slander, the products of British intelligence services.[52] Kanapa's article appeared two weeks before Vermeersch was forced to self-criticism by Lecoeur. Kanapa was denying a substantive reality. The party appeared of one mind in its dedication to the Stockholm appeal and the liberation of Henri Martin but was divided over its relationship with the Socialists. Thorez remained riveted on his experience of the 1930's. He believed it necessary to continue denunciation of the SFIO leadership; by revived class-against-class tactics a new Popular Front would be created. Thorez, therefore, returned to the social-fascist rhetoric of the 1930's and blurred the distinction between socialist leaders and workers; Communists must not lose sight that *the whole of the Socialist party* was the instrument of capital. The influence of Social Democracy over the working class must be liquidated. Even short-term tactical alliances with Socialist functionaries at any local level were at the moment impossible.

Thorez elaborated on his policy in his last speech to the PCF Central Committee a month before the onset of his illness in December.[53] He began by paying lip service to the Peace Movement. War was not inevitable, he said, but peace was hanging by a thread. The imperialist aggressors had only been restrained by the pressures of the popular movement in favor of peace; 14 million French signatures on the Stockholm appeal, part of 400 million world wide, prevented the United States from using the atomic bomb in Korea. The PCF's aim remained the achievement of unity and the creation of a new Popular Front. But the right-Socialists had done the popular movement great damage. They were "valets of U.S. imperialism," confirming at every turn the views of Lenin and Stalin according to which they were the "principal support of the bourgeoisie." It would be impossible to finish with the capitalist system, warned Thorez, without eliminating the influence of Social-Democracy from the workers' movement. The PCF wished to unite with those of different beliefs, but around its own positions. It refused adamantly to lose itself in the morass of electoral politics.

Immediately after Thorez's speech, *L'Humanité* welcomed a local agreement between Communists and Socialists in the municipality of Watten, department of the Nord. The agreement showed, said Fajon, the existence of common aspirations between Socialist and Communist workers. It was wrong to confuse Socialist workers with their leadership.[54] Fajon was clearly advocating policies of the sort that Thorez had just denounced. He appeared regularly thereafter as a leading editorialist in favor of the more moderate line toward the Socialists, also advocated by Duclos and Lecoeur. The sectarian position of Thorez and Jeannette Vermeersch was more clearly identified with Thorez's old associates of the Barbé-Celor group of the 1930–31 period, François Billoux and Raymond Guyot. On October 9 grenades were reported to have exploded at a meeting being addressed by Jacques Duclos. *L'Humanité* immediately linked the incident with the attempted July 1948 assassination of Togliatti in Italy and the murder of Belgian Communist leader Julian Lahaut shortly thereafter. The alleged attempt on Duclos' life became the occasion for the creation of a rival mini-cult in the PCF around the party's second-in-command. The PCF Political Bureau described Duclos the next day as "the indefatigable . . . who puts his immense talent in the service of the humble, in the service of the poor, in the service of justice and peace, Jacques Duclos who assumes, after Maurice Thorez, the heaviest responsibilities in the party."[55] Three days later *L'Humanité* announced that Thorez was bed-ridden, suffering from exhaustion and hypertension. In reality, it was the beginning of a stroke which immobilized Thorez for a period of three years. The PCF, without a clear policy since the conclusion of the Stockholm campaign, was also without its leader.

On November 9, 1950, a team of Soviet doctors arrived in France. On November 13 Thorez accompanied them back to the USSR where rest and treatment uniquely suited to his disability were said to be available. But Thorez's stroke was not medically unusual, and adequate care was available in France.[56] Thorez's movement to the USSR was also explained in terms of fears for his security, given the hysteria consequent upon what appeared to be a wave of assassination attempts against Communist leaders in Belgium, Italy, France, and Japan.[57] But it is not clear why Thorez, ill and limited in his movements, should have been harder to protect in France than when he was in command of his faculties and pursuing his normal round of activities. In the USSR Thorez came to feel a virtual prisoner. In late 1952 he asked Stalin to allow him to return to France; Stalin refused out of purported concern for Thorez's recovery.[58] No historian has yet suggested that Thorez's removal to Russia owed anything to the domestic political scene in France. Yet the hypothesis of a genuine tactical and personal split in the PCF leadership renders his removal intelligible. The Duclos-Lecoeur-Fajon current, in collusion with Moscow, desired Thorez's disappearance and seized upon his illness as the means to accomplish it. The absurd claim of an American attempt to assassinate Thorez during his flight, published by *L'Humanité* a few days after Thorez landed in Moscow, might have been concocted as a means of assuring the Communist leader's well-being while he was in the hands of the Russians.[59] Note, in any event, Lecoeur's double-edged send-off speech on November 8. The replacement of Thorez, Lecoeur said, was at once difficult and easy. It was difficult because in one sense nobody could replace Thorez. But the party would not suffer with comrades of the talent of Duclos and Fajon available to succeed Thorez.[60]

Thorez's departure was the signal for a number of new policy initiatives by the party which he later challenged from his enforced exile in the USSR. His attempts to reassert his control over the party caused confusion throughout 1952; he prevailed after his return to France was made possible by Stalin's death in 1953. The PCF's policy shift in 1950 involved first the attempt to achieve unity with any Socialists, or other French politicians at whatever level, willing to identify with a minimum PCF position on foreign policy. In short, Front national was the line. Entente was possible with Socialist leaders without the mass movement Thorez perceived as necessary to overcome their resistance.[61] Duclos' political attempts at entente were paralleled by trade-union leader Benoît Frachon unashamedly leading the CGT toward a policy of unity with Force Ouvrière and the CFTC wherever any minimal agreement for common action proved possible. On December 2 Duclos announced in the National Assembly that the PCF was ready to support any French government that would renounce nuclear weapons in conformity with the Stockholm appeal, withdraw from the UN side in the Korean conflict, and open negotiations between the great powers. Togliatti made a similiar declaration over a year earlier. Only after a long delay did the PCF finally step into line with other Communist parties in this declaration, which clearly established Soviet foreign policy objectives as the highest priority for the French Communists.[62] Thorez apparently resisted offering PCF support to the government all during 1950, despite Soviet urging.

On November 28, 1950, *L'Humanité* announced the brilliant success of the Communist painter Fougeron's showing of "Le Pays des Mines," a series of canvases depicting the life of French coal miners. The sponsorship of Fougeron, vigorously pressed by Lecoeur, brought the doctrine of socialist realism to its most absurd, making many party intellectuals uncomfortable and the party an object of ridicule among many non-Communist intellectuals. The new policy differed in degree rather than kind in terms of the introduction of Zhdanovian policies in France since 1948. Still, Aragon and Pierre Daix swallowed Lecoeur's new, extremely rigid line with difficulty, and the culturally sophisticated Thorez was known to be hostile to it.[63] Cultural policy was an area in which Lecoeur acted beyond his capacities, and his policy was repudiated firmly by Thorez after the latter's return to France.[64] Finally, Laurent Casanova rejected the policy of neutralism advocated by Hubert Beuve-Marie in *Le Monde,* denouncing its "anti-Soviet prejudice."[65] Neutralism struck a profound chord not only among intellectuals, but in a wide segment of French public opinion after the signing of the Atlantic alliance and the announcement of plans for the integration of West Germany into NATO defense efforts. Right-wing observers attributed the origins of neutralism to the PCF. While it is consistent with known aspects of PCF behavior for the party to have had a hand in its development, neutralism represented an authentic enough current of opinion in France to have rendered any such party effort superfluous. While not sponsoring neutralism, Thorez may well have been, as asserted by some, flirting with it.[66] It was only after Thorez's removal that the PCF came out unequivocally against neutralism.

The differences between Thorez and Duclos remained strategic, not ideological. Thorez was not opposed to the Peace Movement, and Duclos did not oppose a revival of the Popular Front. There was a tension between the two policies; they could not be pursued simultaneously. Thorez hoped to create a genuine mass movement as a basis for a new pro-Soviet foreign policy; he showed less interest in entente with assorted French politicians on minimal objectives such as banning U.S. atomic weapons from France. Duclos reflected Moscow's more limited appreciation of the internal possibilities offered by the French political landscape. Other divergences between the two currents in the PCF were related to the strategic argument. Thorez was more tolerant of an independent role for the Peace Movement, and its advocates, the party's resisters, were trusted men with whom he was close. They aspired, like himself, to rebuild a Popular Front for genuine social change. Duclos zealously wished to subordinate front organizations to the party. On intellectual questions, Thorez was interested in securing the support of prestigious figures in the arts and sciences for left-wing political programs. Duclos pushed the party into the most absurd parody of the Zhdanovian phenomenon in the USSR.

The issue was not decided by Thorez's absence. Duclos remained nominally the head of the party with Lecoeur, as in the war years, his chief assistant, and Fajon now his ideologue. But Vermeersch, Billoux, and Guyot remained loyal to Thorez in the Political Bureau and eagerly awaited his return. Frachon remained secure in his control of the trade unions and now tactically allied to Duclos in their attempt to break down barriers between the CGT and non-Communist unions. Marty remained a splendidly isolated figure, as did Tillon. Tillon was suspected of harboring independent ambitions at the head of the Peace Movement, and his position had been weakened by the purge of the former Resistance heroes. Marty and Tillon shared serious reservations about Duclos' leadership and fell victim to his determined and unquestioning implementation of the Soviet line.

It is hardly surprising that with its leadership weakened and divided, the PCF went through a period of confused and incoherent shifts in its policies in succeeding years. Only the return of Thorez in 1953, with new-found prestige after Stalin's death, could restore a measure of coherence. The years of blunder and vacillation from 1951 to 1953 were in several respects comparable to the excesses of the Barbé-Celor group from 1929 to 1931. There was a similar, if less spectacular, decline in the PCF membership in the 1950's but a much less apparent loss of influence among the Communist electorate. On the whole, the PCF emerged unscathed from its new bout with sectarianism, opportunism, and confusion. Both the emergence of the counter-society and the ingrained loyalty of the party's post-war electorate served to insulate the PCF from the damaging effects its internal divisions and policy shifts might otherwise have been expected to produce. To understand why the party survived its period of confusion with so little damage, it is necessary to examine the structural aspects of the Communist phenomenon in France.

NOTES

1. *L'Humanité,* February 22, 25, 1949.
2. *Le Procès Kravchenko, Comte Rendu Stenographique,* 2 vols. (Paris, 1949), I, 27. Hereinafter cited as *Procès.*
3. Victor Kravchenko, *I Chose Justice* (New York, 1950), 422–23.
4. *Procès,* I, 180.
5. *L'Humanité,* March 10, 1949.
6. *Procès,* II, 417.
7. Martin-Chauffier's testimony is in *Procès,* I, 65–70; Zilliacus' in I, 415–20; Grenier's in I, 79–90; Rémy-Mornet in I, 258.
8. Domenique Desanti, *Les Staliniens* (Paris, 1975), 169–70. See also André Wurmser, *Fidèlement Votre* (Paris, 1979), 359.

9. *Procès*: Buber-Neumann's testimony is in II, 261–75. Nordmann's attempted rebuttal is in II, 584–90.

10. *L'Humanité,* April 5, 1949.

11. Ibid., March 23, 25, 1949.

12. On the April Party Conference see the texts in *Cahiers du Communisme,* May 1949.

13. See the articles in *Cahiers du Communisme* by Roger Roucaute, 6 (June 1949), and Roger Garaudy, 8 (August 1949).

14. See Thorez's speech in *L'Humanité,* October 12, 1949, also his article "Notre Combat pour un Gouvernement d'Union démocratique," *Cahiers du Communisme,* November 1949, 1329–35.

15. Pierre Durand, *Vingt Ans: chronique, 1945–65* (Paris, 1965), 75.

16. *Cahiers du Communisme,* 5 (May, 1949).

17. These themes reappear in G. Cogniot and V. Joannès, *Maurice Thorez, l'homme, le militant* (Paris, 1970), 89–106.

18. *L'Humanité,* February 7, 1949.

19. *L'Humanité,* July 2, 1949.

20. Ibid., July 9, 22, 1949.

21. See Guillon's article in *Cahiers du Communisme,* 26, 9 (September 1949), 1111–20.

22. *L'Humanité,* January 7, 1950.

23. Ibid., January 28, 1950.

24. For a complete overview, United States National Archives (N.A.) Diplomatic Branch, OIR Report No. 5198, March 6, 1950, "Communist Plans to Impede MDAP Shipments to Western Europe."

25. Even before the Martin case the PCF shifted its propaganda to the defense of twenty anti-war protesters arrested in Roanne. See *L'Humanité,* March 25, 27, 1950. On the Martin case see chapter 9.

26. *L'Humanité,* April 21, May 5, May 18, June 2, 1950.

27. See Robert C. Tucker, ed., *Stalinism: Essays in Historical Interpretation* (New York, 1977), in particular Tucker's introduction, xi–xx.

28. See Irwin Wall, "French Communism and its Historians," *Journal of European Studies,* 3 (1973), 255–67.

29. Thus Roger Garaudy's *Les Sources françaises du socialisme scientifique* (Paris, 1950). For a Soviet critique of Garaudy see K. Selezniov, "Les Problèmes de l'Histoire du peuple français dans les Cahiers du Communisme (1947–50)," reprinted from *Voprosii Historii* (No. 5, 1951) in *Cahiers du Communisme,* 28, 9 (September 1951), 1077–91.

30. Personal interview, April 11, 1978. Mme. Gillet once held high posts in the PCF's young women's organization, the Union des Jeunes Filles de France.

31. See, for example, the exchange between Jean Elleinstein and Annie Kriegel in *Le Nouvel Observateur,* No. 660 (July 4–10, 1977).

32. Isaac Aviv, "Le PCF dans le système français des années 1930 à la fin de la IVᵉ république," *Le Mouvement Social,* 104 (July–September 1978), 75–93.

33. See the otherwise incomprehensible Jacqueline Mer, *Le Parti de Maurice Thorez ou le bonheur communiste français* (Paris, 1977), 64–71.

34. Pierre Gaborit, "Contribution à la théorie générale des partis politiques; L'exemple du PCF pendant la cinquième République" (unpublished thesis, University of Paris, N.D.), especially p. 56.

35. For this formulation see Paul Noirot, *La Mémoire ouverte* (Paris, 1976), 91.

36. Pierre Daix, *Aragon: une vie à changer* (Paris, 1975), 357.

37. In Tucker, ed., *Stalinism*, 3–29.

38. Jean Chaintron, personal interview, April 7, 1978.

39. See Hannah Arendt, *On Revolution* (New York, 1965).

40. *Cahiers du Communisme*, 2 (February 1949), 9 (September 1949), 12 (December 1949), 4 (April 1950).

41. *L'Humanité*, April 14, 19, 1950. Laurent Casanova wrote that the Twelfth Congress had given the "force of law" to Thorez's report, and the cult reached its apotheosis with the publication of absurd poems in Thorez's honor.

42. Auguste Lecoeur, *Le Partisan* (Paris, 1963), 247–48.

43. Philippe Bernert, *Roger Wybot et la Bataille pour la DST* (Paris, 1975), 343. Also Gilles Perrault, *L'Orchestre Rouge* (Paris, 1975) so identifies Duclos. For a striking confirmation see the interviews of Arthur London and Sandor Kapasci in *Le Monde*, January 28–29, 1979; London says "we received our directives [during the war] from Duclos."

44. For an account of Thorez's clash with Lecoeur see *Le Partisan*, 205–23. Roger Pannequin insists that Thorez and Lecoeur always despised one another: personal interview, May 2, 1978. And Charles Tillon identifies Lecoeur as the creature of Duclos, personal interview, May 29, 1978.

45. Auguste Lecoeur, *L'Autocritique attendue* (Paris, 1955), 18.

46. *L'Humanité*, September 18, 1950.

47. Jean Pronteau, personal interview, April 25, 1978.

48. The biographies that follow represent a composite of information gleaned from a number of sources. I discovered in the U.S. National Archives, Military Branch, Record Group 226, Military Intelligence report XL21481, translated sketches of members of the Central Committee of the PCF in 1945 compiled by the *Renseignements Généraux*. Especially useful, in addition to the memoirs of Tillon and Pannequin, were G. Willard et al. *De la guerre à la Liberation* (Paris, 1972); Alain Guerin, *La Résistance: Chronique Illustré* (Paris, 1972), especially Vol. I; and Roland Mareuil, *Les contradictions du Parti communiste* (Paris, 1958). Also *Le Parti communiste français pendant la Résistance* (Paris, 1967). Finally Philippe Robrieux was extremely helpful in coming up with some details that eluded me.

49. Georges Cogniot, *Parti Pris* II (Paris, 1979). Marcel Prenant, *Toute une vie à gauche* (Paris, 1980), 308–13.

50. Chaintron, Interview. Philippe Robrieux, *Maurice Thorez, Vie secrète et vie publique* (Paris, 1975), 374. Also his *Histoire intérieure du PCF* (Paris, 1981), II, 278–93.

51. Pannequin, *Adieu Camarades*, 158–65.

52. *L'Humanité*, September 7, 1950.

53. Ibid., September 30, 1950.

54. Ibid., October 7, 1950.

55. Ibid., October 9, 10, 1950.

56. Dr. Pierre Klotz, personal interview, September 18, 1980. Klotz was the first physician to treat Thorez.

57. Philippe Robrieux accepts this view in his *Maurice Thorez*, 396.

58. See Maurice Thorez, *Fils du Peuple* (Paris, 1970), 282. That Thorez felt a prisoner was related to Philippe Robrieux by Aragon—see the Robrieux archive. Klotz visited Thorez several times in Russia and thought him a prisoner in a guilded cage. Interview, September 18, 1980.

59. Thorez landed in Moscow on November 14. On November 16 *L'Humanité* claimed

an American fighter passed within ten meters of Thorez's plane. Thorez had no illusions about the fate of foreign communists in the USSR where he spent the war years. For some speculation about the fate of Thorez, Waldeck Rochet, and possibly anticipated for Marchais in the USSR, see J. F. Revel and Branko Lazitch, "La vrai vie de Georges Marchais," *L'Express,* July 24–30, 1978, 84–91.

60. *L'Humanité,* November 8, 1950.

61. Thus Victor Joannès undertook to explain away Thorez's September 30 remarks: *Cahiers du Communisme,* January 1951, 21–34.

62. *L'Humanité,* December 2, 1950. See Angelo Tasca's analysis in the Tasca Archive (Feltrinelli, Milan), Carton 79, *France,* Elections of June 1951.

63. On Thorez and the arts see Pierre Daix, *Aragon,* and Robrieux, *Maurice Thorez.*

64. Lecoeur admits his incapacities in *L'Autocritique attendue,* 12–15.

65. *L'Humanité,* December 22, 1950.

66. The claim that neutralism was created by the PCF may be found in *Bulletin de l'Association d'Etudes et d'Informations Politiques Internationales* (after 1956 *Est et Ouest* and so noted hereinafter), No. 32 (October 1–15, 1950). Despite its right-wing bias this review was remarkably astute and well informed. Also J. Y. Calvez, "Incertitudes doctrinales du PCF," *Lumière et Vie,* No. 28 (July 1956), 468.

6

INSIDE THE COUNTER-SOCIETY

The structure of the French Communist party has long been recognized as the source of its enduring strength. The PCF's structural uniqueness insured that conflicts among the party leadership, reflected in frequent unexplained shifts in the line, were accepted in a docile manner by the rank and file. Democratic centralism was not simply the implementation of military-style discipline within a democratic façade. Democracy was perceived and practiced by party militants in the cells, where debate was tolerated and secretaries freely elected by the membership. To be sure, most discussions were devoted to ways of better implementing the party line, selling *L'Humanité*, mobilizing people for demonstrations, and recruiting members. But the climate was participatory.[1] Party officials at the next level of organization, the sections, closely watched cell meetings; if the line was discussed too critically, a figure of recognized prestige was quickly dispatched to "explain" the policy and isolate dissenters. A refractory cell could not publicize its views because of the rigid prohibition of lateral contacts, regarded as factionalism and grounds for exclusion. Cell secretaries were judged by their ability to recruit, mobilize, and implement the line; even when pushed forward from below they could not "mount" in the apparatus without approval from above. In committees of party sections, therefore, discipline was much greater and dissent correspondingly rare. According to the PCF's 1946 statistics (the only year available) the mean number of cells per department was 412 and the median 292.[2] The largest department, Paris, had 4475 cells, followed by Seine-et-Oise, with 1396, Bouches-du-Rhone with 1355, and Nord with 1115. The smallest department had 46 cells. The average cell size was a scant 21.4 members. The average number of sections per department was thirty-nine, the median thirty-four.

At the level of the Departmental Federation one encountered the world of the PCF *permanents,* the PCF bureaucrats. Federal organization mirrored that of the party nationally: a federal congress convened annually, a committee at least quarterly, and a bureau ran party affairs from day to day. The Federal Secretary, likely as not to be a member of the PCF's Central Committee, exercised major responsibility and ruled autocratically; secretaries were regarded in Paris as virtual party prefects. Like the party's National Congress and Central Committee meetings, the federal congresses and committees displayed unity and uniformity. Not until the highest echelon of the PCF, the Political Bureau and Secretariat, was debate and discussion with a degree of freedom carried on, and in the latter instances only in secrecy. The PCF thus tolerated a measure of debate at the base and the summit, but stifled dissent at the intermediate levels, where democratic centralism insured that leadership conflict remained unknown to the rank and file and grass-roots sentiment never reached the commanding heights.

Two recent models compete as aids in understanding the PCF: the notion of counter-society, and the functionalist hypothesis. Neither is new. Gabriel Almond's classic, *The Appeals of Communism* (1954) characterized Communism in France and Italy as quasi-autonomous sub-cultures. Almond noted the attractiveness of Communism to persons seeking escape from loneliness or isolation, structured personal relationships at the "inner core" of Communist parties, and trauma involved in breaking with the party, which frequently led to a total severing of previous personal associations. All these themes were reformulated by Annie Kriegel. Jean-Marie Domenach wrote in 1951 that the PCF was "a complete society existing embryonically in the society it wishes to replace," which "deeply corresponds to French realities and needs," a counter-society (although Domenach did not use the term) that paradoxically contributed to the stability of the social order it sought to overturn. Domenach also drew analogies between Communism and Catholicism; but Jules Monnerot rejected obvious comparisons with the Church in favor of Islam which, he argued, like Communism, was "a secular religion in the service of a universal state." A generation later Ronald Tiersky, deeply influenced by Kriegel, called the PCF a Gemeinschaft of shared values and a microcosm of the future order it wished to establish for all society.[3] In the area of Communist studies also, it appears, the more things change the more they remain the same.

Kriegel's counter-society was authentic for those party activists who experienced it; it can only be described in subjective terms, and its importance must not be exaggerated.[4] Jean Rony's counter-society was confined to intellectuals who felt isolated within the party owing to their sense of inferiority vis-à-vis the workers. The Stalin cult, according to Pierre Daix, was largely indulged in by the party apparatus and some intellectuals; workers regarded it with their usual cynicism. Only among intellectuals and apparatchiks was there scandalous reaction to Picasso's allegedly unflattering portrait, published by *Les Lettres Françaises* after Stalin's death. The Communist workers who ran the presses were largely indifferent. It is absurd, says Pierre Durand, to extend the counter-society to the 25 percent of the French electorate who regularly voted for the party. For Domenique Desanti self-made intellectuals of working-class origins were the most deeply immersed in the Communist world: "For a worker the Communist counter-society brought with culture, and an opening to the world, a new sense of his own dignity. To lose this was to founder once again in the grey world of cultural vacuum to which the dominant society relegates the people of the factories, the mines, and the work place."[5]

The counter-society functioned as an agency of assimilation for Jews and other

marginal groups in French society. Kriegel noted that Jews shared several characteristics with politically conscious segments of the working class: urbanity,
cosmopolitanism, a minority sub-culture, and a community of the "elect." For
Jean Elleinstein in 1948 the PCF was a ghetto in which a Jew particularly could
feel at ease. Edgar Morin related his faith in Communism to Jewish alienation
and messianism: Jewish intellectuals were naturally drawn to a small world of
ideologues "uniquely nurtured by a mystical bridge with Moscow." Pierre Abraham was only able to emancipate himself from his "Jewish burden" by joining
the Communist party, although this was an unintended result of his membership,
not a specific goal. André Wurmser proudly refused to hide his Jewish identity
by changing his name, but argued for assimilation with conviction: "the first
duty of a Jew is to wish to disappear as far as Jewish specificity is concerned."[6]
With the advent of Communism, the Jewish question would disappear along with
the Jews.

The psychological comforts of a new ghetto and the hope of escaping from
the Jewish condition were operable in individual cases, but the economic appeal
of Communism to a mass of proletarianized Jews and an equally miserable Jewish
petty-bourgeoisie must not be neglected either. Pierre Aubery noted that the
members of the Yiddish-speaking section of the PCF were fully assimilationist
and showed no concern for the survival of Jewish culture under Communism.
By consciously being militant in Yiddish, they were clearly seeking to escape
economic oppression rather than their Jewishness. The misery of Belleville gave
to the PCF a Henri Krasucki, who rose to leadership of the CGT, and Henri
Fiszbin, who became head of the Paris federation and President of the Communist
group in the Hôtel de Ville. Fiszbin, although a Jew, carried prestige in the party
because of his working-class origins.[7]

Communist intellectuals reaped practical advantages from the counter-society:
honor, adulation, prizes, translations in the Eastern countries, and acceptance
into a community of mutual flattery and encouragement. Membership in the
counter-society was cemented by the fear of rejection back into a bourgeois world
against which one had rebelled. Many authors stressed the psychological support
group membership conferred. For Desanti belonging to a group in possession of
total truth rendered one blind to the outside world; rejection meant total failure,
loss of hope, and social *déclassement*. Paul Noirot found family belonging,
fraternity and friendship, reinforced by immediate familiarity in address or *tu-
toiement* and participation in the "collective delirium" of the cold war. A "Stalinist
clerc" was part of a community united by ideology, history, and devotion and
willing to give his life in the service of the cause. Jean Recanati, orphaned by
the war, found in the PCF a replacement for the family he had lost. For Roger
Pannequin "the society that we wanted, in our minds, had to resemble our group."
One of Harris and Sadouy's interlocutors remarked, "I need to like the persons
around me, to develop a kind of well being around me. Well, I think the party
corresponded exactly to that." Françoise d'Eaubonne experienced "extraordinary,
genuinely visionary moments" in the ordinary: a handshake, a sign of recognition,

a word could become "a way of self-dramatization, one of those modern onanisms born of the need to live at any price with intensity in a world that only offers us the intense in the atrocious, in short that mystifying temptation of the sublime which was so sharply defined in the hearts of the ancient Christians."[8]

The counter-society was concerned not only with politics but also with ambition and love. Philippe Robrieux was bluntly told that as a bourgeois he could only be of service to the party as an accomplished intellectual, which meant he had to keep his mind on his studies. He did. Marriage with "*une bonne camarade*" was "*de rigeur*." Raoul Calas realized "how much the tasks of a militant became easier from the moment that husband and wife are united not only by reciprocal sentiment, but also by common opinions." In André Stil's novel *Le Premier Choc* Henri and Paulette's love for one another is expressed and reinforced by their involvement in party activities. Paulette achieves self-definition and emancipation vis-à-vis Henri after she has led an anti-American demonstration and experienced arrest. Most of the party's prominent women in the early 1950's, including Jeannette Vermeersch, held their positions by virtue of their marriages to highly placed men in the PCF apparatus; in 1968, seven out of nine female members of the Central Committee, noted Kriegel, were married to members of that body.[9] Blanchette Gillet related how a friend in the Communist youth movement, engaged to a Jewish intellectual during the hysteria over the "doctor's plot" in the USSR, was told to break off the relationship. She did.[10] The excluded André Marty complained bitterly that his wife was turned against him while his relationship with his non-Communist brother became cause for suspicion. Noirot had a close friend who was married to an American and forced to choose between political commitment and romantic love. Emmanuel Le Roy Ladurie recalled how pressure was brought on the philosopher Louis Althusser to break with his wife, suspected of deviating from the party line.[11]

With concern for one's love life went a petty-bourgeois moralism which Robrieux compared to the bulk of French Catholics in the 1950's. Sexual looseness and Communist militance were incompatible; homosexuality was a decadent product of capitalist society in decomposition. Communists never departed from established norms in dress and frowned upon their women smoking in public. In Stil's fictionalized account of party life, the headquarters of the Communist women's auxiliary was easily distinguishable from the main office by its cleanliness and feminine touches. Desanti caustically observed: "Our counter-society accepted, unconsciously, the scale of values of official society; it reproduced the 'work-family-fatherland' of the reactionaries, simply adding the adjective 'socialist' without ever explaining existing revolutionary values."[12]

Kriegel's school persists nevertheless in seeing Communist "exteriority" as a potentially revolutionary force: the sub-culture was part of, yet alien to the existing social order, and the counter-society continued the parallel and prolonged existence in France of an incipient dual power. For Tiersky the counter-society's "rigid yet invisible" frontiers demarcating it from the rest of society provided "a structural basis for the negation of the status quo."[13] The PCF resisted integration into the existing social order by virtue of the counter-society, as the Russian Bolsheviks avoided de-radicalization by means of their democratic centralist organization. But neither Tiersky nor Kriegel can demonstrate why the counter-society contributes to, more than it militates against, the PCF's "revolutionary potential." The PCF was analogous to the pre-World War I Social Democracy in Germany, more an example of "negative integration" than of complete alien-ation from the social order in which it functioned. The PCF's specificity for Kriegel, lies in its oppressive internal structure and solidarity with the USSR, including endorsement of Soviet interventions in Budapest and Prague. But these are not the defining characteristics of revolution, and were constants of the PCF during the Popular Front and Liberation, demonstrating that solidarity with the USSR, democratic centralism, and the cult of personality were consistent with Social-Democratic practice. Even when loyalty to the USSR caused the party seemingly to break with the national mainstream, the PCF's alienation turned out to be temporary. The party's flirtation with collaboration in 1940–41 was also more an example of integration with the mainstream of French society than of negation.

Other scholars have used the conservative, immobile aspects of the Communist sub-culture as examples of the PCF's functionalism. For Georges Lavau the PCF is a "tribunitary" party. Its radical ideological rejection of the capitalist system attracts the down-trodden, repressed and alienated elements in French society. The PCF articulates the frustration of society's victims; since most of its daily activity is either standard trade-unionism or electoral politics, the party integrates them and legitimizes the political system through its active participation. Kriegel argued that these functions are "incidental" to the PCF's "real concerns," which lie in the realm of foreign policy. But the PCF's daily functioning in French society clearly assumed more importance than the foreign policy goals it had no chance of realizing. For Lavau the PCF's structure and ties to the USSR remained its last defense against the charge of becoming "a party like the others."[14] Georgio Galli arrived at the same conclusion for the Italian Communist party; after 1945 the ruling group of the PCI behaved in accordance with the principles of rep-resentative democracy, never tried to overthrow the political system, but rather contributed to its stability.[15] Such views have passed into the conventional wis-dom: witness E. Le Roy Ladurie's observation in *Le Monde,* that the PCF performed "immense services . . . [it] has been able to harness certain specific energies which, left free, would have been destructive . . . it has trapped inside an iron cage . . . the generalized anxiety of various groups and youth; without the PCF this anxiety would spread in an uncontrolled manner among different parts of the social organism. Then one would see implanted here and there the metastases of a terrorism which would no longer be comfortably verbal, but tragically expressed in bloodshed."[16]

The contributions of the functionalists have transcended the terms of the Kriegel-Lavau debate. Pierre Gaborit showed how democratic centralism ra-tionalized and preserved the domination of a worker-elite in the party. The PCF interprets "worker" ethnically by social origins, not actual experience in the factories. By this measure, 40 percent of the party's deputies over the years have been workers. Proletarian origins have also been characteristic of 41 percent of federal committee members, 60 percent of party workers and 70 to 75 percent of federal secretaries. The PCF's ideal image of itself can always be found in the social composition of a Communist party congress.[17] Bertrand Badie showed how the party, through its domination of the CGT, transmitted demands from the working class to the French political system in a "functional reciprocal exchange." The CGT tries to stay ahead of the workers in the formulation of demands, canalizes and often inhibits mass action, and downplays any dysfunctional "political" goal to strikes when its internal stability is threatened. In doing so the CGT came to exercise relative autonomy from the PCF.[18] The party attempts to make strikes count politically, using them to influence government policy. Its insistence in the late 1940's and 1950's that mass action could achieve a shift in the parliamentary majority, reorientation of government policy and return of the PCF to a place in the cabinet stemmed from its strike strategy. Neither Gaborit nor Badie agree fully with Lavau, but his work marks their point of departure. Badie rejects orthodox functionalism, which examines every institution from the standpoint of its presumed contribution to the stability of the existing social order, but his model, endorsed in party publications, studies political action in "a situation which is not or is no longer revolutionary."[19]

Domenique Labbé's *gauchiste* (leftist) critique of PCF ideology shows functionalism adapted to left-wing purposes. PCF ideology elaborates the party's relationship to the working class into a "synthetic and fetishized, unchanging notion."[20] Labbé interprets PCF ideology as a total system of grammar, a thought-pattern internalized so that those within its confines cannot formulate a concept that is not a specification of the model. Reduced to essentials, the PCF paradigm was deceptively simple: the Communist party was the vanguard of the working class around which all other exploited groups must rally in the struggle against monopoly capital. After 1958 monopoly capitalism became identical with the personal power of de Gaulle. The PCF world view argued the common interest of 90 percent of the French population against a handful of exploiters. It provided for the internal cohesion of the Communists as a group, masked abandonment of the PCF's revolutionary goals, and placed total emphasis on political power. It also led to a dominance-subject relationship within the party structure socializing the individual to the political paternalism of the capitalist system; Communist ideology paradoxically became a part of the dominant pattern of bourgeois thought.

One need not, perhaps, carry things as far as Labbé, but Lavau observed that it was not dysfunctional in terms of the stability of the system to have at least one party that offered a radical critique. The functionalists offer an attractive alternative to understanding the counter-society in terms of Kriegel's and Tiersky's presumed revolutionary potential. It is a firm tenet of PCF ideology that the revolution will not be "made by the party"; a revolutionary situation makes itself. That in the sixty years of its history since the Congress of Tours the PCF has yet to define a situation as "revolutionary," is in itself eloquent testimony enough. When a revolutionary situation presents itself, arguments about the potential of the PCF counter-society become academic. De Gaulle made the coup d'etat of 1958 while the PCF rallied to the defense of the regime it was blamed for having de-stabilized. Ten years later, the PCF rallied to elections to settle the May events; Mendès-France and the Socialists appeared ready to accept power conferred upon them from the streets. This is not to say the PCF could not find itself in a position of power following a breakdown of legality and a mass movement like May 1968. But the party always knew participation in a democratic coalition was more likely. Neither alternative stemmed from the party's structure and organization.

One of the most noted peculiarities of the PCF was the stability and loyalty of its electorate, as compared to the floating nature of its membership, 15 to 20 percent of whom were likely to leave the party in any given year. The volatile nature of PCF membership argues for a much closer identification between party members and the Communist electorate than previously assumed. Many PCF voters at one time or another have carried their convictions to the point of joining the party, but only a small part of the membership formed the stable core of officials and activists to whom the term "counter-society" may be attached. Defining and counting PCF membership was difficult, since the degree of militancy varied so widely. Kriegel viewed the PCF as a series of concentric circles moving from electors to readers of the press, members, and career officials at the inner core. It would be more accurate to visualize one large colored circle, darkest at the inner core and gradually lightening in color until it blended into the neutral tones of the surrounding matter. As loyal and stable as the electorate appeared to be, there was considerable laxness of commitment at the edges and a higher degree of volatility among Communist voters than had usually been thought.[21]

PCF membership was difficult to estimate because of the party practice of using the number of cards delivered to federations (*cartes delivrées*), rather than the figure of those distributed to and signed by local militants (*cartes placées*). Kriegel estimated the number of *cartes delivrées* to inflate membership by 50 percent; Jean Elleinstein calculated the difference at 25 percent for 1961, but argued that it declined after that, reaching only 11 percent in 1975.[22] Following are Kriegel's figures, based on official party sources:

	cartes delivrées	cartes placées
Jan. 1945		387,098
June 1945		544,989
Dec. 1946		775,352
Jan. 1947	809,030	
June 1947	895,130	
Dec. 1947	907,785	
Dec. 1948	788,459	
1949	786,855	
1954	506,250	
1955	389,000	
1956	429,653	
1959	425,150	

The decline in membership began in 1947 but was masked in that year by the party's switch to *cartes delivrées* in its calculations. Auguste Lecoeur provided Philippe Robrieux with a secret internal document calculating the 1953 low in *cartes delivrées* at 339,269.[23] Lecoeur's rounded estimates of *cartes placées* while he was Organization Secretary were as follows:[24]

1937	225,000
1948	800,000
1951	408,000
1952	330,000
1953	280,000

The treasury normally received an average of six monthly payments per card out of a possible twelve; Lecoeur's efforts to determine membership with greater accuracy failed as he succumbed to pressures to show a membership increase. Robrieux estimates real membership fell to 170,000–180,000 in 1953 and probably did not rise beyond 190,000 by 1960, although the party has never in its history published official figures for *cartes delivrées* lower than 400,000. The turnabout in the party's fortunes occurred only after the 1958 Gaullist coup.

Marcel Servin, Lecoeur's successor, gave revealing information to the Thirteenth Party Congress in 1954. The 506,250 cards delivered to federations accounted for only 2,636,000 stamps sold, or five per card.[25] If full membership were counted by cards sold with twelve monthly stamps, the actual figure would be less than half the official total. Jean-Marie Domenach estimated 60 percent of the post-war influx of new membership was genuinely militant based upon dues payment. Accounts of cell activity in the 1950's demonstrated lethargy. Alain Brayance found in 1952 a typical cell of forty members in the Paris region regularly mustered twelve at weekly meetings. Gabriel Enkiri remarked that fifteen to twenty out of eighty members in his cell in 1956 were active.[26] Official party sources gave a similar picture. In the aftermath of Lecoeur's dismissal in 1954, Charles Pieters, secretary of a cell in Paris' eighteenth arrondissement, complained of the "mechanical" application of Thorez's directive of a party "counted in the millions"; of a hundred members in his cell in 1949 only fifteen or twenty attended meetings. Eighty percent of the cell's adherents lacked five or six stamps on their cards, and some as many as ten. In Stil's novel, cell meetings grew only when a popular political issue required mobilization, such as resisting the unloading of military cargo from an American ship. Jean Baby noted that real accomplishment rested on a tiny group around the cell secretary, while most members remained inactive.[27]

Servin announced a "sample" survey of 153,163 cardholders in an effort to establish the party's social composition in June 1954; it may well have consisted of the total number of cards reactivated by that date, or at least all members who responded to a questionnaire. It is not clear why the party secretary would have taken a sample that large without trying to cover all the party's membership.[28] Given the slow rate at which militants normally renewed their membership— Servin gave the example of a section of 980 members, 200 of whom (19 percent) had not yet renewed by the time of the congress—Servin's sample translates into a solid membership total for 1954 close to Robrieux's estimate of 180,000. Of Servin's sample, 61 percent were listed as eligible for membership in the CGT but only 48 percent were industrial workers; 10 percent worked in nationalized enterprises such as the railroads, electricity, or post and telephone. Half the PCF's membership was not working class, and the party's cells did not accentuate its proletarian character to Servin's satisfaction either. Out of a total of 19,219 cells, 8143 were residential or local, 5924 rural, and only 5152 located in industrial enterprises. Despite the intensive party effort since the "bolshevization" of 1924 to channel working-class membership into industrial cells, Servin was able to report that only 25 percent of his sample were so enrolled. No wonder he lamented, "we cannot be satisfied with the social composition of our party." A comparison of the 1947 to 1954 statistics on cells revealed the smallest loss in industrial cells:

	1946	**1953**	**% loss**
Sections	3,472	2,562	25
Rural cells	12,060	5,924	50
Local cells	15,860	8,143	48
Industrial cells	8,363	5,152	38

The PCF, as electoral geographers have noted, fell back upon its traditional bastions of support in times of crisis. The circulation of *L'Humanité,* estimated as high as 500,000 in 1946, fell to 170,000 by 1951.

Studies of the PCF electorate de-emphasize its social distinctiveness and stress its broad base. In his study of the October 1945 elections Pierre Gaborit argued that the electoral clientele of the party corresponded to a complete cross-section of the French population.[29] Gaborit found the party "stagnated" in its industrial bastions in 1945 while it progressed in rural areas, undergoing a "Radicalization" of its electorate along the lines of the inter-war SFIO. The PCF vote fell from 1936 totals in some urban areas, including Paris, indicating the party had reached a "saturation threshold" among workers. At the same time the PCF progressed in peasant regions, most notably the Center, West (Brittany), Alpine valleys, Mediterranean litoral, and Corsica. In 1936 the bulk of party deputies came from the Nord, Paris region, or South-East. In 1945 the party elected representatives in all but thirteen departments.

The PCF correspondingly modified its discourse to broaden its appeal. Terms like Front unique, Marxism, Leninism, and revolution virtually disappeared in 1945 in favor of verbal appeals featuring slogans such as unity, democracy, and nationalization. A heterogeneous electorate in 1945 was united by its democratic political goals and moderate desire for social transformation. PCF voters shared only a distinctive political consciousness.

François Goguel confirmed Gaborit's study with few modifications.[30] The PCF's former bastions of the Northeast, Center (Berry, Bourbonnais, Marche, and Limousin), Mediterranean, and South-East reappeared in the November 1946 elections, Goguel found, while the West remained largely refractory to the party. But the PCF rarely fell below 10 percent of the vote and never below 5 percent. It penetrated many formerly conservative zones and the variation between its areas of strength and weakness were less marked than they had been before. In rural strongholds of the Center and Midi the PCF now clearly represented the Third Republic's anti-clerical tradition. The 1951 elections marked some strengthening in industrial areas and a partial retreat in newly conquered agricultural regions, showing the PCF to fall back on its traditional areas of support. But the PCF remained for Goguel "of all the French parties not only the one with the greatest membership, but also the party that possessed the largest and most varied territorial bases." The 1956 elections marked some further accentuation of the party's working-class character, but no fundamental modification of the traits shown in 1946. Neither Goguel, nor Gaborit found any correspondence between an electoral map of the PCF and the distribution of industrialization. Mattei Dogan tried to correlate the percentage of the industrial population with the percentage of Communist vote in the 1946, 1951, 1956, 1958, and 1968 elections. In none of these cases did he find any correlation nationally although he found a significant correlation in certain regions. A correlation of the 1946 Communist vote with the level of industrialization reported in the census of that year confirms Dogan's findings: a .0038 Pearson Correlation Coefficient, meaning no significance. A more refined analysis based on the PCF vote in the 1962 legislative elections and the census of that year reveals the following:[31]

	Pearson Correlation Coefficient
Peasants	−0.23
Salaried Agricultural Workers	0.10
Industrial and Commercial Middle Class	0.27
Liberal Professions and High Bureaucrats	0.13
Middle-level bureaucrats	0.24
White-collar workers	0.24
Industrial workers	0.08

These results may not indicate a higher PCF vote among industrial, bureaucrat, and white-collar workers so much as a stronger party vote in areas where those groups are concentrated, that is "dynamic" versus "static" France. François Goguel demonstrated that the PCF vote was higher in departments with a higher productivity index than the national average by 4.2 percent in the 1951 elections and 4.7 percent in 1956. In twenty-seven departments whose productivity accounted for 65 percent of French goods in 1955 the PCF received 22.4 percent as against 18.3 percent in the remaining sixty-three departments.[32] But similar relationships existed for the Socialists and the RPF. Goguel and others were tempted to conclude that the Gaullist-Communist bi-polarity of the Fifth Republic's early years was in some way the fruit of France's technocratic modernization. Events of the 1970's have invalidated that assumption, however.

Local studies and public opinion polls show that the PCF electorate does not differ substantially from party membership, notwithstanding the lack of significant correlation nationally. Duncan Macrae found a high correlation between working-class strength and PCF vote in the larger cities, where the PCF held an estimated 57 percent of the working-class vote in 1947 as compared with 44 percent in the smaller towns. Joseph Klatzmann's study of the working-class vote in the 1956 Paris elections estimated the party's totals as 60 to 70 percent among workers, rising as high as 75 percent in districts where workers constituted a majority of the population. Dogan calculated that 55 percent of the Paris workers voted Communist, and 67 percent of those in the "Red Belt" suburbs of the capital did so.[33] Table 2 lists the nineteen departments on the 1946 census that had 40 percent or more of their population active in industry. They averaged 27.15 percent in Communist vote, just below the national Communist total of 28.89 percent in the November 1946 elections. On the other hand, these same nineteen departments accounted for 43.7 percent of Communist party membership and 45.7 percent of the total Communist vote. If the PCF was not a majority of the proletariat, the proletariat was still close to a majority of the PCF.

Nationally, the relationship between Communist strength and industrial concentration varied strikingly. Dogan calculated the relationship as only .30 in Strasbourg, .28 in Metz, and .24 in Mulhouse, but in Le Havre, it was .62 and in Toulon .87. In twenty-four cities with populations of over 100,000, 50 percent of which was working-class in 1956, the PCF received 25.8 percent of the vote.

Table 2
Industrialized Departments of France, 1946

	% in Industry	Vote Total	PCF Vote %	PCF Members
Nord	62	291,400	28.7	36,116
Pas-de-Calais	56	173,253	21.4	37,000
Meurthe-et-Moselle	54	56,839	24.3	6,993
Loire	53	85,140	29.6	15,762
Seine-et-Oise	53	244,219	34.4	31,324
Loire-Inférieure	52	42,821	13.1	4,540
Rhône	52	106,016	26.5	18,243
Paris	51	839,431	35.3	108,092
Bouches-du-Rhône	48	157,462	38.9	26,726
Haut-Rhin	48	22,732	10.9	2,909
Seine-Inférieure	48	121,212	32.4	8,507
Loiret	45	44,157	26.0	5,195
Vosges	45	41,709	26.6	3,500
Oise	44	64,278	34.3	10,622
Doubs	43	36,367	24.1	5,150
Aube	42	31,982	29.3	5,500
Isère	41	82,019	33.7	15,127
Bas-Rhin	40	40,547	13.6	5,553
Somme	40	74,296	32.7	11,189
Total of 19 Depts.		2,555,880	27.15	358,048
National Total		5,580,649	28.89	819,155

Sources: *Annuaire statistique de la France* (1946); Parti Communiste Français, *Rapports* (Strasbourg, 1947).

If it is assumed that 25 percent of the PCF vote there came from non-workers, then according to Dogan's estimates, 49 percent of France's working class voted Communist. Religion can in some regions be shown to have been a stronger influence on voting behavior than social class. Elsewhere Dogan has shown that the working class–PCF relationship was stronger in "dechristianized" regions than in still largely religious ones, as the correlations for the above-named cities indicate. Strasbourg, Metz, and Mulhouse are in the Alsace-Lorraine area where both regional and religious ties remained strong. Religion has continued to act as a barrier: where its effect remained powerful, the working class-Communist vote relationship was weak. The relative secularization of France in the 1970's led to a strengthening of the tendency toward the left in the electorate culminating in the Mitterrand victory of 1981. But the Communist vote profile as revealed in a March 1978 exit poll did not show that much change: it was 53 percent male, 46 percent under age thirty-four, and 60 percent salaried with industrial workers over-represented. The major sociological difference between left and right in the 1978 elections was not occupation, however, but rather possession of a family patrimony.[34]

The most satisfying explanation of PCF electoral behavior is drawn from the notion of a common political culture or consciousness shared between the party leadership and electorate across socio-economic lines.[35] PCF ideology consistently called for a rally of intellectuals, peasants, and petty-bourgeoisie, both salaried and unsalaried, around the working class against the trusts and monopolies. The party privileges the working class but recognizes the importance of other social categories. Jean Ranger supported Goguel's and Gaborit's finding that the party's new electoral implantations in 1945 were the first to desert in times of crisis. Ranger found the PCF electorate to be the most stable of any French party in terms of geography and social structure although less so than the Italian Communist electorate. French Communist voters showed more loyalty than the voters of other parties. They were and remain more likely to attend electoral meetings and less likely to be undecided on how to vote on election day. According to a 1956 poll, French Communists voted for party, not personality, a confirmation of Pierre Daix's insistence on the absence of personality cult among them.[36] In June 1946 58 percent of PCF voters said the party "perfectly" expressed their views, while 33 percent answered that it did so "*assez bien*" (well enough). According to Ranger, 75 percent of the PCF electorate prefer to identify themselves as workers, which indicates that the Communist political consciousness did have social roots. There is nothing contradictory in this data. If only 50 percent of the PCF electorate actually falls in the "worker" category in terms of occupation, it is likely that housewives, retired workers, agricultural laborers, and even some peasants and members of the salaried middle class who vote Communist also identify themselves as workers. Fifty-five percent of PCF voters gave money to the party during elections and as many as 70 percent attended electoral rallies. Thomas H. Greene noted that the half of the PCF electorate that was working class was not the poorer half. A positive correlation between Communist votes and the census data on the distribution of gas and electricity, television sets, and educational level was obtained in 1956. Richard Hamilton demonstrated that Communist workers were more likely than other workers to own automobiles.[37] The better-paid but alienated workers in the largest industries tended to remain loyal to the party, while poorer-paid workers in smaller enterprises, where the owner worked alongside his workers, displayed more sympathy for their enterprise's fate.

Reduced to its essentials, the content of the Communist political consciousness reflected a belief in the necessity of public ownership of the means of production and exchange combined with a sense of shared destiny with the Soviet Union and the Eastern bloc countries as the major forces working for peace in the world. Dialectical materialism in the pre–1956 period was studied in schematic form from a thirty-page pamphlet by Stalin. The more ambitious read the autobiography and collected works of Maurice Thorez. Even among intellectuals ignorance of basic Marxist writings was commonplace. Diamat, as it was known, was reduced to a number of principles or theses easily committed to memory. It was sufficient to know that Marxism was materialist, dialectical, and scientific; it enshrined the party in its role as the proletarian avant-garde and taught the relativity of all phenomena within the objective framework of the inevitable movement of history. Intellectuals like Henri Lefebvre or Roger Garaudy, who strayed too far in their theoretical writings, found themselves called upon to do self-criticism. Garaudy's non-Stalinist themes of alienation and the young Marx appeared briefly in his work of 1946 and 1947, went into eclipse during the 1950's, and then flowered in the 1960's with Thorez's endorsement. In 1949 the PCF warned against over-estimating the "young and immature Marx": Alienation "cannot stand independently as a distinct moment in Marxist theory."[38] Henri Lefebvre had to apologize in 1949 for referring to Marxism as a sociology. He was only later able to develop his theories outside the party fold.

It is difficult today to understand the frenzy with which PCF intellectuals embraced the phenomenon of Zhdanovism from 1947 to 1954. Party publications defended the biology of Lysenko, advocated "proletarian" as opposed to "bourgeois" science, and insisted that Communist writers embrace the strait jacket of socialist realism. In terms of the novel, socialist realism meant plots must be objectively set in a historical context and demonstrate plausible characters acting in authentic situations. When Communist Pierre Courtade wrote a satirical philosophical tale about Vichy set in a mythical kingdom called *Elseneur,* he was criticized by Pierre Daix for using an "obsolete" literary form. The novel's only positive quality, Daix said, was the extent to which reality intruded despite the mythical setting. Jean Laffitte's simple thriller, based upon a mythical exploit of the Resistance, *Nous retournerons cueillir les jonquilles,* won Daix's praise for containing within it "all the universally important themes of our times." Courtade amused while Laffitte aroused suspense in his audience. It was typically the dry, didactic work of André Stil, *Le Premier Choc,* which did neither, that won the Stalin prize in 1951 and was lauded as one of the century's great novels.[39]

The socialist-realist craze extended to music and art. Music, PCF theorists said, achieved real meaning only when it corresponded to the needs of a social group and exalted the common daily effort of a developing society. Melody, song, and group choral singing were abandoned by decadent bourgeois composers in search of commercialization.[40] The Socialist workers wanted harmonic music, rhymed poetry, and art that depicted the real world. Picasso considered himself a Communist, but André Fougeron was the party's favored painter. Fougeron's *Pays des Mines* was a series of canvases depicting life in the coal-mining regions of the North, the artist's counterpart of Stil's *Le Premier Choc.* The featured canvas in the group, entitled "National Defense," depicted vicious-looking security police with clubs and ferocious dogs assaulting defenseless workers and their women and children at the gates of a mine. The workers were bold, handsome, and draped in Roman garb.[41]

While socialist-realist art reflected a self-taught elite of working-class origins insecure in a world of often incomprehensible bourgeois culture, it also appealed to artists in search of a mass audience. Socialist realism promised to bring together elite and popular culture, simplify high culture to render it comprehensible to the masses, and rescue them from their daily diet of comic books and American gangster movies. If it humbled the intellectual, socialist realism was also intended to raise up the workers. It was the cement that bound the artist to the counter-society. Party-sponsored publications were assured of a captive audience, distribution, and sales. The party promoted its authors and called upon *esprit de parti* in an effort to sell their works. The PCF's cultural output was part of the incessant struggle on all fronts against the hegemony of the bourgeoisie. It was also a vehicle for aspiring novelists of mediocre talent but extravagant pretensions.

Diamat and socialist realism were most likely ignored by the Communist masses. Greene found that Communist voters expressed a "radically humanist" outlook; they were the least racist and anti-Semitic, the most feminist, and in a clear divergence from their leadership, the most opposed to capital punishment of all Frenchmen. These views had little to do with ideology. Pierre Fougeyrollas found that of 150 issues on which they were questioned between 1951 and 1961, Communist voters differed radically on 104 from the majority of Frenchmen. But on basic questions, they shared the same ends: better salaries, lower taxes, peace, and neutrality.[42]

The influence of the Communist party in French society extended beyond its membership and electorate. The PCF insisted that it was not a party "like the others," but it expended a great deal of energy showing how much like the others it was. The party's budget, open for all to see, was presumably based on dues and subscriptions in addition to the salaries of elected officials, which were turned over to the party. Communist Deputies received workmen's wages in return. Jean Elleinstein counted 850 permanent party employees in 1976; Brayance, in 1951, estimated their number at 2000. But these modest numbers ignore the many employees of Communist mass organizations like the CGT or the Peace Movement and the party's commercial and industrial enterprises. In the period of the Fourth Republic the party's auxiliary mass organizations most worried hostile observers. Since then the party's economic holdings have elicited increased scrutiny. The mass organizations were too numerous to list, and their history largely remains to be written.[43] The CGT and Peace Movement were most important; nominally independent, they were tightly controlled by the party. CGT leaders Benoît Frachon and Gaston Monmousseau sat on the Political Bureau although they were not formally members. The Peace Movement's nominally independent activities required the approval of Political Bureau members delegated to run it. Beyond these giant auxiliaries the party maintained, staffed, and controlled organizations for women and youth, sporting clubs and children's organizations, friendship organizations with the USSR and all other Socialist countries, organizations of war veterans, former prisoners, deportees, FTP members, and war widows, associations of intellectuals, the retired, and an emergency assistance group for victims of political persecution. Associations of renters, farmers, small businessmen, artisans, and victims of war damages gave the PCF pressure group leverage in all walks of life.

Jules Moch's public revelations of the Banque Commerciale pour l'Europe du Nord's operation in December 1948 focused attention on the PCF's economic activities, which after the Fourth Republic blossomed into a "capitalist empire of the classic type."[44] In addition to extensive activities in newspaper, magazine, and book publishing, the party ran contracting services to municipalities it controlled and import-export, agricultural, and tourist companies dealing with the Soviet Union and the East-European nations. The party's economic links to the USSR expanded paradoxically as its autonomy became an increasingly critical matter of policy. For the most part the PCF's financial holdings remained disguised. All party enterprises had normal public owners, partners, or stockholders and scrupulously obeyed government regulations. Gentlemen's agreements stipulated that owners who were party militants turn their salaries and dividends over to the party in return for agreed upon wages, but these understandings were maintained outside the formal structure of the enterprises themselves.

An example of how PCF economic enterprise contributed a veiled subsidy to the party's operations was provided by Roger Codou. Codou, while a PCF militant, worked as nominal head of a company dealing in exports to the Polish People's Republic, mostly spare parts for Poland's fleet of Renault trucks.[45] Codou discovered the Polish regime was paying for new engines but receiving rebuilt ones from irregular dealers. The price differential was raked off by the party as a veiled subsidy of its operations. When, in his naiveté, Codou brought this situation to the attention of his superiors, he was rudely reprimanded for mixing in what was not his affair. When Codou was finally summoned to Warsaw to appear before a committee of inquiry set up by the post–1956 Polish regime, the PCF sought to make him bear the blame.

The PCF's commercial enterprises accounted for the alleged power of mysterious figures such as Jean Jerôme, originally Michael Feintuch, a Polish-Jewish Comintern official whose involvement with party finances began with France-Navigation, a merchant-marine company that specialized in running Soviet weapons to the Spanish Republicans. Jerôme, a nationalized Frenchman after the war, was a ubiquitous presence in the highest party councils during the Fourth Republic and after although officially neither on the Political Bureau nor the Central Committee. Jerôme intervened in ideological matters and allegedly was a conduit for Moscow messages and funds. When Antoine Spire applied for a job as a cadre in response to an ad in *L'Humanité*, he was interviewed by Jerôme, who assigned Spire to one of the divisions of Interagra, the huge commercial combine controlled by another curious figure, the "Red Millionaire," Jean-Baptiste Doumeng.[46] Georges Gosnat, who as treasurer of the party supervised its financial operations, also exercised a disproportionate measure of power. Gosnat directed the thousands of employees of the PCF's enterprises, all of whom were sincere and devoted Communists, owed the party their livelihood, and provided the nucleus of ready volunteers for signature collections or demonstrations. All told, estimates of the party apparatus range as high as 14,000.

The autocratic strictures of democratic centralism, frequently criticized by PCF dissidents, were accepted by the docile and obedient apparatus. At the highest levels the PCF leadership was entirely coopted. In the Thorezian era, 75 percent of Central Committee members were reportedly personally chosen by Thorez, 20 percent by Duclos, and 5 percent by Benoît Frachon.[47] The Central Committee normally met to register prior decisions taken in its name by the leadership. None of the memoirs extant recorded much open expression of opinion at meetings of the Political Bureau. Key decisions were taken by the Secretariat, which until 1952 consisted of Thorez, Duclos, Marty, and Lecoeur. Discussion within the secretariat and Political Bureau remained hidden. When the Russians wanted a specific policy or action, it was communicated through Thorez to the Secretariat. At the key words "Les camarades nous disent . . ." ("The comrades tell us . . .") all further discussion was immediately foreclosed. Thorez reigned more as quasi-constitutional monarch than as dictator, however. The position of Duclos, ever in his shadow, was impregnable, and the historic members of the Political Bureau, Marcel Cachin, Etienne Fajon, François Billoux, Raymond Guyot, André Marty, and Charles Tillon could not be removed without major crisis.

Pierre Daix stressed the link between PCF organization and Communist ideology; the leadership commanded obedience by monopolizing information and claiming to hold scientific insight and truth.[48] Stalinism was its mechanism of bureaucratic control, which proved uniquely adaptable to French mental structures and historical tradition, but was also extremely resistant to change. Shaken to its foundations during the crisis opened by Thorez's absence from 1950 to 1953, the system recovered and moved toward integration with the society and politics of the Fourth Republic. With the end of the Vietnam war, the party's liberal posture on colonial policy briefly became the policy of the regime, and the PCF supported the government. Parts of the French political class appeared prepared to live with the PCF's Stalinist practices as the price of the party's support. The PCF's instinctive rejection of destalinization in the USSR coincided with its moment of maximum integration with and acceptance of the parliamentary mechanism of the Fourth Republic. Stalinism for the PCF was fully compatible with Social-democratism in practice, and parliamentary integration of the PCF might have continued to the crisis of the regime in 1958. But the road to integration was long and arduous. Before embarking on it, the PCF had to resolve its internal crisis. The first steps in the process were taken amid the unprecedented and confusing events of 1951 and 1952.

NOTES

1. Maurice Duverger's *Political Parties* (New York, 1954) is still a fine introduction for the English reader. Philippe Robrieux, *Histoire intérieure du PCF*, 3 vols. (Paris, 1980–1982) has the most extensive discussion of organization.

2. Parti Communiste Français, *Congrès de Strasbourg, Rapports* (1947) contains the most extensive statistics the PCF ever published and provides the basis for the computations in this chapter.

3. Gabriel A. Almond, *The Appeals of Communism* (Princeton, N.J., 1954), especially 353–69; Mario Einaudi, *Communism in Western Europe* (Ithaca, N.Y., 1951), 62; Jules Monnerot, *Sociologie du Communisme* (Paris, 1963), 175; Ronald Tiersky, *French Communism, 1920–72* (New York, 1974).

4. See her classic, *Les Communistes français* (Paris, 1968), English edition (Chicago, 1972).

5. Jean Rony, *Trente ans de parti: un communiste s'interroge* (Paris, 1978), 53–54; Pierre Daix, *J'ai cru au matin* (Paris, 1976), 316. Also *Aragon, une vie à changer* (Paris, 1975), 375; Pierre Durand, personal interview, April 6, 1978; Domenique Desanti, *Les Staliniens* (Paris, 1975), 129.

6. *Communismes au miroir français* (Paris, 1974), 179–96; see also her *Les Juifs et le monde moderne* (Paris, 1977); See André Harris and Alain de Sédouy, *Voyage à l'intérieure du PC* (Paris, 1974), 270–72, for the Elleinstein remark; Edgar Morin, *Autocritique* (Paris, 1970), 108; Pierre Abraham, "Mon père, Juif," *Europe* (September 1953). Cited by Pierre Aubéry in his very fine *Milieux juifs de la France contemporaine* (Paris, 1957), which also contains Wurmser's remark, 192.

7. See Henri Fiszbin, *Les Boûches s'ouvrent* (Paris, 1980), 17.

8. Desanti, *Les Staliniens,* 229; Jean Recanati, *Un gentil stalinien* (Paris, 1980), 81; Roger Pannequin, *Andieu Camarades: Les Annés sans suite* (Paris, 1977), II, 73; Harris and Sédouy, 76; Françoise d'Eaubonne, "Reflexions d'une communiste," *Les Temps Modernes,* 153–154 (November–December 1958), 949–54.

9. Philippe Robrieux, *Notre génération communiste* (Paris, 1977), 30; Raoul Calas, *Souvenirs d'un condamné à mort* (Paris, 1976), 144; André Stil, *Le Premier choc* (Paris, 1954); Kriegel, *Les Communistes français,* 52.

10. Personal interview, April 11, 1978.

11. André Marty, *L'Affaire Marty* (Paris, 1955), 49; Noirot, *La Memoire ouverte,* 108; Robrieux, *Notre génération communiste,* 45; Emmanuel LeRoy Ladurie, *Paris-Montpellier, PC-PSU, 1945–1963* (Paris, 1982), 76–77.

12. Stil, *Le Premier choc*; Desanti, *Les Staliniens,* 208, 215.

13. Kriegel, *Les Communistes français,* 94–95; Tiersky, *French Communism,* 266.

14. See Kriegel's critique of the functionalist approach in T. J. Nossiter, ed., *Imaginatinon and Precision in the Social Sciences* (London, 1972), 351–85. Lavau's views now appear in English "The PCF, the State, and the Revolution," in D. Blackmer and S. Tarrow, eds., *Communism in Italy and France* (Princeton, N.J., 1976). He has backtracked a bit in *A Quoi sert le Parti Communiste française?* (Paris, 1982).

15. Georgio Galli, *Il Bipartitismo imperfetto* (Bologna, 1966).

16. See Leroy Ladurie's review of E. Todd, *Le Fou et le Proletaire* in *Le Monde,* February 20, 1979.

17. Pierre Gaborit "Contribution à la théorie général des partis politiques: L'example du PCF pendant la cinquième République." (Thèse pour le doctorat d'état en science politique, Université de Paris, 1976), 56, 136, and the Appendix.

18. Bertrand Badie, *Stratégie de la Grève: Pour une approche fonctionnaliste du PCF* (Paris, 1976), 1–2 and passim. George Ross, *Workers and Communists in France* (Berkeley, Calif., 1981).

19. See "Entretien avec Bertrand Badie," *Cahiers d'histoire de l'Institut Maurice Thorez*, 23 (1977), 163–74.

20. Dominique Labbé, *Le Discours Communiste* (Paris, 1977), 185 and passim.

21. William Ascher and Sidney Tarrow, "The Stability of Communist Electorates: Evidence from a Longitudinal Analysis of French and Italian Aggregate Data," *American Journal of Political Science*, XIV, 3 (August 1975), 475–501.

22. Jean Elleinstein, *Le PC* (Paris, 1976), 96–97. Kriegel's discussion of membership is in *Les Communistes français*, 29–38.

23. Robrieux, *Histoire intérieure*, II, 374.

24. Auguste Lecoeur, personal interview, July 12, 1978.

25. See *Cahiers du Communisme*, 6–7 (June-July 1954), M. Servin, "Rapport sur les questions d'organisation," 729–58.

26. Einaudy, *Communism in Western Europe*, 84–115; Alain Brayance, *Anatomie due PCF* (Paris, 1952), 206; Gabriel Enkiri, *Militant de Base* (Paris, 1971), 37.

27. Jean Baby, *Critique de Base* (Paris, 1960), 154–55. *L'Humanité*, May 17, 1954.

28. See the analysis in *Bulletin de l'Association d'Etudes et d'Informations Politiques Internationales* (BEIPI, *Later Est et Ouest*), 115 (Sept. 16–30, 1954). Also Robrieux, *Histoire intérieure*, II, 374.

29. Pierre Gaborit, "Le PCF et les élections à la constituante de 1945 en France metropolitaine," (Memoire pour le diplome d'études supérieurs de sciences politiques), 3, and *passim*.

30. François Goguel, *Géographie des élections françaises sous la troisième et la quatrième République* (Paris, 1970), 101–85.

31. I have used the Census of 1946 and the PCF Party Congress of Strasbourg, 1947, and the election returns of 1962 and Census of that year to assemble these data.

32. Goguel, *Géographie des Elections*, uses percentage of those eligible to vote rather than those actually voting (*suffrages exprimés*), which accounts for the lower figures.

33. Duncan Macrae, Jr., *Parliament, Parties, and Society in France, 1946–58* (New York, 1967), 251–58; Joseph Klatzmann, "Comportement électorale et classe sociale," in M. Duverger and J. Touchard, eds., *Les élections du 2 Janvier 1956* (Paris, 1957), 265; Mattei Dogan, "Covariance Analysis of French Electoral Data," in M. Dogan and S. Rokkan, eds., *Quantitative Ecological Analysis in the Social Sciences* (Cambridge, Mass., 1969), 285–98.

34. The state of the art may be examined in two key works: Guy Michelat and Michel Simon, *Classe, religion et comportement politique* (Paris, 1977), and Jacques Capdevielle et al., *France de gauche vote à droite* (Paris, 1981).

35. Pierre Fougeyrollas, *La Conscience politique dans la France contemporaine* (Paris, 1963).

36. Jean Ranger, "L'évolution du vote communiste en France depuis 1945," in *Le Communisme en France* (Paris, 1969), 208–35; Jean Stoetzel and P. Hassner, "Résultats d'un sondage dans le premier secteur de la Seine," in Duverger and Touchard, *Les élections du 2 Janvier, 1956*, 211. Of the respondants 87 percent put party first, only 5 percent personality.

37. Thomas H. Green, "The Electorates of Nonruling Communist Parties," *Studies in Comparative Communism* IV, 3–4 (July–October 1971), 68–103; Richard Hamilton, *Affluence and the Worker in the Fourth French Republic* (Princeton, N.J., 1967), 158–64.

38. *La Nouvelle critique,* No. 4 (March 1949), contains "Autocritique" by Henri Lefebvre; No. 5 (April 1949) has Garaudy's recantation.

39. Pierre Courtade, *Elseneur* (Paris, 1949), reviewed by Pierre Daix in *La Nouvelle critique,* No. 3 (April 1949), 66–75; Jean Laffitte, *Nous retournerons cueillir les jonquilles* (Paris, 1948), reviewed in *La Nouvelle critique,* No. 1 (December 1948), 90–95.

40. Ibid., No. 4 (March 1949).

41. See *Auguste Lecoeur et André Stil présentent Le Pays des Mines d'André Fougeron* (Paris, 1951).

42. See note 37 above. Confirmed by Capedevielle, *France de gauche vote à droite*.

43. For a list see Brayance, 130–70, and Jean Montaldo, *La France Communiste* (Paris, 1978).

44. See the recent work by Jean Montaldo, *Les Finances du PCF* (Paris, 1977).

45. Roger Codou, personal interview, July 18, 1978.

46. Antoine Spire, *Profession permanente* (Paris, 1980), 57.

47. Jean Pronteau, in the Robrieux archive.

48. Pierre Daix, *La Crise de PCF* (Paris, 1978).

7
COLD WAR DELIRIUM, 1952

Thorez's absence from December 1950 to March 1953 opened the most confused and tormented period in party history, a collective hysteria induced by the Cold War. Hostilities continued in Vietnam and Korea with the clear danger of direct East-West confrontation. The PCF's anti-war effort appeared as futile as the Peace Movement's propaganda against alleged American germ warfare in Korea. American McCarthyism, coupled with Cold War election rhetoric and open discussion of preventive war against the USSR, frightened readers of the French press. The June 1951 elections brought a right-wing shift in French politics. In a French version of McCarthyism, successive governments bothered the PCF with searches, seizures, law suits, and arrests. Under the government of Antoine Pinay (March-December 1953) anti-Communism reached a high point. Pinay was one of the most popular politicians of the Fourth Republic; his politics of austerity received credit for stopping inflation and initiating the economic upturn of 1952. His anti-Communism convinced the Communists that a "fascisation" of the regime would culminate in their suppression.

The new conservatism had contradictory effects on the PCF; it strengthened the hand of sectarians while it opened new perspectives for an alliance strategy, leading the party toward moderation in the hope of a renewed Popular Front. Conflict erupted in the PCF's Political Bureau; rival strategies were confused with personal ambitions in the context of an expected succession, and PCF policy underwent a number of sharp and confusing shifts or *tournants,* as two different factions gained momentary political advantage. Compounding the confusion were Thorez's effort to influence policies from exile and Duclos' purge of two historic leaders, Marty and Tillon. Thorez relied on Jeannette Vermeersch, François Billoux, and Raymond Guyot, for whom Stalinism was a total world view as well as a mechanism of bureaucratic control. Stalinism for the Thorez group was not necessarily what the Russians, even Stalin, said it was at any given moment. In 1952 Stalin remained silent while intrigue dominated the Soviet Politburo. Duclos and his lieutenants, Auguste Lecoeur and Etienne Fajon, tried to keep PCF strategy anchored to an inconsistent Soviet foreign policy.

Four separate phases of PCF policy can be discerned during the period of Thorez's absence. From Thorez's departure until February 1952, Duclos kept the PCF on a moderate course of Front national including overtures to the

Socialists. Auguste Lecoeur initiated reforms in PCF organization designed to bolster membership by encouraging inactive militants to retain a nominal affiliation with the party. A second, sectarian period began in February 1952 under the impulse of Thorez: enunciated in a May 1952 article in *Cahiers du Communisme* by François Billoux, it culminated in the demonstration against the Paris arrival of American General Matthew Ridgeway on May 28. Duclos chose the moment of the Ridgeway demonstration to initiate the removal of Charles Tillon and André Marty from the Political Bureau, clearing the way for his control of the party following the demonstration's anticipated failure. On the evening of the manifestation Duclos was arrested; Lecoeur and Fajon repudiated the radical line, opening a third period during which the moderate policies of 1951 were resumed. But Duclos' opportunism was barren of results and abhorrent to Thorez. In September 1952 the moderate line was rejected and a fourth and final phase proclaimed partially reaffirming the sectarian line of May. Thorez's return, the weakening of Duclos, and elimination of Lecoeur followed with Stalin's death. The resolution of conflict was barely accomplished in 1954 when the PCF was buffeted by the new challenge of de-Stalinization in the USSR.

The Peace Movement's successor to the Stockholm ban-the-bomb appeal was a national "consultation" on the subject of German rearmament. Opposition to a reconstructed Wehrmacht was widespread in France; the PCF and CGT threw themselves into the campaign with enthusiasm, and signatures mounted faster than ever before: 2 million by February 1951.[1] The Political Bureau subordinated everything to the quest for signatures, including working-class economic demands. Following a demonstration against General Eisenhower on January 24, Fajon demanded the campaign be carried to all the foyers of France while the Central Committee declared no task more urgent than opposing a revengeful Germany, the linchpin of American plans for aggression. The campaign was popular and may have helped reverse briefly the PCF's membership decline; on February 21 Lecoeur announced new members were joining at the rate of 1000 per week.[2]

Within days, however, the World Peace Council announced a new campaign in favor of a Five-Power Pact between the USA, the USSR, China, Britain, and France. The PCF, surprised by the sudden reversal of emphasis, shifted gears abruptly, but with difficulty. The struggle against the "new Wehrmacht" disappeared from party propaganda, and the signatures collected on its behalf were dumped. Stalin had decided to rebuild the Wehrmacht in East Germany.[3] Other complications quickly ensued. France was in a pre-electoral period, and the campaign for "popular assemblies" to "ratify" the Five-Power pact threatened to interfere with the election effort. Could Communists use these assemblies for electoral purposes? Absolutely not, *L'Humanité* warned: the assemblies were for non-partisan peace aims. The party's electoral message must be gotten across separately.[4] Opposing German rearmament was a popular issue aimed at Paris and easily attuned to the rhetoric of French nationalism. A vague Five-Power

Pact, the foci of which were Washington and Moscow, was an intangible abstraction by comparison.

PCF militants protested the change, despite clumsy attempts in the Communist press to link the German rearmament drive to the Five-Power Pact. Charles Tillon spearheaded the opposition, arguing for an independent Peace Movement separately organized and insulated from the party's control. To enlist support Tillon approached André Marty with whom he had good relations in the past. Their meeting led to charges of factionalism a year later. Tillon's plans were denounced by Laurent Casanova and the disagreement brought to the Political Bureau; it decided against Tillon, who became the PCF's last major obstacle to the new Soviet policy on German rearmament, his removal only a question of timing.[5] The Soviets tried to strengthen the loyal French peace partisans: Frederic Joliot-Curie and Eugénie Cotton were awarded the Stalin Peace Prize. *L'Humanité* called the awards a glory for France.[6] They were rather a pointed reminder of where Soviet priorities lay. The subordination of the PCF to Moscow's policy was further underlined by a simultaneous Soviet critique of nationalist deviation in PCF ideology.

In February 1951 *Cahiers du Communism* reprinted an article from the Cominform organ, *For a Lasting Peace,* attacking the French Communist review's ideological failures. The Cominform found *Cahiers du Communism* lacking in its coverage of the People's Democracies, the anti-Tito campaign, the struggle against Social Democracy, and most critically, Marxist theory. The publication of works by noted French Communist scholars Henri Lefebvre and Georges Politzer was criticized as theoretically inadequate. *Cahiers du Communism*'s editor, Victor Michaut, responded by admitting to "a certain ideological lack of preparation, a lack of theoretical depth in the treatment of burning issues," and promised ameliorative measures.[7] In September an article reprinted from *Voprossi Istorrii* criticized the PCF's nationalist orientation. The article noted *Cahiers du Communism*'s importance as the vehicle for Duclos' critique of the American deviation, Browderism, in 1945. All the more serious its insensitivity to "deviations" from Marxist-Leninist theory. Albert Soboul's work on the history of the French revolution was written "in the spirit of idealism." Roger Garaudy's *Sources françaises du socialisme scientifique* exaggerated the importance of the French utopian socialists and underestimated that of Marx and Engels. Garaudy was known to be a protégé of Thorez and had published a self-critique in 1949 when an amended version of his book was brought out placing emphasis on the failings of the French utopians as compared to the scientific breakthrough of Marx and Engels.[8] The criticisms were irrelevant to Garaudy, therefore, but made sense only in terms of a general Soviet critique of PCF "nationalism" and an indirect slap at Thorez.

Duclos tried to dispell any suspicion of PCF nationalism in the 1951 election campaign: "the struggle for the defense of peace constitutes, in all circumstances, in our epoch, the central and decisive task, to which Communists subordinate the ensemble of their activity." The PCF, Duclos went on, was ready to participate in or support any government committed to signing a Five-Power Pact, ending all special treaties with the USA, reaching peace with a united Germany, ending the Vietnam war, banning nuclear weapons and war propaganda, achieving arms reduction, and protecting democratic liberties.[9] There was little mention of traditional working-class concerns in Duclos' formulation, and the call for a peace treaty with a united rearmed Germany angered French nationalists, including those in the PCF. Hostile observers noted even a reactionary government committed to the PCF's foreign policy aims could count on Communist support.[10] Duclos unashamedly advocated fiscal conservatism: the PCF wanted fiscal reform without new taxes, the protection of private property ("the fruit of labor and savings"), democracy, and lay education. The issue in the elections was not collectivization, wrote Pierre Courtade, but rather preventing a nuclear holocaust which would leave nothing in France to socialize except ruins and corpses.[11] The party protested the complex system of voting adopted by the Third-Force parties in the June 1951 elections to reduce the number of Communist and Gaullist seats in the Assembly. But even with this "electoral swindle" the PCF remained "resolutely attached to democratic liberties, the usage of which facilitates the struggle of the proletariat for the abolition of classes."[12]

The party's emphasis on international affairs during the 1951 elections left working-class demands ignored. The CGT was caught napping by a mini-strike wave in March 1951, which spread rapidly from Parisian transport to the Renault factory and the national railroads. Awkwardly noting the spontaneity of the movement, the Communist union "recommended the formulation of demands in every enterprise," thus admitting it had none of its own. The Political Bureau declaration of March 22 ignored both strikes and elections, underlining instead the "enormous importance" of the Five-Power Pact and the "key role" of France in the international Peace Movement.[13] Front national was triumphant; Thorez's hoped-for Popular Front lay dormant.

The French Communist electorate demonstrated its fidelity in June, delivering 5,000,000 votes to the party, 26.6 percent of the total. Because of the new electoral system, however, the votes translated into only 102 Communist seats as opposed to 151 in the outgoing legislature. The Political Bureau made its ritual condemnation of "the electoral swindle which has given birth to a ferociously reactionary majority," but repeated the party's readiness to support any government willing to commit itself to a Five-Power Pact.[14] Despite the conservative turn of French politics, the PCF continued its opportunistic pursuit of Soviet foreign policy aims. Passage in September 1951 of the *Loi Barangé,* which extended government aid to Catholic schools, caused no shift in PCF policy. The October cantonal elections became a plebiscite only on peace, and Duclos offered PCF support on the second ballot to any candidate willing to make a declaration in favor of the party's peace program. The offer was accepted, according to *L'Humanité,* by eighteen Radicals and Socialists.[15] The party slipped to a total of 78 seats on cantonal councils nationally as compared to the 351 places it held in 1947 and 204 in 1949. But despite clear election manipulation the Communist electorate held firm, and returns showed a portion of the left Socialist vote willing to support Communists rather than allow "reactionaries" a victory.[16]

The PCF carried its policy of détente from the political to the social arena. The CGT ceased attacks on leaders of rival unions and offered to negotiate a common program. On September 1, agreement was reached with Force Ouvrière, the CFTC (Christian unions), and the Confédération Générale des Cadres co-ordinating efforts to achieve a 23,600-franc minimum wage. On September 11, the CGT invited the independent FEN (National Teachers' Federation) to join the discussions.[17] These were not Popular Front tactics, however; the party had no intention of limiting itself to organizations of the left. On September 13 Fajon called for common action "larger than ever," including not only the middle classes, but also French business interests who were "facing ruin by the American grasp [*mainmise*] on the French economy." Fajon's target was the Schuman plan for the European Coal and Steel Community;[18] an open letter signed jointly by René Damien, head of the Nord Steel trust Usinor, and Usinor's Communist Committee of Enterprise warned the Schuman plan would establish German industrial domination and lead to French servitude and decadence. Duclos' reply, called by Fajon a "document of the highest importance," noted that individual members of management had distinguished themselves in the Resistance: "and when for reasons of their own representatives of management declare their opposition to this plan [the Schuman] we are not at all embarrassed, on the contrary."[19]

If the PCF could come to terms with the trusts, it could do no less with the Socialists. Individual Socialists had agreed to joint action with the Communists on the basis of the PCF's program for the cantonal elections. Middle-level Socialist party officials were showing increased hostility to the government's policy and greater readiness to cooperate with the PCF on specific issues. As the European Coal and Steel Community and the plan for a European army became issues of overriding importance, the PCF sought the cooperation of influential Socialist politicians like Jules Moch and Daniel Mayer who opposed these schemes. Moch's role in the 1947–48 strikes was conveniently forgotten. On January 2, 1952, Etienne Fajon signaled a change in PCF attitudes toward the Socialists, warmly welcoming a local agreement in the Gironde between a Socialist section and a Communist cell.[20]

The PCF's earlier sectarian line had been costly in terms of party membership: the decline was continuous since 1947. August Lecoeur, organizational secretary since 1950, came under increasing pressure to reverse the trend. The circulation of the Communist press was also poor. *L'Humanité* reported average sales of less than 200,000 daily issues in 1951, and a special effort toward the end of the year netted the newspaper a gain of only 15,000 additional subscriptions.[21] Despite exhortations a majority of cells and sections did nothing to increase their press circulation; lethargy was evident and alarming; numbers of Communists were staying away from meetings and dropping their membership. Lecoeur responded with an open letter to local Communist officials suggesting ways of increasing membership totals.[22] Blaming "sectarian tendencies" for the decline, Lecoeur instructed party officials to seek out members who missed meetings and inquire about absences. If cards were not renewed, visits must be made to homes. All cells were told to appoint "political instructors" to discuss issues with inactive Communists, convince them to turn out for meetings, and keep them enrolled in the event they failed to do so. If attending cell meetings was one part of party activity, Lecoeur said, individual effort was another, and failure to take it into account was causing the unnecessary membership declines.

Lecoeur's initiative was accompanied by a campaign to promote his personality. Numerous articles were devoted to the new system; all quoted Lecoeur, many printing his name in block letters for increased emphasis. The innovation became a pretext for Lecoeur's downfall but it was not original and was in use in the Czech and Polish parties.[23] It was, moreover, only an institutionalization of an existing PCF trend. There was nothing very Leninist, Lecoeur never tired of pointing out later, about Thorez's original slogan of a party that was to be counted in the millions. Yet Lecoeur's initiative was part of a total package of policies easily labeled "opportunist," which Thorez surveyed with increasing frustration from the USSR where his enforced convalescence resembled imprisonment.

By late 1951 Thorez was isolated from party affairs and making little progress toward recovery. His stroke impaired the use of his right arm and leg, but his mind was unaffected.[24] Communications with Paris were difficult and visits infrequent. The Soviet embassy pressured Jeannette Vermeersch to visit her husband more often, but she experienced the isolation of his "cure" with distaste.[25] To maintain his position during his absence, Thorez sought to give a new spurt of enthusiasm to the cult of his personality. His close associates François Billoux, now in charge of ideology, and Georges Cogniot, an influential party intellectual, directed the enterprise. In October 1951 a year of "individual study" of Thorez's writings was announced to raise the educational level of party militants. Monthly outlines of suggested reading in Thorez's *Oeuvres* and *Fils du Peuple* appeared in *Cahiers du Communisme,* replete with study questions and reading guides. Cells were encouraged to appoint counselors to assist less sophisticated comrades with their course of study. The vulgar aspects of the cult were not neglected either, as was apparent in the following song:[26]

Millions of happy voices
Chant this joyous refrain:
Good health, Good health, Maurice!
Good health and happy birthday!
Comes the day of your return, Maurice!
To spread joy in the hearts of proletarians;
To the four corners of your homeland of France
The skies are cleared and the winds have sung
To the son of the people, to the son of hope

Good health, Good health, Good health.
Return . . . with you for our guide,
We go forward to save the peace
Thirty years, your patriotism
And your superhuman struggle
Toward the march to Socialism
Have shown us the way.

Poems and paintings celebrated the leader's impending return, and the PCF pridefully referred to itself as "the party of Maurice Thorez."

The study of Thorez's *Oeuvres* caused problems for Duclos. Thorez's articles of 1931–32 could be read as implicit criticism of current line, motivating Duclos to warn in *France Nouvelle* against a too "sectarian" reading of Thorez. *France Nouvelle,* edited by Florimond Bonte, supported Duclos against the radical line enunciated by Thorez and François Billoux. Militants must avoid the impression of dogmatism conveyed by out-of-context quotes, wrote Duclos. The "class-against-class" doctrine did not imply opposition to political alliances to protect French independence. At present elements of the French bourgeoisie understood the danger of American domination, and the PCF was correct to ally with them as it had done in the Popular Front.[27] Duclos was obscuring the issue; for Thorez class-against-class rhetoric led to the Popular Front through mass mobilization, applying pressure against Socialist leaders from their own ranks. Thorez now tried once again to impose this policy on the PCF and prepare the way for his return. The aim of a Popular Front paradoxically underlay the sectarian turn of May 1952.

The PCF's new militancy was evident in February when the Political Bureau rejected prohibition of a demonstration to commemorate the Popular Front manifestation of February 12, 1934. Lecoeur, despite his ties to Duclos, was the immediate instrument of Thorez's new policy, returning from Moscow to announce Thorez was "in full form" with the lucidity of judgment and authority of always, ready to resume leadership of the party.[28] The Political Bureau initiated a campaign of work stoppages and petitions to protest prohibition of the demonstration, and threatened a general strike. Thorez's aim was to make 1952 a replay of 1934; the Popular Front was to emerge from a mass movement, Front unique become Front populaire. The February 12 strike was billed as a demonstration of republican defense and anti-fascism. It was not successful but was meant only as a beginning. Lecoeur told the Central Committee on February 14 that the struggle for peace was the struggle for Socialism; the "treason" of the French bourgeoisie was a permanent feature of French politics. This was the new theme: Duclos' appeal to the nationalism of French industrialists was ended. André Marty called for renewed support for colonial peoples; the party now supported their self determination "up to and including separation from France."[29] Duclos announced a resumption of the campaign against the manufacture and transport of war materials for Vietnam.

The new line was justified on a number of grounds. Duclos' national front was a demonstrable failure. Membership continued to lag, and French politics veered sharply to the right. The Pinay government of March 1952 included the Gaullists and excluded the Socialists. As Pinay began to persecute the Communists, the Socialists moved to the opposition. The themes of anti-fascism and republican defense reflected the PCF's fear of suppression. The USSR exploded its atomic bomb in 1949; with Soviet security assured, it no longer appeared necessary to sacrifice internal interests to Soviet foreign-policy goals.[30] The PCF's violent response to the arrival of General Ridgeway in Paris on May 28, 1952, is usually ascribed to hysteria over a presumed new danger of war. But the sectarian line was adopted by the PCF when the Soviet Union began showing a conciliatory bent in international affairs. On March 10, 1952, days before Billoux's arrival in Moscow to plan with Thorez the PCF's new line, Stalin proposed a unified neutral Germany. While Billoux was with Thorez in the Crimea, Communist press outlets publicized Stalin's April 2 statement to an American journalist: coexistence was possible, and the danger of war was not greater than two or three years earlier.[31]

Thorez's new sectarianism thus ran counter to Soviet foreign policy, and it was resisted by Duclos, Fajon, and Lecoeur, although they occasionally were forced to follow along publicly. Stalin's March 10 declaration on Germany caused upheaval in the Peace Movement; Duclos suppressed its popular newspaper, *Action,* for continuing its opposition to German rearmament. Cloudy circumstances surrounded *Action*'s demise. Pierre Hervé, a well-known journalist and Resistance leader, had just won André Marty's praise for his contribution to peace.[32] Yves Farge, fellow-traveller and Resistance hero who also wrote for *Action,* had close ties to Charles Tillon. Farge's anti-Germanism reportedly overcame his pro-Soviet sentiments, and *Action* was suppressed just as Duclos was beginning the Marty-Tillon affair. Farge went to Moscow intending to protest Duclos' moves against the Peace Movement; he also carried a letter from André Marty protesting the East European purge trials.[33] Farge died in an automobile accident in the USSR in January 1953; Pierre Hervé attributed his death to the KGB.

François Billoux returned from Russia in April 1952 carrying a set of notes of his conversations with Thorez. Billoux's notes became the basis for the PCF's harder line and the May 1952 *Cahiers du Communisme* article. The Political Bureau discussed Billoux's visit with Thorez on April 11 and 17 and again on May 16, 1952. As a result of Duclos' arrest on May 28 notes of these discussions fell into the hands of the French police. Their content became the basis of a government attempt to lift the PCF's parliamentary immunity and prosecute its leaders for sedition. Whatever their judicial uses, Duclos' notes afforded a rare glimpse of the internal divisions in the Political Bureau.

Billoux stated the new interpretation of events developed with Thorez. The French bourgeoisie *en bloc* was the enemy, and the Peace Movement was a legitimate weapon only to the extent that it led directly to Socialism. Duclos' policy of alliance with the nationalist bourgeoisie was condemned: "our self-criticism remains to be done."[34] A total reorientation of French politics was to be achieved by direct working-class action against the Vietnam war. Billoux invited government prosecution, declaring that "We are working for the defeat of this [the French] army in Vietnam, Korea, and Tunisia." He criticized the party's primary emphasis on the Peace Movement which was a vehicle of compromise; the transition to Socialism depended upon direct party action.

Duclos and Fajon challenged Billoux's analysis. Fajon ritually praised Thorez's "deep political reflection" but warned against "giving the impression of '*un tournant*' " in PCF policy. The PCF must continue to emphasize the Peace Movement, or the party would fall into total isolation and impotence. Duclos rejected Billoux's analysis of the transition to Socialism: the PCF must not "make of the acceptance of Socialism, the condition of union [by others with the PCF] in the defense of peace and the reconquest of national independence." The PCF's internal conflict between the strategies of Front national and Front populaire emerge clearly in Duclos' notebook.

The victory of the Billoux-Thorez line was announced by Jeannette Vermeersch in *France Nouvelle*. Vermeersch questioned whether the unions or the Peace Movement had contributed to peace; direct working-class action was necessary, and it was sadly insufficient. The Popular Front showed that success depended upon subordinating everything, including labor's demands, to "the decisive question of the moment," in the 1930's, anti-fascism, today, peace.[35] As Thorez and the Barbé-Celor group said in the 1930's, the struggle for beefsteak was passé. Thorez, in the Crimea, now vicariously sought to relive the enthusiasm of the class-against-class years. Vermeersch also criticized Lecoeur for his leadership of the PCF's Pas-de-Calais federation, avenging his criticism of her work in 1950. Conflict was now overt, the tide had turned and Thorez, Billoux, Vermeersch, and Guyot were in control. Publication of the Billoux article signalled the violent confrontation between party militants and the police on May 28, 1952.[36] Billoux stridently called for defeat of the "war-mongers" and French entry into the Soviet camp, declaring proudly that: "the working class is struggling for Socialism." Restatement of an eternal verity of the left in May 1952 sounded like a new and defiant battle cry. Billoux charged the bourgeoisie with treason, but exempted capitalists participating in a Moscow trade fair. Still, the message seemed clear. Paul Noirot remembered rallying to Billoux's themes with joy; Pannequin, who helped Billoux write the article, noted a new burst of rank-and-file enthusiasm.[37]

There was nothing insurrectionary in the Ridgeway manifestation of May 28, 1952, even if some naive militants thought it a signal by Stalin for a Communist seizure of power. There was a new level of defiance, meant to dramatize the party's commitment to peace and Socialism and to win support for a revived Popular Front. From the April 29 appointment of Ridgeway as American commander in Paris, the Communist press denounced him as responsible for germ warfare in Korea, a "microbian killer" and advocate of the extermination of peoples, whose his appointment was a provocation.[38] The Paris Communists organized the demonstration "to shake up the odious government in power in our country." The Peace Movement endorsed it, but it was a party affair. To overcome government prohibition of the demonstration, secret coded instructions were circulated to militants on where to rendezvous and metallic signs, useful as shields, distributed. Demonstrators armed with clubs successfully resisted police efforts to disperse them.[39] By late evening Communist militants experienced the heady sentiment of controlling the streets, but their total number did not exceed 10,000. Participants had no instructions on what to do once they had successfully stood their ground against the police; eventually they dispersed and went home. There was one death, an Algerian, on the night of the demonstration, although another participant died two years later from head wounds.[40]

Hardly a success by any standard, the Ridgeway demonstration was overshadowed by the arrest of Jacques Duclos on trumped-up charges of planning an insurrection. Duclos took no precautions, relying on his parliamentary immunity despite the Pinay government's arrest of André Stil, an editor of *L'Humanité,* two days before. When police searched Duclos' car, they found a revolver, a radio, and two wrapped dead pigeons. Government prosecutors claimed they were carrier pigeons, but Madame Gilberte Duclos said they were destined for a dinner with *petits pois* (green peas). The police confiscated Duclos' notebooks, which became the basis of the alleged *complot des pigeons* (conspiracy of pigeons), but they rather testified to the nonchalance or diffidence with which Duclos regarded the demonstration.

Disarray followed Duclos' arrest. Power fell to Lecoeur and Fajon who each gave conflicting directives to the party press.[41] The liberation of Duclos gave rise to conflicting views over whether the party's attitude toward the Socialists should continue to be one of vituperation (Lecoeur) or dialogue (Fajon). Nominal authority should have fallen to the third of the historic leaders on the Secretariat, André Marty. But Duclos had curiously chosen the eve of the Ridgeway manifestation, May 27, to launch the Marty-Tillon affair.

The exclusion of Marty and Tillon remains symbolic of the PCF's Stalinist heritage to this day. Marty and Tillon were fiercely independent in spirit, autonomous in their realms, and allied with neither of the competing factions. Both were nationalists and Stalinists at the same time, and each sponsored a personality cult. The juxtaposition of their cases was circumstantial, but the similarities compelling; the link between them became a matter of logic if not fact. Both admitted meeting to discuss problems in the Peace Movement in 1951, thus violating the principles of democratic centralism. Both were heroes of the Black Sea mutinies against French intervention in the Russian Civil War in 1919 and went on to distinguished careers on the party's behalf: Marty heading the International Brigades and Tillon leading the military arm of PCF Resistance, the FTP. Each engaged in cloudy practices and made enemies: Marty's alleged ruthlessness was immortalized by Ernest Hemingway in *For Whom the Bell Tolls*; Tillon's rumored role was in the "Special Organization" (OS) of 1939–41.[42] Both were personally popular but isolated following the sectarian turn of 1947. Tillon created the French Peace Movement only to see it domesticated to Russian needs. He despised Duclos and Lecoeur since the confrontation between the party's military and civilian branches during the war. Marty bruised many by his habit of generously distributing personal insults. Both crossed Jeannette Vermeersch and therefore lost the protective mantle of Thorez, whom they later criticized severely. But Thorez had little to gain by their removal, which worked to the advantage of Duclos.

The connection of the Marty-Tillon affair and the East-European trials remains obscure. Robrieux says Stalin agreed to their removal in a meeting with Duclos in the summer of 1951. Jeannette Vermeersch denied Stalin did anything more than reluctantly assent, while Thorez had no part in the affair at all.[43] Marty and Tillon opposed Soviet policies: Tillon protested German rearmament and was removed as head of the Peace Movement in September 1951; Marty objected to the anti-Tito witch hunt. But the East-European trials had different results in each of the satellite nations and hinged more upon internal issues of the parties concerned than on Soviet desires.[44] Sometimes the nationalists purged the orthodox Stalinists rather than the reverse. The anti-Tito phase was over in 1952 when the Marty-Tillon trials occurred; the Slansky case in Czechoslovakia, which took place later in 1952, had anti-Semitic overtones and bore little resemblance. Raymond Guyot was the brother-in-law of Arthur London, a prominent victim in the Slansky case, to whom Duclos was also closely connected through Maurice Tréand. But neither Guyot's nor Duclos' connections with the Czech accused worked to their disadvantage. Duclos' move against Tillon was internal, the logical completion of the purge of former Resisters begun in 1950 at the Twelfth Party Congress and a final settling of accounts for divergences of the war years, particularly the critical period of Duclos' pseudo-collaboration in 1940–41.[45]

Marty's interrogation began on May 26 in the presence of Duclos, Fajon, and Lecoeur with Léon Mauvais acting as prosecutor. Marty and Tillon were charged with "fractional" activity and concealed political disagreements with the party line. The chief prosecution witness was Georges Beyer, Marty's brother-in-law, a veteran of the OS and the Resistance, and a 1950 purge victim. Beyer testified that Marty met Tillon at Beyer's home in June 1951 to discuss making the Peace Movement independent of the party. Marty denied the meeting occurred, then admitted it when confronted with Tillon's separate confession. The initial falsehood weakened Marty's subsequent defense. Beyer also claimed Marty was planning publication of an oppositional bulletin to the party line in 1949 and opposed Thorez's "no war against the USSR" statement. Marty denied all substantive charges, admitting only his frequent use of derogatory terms to describe other party leaders.[46]

Only one charge was serious: that the two leaders met to discuss the Peace Movement with the aim of making it an autonomous pressure group. Tillon was removed in 1951 from administration of the Movement and his self-criticism was on record. He later reflected bitterly that his actions in the Peace Movement had always been supported by Jeannette Vermeersch and Maurice Thorez, both of whom, he assumed, were now hypocritically charging him with crimes of which they were guilty.[47] But if Thorez's complicity was apparent to Tillon, it must have been equally so to Duclos and the other PCF leaders who were prosecuting Tillon in Thorez's absence. Duclos was linking Thorez, by implication, with the PCF's nationalists.

The affair was concluded in a manner that would have been inconceivable in any of the Communist parties in power. This is not to minimize the psychologically devastating impact on Marty and Tillon, charged with treason by the movement to which they owed their identities. But the objective realities belied their subjective experiences. The PCF did not have available to it the mechanisms of Communist parties in power: it could not conduct show trials, torture the accused into confessions, or carry out "legal" execution. Neither Marty, Tillon, or Lecoeur later made "confessions." Marty offered several documents of self-criticism, which were rejected by Duclos because they admitted to only a small portion of the "crimes" with which Marty was charged and contained counter-charges against the party leadership. Marty attributed the allegations against him to machinations of the "class enemy" within the party, a "*coup monté*" or conspiracy by the right, aimed at weakening the PCF through the removal of one of its most effective leaders.[48] He confessed to lack of enthusiasm for the Peace Movement's signature campaigns and the cult of Maurice Thorez, but condemned the "fiasco" of the February 12 strike and the Ridgeway demonstration. Charged with opposing the dissolution of the patriotic militia in 1944 and the *tournant* of 1947, he demanded the PCF re-examine its participation in power of 1945–47.

Tillon refused to make any confessions and instead took refuge in silence, facetiously offering Duclos only an open and joint examination of the party's "errors" in 1940.[49] Tillon was removed from his official positions but not excluded, and he returned to full membership in 1957 only to resign in 1970. Too many shared secrets existed between the PCF and its excluded figures for an open confrontation to be of use to either side in their disputes.

Other less known cases occurred simultaneously with the Marty-Tillon affair, highlighting the PCF's difficulties with its former resisters. Louis Prot, a PCF Deputy from the Somme, became aware of impending charges against himself, accused the party in turn of thefts, arson, and various other crimes in 1944, and threatened to make public damaging information about Duclos' activities during the war. The charges against Prot were withdrawn, and he was allowed to retain his local office as mayor.[50] The most bizarre case involved Georges Guingouin, guerrilla leader in the Limousin and resister when the party policy was pseudo-collaborationist in 1940–41. Guingouin reigned as a war-lord during the Resistance, ignoring party directives and presiding over bloody reprisals against collaborators in 1944 that went too far for the party's taste.[51] When attempts to restrain him failed, the party sent a mission to the Limousin to liquidate him, but it was unable to penetrate his bodyguard. After civil authority was restored, further attempts were abandoned. The PCF excluded Guingouin in November 1952 following mutual charges and counter-charges; *L'Humanité* dignified with a denial Guingouin's charge the party tried to kill him: "Communists reprove, condemn, and struggle against such methods."[52] In February 1954 Guingouin was prosecuted by the French government and spent a period in prison before the charges were dropped for lack of evidence. The party was silent during his imprisonment and rumored to have fed damaging information to the prosecution, although many Resistance heroes rallied to Guingouin's defense. A mutual silence prevailed between Guingouin and the party thereafter. In 1978 he was said to be negotiating a return to the fold.

The Marty-Tillon affair eliminated two of Duclos' rivals; it also became a retrospective justification of the PCF's line since 1939. All "errors" and "deviations" were attributed to the two fallen leaders. The Political Bureau's summary of the affair revealed real political differences.[53] The party repudiated Tillon's independent Resistance role from 1939 to 1941, asserting that maintaining Franco-Soviet friendship was the only policy then in the French interest. The PCF claimed leadership of the Resistance "from the first day of the occupation." Marty, by "discriminating" between Communists who spent the war years in France and those who were in Moscow or elsewhere, "played the game of de Gaulle and the reactionaries." It was a crime, the PCF said, for Tillon to oppose the FTP to the party's civilian leadership in 1944; the FTP had been created by the party, Thorez and Duclos, to whom the glory of the Resistance belonged. At the Liberation "excellent comrades believed, on the basis of an erroneous appreciation of the rapports of strength at the time, that the working class should have taken power. . . . The Communist party . . . is conscious of not having allowed any historical possibility of escaping it, and at any moment and in all circumstances to have done its duty." This was Duclos' defense of the PCF line against the Yugoslavs at the founding conference of the Cominform in 1947, now vindicated with removal of the French Titoists. Marty allegedly minimized the Soviet Union's role in the Liberation of France. Tillon developed an independent conception of the Peace Movement, opposed German rearmament when it was no longer party policy to do so, and resisted the campaign for a Five-Power Pact. Marty took the blame for the PCF's hesitations in accepting the Cold War reality in 1947 and the Peace Movement thereafter. He was charged as well, as the PCF had just been, with Blanquist nationalism and ideological deviation.

Marty and Tillon's most serious "deviation" was sharing in the generalized aspiration for social renovation prevalent among Resistance forces after the war. Titoism was not at issue but Browderism, not insurrection but rather the merger of the party in a broad movement of patriotism and social concern. Marty and Tillon refused to accept the PCF's ghetto after 1947 and tried to recapture the spirit of the Resistance. Paradoxically, Tillon once again anticipated the correct party line; the Peace Movement restored to the PCF a national audience it had been in danger of losing. As in the case of the Resistance, however, the PCF sapped the foundation of the Peace Movement by domesticating it to Soviet policy. Tillon was right once too often.

By proceeding with the Marty-Tillon affair and failing to take precautions the evening of the Ridgeway demonstration, Duclos helped bring about the failure of the Thorez-Billoux policy. He now lost no time in seeking to reverse the PCF line. Lecoeur and Fajon, now in policy-making posts in the party's Secretariat, called for a general strike on June 4 in an effort to secure Duclos' release. It failed abysmally. The proletariat could not be mobilized at will for political causes. "You are throwing us into the water," Frachon warned the Political Bureau, "without knowing whether we can swim."[54] Two days later the PCF shifted gears. Lecoeur and Billoux denied the Billoux-Vermeersch articles and Ridgeway manifestation meant a change in the PCF line. There had been no insurrectionary content to the Ridgeway demonstration; sticks and signs did not make a revolution. The aim had been to show Ridgeway that he was unwelcome in France. President Auriol in his past had also participated in illegal demonstrations, Lecoeur noted.[55]

The repudiation of Billoux and return to the Duclos line were announced in Etienne Fajon's Central Committee report on June 18, thus opening the third phase of the 1952 drama.[56] Fajon began by returning to the theme of internal conflicts among the bourgeoisie. Some capitalists went to the Moscow trade fair; others opposed German rearmament. It was a mistake to condemn all the French bourgeoisie as the enemy. Serious errors were made both in the February 12 strike and the Ridgeway demonstration, causing the party to lose its necessary liaison with the masses. But the most serious difficulty came with the May article in *Cahiers du Communisme*. "Written in our name by Billoux," Fajon said, it had engaged the responsibility of the entire Political Bureau. The article could be interpreted to indicate a turn in PCF policy as conservatives charged, because its message was "insufficiently clear and complete." Billoux had been guilty of "our most tenacious error," sectarianism, in wrongly identifying the peace struggle, the immediate task, with Socialism, "our program of the future." Fajon called upon the party to take neutralist sentiment more seriously, broaden its appeal and ally with non-proletarian elements of the population. Not to do so was to adopt "perspectives abandoned for twenty years." The PCF must not disdain workers' economic needs; directly criticizing Jeannette Vermeersch, Fajon denied the material demands of the workers were obsolete. The Socialists were still the "principal support of the bourgeoisie," but this last holdover of Thorez's policy was not to endure much longer.

According to Roger Pannequin, a majority of the Central Committee were disappointed to hear Billoux and Jeannette Vermeersch rise to repudiate their policies in self-criticism.[57] But the failure of the Ridgeway demonstration, absence of any perspective of a Popular Front, and difficulty of communications with Thorez appeared to leave no alternative. The May article, Billoux admitted, erred in treating the French bourgeoisie *en bloc* and linking the Peace Movement with

Socialism; it lost sight of workers' needs to align themselves with other strata of the population. There had been no policy turn intended; only a warning against opportunist tendencies. Jeannette Vermeersch also repudiated the article she published in *France Nouvelle*.[58]

Neither Lecoeur nor Fajon subsequently admitted to any serious disagreements in the party leadership in 1952. The oscillations in the party line were supposedly due to the pressure of events, Thorez's absence and Duclos' arrest. According to Lecoeur, Thorez tried to moderate each tendency; he did not intend Billoux to codify dogmatically their conversations and made known his displeasure after the May article. Fajon received a message from Thorez after the Central Committee's June meeting: Fajon had done well to criticize Billoux, but went a bit too far.[59] The still-committed Communist, Fajon, and the former party member become anti-Communist, Lecoeur, agreed on the need to preserve the appearances of democratic centralism. But the evidence of disagreement on the Political Bureau was clear from Duclos' notebook. Billoux's article only restated the policy in effect since February and was endorsed by Thorez after his return to France in 1953. The issues were not simply tactical. The struggle for peace either was or was not linked to the final goal of socialism. From February to May 1952 the PCF linked the two and it unlinked them in June. Fajon's rebuke by Thorez after the June meeting of the Central Committee was consistent with Thorez's reassertion of the Billoux line upon his return and Fajon's self-criticism delivered prior to the Thirteenth Party Congress in 1954. But if Fajon received such a message from Thorez, which is likely, in the short run it was ignored. PCF policy veered more sharply to the right in June 1952 than at any time since the party's exclusion from the government in 1947. In the retrospective of twenty-five years of subsequent PCF history, moreover, it was the turning point of June 1952, although several times criticized by Thorez, that appeared definitive.

The critical aspect of Fajon's return to moderation was his attempt to resolve the PCF's ambiguity toward the Socialists. Since 1947 the PCF had villified the Socialists to the point of insisting upon their "liquidation." Communists well knew, nevertheless, that the Socialists would not disappear, and their cooperation remained essential for the PCF again to become an influential force. Class-against-class rhetoric was always intended to prepare for an alliance with the Socialists once they were sufficiently mellowed by rhetorical pounding. In June 1952 Fajon declared that the moment had come to conclude an alliance. The arrest of Duclos was the precipitant. Attempts to liberate Duclos through mass pressure only revealed the weakness of party support while stiffening the anti-Communism of the French right. Use of the mechanisms of "bourgeois democracy," in particular the legal system, was more promising. The PCF needed the support of the most progressive segments of French opinion and the benevolence of the judiciary. Many judges were Socialists. While developing his legal appeal from his prison cell, Duclos called for an end to attacks on the Socialists by his party.

In the June 1952 issue of *Cahiers du Communisme*, Victor Michaut signaled the PCF's transfer of its efforts to the legal system. Duclos' liberation and the struggle for peace were the two most significant tasks facing the party. The June 4 strike failed because it was political and did not articulate working-class economic demands. "The PCF," said Michaut, "will now struggle for the defense of its legal positions." From his prison cell, Duclos denounced the violation of his parliamentary immunity and denied that Communist parties ever intended coups.[60] Duclos' physician testified that imprisonment was having deleterious effects on the Communist leader's health. Duclos also appealed directly to the Socialists. He thanked those who were joining in common action with the Communists in favor of his release, recalled unity of action of 1934 and 1935, and evoked the common martyrdom in the Resistance of Communist and Socialist militants. Common action was to the advantage of both parties, and unity at the base must make itself felt at the leadership level. In *L'Humanité,* Lecoeur called for unity between Communists and Socialists at the summit while Benoît Frachon appealed for CGT unity with Force Ouvrière and the Christian unions.[61] Attacks on the Socialists again disappeared from the Communist press. The PCF took its first step in a policy of attempted unity with the Socialists, a policy that was to be doggedly, if inconsistently, pursued until it reached fruition in the Gaullist era of the 1960's and 1970's.

Not simply the Socialists but the democratic system as a whole was at issue. Duclos was released on July 2. Citing the joy of the workers at this great victory, Fajon saluted the judges who used "soul and conscience" in their decision. Fellow-traveller Pierre Cot in a widely noted and later criticized article, contrasted the failed attempt to create a direct working-class response to Duclos' arrest with the "conscience and probity" demonstrated by the judges in Duclos' case. The independence of the judiciary liberated Duclos, not the combativeness of the workers.[62] A healthy part of the bourgeoisie was committed to republicanism and against fascism: the Communists had failed to take this into account. Cot went beyond simply playing upon the internal contradictions of the bourgeoisie. Coexistence in the international sphere must be matched by internal coexistence; the working class needed alliance, compromise, and unity with the Socialists. Fajon's criticism of the Billoux line in June 1952, Cot said, was the essential beginning of the new policy.

Thorez was not publicly heard from during the summer of 1952; the absence of a telegram of congratulations to Duclos upon his release from prison was curious. Thorez's confederates continued to promote his personality cult. On June 3, 1952, a show opened in the *Mutualité* entitled *"Celui de France que nous aimons le plus"* (The Frenchman we love the most), by Henri Bassis.[63] A taudry drama set to music, it might have been dismissed as another absurdity of the PCF's Stalinism were it not for the attacks on the Socialists in the play's text, which also repeated the message of the Billoux article in *Cahiers du Communisme.* Bassis' play contradicted the moderate policies Duclos and Fajon had just begun to implement. Concentrating on World War I, the play denounced the perfidy of Social-Democracy, and accused the Socialists of welcoming and perhaps causing the death of Jaurès:

Jaurès was the first to die for *la patrie*
The empty corps of Social-Democracy
Rots away in the tempest
They have silenced the prophet
And joyfully they bury his prophecy
Nothing henceforth will stop them
This death, for them, is a holiday
They have lied, forgotten all
Soiled the hopes of the workers
The social-traitors from across the Rhine
Beat the same refrain
They have liquidated the party
Destroyed our arm and our tool.
Their socialism is rotted away
They preach crime and barbarism

The Socialists in Bassis' play taunt Lenin in the same way the Jews in the passion plays torment Christ. But salvation was achieved through Thorez:

We will know, we do know
Who traces a socialist way for France
A just and sure way, that passes through peace.
It is true. Ah! What love for him, and respect
He said to us, This is the decisive question
We must win the peace so that France may live.
Oh when will he return? He is here, in person,
In the head and the heart of each of us.

Stalin was mentioned only twice in the entire play. In contrast, the text attributed to Maurice Thorez the charting of a French way to socialism, vintage 1946, that passed through vituperation of the Socialists and the struggle for peace. Bassis' play continued through the summer of 1952 while Duclos was writing letters from prison to his "Socialist brothers" and Cot was paying tribute to the probity of Socialist judges.

Thorez and Billoux awaited their opportunity to return to the offensive. How they re-established control remains obscured. The most likely interpretation is the simplest. The continuation of the Duclos line of cooperation with the Socialists was conditional upon its success. The SFIO had formally condemned the Pinay government. The basis for an accord existed between Communist and Socialist workers and their parties. For once, the PCF was willing to take Guy Mollet's declarations as a genuine expression of the workers' views. Fajon and Lecoeur both commented favorably upon the Socialist party's stand.[64] But when the overtures failed to bring a response, Fajon complained of the "pernicious policies" of the Socialist leaders, whose anti-Communism had prevented any concrete moves toward unity.[65] At the September 1952 meeting of the Central Committee the PCF abandoned the entente with the Socialists. The efforts of Socialist workers had not been sufficient to force a change by their leadership. It was once again necessary to unmask the treasonous role of the Right-Socialists who were playing the game of Pinay.[66] Duclos' position was compromised by the failure of his policies. In a veiled critique of his actions, he declared the party had underestimated the "fascist nature" of the Pinay government. Lecoeur denounced the "opportunism" of the recent period; we must again show the Socialist workers their leaders are traitors. Pierre Cot's call for internal coexistence in French politics had been wrong, just as Billoux had been inexact in equating the Peace effort with the march toward Socialism.

Duclos announced that Thorez's return to France was certain to occur prior to the next Central Committee session. This information could account for the ambiguity discernible in PCF policy toward the end of the year. Still in charge, Duclos was constrained to abandon efforts to ally with the Socialist leadership, but he did not yet return to the discredited Billoux policies of May; the fourth and final phase of PCF policy came hesitantly. For Duclos, Front national was still the basis of PCF policy. The paramount danger to France again became German rearmament, which the American-sponsored plans for a European Defense Community (EDC) promised shortly to make into a frightening reality. Plans for the EDC, Duclos noted, were causing internal contradictions to appear once again among the French bourgeoisie. Communists must pursue a policy of Front national *uni* (united), Duclos declared, rallying patriots from all social categories, opinions, and beliefs, against the war-mongering policies embodied in the EDC.

Lecoeur laid the blame for the recent "opportunism" in party policy flatly on the Central Committee, which had failed to criticize actions of the Political Bureau. Even now too few party officials had risen to speak. Was the Committee not aware, Lecoeur asked, of the "lack of balance" in PCF policy proceeding and following the 28th of May 1952? The source of the PCF's vacillation was clear: lack of vigilance in guarding against the double-edged danger of opportunism and sectarianism. Lecoeur criticized the extreme tone of some Communist articles preceding the Ridgeway demonstration and the "outrageously sectarian" strikes of February 12 and June 4. The party had not yet carried out a retrospective analysis of these events and as a result weakened its liaison with the masses: "If we had observed the errors of February 12," said Lecoeur, "we would not have repeated them on June 4." Nor could the Billoux article, which had been meant to warn against the opportunist danger, be cited as a pretext for these errors. "The Political Bureau is not composed of half opportunists and half sectarians trying to prevail one over the other," Lecoeur said; the faults were being committed by the same leadership. Lecoeur's attempt to lay the blame for his, Duclos', and Fajon's actions on the Central Committee was as false as his denial of a split on the Political Bureau.

Existence of the split was virtually admitted to publicly in 1954. It remains problematic how it related to divisions in the USSR's leadership. The Rival clans in the Soviet Politburo may have conducted their struggles by extension at the interior of the PCF or, more likely, permitted the internal factions in the French Political Bureau to struggle among themselves without outside interference. *Pravda* reported the Ridgeway demonstrations and the arrests of Stil and Duclos but said nothing of the Fajon-Billoux debate. Its coverage of the Marty-Tillon affair was limited to summaries of the PCF's official declarations. The Cominform organ, *For a Lasting Peace,* printed excerpts of Fajon's June 18 speech, but omitted his critique of Billoux.[67] The Soviet Politburo was divided from 1952 through 1955 and very likely earlier. Lecoeur and Duclos were most likely linked to Beria and Malenkov, who were, paradoxical as it may seem, advocates of conciliation in international affairs. Thorez and Billoux preferred the politics of the more sectarian Molotov group.[68] This is consistent with Thorez's later alliance with the so called anti-party group in the USSR and efforts to block Khrushchev's de-Stalinization. One may extend the parallel backward in time as well and link Thorez to the so-called party revival in the USSR headed by Molotov and Zhdanov immediately after the war. Zhdanov's elimination in 1948 and the Leningrad purge of 1949 preceded the eclipse of Thorez in 1950. Zhdanov could have been a supporter of Tito's left-sectarian national Communism.[69] Thorez also became tainted by the nationalist heresy, which explains his "imprisonment" in the USSR.

The divisions in the PCF Political Bureau were compounded by personal ambitions. Fajon and Billoux were rivals for the succession to Thorez and Lecoeur asserted his claim to leadership if the ill Thorez stepped up (to an honorary presidency) or down.[70] It would be a mistake to dismiss any of these aspirations on the basis of the theoretical operations of democratic centralism. Communist leaders also had clay feet; considerations of personal ambition crossed their minds. The proportions of personal ambition to political difference can never be calculated. What may one day be revealed is the means by which the Thorez group reasserted its control.

Reassertion of the PCF's sectarian line again was counter to developments in the USSR. The Nineteenth Congress of the Communist Party of the Soviet Union (CPSU), held in October 1952, was consistent with Duclos' national front of September; the Soviet Union recognized Western capitalism had reached a phase of stabilization and committed itself to peaceful coexistence.[71] Foreign Communist parties were to continue the peace effort and support democratic freedoms and neutralism. On one issue agitating the French Stalin pronounced clearly: the struggle for peace was not the struggle for Socialism. Billoux's May 1952 article in *Cahiers du Communism* thus stood condemned. The French delegation, composed of Lecoeur, Roger Garaudy, Georges Cogniot, and Thorez, could not have been pleased. Despite the moderate tone of the CPSU Nineteenth Congress

Lecoeur returned to France again the instrument of a Thorez-inspired leftward thrust in PCF policy. PCF diatribes against the Socialists reached a new level of invective; the Socialist International was made up of traitors, the SFIO's hostility to Pinay was hollow, designed to mask its role as servant of the grand bourgeoisie. The non-Communist trade unions were "instruments of the class enemy." A year of effort by Benoît Frachon to rebuild unity with their leaderships was repudiated. The only unity possible must be based on the positions of the CGT.[72]

On September 17 sanctions were announced against Marty and Tillon, now unmasked as agents of imperialism. For months since May, while the investigation of their "crimes" was under way, not a word escaped the Political Bureau, attesting to the efficacy of democratic centralism. Now each passing day revealed examples of the treasonous behavior of the two Communist heroes. Marty had been a police agent; his exploits in the Black Sea were built on lies. How could the party have peddled this mythology for so many years while harboring the traitor in its leadership?[73] This question was never posed by the sub-culture's adherents who had other concerns.

On November 22 *L'Humanité* denounced the Slansky group in Czechoslovakia which, along with Tito, Kostov in Bulgaria, and Rajk in Hungary, allegedly had been using their high posts to restore capitalism. The French party leadership, Eastern Europe and the USSR (once the doctors' plot was uncovered in 1953) were riddled with spies, Trotskyists, bourgeois nationalists, and Zionists. The discovery that Israel and world Zionism were agents of American espionage was another blow to a party harboring many Jews in its membership. The PCF had welcomed the birth of Israel in 1948 as a blow against imperialism. The charge of anti-Semitism stung the party; yet its propaganda began to echo some of the historic stereotypic imagery which depicted Jews as an international conspiracy of capitalist financiers.[74] The PCF stressed that the Rosenbergs were Jews; their conviction in the USA had no counterpart in Eastern Europe, where anti-Semitism had been explicitly outlawed. But in the same breath with which it demanded the release of the Rosenbergs *L'Humanité* insisted Slansky receive the death penalty. In the delirium of the Cold War the rival cases of these Jewish Communists canceled one another.

Persecution of Communists in France was in any case the real issue. On October 16 the French government sought to lift the parliamentary immunity of Duclos, Billoux, Fajon, Guyot, Marty, and Léon Feix. The pretext was the Duclos notebook; legal proceedings continued for a year before the case was thrown out of court. *L'Humanité* welcomed the opportunity to create new figures of martyrdom. The inclusion of Marty in the indictment, however, went unmentioned in the Communist press; he was on his way to becoming a non-person in the Communist sub-culture. Lecoeur was also missing from the list. An explanation was offered by a self-styled organ of dissident Communists, *Unir,* which pointedly accused Lecoeur of being a police agent.[75] From its inauspicious beginnings *Unir* was able to win a respected position in the world of the non-

Communist left and the collaboration of dissident Communists who turned it into a recognized organ for the critique of party policy. Only in the 1970's was *Unir*'s genesis in the services of the French police exposed; it was the obverse of the Pinay government's legal campaign of petty persecution. Whether or not *Unir* contributed materially to the weakening of Lecoeur's position, the French government probably omitted him from the indictment in an attempt to undermine him.

The December 1952 Central Committee meeting showed the party in the greatest depths of the ghetto mentality, setting the stage for the fourth phase and triumph of the modified sectarian line. François Billoux, not a member of the Secretariat, delivered the major report; Georges Cogniot, not even a member of the Political Bureau, delivered a parallel address on the CPSU Nineteenth Congress. Duclos, Fajon, and Lecoeur, all on the Secretariat, played no prominent role in the December proceedings. In September Lecoeur had criticized both opportunist and sectarian tendencies in the PCF leadership. Now the PCF's opportunism alone was the target. Stalin had determined the Peace Movement would not lead to Socialism; in this respect Billoux had to admit he had been in error.[76] But in its broad outlines his May article was correct: the enemy was the entire French bourgeoisie. The strike of February 12, 1952, condemned by Lecoeur and Fajon, was correct. Billoux criticized Fajon and defended the Ridgeway demonstration. The Political Bureau had failed to appreciate the harshness of the fascist Pinay government and weakened the struggle against Social-Democracy. Duclos, who bore direct responsibility for all of these mishaps, stood explicitly condemned.

Duclos admitted the justice of Billoux's criticism and took personal responsibility for the failure to take necessary precautions during the Ridgeway demonstration. He had underestimated the Pinay government's willingness to resort to extreme measures; his arrest obscured the "victory" of May 28 and resulted in the slide into opportunism. The Central Committee resolution pledged the "liquidation" of the opportunist tendency manifest in party policy and criticized the leadership for relaxing the struggle against Social Democracy and abandoning the correct line of the Billoux article. Duclos', Fajon's, and Lecoeur's policies were condemned. Lecoeur escaped direct criticism for the moment; by making him the messenger of the sectarian line in February and November, Thorez played the Stalinist game of choosing the known advocate of a particular policy to be the instrument of its condemnation. The connection between Lecoeur's "political instructors" and the ensemble of Duclos' opportunistic policies was a matter of logic; in 1953 Thorez made it explicit and it became the reason for Lecoeur's downfall. But the Central Committee first needed to dispose of the Marty affair. All those who had been closely associated with or worked under Marty in the past now joined the chorus of his condemnation. In December 1952 the PCF was not implementing Stalin's policy, but it remained a Stalinist party.

Neither the oscillations in the party line, the crisis in the leadership, or the Marty-Tillon affair, caused noticeable erosion of Communist influence or support.

One of the most notable characteristics of the PCF is that its support has been consistently loyal, no matter what the specific policy options of the leadership at any given moment. PCF support, until 1981, reflected structural aspects of French society over the long run rather than the immediate impact of short-term events. The party's policies were important nonetheless. What Communist leaders did with their support was as significant as its sources. The PCF's ability to influence French politics in 1952 appeared to be severely impaired if not destroyed; yet by 1954 the party once again became a significant force in French politics, playing a critical role in the achievement of peace in Indochina, the defeat of the European Defense Community, and the beginning of decolonization. The reintegration of the PCF into French political life occurred after Stalin's death and Maurice Thorez's return to France. These events provided the necessary setting for the party's return to a position of influence and opened a new era in party history.

NOTES

1. *L'Humanité,* February 10, 1951.

2. Ibid., January 19, 20, 24, 1951; February 10, 15, 16, 17, 21, 1951.

3. Charles Tillon, *On chantait rouge* (Paris, 1976), 486.

4. *L'Humanité,* May 17, 1951.

5. Charles Tillon, *Un procès de Moscou à Paris* (Paris, 1974), 70; personal interview, Roger Garaudy, September 12, 1980.

6. *L'Humanité,* April 9, 1951.

7. *Cahiers du Communisme,* 2 (February 1951), 9 (September 1951).

8. See Garaudy's self-criticism in *La Nouvelle Critique,* 5 (April 1949) and the two editions of *Les Sources françaises du Socialisme Scientifique* (Paris, 1948 and 1949). Georges Cogniot, *Parti Pris: De la liberation au Programme commun,* II (Paris, 1976) says Thorez was aware of Garaudy's "idealism" yet allowed his personal sympathies for the latter to get the better of him, 88. Garaudy agrees that the 1951 attack was aimed at Thorez. Interview.

9. *Cahiers du Communisme,* 6 (June 1951), *L'Humanité,* May 18, 1951.

10. See *BEIPI,* No. 51, July 16–31, 1951. Also Marshall Schulman, *Stalin's Foreign Policy Reappraised* (New York, 1965), 206.

11. *L'Humanité,* June 4, 11, 1951.

12. J. Berlioz, *Cahiers du Communisme,* 3 (March 1951).

13. *L'Humanité,* March 22, 23, 1951.

14. Ibid., June 23, 1951.

15. Ibid., September 10, 28, 1951, October 8, 15, 1951.

16. Handwritten manuscript by Angelo Tasca in the *Fonde Angelo Tasca,* Fondazione Feltrinelli, Milan. Also *L'Humanité,* October 16, 1951.

17. Pierre Grimaud, *Nous avons payé trop cher,* (Paris, n.d.) in the Institute Maurice Thorez (mimeographed). Grimaud's work interprets the 1950–52 period in terms of a struggle within the PCF leadership, the first to do so, to my knowledge, from a party source.

18. *L'Humanité,* September 1, 11, 13, 1951.

19. Ibid., December 5, 1951.

20. Ibid., January 2, 1952.

21. Ibid., December 15, 1951.

22. Auguste Lecoeur, personal interview, July 11, 1978; *Autocritique attendue* (Paris, 1955), 24. The text is in *Cahiers du Communisme,* 2 (February 1952), 188–92.

23. Lecoeur interview.

24. Interview with Dr. Pierre Klotz, Thorez's physician, September 18, 1980.

25. Aragon interview in Robrieux archive; Lecoeur interview, July 12, 1978. See Philippe Robrieux, *Maurice Thorez, vie secrète et vie publique* (Paris, 1975), 396–400.

26. The text may be found in *L'Humanité,* April 28, 1952. (My translation from original.)

27. *France Nouvelle,* January 12, 1952.

28. *L'Humanité,* February 2, 4, 11, 13, 1952. Lecoeur also met with members of the apparently divided Soviet leadership.

29. Ibid., February 14, 16, 1952. *Cahiers du Communisme,* 2 (February 1952), 3 (March, 1952).

30. Lecoeur interview, July 12, 1978.

31. Pierre Durand cited the war hysteria in France as a reason for the PCF's turn in policy: personal interview, April 6, 1978. On Stalin's proposals see Schulman, 210–25. Roger Pannequin noted the divergence of the Thorez-Billoux initiative from Soviet policy in *Adieu Camarades* (Paris, 1977), 271. See also *L'Humanité,* April 2, 1952.

32. See Pierre Hervé's version of events in *Lettre à Sartre* (Paris, 1956) and *Dieu et César sont-ils communistes?* (Paris, 1958).

33. Vilem Kahan knew of Marty's protest through Czech party sources. Personal interview, August 16, 1978.

34. A Bowdlerized version of Duclos' notebook was published under the title *La Signification politique du cahier Jacques Duclos* (Paris, 1952). The whole is in France, Assemblée Nationale, *Documents parlementaires,* No. 4415 (October 15, 1952). This is the account I have used here.

35. *France Nouvelle,* May 31, 1952.

36. For the text, entitled "Les taches du Parti deux ans après le xiie Congrès: Organiser et diriger l'action unie des masses pour imposer une politique de paix et d'independence nationale," see *Cahiers du Communisme,* 5 (May 1952), 453–68.

37. Paul Noirot, *La Memoire ouverte* (Paris, 1978), 108–17. Pannequin, *Adieu Camarades,* 273.

38. *L'Humanité,* April 29, 1952, May 8, 14, 19, 24, 1952.

39. Pierre Daix, *J'ai cru au matin* (Paris, 1976), 285–95, interview, May 5, 1978. Noirot, *La Memoire ouverte,* 108–17. Marty, *L'Affaire Marty* (Paris, 1955), 39.

40. Ironically the wife of this worker, then pregnant, died during the anti-OAS demonstrations of February 8, 1962, thus fully orphaning her nine-year-old son. Her name was Fanny Dewerp. See Cogniot, *Parti Pris,* II, 456.

41. Pierre Daix, then editing *Ce Soir,* and Pierre Durand at *L'Humanité* both reported they received conflicting directives from Lecoeur and Fajon until the line was clarified on June 18. Personal interviews.

42. For a good summary of their careers, see Yves Le Braz, *Les Réjetés* (Paris, 1974).

43. Philippe Robrieux, *Histoire intérieure du Parti communiste français* (Paris, 1981), II, 337.

44. Lilly Marcou, *Le Kominform* (Paris, 1977).

45. Tillon, interview, May 29, 1978.

46. Minutes, Political Bureau meetings, and texts of the "confessions" are in *Archives André Marty* (AAM) (Microfilm collection), Reel 22, May 26–27, 1952.

47. Charles Tillon, *Un procès de Moscou à Paris* (Paris, 1970), 70.

48. AAM, Reel 22, August 24, 1952. Also *L'Affaire Marty*. The French police were not above this sort of thing. See the analysis of the role of *Unir*, below.

49. *Un Procès de Moscou à Paris*, 132. An act which detracts considerably from the veracity of the title.

50. On the Prot affair see Claude Harmel, "Les Scandales du PCF," unpublished manuscript, Robrieux archive. An account also appears in the U.S. National Archives, State Department File 851.00B, April 28 and July 25, 1949.

51. There is a folder on the Guingouin affair in the Tasca archive, and accounts appeared in *Le Figaro* May 12, 1952, and *L'Aurore*, September 14, 1952. Also Robrieux, *Histoire intérieure*, II, 308–10.

52. *L'Humanité*, November 14, 1952.

53. The text appears under the heading "Documents: Les Problèmes de la politique du parti et l'activité fractionelle des camarades A. Marty et C. Tillon," in *Cahiers du Communisme*, 29, 10 (October 1952), 935–55.

54. Roger Pannequin, personal interview, May 2, 1978.

55. *L'Humanité*, June 2, 5, 6, 7, 14, 1952.

56. Ibid., June 19, 1952, carried the text.

57. Pannequin interview.

58. *L'Humanité*, June 19, 1952.

59. Lecoeur interview, July 12, 1978; Fajon interview, April 10, 1978. See also Auguste Lecoeur, *Le Partisan* (Paris, 1961), 256–58.

60. *Cahiers du Communisme*, 6 (June 1952), 8 (August 1952).

61. *L'Humanité*, June 25, 1952.

62. *Les Lettres Françaises*, July 18–25, 1952. *L'Humanité*, July 2, 1952.

63. Henri Bassis, *Celui de France que nous aimons le plus* (Paris, 1952).

64. See *France Nouvelle*, July 26, 1952.

65. *L'Humanité*, July 23, 26, 1952, August 1, 1952.

66. *L'Humanité*, September 4, 1952. Also *France Nouvelle*, September 6, 1952.

67. *Pravda*, May–June 1952, *For a Lasting Peace*, July 30, 1952.

68. Pannequin, *Adieu Camarades*. Also, personal interview. Robrieux, *Histoire Intérieure*, II, accepts Duclos' link to Beria. On Thorez's resistance to destalinization see also his *Maurice Thorez* and chapter 10 below.

69. See, notably, Isaac Deutscher, *Russia After Stalin* (London, 1953). Also Lilly Marcou, *Le Kominform*, 285–86, and William McCagg, *Stalin Embattled, 1944–48* (Detroit, Mich., 1978). Robert Conquest, *Power and Policy in the USSR: The Struggle for Stalin's Succession 1940–1960* (New York, 1967) notes Zhdanov's possible connection to Titoism: See in particular pp. 100–10.

70. Pierre Daix, personal interview, May 5, 1978, also *J'ai cru au matin* (Paris, 1976).

71. Schulman, *Stalin's Foreign Policy*.

72. *L'Humanité*, October 30, 1952, November 12, 1952, December 5, 1952.

73. Lecoeur wrote that he asked Duclos if the charges against Marty's Black Sea heroism were true—Duclos confirmed them as originally made by the Socialist deputy Max Lejeune in 1951. If true, this is a remarkable indication of both the ignorant credulousness of young and ambitious Communists and the cynical manipulation of the mythology in which they believed by an old guard. See *Le Partisan*.

74. *L'Humanité,* November 22, 25, 27, 28, 29, 1952.

75. An almost complete collection of *Unir* is in the Robrieux archive; its police origin, which the party denounced as early as 1953, is still a sore point among some dissident ex-Communists. For the attack on Lecoeur, No. 3 (December 1952).

76. It is interesting to compare the accounts of the Central Committee meeting in *L'Humanité,* December 6–9, 1952, and *France Nouvelle,* December 13, 1952. The former features Billoux's return to the May line; the latter stressed his few words of self-criticism ignoring the more serious and extensive *mea culpa* of Duclos. This would tend to confirm Pannequin's assertion that *France Nouvelle* was run by the Bonte clique who were friendly to Duclos and not to Thorez.

8
THE ROAD TO INTEGRATION, 1953–1956

The collective delirium of the Cold War climaxed early in 1953, just prior to Stalin's death. Never had the Communists been so isolated; never had their politics appeared so absurd. Yet in eighteen months' time, the PCF found itself participating again in the political process, offering Communist votes to the Mendès-France government to end the Indochina war and comprising part of the majority that defeated the scheme for a European Defense Community (EDC). The transformation began after Stalin died and Thorez returned to France, two events which were not coincidental. Stalin's death signalled a reversal in Soviet policy evidenced by the abrupt dismissal of charges against Jewish doctors accused of attempting to poison the Soviet leadership. While the Politburo moved toward collective leadership and a cautious approach to foreign affairs, Thorez reasserted control in the PCF and implemented a more independent line. Thorez still hoped to recreate a version of the Popular Front: "class against class" would give way to Front populaire when the time was right. In the meantime a period of "softening up" the Socialist leadership was necessary; attacks in the Communist press continued while PCF militants made friendly offers of cooperation to Socialist dissidents and rank and file. Thorez remained confident the SFIO leadership could be made to rejoin Communist positions. Potential issues for agreement existed: the Socialists were alienated from the conservative majority and disturbed by the Vietnam war.

The same intentions had been behind Billoux's famous May 1952 article in *Cahiers du Communisme*. To establish his control over the party, Thorez had to force acceptance of the Billoux line as correct; Duclos, Lecoeur, and Fajon must be made to repudiate their criticism and displays of "opportunism" in the party line. Lecoeur, who asserted his candidature to succeed Thorez, was removed from the leadership and expelled. The factional struggle reached its denouement at the Thirteenth Party Congress in June 1954; self-criticisms by Duclos and Fajon, the ousting of Lecoeur, and triumphant posturing of Billoux and Guyot were then publicly exposed. Thorez's efforts to achieve a Popular Front, however, could not be consistently pursued. The June 1953 bid by Pierre Mendès-France to become Premier was premature; the August 1953 strike movement caught the PCF by surprise, was of unexpected dimensions, and could not be dealt with on the parliamentary level. In September 1953 Thorez was constrained to abandon

Front populaire in favor of Front national: the EDC, with its threat of German rearmament, outraged his Jacobin nationalism and led to a renewed PCF quest for allies on the nationalist right. Opposition to the EDC and the Indochina war brought the PCF into a developing national majority on these issues in 1954. During the government of Pierre Mendès-France, the PCF was in a position of influence it had not enjoyed since 1947. But on questions of internal party organization and policy toward the International Communist Movement Thorez remained uncompromising. His victory over Duclos, Fajon, and Lecoeur was followed by an intensification of his personality cult. Thorez claimed an international position as a Marxist theorist and became a major obstacle to Soviet efforts at de-Stalinization.

There were early signs that the PCF hoped to escape political isolation. The party's 1953 New Year's declaration asserted that the choice facing France was not between Socialism and submission to the USA; a third alternative of peace and national independence was possible. Publication of Volume 10 of Thorez's works, dealing with the formation of the Popular Front, showed how the PCF became "an essential factor in the life of the French people" after leaving the "isolation of the Barbé-Celor group."[1] These conciliatory statements coincided with Stalin's declaration to the *New York Times* that he believed the USA and the USSR could live in peace.

Moderation was eclipsed by the madness of the alleged "doctors' plot" which Soviet security services uncovered on January 14, 1953. The Jewish question was already a matter of polemics because of the Slansky and Rosenberg trials, both involving Jews accused of treason, a sensitive subject in France since Dreyfus. To complicate matters, France was now governed by a representative of the Jewish haute-bourgeoisie, René Mayer. The opportunity was too much for *L'Humanité* to ignore; the criminal Soviet doctors were "corrupt Jewish bourgeois nationalists," responsible for the death of the beloved Zhdanov in 1948 and working for American secret services and the Zionist distribution committee, the "Joint," in a plot to kill Stalin. Roger Garaudy compared the accused physicians to Nazi concentration camp doctors, many of whom he said had also been Jews.[2] The Communists went to great efforts, however, to neutralize the charge of anti-Semitism against themselves. On February 14 Billoux, Guyot, Fajon, Lecoeur, and Duclos attended a massive rally for the Rosenbergs, described as victims of the "real" anti-Semitism inherited from Hitler. "We, Communists, defend Julius and Ethel Rosenberg who are Jews," Duclos declared. Those who defended Slansky and the white-coated murderers in the USSR were uninterested in the fate of the Rosenbergs; Jules Moch, Daniel Mayer, and Oreste Rosenfeld (three Socialists with visibly Jewish names) instead defended traitors.[3] Lecoeur called upon Jewish workers to lead the struggle against this "odious exploitation of racial prejudice by the defenders of espionage working within Joint and Zionism." Annie Besse, herself Jewish, denied that anti-Semitism had any connection with the Slansky case or the doctors' plot. Espionage was the only issue; if anti-Semitism suggested itself, the fault lay with the accused, who had excluded themselves from their national communities, stripping themselves of all except their Jewish identities. Zionism was racist and Israel a tool of the U.S. State Department. No Marxist text recognized the Jews as a nation; their liberation could only come with assimilation.[4]

Annie Besse's themes suggested Jewish self-hatred; Pierre Hervé's pieces in *Ce Soir* indulged in traditional anti-Semitic stereotypes. Hervé claimed he was ordered to do the articles by Duclos, the material supplied by Jewish comrades.[5] Hervé traced Jewish anti-Communist plots back through the 1930's, the death of Gorky "by the same methods" as the doctors allegedly had used, Trotskyism, and the attempt to kill Lenin by Dora Kaplan in 1918.[6] The Jewish diaspora was a war arm in the service of the U.S. State Department; Jewish financiers aided Hitler's rise to power and Israel, Hervé wrote, was a "parasitic state," consisting of a transplanted petty bourgeoisie. Anti-Semitism was a diversion; the U.S. State Department had "made of Judaism (not Zionism) a banner of militarism" engaging in sabotage, murder, conspiracy, and espionage. The PCF's Jewish intellectuals and doctors were forced to sign telegrams expressing support for the Soviet leadership and Stalin for their vigilance in exposing the "white-coated murderers" and the Zionist plot. Suspicion nevertheless fell upon the party's Jews amid the general Cold War hysteria; several Jewish party members were denied promotions and in one case a woman was advised to break her engagement to a Jewish intellectual if she wished advancement.[7] The climate only dissipated when the doctors' plot was exposed as a fraud. Thorez remained silent during the affair, in contrast to Duclos and Lecoeur. Several of the accused Soviet doctors had treated Thorez, and he regarded them as friends.[8]

The anti-Zionist campaign was paralleled by the uninhibited outpouring of tributes to Stalin in the Communist press following his death. Workers, peoples of all the world were in mourning, *L'Humanité* announced; *France Nouvelle* declared boldly that "Stalinism lives, it is immortal; the sublime name of the genial master of world communism will shine with brilliant clarity across the centuries and will always be pronounced with love by a grateful humanity; we will remain loyal to Stalin forever . . . eternal glory to the great Stalin, whose imperishable masterful scientific works will help us to rally a majority of the people and become the guiding force of the nation."[9] The PCF Conference combined a tribute to Stalin with devotion to Thorez, linking the two personality cults in a way the PCF leader would later find embarrassing: "In your works [Thorez's] we have learned to conduct our battles victoriously. . . . According to your example we have learned to love the Soviet Union, to love Stalin with that love with which one loves the future when it appears with its most shining visage. . . . You taught us that it was the honor of our lives to deserve ever more the beautiful title of 'Stalinist.' " The statement in poetic form was attributed to Aragon.

On March 18 the PCF Political Bureau "categorically disapproved" of a Picasso portrait of Stalin published as an intended tribute by the monthly *Les Lettres Françaises*.[10] The sketch arrived barely in time to make the publication deadline and was quickly approved by editors Aragon and Pierre Daix, who saw in Picasso's rendition an affirmation of Stalin's perennial youth. But Lecoeur saw implicit defiance of the socialist-realist line in culture, of which he made himself the self-appointed guardian. The Secretariat also condemned the portrait "without doubting the sentiments of the great artist Picasso whose attachment to the working class is well known." Letters of protest by indignant Communists were received by Aragon who was forced to read them publicly at a Parisian meeting. According to Pierre Daix one letter was withheld—a message from Thorez disavowing the Secretariat and approving the Picasso portrait.

By orchestrating the anti-Zionist campaign and the Stalin cult while humiliating Thorez's favorite, Aragon, Lecoeur appeared to be presenting himself to Moscow as a likely successor to the PCF leadership. The exposure of the doctors' plot also threatened Beria, with whom Duclos and Lecoeur were linked.[11] By their zealous fanaticism the two leaders hoped to survive that connection and consolidate their control. In effect they accomplished the opposite. Resentment grew in the party against Lecoeur's autocratic methods, ultimately playing a role in his downfall. Duclos, Fajon, and Lecoeur misread the internal Soviet situation; the USSR reversed directions dramatically and on April 6 announced the rehabilitation of the Soviet doctors. Four days later Maurice Thorez returned to France.

L'Humanité reported that the doctors had been falsely arrested and their confessions obtained by illegal and inadmissible methods. Dismissal of the charges demonstrated the superiority of Soviet justice, which admitted its errors and rehabilitated those wrongly accused. The accusations were the work of anti-Soviet plotters who wished to "sow racial hatred in the USSR."[12] In its attempt to turn black into white the PCF admitted the use of "inadmissible" procedures (that is, torture) in the USSR and the existence there of a fertile ground for "racial hatred." The rehabilitation of the doctors was clearly, in retrospect, the signal for the beginnings of de-Stalinization in the USSR. But the return of Thorez to France opened the way for a different process in the PCF. Thorez intensified the party's Stalinist characteristics while differentiating its policy from the USSR and trying to lead it toward integration with the French political system.

A beleaguered Aragon sensed in Thorez's return a way out of his predicament. The poet's celebration of the event was not simply servile flattery but rather showed the uses of the Thorez cult in the party's internecine struggle. Two years of party policies, Aragon wrote, were affected by Thorez's return, which alone promised a future of happiness for all: "And one already can hear tomorrow sing."[13] Duclos, Lecoeur, and Fajon, who suppressed Thorez's criticism of their handling of the Picasso portrait affair, were understandably disturbed by Aragon's poem,[14] with good reason, for Thorez's return brought not only Aragon's immediate rehabilitation but a deep-seated shift in PCF policy.

Duclos hinted at what was coming during the March Party Conference; he endorsed the December 1952 resolution of the Central Committee, affirmed the line of the May article by François Billoux, and denounced the "opportunism" in the PCF line since June 1952.[15] Duclos was in effect repudiating his stewardship of the party during the previous year. With Thorez's return vindication of the Billoux line against "opportunism" became the means of discrediting Duclos, Fajon, and Lecoeur.

Paradoxically, while condemning opportunism, Thorez led the party to more moderate policies than at any previous point in its history. The apotheosis of this policy came in 1956 when the PCF rejected Khrushchev's de-Stalinization in the USSR and at the same time supported the Socialist government of Guy Mollet in the hope of achieving peace in Algeria. Political integration and continued internal Stalinist practice were characteristic of the PCF's internal dialectic: Stalinism disciplined the party's revolutionary energies and channeled them toward what the leadership perceived as constructive political change. De-Stalinization would have brought the party closer to the revolutionary left, as almost occurred later on in the struggle against the Algerian war. It was no accident that in 1961 the French Khrushchevites, Servin and Casanova, advocated a policy that by-passed the Socialists in favor of an entente with intellectuals, students, and an emerging new left at the same time they called for an internal relaxation of party controls. Thorez was to deal with them as he had with the similarly pro-Soviet Lecoeur in 1953–54.

Lecoeur was in trouble immediately upon Thorez's return. Duclos questioned his action in the Picasso portrait affair: "we can even ask ourselves whether the declaration [of the Secretariat] relative to a portrait by Picasso has not to an extent permitted our enemies to campaign among intellectuals whom they seek to turn away from us. . . ."[16] Duclos' comment implied self-criticism; it was elaborated upon in coming months until the consolidation of Thorez's control in the party was apparent. The softened party line on intellectual questions was accompanied by a cautious step toward the Socialists. During the municipal elections of April 1953, the PCF offered to facilitate the election of Socialists on the second ballot. Communists would support any Socialist accepting a minimum program that included a reduction in military expenses, the satisfaction of working-class demands, an end to the Vietnam war, the rejection of the Bonn-Paris agreements, and détente. Where the left was a majority, the Communists were prepared jointly to elect a mayor from whichever of the two parties held the most seats. But the Communists permitted no relaxation as yet in their rhetoric toward the Socialists: the Socialist leaders still profited from votes of honest workers to betray the working class and the national interest.[17]

Observers placed diverse interpretations on the party's policy turn after Thorez's return. Pierre Hervé, contrasting the PCF's attitude with more conciliatory statements made toward Social Democracy in Italy by Togliatti, saw Thorez's sectarianism drifting away from the policies of the USSR. Roger Pannequin called Thorez's first speech after three years away from France one of the best examples of sectarianism in PCF history, reaching a level of invective toward the Socialists unsurpassed in twenty years. But Pierre Grimaud observed that Thorez offered an olive branch to the Socialists on the same occasion, designating unity the "decisive question of the hour" and entente between leaderships both possible and desirable. For Grimaud, Thorez's return marked a "decisive transformation in the opposite direction," a real and durable transition to a conciliatory policy toward the Socialists after two years of oscillation.[18] The contradiction was more apparent than real. The PCF's sectarian resistance to de-Stalinization was, for Thorez, the condition of the party's political integration in France. Thorez was pursuing the only policy he understood, Front unique as a prelude to Front populaire, entente with Socialists on the local level as a prelude to entente with the Socialist leadership. In April 1953 Duclos explained Thorez's class-against-class tactics in the 1930's had been essential to establish the role of the working class as an independent force; that phase completed, the PCF was able to become the defender of democratic liberties. In June Thorez lauded unity and the Popular Front, which, he said, the Communists had initiated and animated. The June 1953 resolution of the PCF Central Committee explicitly called for a new Popular Front, recalling that unity had been created in 1934, despite Socialist objections, as a result of mass pressure.[19] The PCF desperately wanted unity with the Socialists, but the Socialists must rally to minimum Communist positions which were ipso facto the positions of the working class.

The issues upon which unity could be achieved were an end to the Vietnam war and satisfaction of trade-union demands. The PCF tried to form a coalition on both these questions during the abortive effort by Mendès-France to form a government in June 1953 and the strike wave of August. The party was reproached over these incidents. Critics charged its failure to support Mendès-France destroyed an opportunity to terminate the Vietnam war. By failing to capitalize on the strikes, the PCF allegedly missed an opportunity to achieve structural reforms.[20] In both crises the PCF was searching for the Stalinist mean, trying to negotiate the narrow path between the Scylla of opportunism and the Charybdis of sectarianism, with the usual result: immobility. In both cases the party argued that any attempt at precipitate action on its part would have been premature. *L'Humanité* regarded Mendès-France with suspicion; he had opposed the Vietnam war but supported the arch-conservative Paul Reynaud and was known as an advocate of constitutional revision, code words to the PCF for dictatorship. Yet on June 3 *L'Humanité* declared the investiture of Mendès-France "uncertain"; clearly, the party had not decided whether to make his majority possible. Parliamentary spokesman Jean Pronteau criticized Mendès-France for proposing a "reactionary" social program but asked clarifications of his foreign policy. "Will you take the initiative to negotiate with the Vietnamese?" Pronteau asked. The Communist party for its part would support any initiatives by the French government toward peace.[21]

The PCF refused to back Mendès-France because he did not provide the necessary guarantees. "You have recognized the seriousness of the illness from which France suffers," Duclos told him, "but you have not gone on to research the causes," explaining that the "Marshallization of France" was the culprit of the nation's ills. But the PCF was nearer to supporting Mendès-France than

Duclos implied. Replying to the Socialist *Le Populaire* after the crisis, *L'Humanité* noted that Mendès-France was unable to promise French departure from Indochina: "It is evident that if M. Mendès-France had promised to adopt this policy . . . a different situation would have resulted. That would not have failed to enter into our considerations, for the Communists have as a rule always to determine their conduct in relation to the essential problem of the moment."[22] The PCF appeared to say it would exercise independent judgment, based on considerations of French politics rather than Moscow, in deciding whether to support the government. Despite the conservative election results of 1951, developments in the National Assembly now offered the prospect of departure from the reflex negativism that characterized the PCF in recent years. With its general strategy fixed, the PCF had to make its tactical decisions in Paris if only because of the rapidity with which political crises occurred.

Attacks on the Socialists continued in the Communist press, but in the summer resurgence of labor unrest, the Communists saw the possibility of creating the necessary mass pressure on the Socialist leadership to make cooperation between the two parties possible. The August strikes began in the postal service among Socialist-leaning militants of Force Ouvrière; the issue was rumored deflationary decree laws under consideration by the Laniel government. The Communists quickly recalled unitary Socialist-Communist action in 1935 while the CGT, which had been seeking cooperation with Force Ouvrière and the CFTC since April, asked to be received by Laniel's office to negotiate a settlement. According to some sources the Communist union offered a return to work in exchange for government recognition on a par with the non-Communist unions, FO and CFTC. A transparent example of the Communists' desire for integration into the system, the offer was also a reflection of the labor organization's miscalculation of the meaning of the strikes.[23] By August 8, 2 million workers had left their jobs and enterprises in which the CGT was dominant among workers had been affected. Auguste Lecoeur castigated the Communist unions for their opportunism: they had failed to judge correctly the depth of working-class combativeness and discontent, missing an opportunity to strike "crushing blows" against the government.[24] Lecoeur very likely spoke for himself in this outburst: the PCF was caught without a response to the strikes. It could do no better than to associate with Socialist demands for a special session of parliament. In a letter addressed to "Comrade" Mollet the Communists suggested a joint initiative with the SFIO while the CGT extended the strikes to the construction industry, textiles, chemical plants, and ports as a means of insuring its control. Frachon demanded Laniel meet with the CGT and the other labor unions "in the image of what was done in 1936," when the Matignon agreements were signed. The Political Bureau expressed its full support of the strikes and condemned efforts at "political repression." The PCF demanded that parliament vote higher salaries for government workers and declared the strikes constituted popular rejection of the Marshall Plan and NATO.[25] At its peak the movement reached 4 million workers, the largest strike of its kind to date in French history.

Laniel refused to compromise with Communism. He would not receive the CGT but negotiated a return to work with FO and the CFTC on August 22, leaving the CGT no recourse but to denounce the other unions for their "treason." Meanwhile Assembly President Edouard Herriot stopped counting telegrams from Deputies when the total approached the statutory 206 required for a special session. The PCF protested but purely for public consumption. The National Assembly was due to convene in a month anyway, and its conservative majority was sure to stand firm against the strikers. The CGT called for a return to work on August 25, the same day the government released four prominent Communists it had been holding in custody, including Alain Le Léap and André Stil. André Marty and *Unir* saw a sordid arrangement but the two acts may have been mutual gestures of tacit good will: Marty was no longer in a position to know and *Unir* wasn't necessarily telling the truth.[26] Even as gestures of mutual forbearance, the coincidence made the August strike movement a milestone in the integration process.

But the attempt to recreate a Popular Front had momentarily failed. Unity at the base had been insufficient, the PCF said; but the Socialist leaders could still be made to cooperate, for "the idea of unity has become a material force by spreading among the masses."[27] Within days, however, another sudden shift in PCF policy took place: on September 12 the Political Bureau called for a front of struggle against ratification of the 1952 Bonn and Paris treaties instituting the European Defense Community. Front populaire again quickly gave way to Front national; the Peace Movement called upon its members to struggle against the treaties. Duclos told the Central Committee that the Communists were ready to unite with anyone to block the creation of a new Wehrmacht, once again an "essential problem of the moment." Unity between Communists and Socialists had been superceded: Thorez declared "Nothing is more important, nothing is more urgent, than the rallying of all good Frenchmen in order to defeat the Bonn-Paris agreements."[28] In an interview with the *Nouvel Observateur,* Thorez now referred to the abortive Front français of September 1936 rather than the Front populaire of June.

Thorez was perhaps helped to the conviction of the overriding importance of foreign policy by new Russian pressures. Soviet policy resumed a militant posture after the fall of Beria in July 1953. But the September 1953 shift to Front national came after a two-fold failure of the Popular Front in the Mendès-France episode and the August strikes. Internal rejection of the PCF's efforts at integration, as in the past, forced the party back toward the International Movement. Opposition to a new Wehrmacht was also a Jacobin-nationalist theme, popular with the PCF, the issue the Soviets had forced the party to abandon for the Five-Power Pact in 1951. Soviet and French concerns were now consonant from the PCF's point of view. Thorez was not conceding ground to the die-hard pro-Soviets in the Political Bureau, Duclos, Lecoeur, and Fajon, with the turn in policy. Thorez remained in control, as he made clear by ridding the party of his presumed heir apparent, Auguste Lecoeur.

The Lecoeur affair had been building since Thorez's return. Thorez's resentment of Lecoeur's ambitions was exacerbated by the latter's attack on Aragon and dogmatic implementation of the Soviet ideological line. Thorez opposed sectarianism on cultural matters; the cultural thaw in the USSR enabled him to follow his inclinations in France. Following Duclos' criticism of the Secretariat in the Picasso portrait affair, Thorez rehabilitated the French biologist and resister, Marcel Prenant, who had opposed Lysenko's theories. In July 1953 the Lysenko campaign was dropped, and Thorez remarked to intimates that Lecoeur had been seeking to bury him before he was dead.[29] Lecoeur suffered from his link to Beria, the removal of whom the PCF leadership celebrated along with the Russians in July. Lecoeur's explanation of his undoing was of interest: his problems, he said, began with Stalin's death. Having perceived the liberalization policies in the USSR, he advocated similar policies in France, becoming a Khrushchevite before his time. Lecoeur proposed to Thorez the democratization of PCF internal practice and an attenuation of the personality cult in the French party. He suggested Thorez permit militants to elect their leaders and cells be renamed "sections," bringing PCF practice in line with French working-class tradition.[30] Lecoeur's proposal to rename cells became one of the charges of "opportunism" later brought against him. Lecoeur may well have suggested liberalization in the PCF along the lines Beria implemented in the USSR before his death. Lecoeur always staked his future, as Duclos' lieutenant, on the correct anticipation of the Soviet line; if Beria's removal marked a return to more Stalinist practices in the USSR (with which Thorez was more comfortable), it was also the signal for Lecoeur's ouster in France.[31] Lecoeur angered Thorez in the anti-Zionist and socialist-realist campaigns; he now appeared the champion of an equally unwelcome liberalization. Not surprisingly, Lecoeur was charged with the dual evils of opportunism and sectarianism.

Lecoeur's downfall began at the Central Committee meeting of Drancy, in October 1953. Duclos reaffirmed the "correct" analysis of Billoux's article of May 1952 and warned that the self-criticism of the party leadership for the opportunist errors of 1952 had not been completed. There had been no examination of organizational problems which "one had believed could be resolved separately by methods which resulted in the abandonment of Leninist principles with regard to the functioning of the leadership of cells. . . ." Duclos was referring to the system of "political instructors" in the cells, which he and Lecoeur had implemented in 1952. In Stalinist fashion, Duclos now called upon Lecoeur to be the chief critic of his own policies. The system of political instructors, Lecoeur admitted, was an opportunist deviation and a violation of collective leadership.[32] It legitimized the creation of a category of members who paid dues, but were otherwise inactive, a violation of Section 2 of the party statutes according to which members of the PCF must participate actively in the life of the cells. Side-stepping the issue of his own responsibility, Lecoeur asked the Central Committee "to criticize us [the Political Bureau] without regard to personality." But François Billoux, who dealt with ideological questions at Drancy, criticized

Duclos and Lecoeur directly. Billoux also raised again the Picasso portrait affair, accusing Duclos of creating a false impression of the relationship between the Communist party leadership and its intellectuals. Following the Drancy meeting, Lecoeur offered his resignation as party Secretary for Organization, but for the moment it was refused. As Marcel Prenant had found out earlier, one never resigned high PCF functions; one was relieved of them at the party's pleasure.[33]

The Lecoeur affair dragged on until the PCF Thirteenth Congress in June 1954. Orchestrated by Thorez, it had two aims: making Lecoeur admit his errors and justifying the Thorez-Billoux line of 1952. Lecoeur was pressured but refused to "confess" and submit to a "trial" of the kind Marty and Tillon had undergone. Instead he wrote an article condemning the device of "political instructors" in cells but again omitted his role in implementing the policy.[34] If Thorez wanted more than that, Lecoeur said, then the Communist leader must recognize the opportunism explicit in his slogan of 1947, calling for a party "counted in the millions." The use of political instructors, Lecoeur claimed, had been sanctioned by practices in the People's Democracies, approved by the PCF Political Bureau, and in line with Thorez's earlier policies. Thorez used the Lecoeur affair to humiliate Duclos and Fajon and establish who had been right and wrong in the confusing events of 1952. As a by-product of the process, Thorez emerged in undisputed control of the PCF, able to lead it in a direction opposed to the desires of the USSR.

The public indictment of Lecoeur took place at the Central Committee meeting of Arcueil in March 1954. Lecoeur refused to attend; Thorez also stayed away, leaving the unpleasant work to his subordinates. Lecoeur was replaced as Secretary for Organization by Thorez's personal aide, Marcel Servin. Duclos explained the change to the assembled delegates, charging that "serious deviations" had existed in party organizational work since 1952.[35] Lecoeur had dealt with these deviations in an impersonal way, masking his responsibility for the party's opportunist errors. Lecoeur had spread the noxious idea that the party was "isolated," reducing it tactically to a supporting role for one or another of the quarreling factions of the bourgeoisie. At the same time he established activist minorities, a clear example of sectarianism, adventurism, and the un-Leninist "cult of spontaneity." Lecoeur's proposal to suppress the term "cell" was a clear example of "liquidationism." He had sought to promote his own followers to positions of power and built his organizational apparatus into a substitute for the party's regular organs of authority. In Duclos' analysis, Lecoeur was nothing less than an aspiring French Stalin.

Billoux attributed to Lecoeur the blame for the party's twists, turns, and defeats in 1952. The article of May 1952 was correct; the demonstration against Ridgeway was the "honor of the proletariat." Duclos, who had sabotaged the demonstration, and Fajon, who had later criticized it and the Billoux article, were both clearly in the wrong. According to Billoux, Lecoeur committed two grievous errors in 1952. First, on his own authority, he ordered the abortive general strike of February 12, 1952, "against the will of the Political Bureau," in a violation of collective leadership. Second, following Duclos' arrest, Lecoeur "monopolized the leadership" of the party and diverted it onto the path of becoming a mere auxiliary source of support for a faction of the bourgeoisie.[36] Duclos was clearly implicated in Billoux's charges; Billoux left no doubt when he condemned the attempted strike of June 4, 1952, aimed at securing Duclos' release.

Several Central Committee members who had worked closely with Lecoeur were forced to condemn him and their prior association with his actions. André Stil, recipient of the Stalin prize for literature, arose to condemn Lecoeur's *ouvrieriste* popular demogogy in the domain of cultural affairs. Conspicuous by his absence, however, was René Camphin, Lecoeur's close associate in the Pas-de-Calais federation of the party and the Resistance. Camphin was found dead in his room the night before; the party's version of his death, accepted by the police, attributed it to an accident. Camphin went to sleep with a gas heater on; somehow, the flame had been extinguished causing him to die of asphyxiation.[37] Camphin was a Deputy, member of the Central Committee, and secretary of the Pas-de-Calais federation (which Lecoeur was now also charged with disrupting). He also had a major role in the party's post-war plans for clandestine organization in the event of political suppression. Former members of the PCF believed he committed suicide or was murdered.[38] Camphin was revolted by the prospect of publicly testifying against Lecoeur and had terminal cancer. But his family ties and stubborn independent spirit made suicide unlikely. He also possessed unspecified secrets, compromising for the party, which he may have threatened to divulge if forced to join in Lecoeur's denunciation. The gas meter was located in the hall; a simple closing and reopening of the switch would have sufficed to put out the flame, allowing gas to permeate the room. The last person to see Camphin alive was Central Committee member Roger Roucaute, who also discovered his body. Roucaute allegedly participated in the attempt on Guingouin's life and ironically had just published a denunciation of the "reactionary" press exploitation of "shameful acts" that occurred in the Limousin after the war, with which he insisted the Resistance had nothing to do.[39]

Lecoeur was not expelled from the PCF until 1955, following the publication of his *Auto-critique attendue,* in which he openly attacked the policies of the leadership. He became active in the Socialist party, then joined the Gaullists. He polemicized against the party throughout his subsequent career but always regarded certain subjects as off-limits. Of the party's real relationship to the USSR he revealed next to nothing. He acknowledged the existence of various scandals in party history analogous to the Camphin affair, but refused to provide details. His silence, a characteristic shared by other ex-Communists, could have stemmed from a tacit agreement with the leadership, although exposure of the less attractive aspects of party history would have damaged Lecoeur's reputation as well. Lecoeur may also have feared for his life; an alleged attempt to kill him occurred at a Socialist meeting during which he was scheduled to speak at Henin-Liétard in 1956.[40]

Camphin's death demonstrated the serious nature of the upheaval occurring among the PCF's leadership. The crisis involved a final confrontation between Thorez and the faction led by Duclos and Fajon. After losing their closest collaborator, Duclos and Fajon were forced to undertake a more thorough self-criticism than any they had previously done. The new organizational secretary, Marcel Servin, raised the question of Duclos' shortcomings shortly after the Central Committee meeting. Lecoeur's deviant reform came from the Secretariat, Servin said, despite the opposition of the Political Bureau; Duclos, as head of the Secretariat in 1952, shared responsibility with Lecoeur.[41] In December 1952 the party had repudiated its opportunist line, but Lecoeur continued his "Menshevik" policies in organizational work even after he was criticized and "unmasked" by Thorez at Drancy (October 1953). According to Servin, then, Thorez, after his return to France in April 1953, was unable to have his views prevail in the party. On organizational questions and cultural affairs Lecoeur, backed by Duclos, retained control for some months after Thorez's return. Waldeck Rochet, a close personal associate of Thorez, explained that Lecoeur implemented his independent policies by means of the creation of a separate organizational apparatus, the network of political instructors, which usurped the powers of the Political Bureau.[42]

In reasserting his control of the party, Thorez promoted his personality cult, notwithstanding the emphasis on "collective leadership" in the USSR, and claimed a role as theorist in the International Communist Movement once reserved only to Stalin. In March 1954 he repudiated the self-criticism he had done in 1947. It was not opportunism that had been at fault but the policy shift of 1947. The party's handling of the strikes of 1947 and 1948 had been riddled with errors because of Lecoeur, who repeated those errors again in the failed attempt at a general strike on February 12, 1952. The Central Committee emphasized Thorez's infallibility in its birthday message to the Communist leader on April 28, 1954: "With your help and under your leadership," the message declared, "the party corrects its insufficiencies, its errors, its mistakes, which were facilitated by the illness that struck you."[43]

Thorez must have orchestrated the series of criticisms directed at Duclos and Fajon that appeared in the "tribune" column of *L'Humanité* prior to the Thirteenth Congress. The articles were unusual in their frankness and may well be without parallel in the rest of party history. On May 18, 1954, the "Ernst Thaelmann cell" asked how Duclos could have blamed Lecoeur alone for the mistaken attempt at a general strike in February 1952. Why had the Political Bureau not reacted? How could Lecoeur's errors have been allowed to go on for so long? Other articles asked why there had been no resistance among the leadership to Lecoeur's disastrous policies. Fajon responded on May 31: "I think that the reproach that has been made to us is well-founded, and that our self-criticism has not yet really been undertaken."[44] Lecoeur's errors should have been exposed much earlier; by failing to do so the leadership had facilitated Lecoeur's harmful actions. Fajon was further embarrassed, he said by his justification of the February 12, 1952, strike and found the re-reading of his article in *L'Humanité* "a painful experience."

Raymond Guyot admitted he had been too timid to challenge Lecoeur; in the aftermath of Thorez's illness the Political Bureau as a whole had been prevented from fulfilling its role properly. Fajon, Guyot charged, seized control of the party with Lecoeur after Jacques Duclos' arrest and led it into its deviationist course. Under the guidance of Maurice Thorez, the deviation was exposed in December 1952. But in 1953 the lesson was only assimilated mechanically and errors persisted until Lecoeur was finally eliminated at the Central Committee meeting of Arcueil in March 1954.

In the same article as his criticism of Fajon and Lecoeur, Guyot noted the errors of a little-known party official from the fifteenth section of Paris, Georges Marchais. Marchais, a trade-union leader in the Citroen plant, was criticized for his part in the April 25, 1954, attempted twenty-four hour general strike. The strike was a failure, and Frachon was forced to repudiate it at the forthcoming Thirteenth Party Congress in June. Marchais, who had only been a member of the PCF since 1947, had risen sufficiently in importance so that along with Lecoeur and Fajon, he was chastised by Guyot for advocating the theory of spontaneity and neglecting mass action. Marchais did his self-criticism and eventually overcame his association with Lecoeur, as well as his cloudy past during the war, to rise rapidly in party ranks; how he did so is not understood.[45] But the legacy of the factional disputes characterizing this period remained with him throughout his career. Marchais remained cool toward Thorez, renaming the Maurice Thorez Institute the Center of Marxist Research in 1979. He kept Fajon as a member of the Political Bureau through the 1970's, sponsored Jacques Duclos as the party's presidential candidate in 1969, and retired Billoux and Guyot from the Political Bureau at the Nineteenth Party Congress in 1972, when Marchais was confirmed as the PCF's Secretary-General. Marchais was Lecoeur's successor in Duclos' affections; arriving on the scene later, he succeeded in rising to the party leadership where Lecoeur failed. Lecoeur's resentment of Marchais' success could have fueled the offensive Lecoeur carried on for a decade over Marchais' murky past.

Guyot virtually admitted publicly that the events of 1952 were the consequence of a hidden struggle for leadership. Internal struggles in the PCF were also noted by observers at the time. Yet the existence of such conflict remains to be accepted by modern historians, who, riveted on the functioning of democratic centralism in theory, ignore how the system worked in practice. Even for Gramsci, the Leninist (Stalinist) party was the Modern Prince, arising under capitalism and reflecting the need of capitalist man to both rule and be ruled. Struggles for power must necessarily, then, occur within it. Not permitted to occur openly between organized factions, power struggles in Communist parties remained hidden, appearing later to observers as unexplained and obscure shifts in the party line. The defeated faction later paid by self-criticism or, as the case demanded, expulsion. The PCF Congress of Ivry in June 1954 saw the resolution of the PCF's internal struggle and the consolidation of Thorez's control.

The retrospective analyses of the events of 1952–53 and the Lecoeur affair were repeated at great length at the June Party Congress. Duclos' admission of his errors was remarkable. Accepting criticisms raised in the "tribune" column of *L'Humanité,* Duclos noted the Central Committee and the Political Bureau should have blocked Lecoeur's errors before Thorez's return. The leadership had not displayed the necessary vigilance; opportunism dominated the party, leading to a deviation from the line of the Twelfth Congress of 1950. "We must not be surprised," Duclos said, "that at every aggravation of the class struggle different divergent currents manifest themselves in the ranks of the working class, and that (these) cannot fail to have their extension in the interior of our party."[46] Like Guyot, Duclos publicly admitted the existence of internal conflict.

A document extant in the archives of Angelo Tasca at the Feltrinelli Foundation in Milan describes the dramatic resolution of the PCF's internal struggle at the Thirteenth Party Congress. The events in question allegedly occurred at the meeting of the party's "Political Committee" which convened to ratify the choice of candidates for leadership. The anonymous author was a police agent, informed by circles close to Léon Feix, head of the PCF's colonial section since the ouster of André Marty; his accuracy in personal details lends plausibility to the events recounted. The document contains exaggeration and apparently invented dialogue; it is cited here as confirmation of how the existence of internal conflict in the PCF impressed itself on astute and well-informed observers in 1954.[47] Even if the events described never occurred, they remain plausible imaginative reconstructions of what did.

According to the account, in a long, stormy, and unprecedented session of the Political Committee, Duclos and Billoux confronted one another angrily, each admitting his personal dislike. Both eventually did their "self-criticism," but only Duclos' was substantive. The two leaders were reconciled after Thorez resolved their dispute in favor of Billoux. Billoux's only fault, Thorez said, was that after he correctly perceived the necessary line to follow in 1952 and was implored by some party leaders to stand firm, he failed to stick to his position. As a result, the party had been allowed to lapse into opportunism. Thorez was liberal with reproach: the leadership as a whole, during his absence, had been unworthy; the Political Bureau, preoccupied with his succession, was unable to prevent the opportunist victory. Thorez held Duclos chiefly responsible and regretted that while ill, he allowed Duclos to influence him. Duclos, Lecoeur, and Fajon became fascinated by the parliamentary game and the possibility of partial agreements with segments of the French bourgeoisie, reducing the PCF to the status of an auxiliary source of support for one or another of the bourgeois parties and neglecting the leading role of the working class. The quest for unity "at the base" was ignored and the working class demoralized. Had Lecoeur the courage to defend himself at the Congress, Thorez said, he would have admitted he acted in league with Duclos. Finally, Thorez noted, Fajon's responsibility was substantial as well. Hopeful of succeeding Thorez, Fajon attached himself to Duclos, the stronger figure in the conflict. Fajon led in the criticism of Billoux, even after realizing Billoux's ideas were correct. Following Thorez's analysis

Duclos and Fajon proceeded to do their self-criticisms. Fajon admitted to ideological weaknesses, engaging in a personal vendetta against Billoux and being unworthy to serve in the Secretariat. Satisfied with Duclos' and Fajon's performance, Thorez then reappointed them to the Secretariat along with Billoux and Marcel Servin. Balance was restored on the Secretariat between advocates of the sectarian and opportunist lines, with Thorez now in a position to arbitrate.

Two further examples of conflict emerged in public view at the Congress. CGT leader Benoît Frachon condemned the twenty-four-hour general strike of April 28, 1954, and Louis Aragon restated the PCF's position on cultural problems, repudiating the vulgar Zhdanovian socialist-realism championed by Lecoeur. Frachon, like Duclos, was untouchable by virtue of his wartime role, expertise, and talents in trade-union leadership. He resisted personal involvement in the cult of Thorez and tried to insulate the CGT from the conflict occurring in the PCF leadership.[48] The counterpart of Frachon's quest for relative autonomy for the CGT was a constant effort toward unity with FO and CFTC, evident since 1951, and resistance to the politicization of strikes. Frachon supported Duclos' opportunist line. In the spring of 1954 the CGT launched a plan for a twenty-four-hour general strike for a minimum wage of 25,166 francs. The strike was set for April 28; by the time it took place economic demands were eclipsed by the campaign against the European army and support of the Geneva negotiations on Indochina.[49] The strike was ignored by most workers despite long and methodical preparation. Frachon, like Duclos, found himself charged with opportunism; at the Congress, he admitted the CGT had failed to link working-class economic demands with European rearmament and colonial repression. Frachon linked the April 28, 1954, strike to the "errors" of Lecoeur and resolved to pay greater attention to the political context of strike action in the future, in other words, to coordinate his policies with Thorez and not Duclos.[50]

Having asserted his control over trade-union policy, Thorez turned his attention to cultural questions. Aragon soundly condemned Lecoeur's crude Zhdanovism as an example of the cult of spontaneity, sectarian adventurism, and liquidationism. There was a relationship between artistic creation and the working class. But the party could only define a tendency; it was up to the artist to translate directives into cultural reality. Party art was possible, but it must not be sectarian, vulgar, schematic, or crudely declarative, nor could it be confused with individual works by party members; one could be in the PCF and still not do party art (presumably like Picasso). Lecoeur had opposed form to content and condemned emphasis on form alone as decadent. This was contrary to Marxism; form and content were interrelated. Even an abstract work of art, devoid of form, might express class content. Hardly a charter of complete cultural freedom, Aragon's strictures represented the more tolerant and sophisticated approach to cultural questions of Thorez.

Aragon's manifesto of cultural affairs was followed by a reorganization in the staff of the PCF's ideological weekly *France Nouvelle*. Editor Florimond Bonte was hostile to the Thorez-Billoux line; on November 3, 1954, Duclos pointed out the need for "improvement" in *France Nouvelle,* which carried an insufficient number of articles on the party's internal life. Waldeck Rochet and Marcel Servin linked *France Nouvelle* to the Duclos-Fajon-Lecoeur trio: there had been "gross errors" in the content of the PCF weekly, which had to be corrected as part of the party's struggle against opportunism. A new editorial committee was appointed, including Fernand Dupuy, another personal associate of Maurice Thorez.[51] Thorez thus consolidated his personal control at the Thirteenth Party Congress over the party's cultural policy, trade unions, and the press.

Unlike the Twelfth Party Congress of 1950 few personnel changes were necessary in 1954. The Secretariat was expanded; Marty and Lecoeur were replaced by Billoux, Servin, and Fajon, who joined Thorez and Duclos. Victor Michaut, editor of *Cahiers du Communisme* and an associate of Duclos, was eliminated from the Political Bureau, as were the disgraced Marty, Tillon, and Lecoeur. Promoted in their place were Léon Feix, head of the party's colonial section, Georges Frischmann, head of the postal division of the CGT, and Marcel Servin. The others continued in their functions: those eliminated from the Central Committee included three close associates of Lecoeur, Roger Pannequin, Theo Vial, and Joseph Legrand. Marius Patinaud, who had been Undersecretary of Labor in 1946–47, also lost his position on the Central Committee, allegedly for having hidden his disagreement with the Nazi-Soviet pact in 1939.[52] If so, this would have been the final laying to rest of closet skeletons from the war years.

The consolidation of Thorez's control and settlement of the party's internal factional disputes were accompanied by the most far-reaching attempt since 1947 to achieve a re-insertion of the PCF into French political life. The PCF had passed a milestone in its quest for unity; it now gave full attention to the pursuit of integration. The effort was consistent with Soviet foreign policy. The USSR wanted the French parliament to reject the European Defense Community. Thorez resorted to traditional Stalinist tactics; having defeated his rivals, he became the ardent champion of their policies, placing Front national over Front populaire. Thorez was not necessarily bowing to Soviet pressure: independent agreement existed between his Stalinist chauvinism and Soviet ties. Indeed, Thorez opposed the USSR's de-Stalinization in 1954 as he tried to integrate the PCF, on the issues of Indochina and the EDC, into France's governing majority. Had Thorez been successful in these efforts, the result could only have been as in 1946, even further independence and differentiation of the party from the USSR.

The potential for disagreement was revealed in a minor incident over a *Pravda* article, published by *L'Humanité* on December 11, 1953, and intended to encourage French assertiveness in foreign affairs. *Pravda* applauded French efforts to restore French independence and "*grandeur,*" noted progress toward independence from the USA, and commented favorably on statements hostile to the EDC by Herriot and de Gaulle. André Stil noted the "exceptional importance" of the *Pravda* article; the USSR supported great power status for France while the Americans sought to diminish its prestige. During the next few days, however,

Stil found himself under attack.[53] The *Pravda* article was not to be interpreted as favorable to the economic policies of French governments since the war; growth had been at the expense of an exploited proletariat whose condition worsened. The inherent tension between Soviet approval of French foreign policy and PCF efforts to remain a party of opposition, characteristic of the 1970's, was already present in 1954.

In December 1953 PCF deputies supported Socialist Marcel Naegelen in the presidential election for a successor to Vincent Auriol. PCF support for Naegelen remained unflagging through twelve National Assembly ballots, until conservative René Coty secured a majority. Naegelen was an Alsatian nationalist on the right wing of the Socialist party. He previously distinguished himself as Resident-General in Algeria by manipulating elections and repressing Muslim nationalism. But the PCF overlooked Naegelen's past because he was hostile to the EDC and in the interest of facilitating unity with Socialist workers.[54] In *France Observateur,* Claude Bourdet noted the presidential election encouraged the PCF to participate in parliamentary politics; the party denied it needed encouragement. In January the PCF provided the votes necessary to elect the Socialist, André Le Troquer, President of the National Assembly, over a supporter of the EDC, Pierre Pflimlin. Le Troquer was also a right-Socialist who caused a scandal during the 1946 elections by charging Thorez with desertion. But the party knew that neither Naegelen nor Le Troquer were "lovers of Communism"; in voting for them, it facilitated unity with the Socialists while opposing the EDC. The PCF noted approvingly Jacques Fauvet's observation in *Le Monde* that it had been readmitted into the parliamentary club. PCF backing in the Assembly was no longer likely to be refused.[55]

The PCF was careful in its approach to the anti-EDC campaign and opposition to the Vietnam war. These two issues dominated French politics in the spring of 1954; observers noted of the EDC that passion was on the side of its adversaries and reason with its defenders. But the PCF eschewed the more demagogic aspects the debate often assumed.[56] For the Communists, the EDC was an American-sponsored plan to rearm Germany as an anti-Communist bastion, revengeful advocate of aggression against the USSR, and vehicle for American domination of Europe. But the party refused to repeat the false charges that the treaty contained secret annexes providing for German domination of French military strategy. The party's position on Indochina provided an instructive parallel. Left-wing critics regularly accused the PCF of having sacrificed the anti-colonial struggle on the altar of Soviet security needs in Europe. Such views ignored the extent to which German rearmament offended the PCF's own native Stalinist-Chauvinist sentiments and failed to evaluate the PCF's anti-colonial sentiments accurately. Since 1934 the PCF had never unconditionally supported the aspirations of colonial peoples for independence. On Indochina the PCF had repeated with monotonous regularity since 1946 that negotiations and peace did not mean the end of Franco-Vietnamese ties. On the contrary, a negotiated settlement offered the best means of providing for a new and lasting relationship based on reciprocal equality, including economic and cultural links, within the framework of the French Union.

In the spring of 1954, the drama of Dien Bien Phu drove the issue of the EDC off the front pages. *L'Humanité* again avoided demagogy, took no satisfaction in the French defeat, and only decried the spillage of blood. The PCF enthusiastically supported French attendance at the Geneva conference on April 26, denounced the responsibility of Georges Bidault and his collaborators for seven years of useless war, and declared it would support any sincere efforts for peace.[57] At the Thirteenth Party Congress, Thorez's cloture speech defined three great national imperatives of French foreign policy: rejection of the EDC, peace in Indochina, and European security. With the satisfaction of working-class demands and the defense of democratic liberties these foreign-policy goals comprised a coherent total program. "The Congress has confirmed," Thorez said, "that the Communists are always ready to support, in Parliament or in the country, any effective step forward, any disposition conforming to the interests of the working class, to the interests of the people, to the interest of peace."[58]

The party's support of Mendès-France's successful attempt to form a government in June 1954 followed logically. The PCF hoped to become part of the emerging new majority, one of the pillars upon which a government of peace must stand. "In voting for you," Billoux told Mendès-France in the National Assembly, "we are giving you the possibility to translate words into acts and bring peace to Indochina."[59] Comprising part of Mendès-France's majority was intended as a dramatic consummation, a successful resolution for Thorez of a long period of struggle simultaneously to reassert his control over the PCF and achieve its reintegration into French political life while preserving its Stalinist purity in ideology and organization. Political realities blocked Thorez's hopes in 1954. Mendès-France refused to count Communist votes in his majority; if forced to rely on the Communists, he declared, he would rather resign. The party protested that Mendès-France's attitude toward the PCF was not the issue, but peace; the PCF's votes counted whether Mendès-France thought so or not. But the party was disappointed and never forgave Mendès-France his insult. The new government resolved two of the PCF's most pressing concerns, Indochina and the EDC. But Mendès-France would not offer an opportunity for integration of the PCF into French politics. Even on these two issues, the romance was short-lived. The Indochina peace gave only a respite of a few months until rebellion flared anew in Algeria and rejection of the EDC was followed by the immediate negotiation of new agreements providing for German rearmament in a non-integrated format. But the PCF did not stop trying. It sought a way into the majority on Algeria as on Indochina. The party's attitude on colonial questions cogently revealed the depth of the PCF's aspirations to share in a kind of consensus with the French political elite. With the outbreak of the Algerian war, the relationship between Communism and decolonization became a central issue in French politics.

NOTES

1. *Cahiers du Communisme,* 1 (January 1953).
2. *L'Humanité,* January 14, February 2, 1953. Garaudy remains more troubled by this article than anything else he ever wrote: personal interview, September 11, 1980.
3. Ibid., February 14, 18, 1953. Rosenfeld was not Jewish.
4. *Cahiers du Communisme,* 2 (February 1953). Annie Besse is now the noted historian, Annie Kriegel.
5. Pierre Hervé, *Dieu et César, sont-ils Communistes?* (Paris, 1956), 45.
6. The articles appeared in *Ce Soir* from January 27 to February 6, 1953.
7. Dr. Pierre Klotz, personal interview, September 18, 1980. Blanchette Gillet, personal interview, April 11, 1980.
8. Philippe Robrieux, *Maurice Thorez, vie secrète et vie publique* (Paris, 1975), 412.
9. *L'Humanité,* March 9, 1953; *France Nouvelle,* March 9, 1953.
10. *L'Humanité,* March 18, 1953. For a full analysis see Pierre Daix, *Aragon: une vie à changer* (Paris, 1975), 371–76.
11. Philippe Robrieux notes Duclos' link to Beria as the probable source of his power: *Histoire intérieure du PCF,* II (Paris, 1981), 337–45.
12. *L'Humanité,* April 6, 8, 1953.
13. Ibid., April 8, 1953. Daix, *Aragon,* 380.
14. A. Lecoeur, *L'Autocritique attendue* (Paris, 1955), 8–12.
15. *L'Humanité,* March 9, 1953.
16. Ibid., May 8, 1953.
17. Ibid., April 28, 30, 1953.
18. Pierre Hervé, *Lettre à Sartre* (Paris, 1956), 36–38; Roger Pannequin, *Adieu Camarades* (Paris, 1975); Pierre Grimaud, *Nous avons payé trop cher* (Paris, n.d.), 90–91.
19. *Cahiers du Communisme,* 4 (April 1953), 6–7 (June-July 1953).
20. André Marty, *L'Affaire Marty* (Paris, 1956), 130–34.
21. *L'Humanité,* May 29, June 3, June 4, 1953.
22. Ibid., June 5, 11, 1953.
23. Georgette Elgey, *La République des contradictions* (Paris, 1968), 151–68. *L'Humanité,* August 6, 18, 1953.
24. *L'Humanité,* August 10, 1953.
25. Ibid., August 26, 1953.
26. Archives André Marty, Reel 22, memo dated September 16, 1953. *Unir,* October 1953. See also *L'Humanité,* August 25, 1953.
27. *Cahiers du Communisme,* Editorial 7–8 (July-August 1953).
28. *L'Humanité,* September 11, 12, 1953; October 5, 23, 24, 1953.
29. Louis Couturier, *Les "Grandes affaires" du PCF* (Paris, 1972), 58.
30. Auguste Lecoeur *Le PCF: Continuité dans le changement* (Paris, 1977), 157–58. Personal interview, July 12, 1978. Lecoeur denied any personal link to Beria, but attributed such a connection to Duclos.
31. Isaac Deutscher, *Russia in Transition* (London, 1953) speculated that Beria, paradoxically, headed the liberal faction responsible for exonerating the doctors.
32. *L'Humanité,* October 23, 26, 28, 1953.
33. Lecoeur, *L'Autocritique attendue,* 23. Marcel Prenant, *Toute une vie à gauche* (Paris, 1980), 293.
34. *Cahiers du Communisme,* 1 (January 1954). Personal interview, July 12, 1978.

35. *Cahiers du Communisme,* 3 (March 1954).

36. *L'Humanité,* March 9, 1954.

37. Ibid., March 8, 1954.

38. Roger Pannequin asserted Camphin was murdered; Lecoeur believed it was a suicide. Personal interviews, May 2, July 12, 1978. See also Robrieux, *Histoire intérieure,* II, 360–62.

39. *L'Humanité,* February 20, 1954. On the Guingouin affair see Chapter 7.

40. Auguste Lecoeur, *Le Partisan* (Paris, 1963).

41. *L'Humanité,* March 25, 1954.

42. Ibid., March 31, 1954.

43. Ibid., March 26, April 28, 1954.

44. Ibid., May 17, 18, 31, 1954.

45. See *Est et Ouest,* April 1–30, 1980; Nicolas Tandler, *L'Impossible biographie de Georges Marchais* (Paris, 1980); Auguste Lecoeur, *Stratégie de mensonge* (Paris, 1980).

46. *L'Humanité,* June 3, 1954.

47. The document is untitled and undated. See Fonde Angelo Tasca (Fondazione Feltrinelli), Carton 165, Folder marked "XIII Congress of PCF." Tasca integrated the document into his own analysis of the Thirteenth Congress. I have discussed it with various witnesses and received partial confirmations of the veracity of its contents.

48. Angelo Tasca, "Le XIIIᵉ Congrès, la situation, la politique, la tactique et les perspectives du PCF," *Fonde Angelo Tasca,* 165. *BEIPI* (July 1954), *Unir* (April 1956), Pannequin, interview.

49. *L'Humanité,* April 28–30, 1954.

50. *Cahiers du Communisme,* 6–7 (June-July, 1954).

51. *L'Humanité,* November 3, 1954.

52. See *BEIPI,* July 1954.

53. *L'Humanité,* December 11, 12, 18, 1953.

54. Ibid., December 19–25, 1953.

55. Ibid., December 31, 1953; January 13, 14, 1954.

56. See Elgey, *La République des contradictions,* 260–338; also John Marcus, *Neutralism and Nationalism in France* (New York, 1954).

57. *L'Humanité,* May 12, 13, 1954.

58. *Cahiers du Communisme,* 6–7 (June-July 1954).

59. *L'Humanité,* June 12–18, 1954.

9
COMMUNISM AND DECOLONIZATION

Communism and decolonization account for many twentieth-century political upheavals. After World War II, France became a domestic battleground for these forces: the French absorbed one of the largest Communist parties in the non-Communist world while losing one of the greatest colonial empires. The relationship between these two processes has received increased scrutiny from historians in recent years, and some long-held views have been revised. Alfred Grosser argued Communism and decolonization created a double cleavage in French politics under the Fourth Republic; a powerful, dictatorial, political force challenged the system while violent anti-colonial movements erupted abroad, rendering a liberal colonial policy unworkable and leading to ministerial instability, drift, and collapse of the regime.[1] But the political elite of the Fourth Republic lacked neither a consensus nor a policy on colonial issues. The consensus held that if France was to avoid a future of diminished prestige and growing decadence, it must retain its colonial possessions.[2] The policy of forcible opposition to movements of colonial independence was systematically pursued by a majority ranging from the Mollet Socialists to the extreme right. It was not, as de Gaulle later claimed, the lack of a policy that undermined the regime. The Fourth Republic collapsed from the determined implementation of a policy of colonial repression.

The French Communists dissented from the regime's policy, but they did not challenge the consensus. They cannot be held responsible for the regime's collapse. The PCF used the decolonization issue to achieve integration into the political system; by May 1958 the Communists were the Fourth Republic's most loyal defenders. Left-wing critics attacked the PCF's abandonment of the eighth condition of 1919 Comintern membership, according to which Communists must unconditionally support all national liberation movements.[3] But the Comintern dictum was rarely relevant to actual PCF behavior; colonial issues remained a minor priority among Communist concerns. The PCF leadership shared the colonial myth that indissoluble ties bound France to its overseas possessions. The party revived a modified anti-colonial rhetoric in difficult periods like 1939–41 and 1949–52, but its turn to Jacobin rhetoric in the 1930's was definitive.[4] At the PCF Congress of Arles in December 1937 Thorez told colonial peoples of the French empire that their interests were best served by union with France, where liberty and racial equality still were protected.[5] The PCF resurrected the same policy in the immediate post-World War II period: the United States replaced the Axis as the imminent threat to colonial peoples unfortunate enough to slip away from French protection. Among French parties, the Communists had the "most soundly humanist position on colonial questions"; they "alone recognized early the kind of flexibility a successful post-war imperial policy must possess."[6] The PCF recognized the self-defeating nature of the forceful policy consistently deduced by other parties, including the Socialists, from the colonial consensus. Within the context of the era, Communist policy was farsighted. It was not sufficiently so to save the Fourth Republic, but the Communists bore less responsibility than any of the other parties for the Republic's collapse.

In the absence of Soviet interest in the fate of the French empire, PCF colonial theory developed pragmatically and autonomously, taking into account the French colonial myth and the constitutional mechanism of the Union française. The PCF remained Leninist: imperialism was the monopoly-stage of capitalism, and Communists supported the right of all peoples to self-determination. But general principles had to bend in the face of historic circumstances. The separation of colonies from the ruling country, far from always being a progressive solution, was the exception rather than the rule. "The right to divorce," as Lenin said, "was not the obligation to divorce."[7] History made natural mates of France and its overseas territories; organic ties were strengthened by the common struggle of the French working class and the colonial peoples against monopoly capitalism. Emancipation of colonial peoples and social progress in the metropole were related questions. France and its territories faced common questions "posed by history," soluble only by continued association and regular contact.

French tutelage was essential until the colonies were prepared for independent, equal association with the metropole. The PCF accepted the four-fold categorization between overseas departments and territories and associated territories and states, written into the constitution of the Fourth Republic and the French Union. The PCF advocated departmental status for France's oldest colonies, Martinique, Guadeloupe, and Réunion; they shared the historical experience of the French Revolution, and their tiny size precluded independence. The party designated black Africa for overseas territorial status because of its low level of industrial development and national consciousness. While deserving locally elected territorial assemblies, black nationalism did not warrant the degree of autonomy thought suitable for North Africa as associated territories: full local autonomy with freely elected Assemblies and governments, but foreign policy and defense excluded from their competence. The Communists reserved the highest category of associated state, denoting equal and independent status within the French Union, for Vietnam. The Vietnamese earned self-government during their struggle against the Japanese; theirs was the homeland of an ancient and great people and a distinguished civilization.[8]

Communist party organization in the French Union became a corollary of colonial classification. The overseas departments had regular sections of the PCF.

Tunisia, Morocco, and Algeria had independent Communist parties under the close supervision of the PCF, which had founded them. The Algerian Communist party became formally independent in 1936 but it was advised by André Marty until 1952.[9] In black Africa the PCF preferred to work through the national bourgeoisie in the Rassemblement Démocratique Africain, while organizing Communist study groups for the instruction and training of local intellectuals. An indigenous Communist party had long existed in Vietnam; Ho Chi Minh had been a founding member of the PCF, a fact to which the PCF, however, rarely referred. By 1946 contacts between the two parties were scant and relations not the best, complicating matters when the Indochina war broke out.

The ultimate goal was national self-determination, but "fraternal union" with the metropole would continue as long as it was "freely consented to." The PCF occasionally cited the constitution of the USSR as a model, but insisted upon two crucial differences: France would inevitably decolonize before it achieved socialism, rendering the Soviet solution inapplicable in the short run, and because France and its overseas territories were not contiguous in territory, new forms of association would evolve in the socialist future.[10] The colonial question thus buttressed the general theoretical argument, often stated by Thorez in 1946 and 1947 and again after 1956: France did not have to repeat the experience of the USSR or the People's Democracies, but could find its own unique way to Socialism.

The PCF did not expect an independent Vietnamese state to be viable in 1945, fearing it would fall under American influence. The Political Bureau limited itself to taking note of the Vietnamese declaration of independence in September 1945 and qualified its expression of support with the understanding that Vietnam would enter the "democratic family of the French Union." The PCF supported the dispatch of French troops to Indochina in 1945 while Moscow did not comment on Vietnamese developments until February 1946.[11] Harold Isaacs found the Vietnamese cynical about the Russians and suspicious of the PCF. The French Communists, he was told, "are Frenchmen and colonialists first and Communists after. In principle they are for us, but in practice? Oh, that is quite another thing." The PCF warned the Vietnamese against any "premature adventures" and advised patience until the growing influence of the party in metropolitan France brought about a favorable settlement in the colonies.[12] The Vietnamese accepted this advice for a trial period but angered the French by dissolving the Communist party of Indochina into a broader grouping of nationalist forces, violating Duclos' warnings against Browderism.[13] The Vietnamese became impatient with the PCF's liberal colonial policy during 1946. The PCF rallied to the March 6, 1946, agreements, in which Ho Chi Minh accepted independence within the framework of the French Union, but reacted with only verbal condemnation when the French government violated the accords in July. The PCF did not comment during the bombardment of Haiphong in November 1946, and when open warfare erupted in December 1946-January 1947, relations between the two parties collapsed, not to be resumed until 1949.[14] In December 1946 the

PCF rallied to Blum's ominous warning that order must be restored prior to any negotiations; on March 18, 1947, it abstained rather than vote against the government request for war credits. Thorez backed the Bollaert peace mission; when it failed, the Communist leader appeared to have condoned repression in Vietnam. Thorez, however, later insisted Bollaert's instructions formally excluded military operations of conquest or reconquest.[15]

After the historic *tournant* of 1947, the Vietnam war forced the party to assume an anti-colonial posture, but it mounted no real challenge to the colonial consensus. From 1947 to 1949 opposition to the war remained verbal, reaching an unusual level of intensity only in January 1949 with the campaign against the arrest of Tran Ngoc Danh, president of the Democratic Republic of Vietnam's delegation in France. The October 1949 victory of Communist forces in China signalled an intensified effort against the war, but as part of the International Peace Movement. The effort to block the transport of war materials to Indochina was subsumed under the broader campaign against the U.S. sponsored Mutual Defense Assistance Treaty. The party insisted upon the legality of its protest actions, and when the French government passed repressive legislation, the strikes abruptly ceased. In January 1950 the Soviet Union recognized the Democratic Republic of Vietnam; Communist functionary Leo Figuères visited Vietnam, restored friendly relations between the PCF and the Vietminh, and held a press conference to announce an offer by Ho Chi Minh to exchange prisoners.[16] The French government responded with a warrant for Figuères' arrest, but showed reluctance to find him. Some years later, while conducting party propaganda activities openly, Figuères had to remind his listeners that he was still technically a fugitive from the law.

On January 27, 1950, Jeannette Vermeersch charged French soldiers in Vietnam were committing atrocities "comparable to the frightening [German] examples of Oradour-sur-Glane and Ascq."[17] The party previously blamed atrocities on mercenaries and the French foreign legion; the Assembly was scandalized and several deputies demanded that Vermeersch be censured. But Communist arguments against the war never challenged the carefully constructed colonial consensus. The PCF labeled the war immoral, illegal, in violation of the constitution of the French Union and the charter of the United Nations, and contrary to the national interest. The Communists repeatedly emphasized the costs of military operations in terms of both lives and francs, linking them to insufficient social expenditure and inadequate wages at home. Ho Chi Minh had been received in France as head of state, held the allegiance of his people, and controlled 90 percent of Vietnamese territory. He wanted nothing more than full implementation of the March 1946 accords, which guaranteed Vietnamese independence within the French Union. Continuation of the struggle would inevitably lead to defeat and replacement of the French presence by U.S. imperialism, in whose real interests the war was being waged.[18]

To underline the quest for consensus, the PCF campaigned for the freedom of Henri Martin, a sailor arrested for anti-war activity.[19] The issue was the government's violation of civil liberties; by focusing on the military, the Martin campaign served to publicize the party's hostility to conscientious objection, desertion, and sabotage. Conscientious objection, the party said, while coura-geous, was individualist and unsuitable for mass emulation. Desertion was cow-ardice and sabotage treason. Lenin taught that the duty of a Communist was to depart for any war into which he had been conscripted and carry on the (party) struggle where circumstances placed him. Martin was accused of sabotage but acquitted; another sailor was convicted of sabotage, but the PCF charged he was the victim of government provocation seeking to discredit the anti-war movement as a whole. Martin's act was an expression of patriotic duty; André Marty complained that PCF propaganda over-emphasized Henri Martin's Communist party membership at the expense of his role as a former resister and patriot. The French government helped the campaign by clumsily staging several trials. The cause of this martyred sailor during his three years in prison captured the imag-ination of France's intellectual, university, and scientific community. It allowed anti-Stalinists of the left to put their dislike of colonial war above their hostility to the PCF and enabled the party to fashion a genuine mass movement.

A renewed militant anti-colonial policy coincided with the PCF adoption of a more sectarian stance from February to May 1952. Billoux's dramatic pro-nouncement that the peace struggle was part of the struggle for socialism found a parallel in an article by Léon Feix, calling for redoubled activity including demonstrations and strikes to block the transport of war materials to Indochina.[20] Billoux called for the defeat of the French army in Vietnam and North Africa, and Fajon added that Communist demands for the right of self-determination of peoples included the possibility of separation from France. But Feix admitted the level of anti-war activity in 1952 remained inferior to 1949 and 1950. He eschewed sectarianism and called for unity with Christians, Socialists, and mod-erates whose consciences were outraged by the slaughter. The 1952 direct action campaign was a pale imitation of its predecessor, which had fizzled out inglo-riously in 1950.

The party welcomed the commutation of Henri Martin's sentence in August 1953 as a major step forward, condemned the "*coup de force*" in Morocco by the Laniel government, which resulted in the deposition of the Sultan, and offered its support to any government willing to negotiate peace in Indochina. PCF moderation in the spring of 1954 was exemplary. The party avoided any display of *Schadenfreude* or joy when the garrison fell at Dien Bien Phu and supported Mendès-France. *L'Humanité's* reports of the Geneva negotiations were a model of objectivity; the newspaper stressed that an independent Vietnam within the French community was still a possibility. Negotiations with qualified represen-tatives of the national movements in Tunisia and Morocco, the PCF said, were the best means of safeguarding the economic, political, and cultural interests of France in those countries as well. The party greeted the Geneva agreements as the fruit of eight years of struggle: "our combat has imposed the Indochina peace," Duclos proclaimed.[21] *L'Humanité* bitterly attacked the Algerian nationalists for their rejection of the Indochina agreements and charge of treason against the PCF while it praised the Geneva agreements as a victory for the world-wide forces of peace and a success for national liberation movements. The signing of the agreements was a popular victory to which the PCF was proud to have "contributed with all its strength."[22]

French black Africa lacked a violence-prone independence movement, and the PCF had no sections or affiliates there. Efforts to promote Communist influence began in the 1930's with the creation of study groups, and the PCF aided in the creation of the Rassemblement Démocratique Africain (RDA), the most significant political force to develop in French West Africa after World War II. The Communists were rewarded when African Deputies contracted a tactical alliance with the PCF in the National Assembly at the founding Congress of the RDA at Bamako in 1946.[23] But efforts to convert the *apparentement* into a stronger alliance backfired. At first the RDA sought to implement Communist methods of organization.[24] Gabriel d'Arboussier, Secretary of the movement from 1946 to 1950, was sympathetic to Communism, if not a *sous-marin* (hidden party member). When the PCF returned to the opposition in 1947, the RDA suffered repression, which further solidified the movement's ties to the PCF. By the Abidjan, January 2–6, 1949, Congress, the PCF seemed to have colonized the RDA.[25] An *école des cadres* (training school for militants) was created, within which d'Arboussier instructed students in historical materialism. The Congress stressed the importance of mass action, elimination of those "betraying" the movement, subordination of elected officials to the party, defense of African workers, and consolidation of the movement through the creation of local committees of workers and peasants. The RDA reaffirmed its alliance with the French working class and endorsed PCF representative Waldeck Rochet's call for a new French government of democratic union.

But despite PCF efforts to portray it as an "original" movement, the RDA remained the opportunistic arm of an assimilationist elite of blacks. President Félix Houphouet-Boigny was never a Communist; his willingness to collaborate was stimulated by the brief presence of a Communist governor-general in the Ivory Coast and the party's presence in the French government. With the Communists in opposition the alliance brought no further advantages, and it made little sense to RDA militants to suffer persecution from rightist governments using anti-Communism as a pretext. In July 1950 the RDA broke with the PCF, and in 1952 it entered the conservative government of Antoine Pinay. The PCF condemned the RDA's defection as a victory for imperialism: Pinay corrupted the Parisian political leadership while colonial authorities bought the collaboration of the black bourgeoisie overseas. Léon Feix called upon RDA militants to dissociate themselves from their leadership's betrayal.[26] D'Arboussier remained loyal to the PCF, but he was vulnerable. Houphouet-Boigny, seeking his ouster in July 1952, denounced him as a refined bourgeois, a lover of luxury and opulence "who imagines himself a proletarian."[27] As a mulatto, Houphouet charged, d'Arboussier was unsuitable as a mass leader in Africa and incapable of understanding African reality. The RDA, Houphouet emphasized, had never been Communist. Its alliance with the PCF was "entirely derived of political opportunism, [and] had never implied an ideological choice." Communism, wrote RDA deputy Gabriel Lisette, was alien to African Islamic and Animist traditions; its rejection was an affirmation of the African personality.

The PCF continued, nevertheless, to support the RDA; the liberal consensus that underlay the October 1946 constitution remained the basis of both organizations despite altered circumstances. With the advent of the Mollet government in 1956, which briefly enjoyed Communist support, Léon Feix renewed the party's call for *"une veritable Union française"* (a true French Union), based on equality of rights and mutual interest between France and black Africa. France remained the country of human rights; admiration for its culture persisted throughout French Africa along with a practical need for technicians, doctors, teachers, and jurists. The PCF voted for the statute for black Africa introduced by the Mollet government in June 1956. The new legislation enlarged suffrage, provided for a single electoral college, expanded the powers of local assemblies, and created an indigenous executive power. The PCF would have preferred more far-reaching legislation, but supported Mollet's bill as still representing genuine progress.[28] The break with Mollet in July 1956 over Algeria still did not lead the party to espouse African independence. Only after the Bamako congress of September 1957, when the RDA first demanded African independence, did the PCF then declare that African independence was ineluctible and would be achieved either with French assistance or in opposition to France. The slogan of a *"veritable Union française"* now was quietly dropped, and the PCF promised full support of the African cause. The African masses were appreciative of France and the heroic record of the PCF on their behalf, and would remain so after new ties, based on independence and equality, were negotiated by de Gaulle.[29]

The PCF's policies in French Africa highlighted the party's commitment to the colonial consensus of France's ruling elite. The PCF campaigned for the abolition of forced labor and other social reforms and supported progressive legislation like the statute of 1956. But in so doing, it invited the charge of paternalism and insensitivity to the aspirations of black people. The black poet Aimé Césaire resigned from the PCF in 1956 over the PCF's position on Algeria and Khrushchev's revelations of Stalin's crimes but complained that the aims of Communism and the cause of black peoples could not be identified. The anticolonial struggle was of a totally different nature than the struggle of the French workers against capitalism; the PCF had embraced the assimilationist doctrine and contributed to the artificial separation of Guadaloupe and Martinique from black Africa.[30] For Césaire, the struggles of black people everywhere were joined to one another. His charges made an impression: the PCF abruptly changed position toward the West Indies in 1957, advocating that the people of Martinique be granted the right to administer their own affairs.[31] But Martinique's autonomy must still remain within the framework of union with France, or it risked being swallowed by the USA. Autonomy was only viable in the context of alliance with the French proletariat and conditions of struggle "infinitely better than those capable of existing in almost the totality of countries of the new world."

For the Communists, as for all other Frenchmen, Algeria was regarded as a special case. The PCF rejected the fiction indulged in by official French policy makers that Algeria consisted of three French departments as inseparable from the metropole as Normandy or Poitou. Algeria was a classic case of colonial oppression, its appalling poverty the result of imperialism and a one-crop economy imposed by an alien elite. Land needed for wheat production was diverted to wine for export while native Muslims, ironically forbidden alcohol, were left to starve.[32] But the presence of over 1 million inhabitants of European origin was a historical fact, and the PCF could not envisage their emigration. Most of the settlers were workers, artisans, and shopkeepers, as much victimized by the colonial interests as the Muslim population. The PCF refused to admit the nationalists' thesis that an Algerian nation had existed prior to the arrival of the French. Contemporary Algeria, like France before 1789, was a mixture of nationalities including Europeans, Jews, Arabs, and Berbers; a "nation in formation" as Thorez said in 1939, its personality yet to emerge from a process of racial fusion.[33] The Communists distrusted Islam and regarded the Algerian national movement as sectarian and chauvinist. Ferhat Abbas represented the Islamic bourgeoisie, which wanted to separate Algeria from France in order to bring it into the American orbit. André Marty regarded Abbas as an American agent.[34] The only party that successfully united Arab, Berber, European, and Jew was the Algerian Communist party. The PCF did not uniquely apply the idea of multi-national fusion to Algeria in the 1940's; it welcomed the birth of Israel in 1948 on similar grounds.[35] The presence of the Jewish population in Palestine, like the French in Algeria, was an irreversible historical fact. A process of bi-national fusion was possible if a progressive French colonial regime consciously sought to bring it about. These views were imperative for the Algerian Communists, who remained primarily a settler party as late as 1952.

The Algerian Communists committed a fatal error in calling for the rapid and pitiless punishment of inciters of the May 1945 riots in Setif and Constantine. Coinciding with the May 1945 armistice, the riots appeared a fascist plot; neither the PCF nor the Communist party of Algeria (PCA) could foresee the demonstrations would assume a hallowed place in nationalist mythology. The Communists did denounce the excesses of the ensuing French repression and called for universal equal suffrage, a constituent assembly, the recognition of Arabic as a national language, and financial autonomy. As a result, they won 20 percent of the vote in the second college in the elections of October 1945. But the PCA again erred in advocating associated territorial status for Algeria and accepting implementation of the two-college system, which gave the settlers and the much larger indigenous population equal representation. These policies alienated the PCA from the nationalist movement; an attempt to build a united Algerian front collapsed in 1952 even though the PCA achieved a Muslim majority in its membership and denounced the French colonial administration's manipulation of elections.[36] The PCA was further buffeted by the Marty affair (Marty enjoyed great popularity among Algerian Communists as head of the PCF's colonial section) and the PCF's support of Marcel Naegelen in the December 1953 presidential elections. As Resident-General of Algeria, Naegelen was responsible for electoral manipulation to preserve settler dominance. A "colonial counter-society" fully committed to reformist and legal behavior, the PCA, like its parent PCF, was completely surprised by the Algerian national insurrection which began on November 1, 1954.[37]

Ever since Sartre's 1956 indictment of the PCF's "spinelessness" in its opposition to the Algerian war, the view that the party did not oppose the war has proliferated.[38] But the French Communists, within the means available to them, and constrained by the parameters of their own best judgment, did oppose the war; the prevailing misinterpretation of the PCF position stems from the party's lack of success. It is doubtful that the PCF's effort against the war helped bring the conflict to an earlier conclusion. On the other hand the PCF's anti-war effort almost brought the party to full political integration into the political system of the Fourth Republic. Indeed, the PCF was near enough to power in 1958 to render plausible the notion that the Fourth Republic was destroyed in part to make that integration impossible.

The Algerian insurrection began during the party's failing romance with Mendès-France. After the Indochina peace, Tunisia received autonomy; the PCF criticized the Algerian nationalists for their obtuseness in failing to recognize that benefits might accrue to them as well from a moderate approach.[39] The belief that the Algerian violence was caused by "provocateurs" was consistent with the PCF's posture and outlook. The Political Bureau refused to condemn the rebellion, however, and called for negotiations with qualified representatives of Algerian opinion, alone among major French parties in doing so.[40] France and Algeria were bound by indissoluble ties, but the links needed to be transformed: the colonialist relationship must become a freely negotiated one based on reciprocal equality. While condemning French repression the PCF also repudiated "individual acts [of terrorism]" by rebel forces, which were calculated to play into the hands of the most reactionary pro-colonial elements in the metropole. In subsequent years the PCF did not deviate from this line in any substantial way. It adapted its call for negotiations to the reality of domination of the rebel forces by the Algerian National Liberation Front, but the issue of terrorism estranged the party from the nationalist leadership.

In September and October 1955 protests occurred among draftees destined to serve in Algeria; the Communists reacted sympathetically, Marcel Cachin pleading in the National Assembly: "Listen to the voice of our youth, called to the colors." Jacques Duclos blamed the war on French failure to recognize the existence of an "Algerian national problem" and saluted the draftees for calling attention to the need for negotiations. Etienne Fajon defended "the legitimate desire of soldiers not to risk their lives in an unjust war that was contrary to the national interest."[41] Critical developments were also occurring beneath the surface. The Algerian Communists rallied to the cause of independence in June 1955; now dominated by a Muslim majority, the PCA differentiated itself from the parent French party. Yet the parallel between its actions and the PCF suggests a concerted effort by the two parties to present themselves as the last remaining bridge between the French government and the nationalist movement.[42] Communism alone could capitalize on the historic ties between the proletariat and the oppressed colonial peoples, both of whom shared the same enemy in French monopoly-finance capitalism.

The PCF joined the "Republican Front" led by Pierre Mendès-France to contest the 1956 elections on a program of peace through negotiations. During the campaign Socialist leader Guy Mollet condemned the war as "imbecilic and endless," sufficient basis for agreement with the PCF. The party hoped for a new Popular Front; opposition to the Algerian war might yet offer the occasion for mass mobilization to overcome the Socialist leaders' resistance to an alliance. The Algerian Communists similarly sought a coalition with the National Liberation Front (FLN); the parallel was evident. If successful, the PCF and PCA might offer a way to bring the French government and the Algerian National Liberation Front into negotiations. Neither party succeeded. For Mollet, the Communists were still not so much on the left as to the east, and his commitment to negotiations was short-lived. The FLN refused to allow the PCA to join the insurrection on an equal basis and demanded that the PCA disband its organization and have its members join individually.[43]

It is in the context of parallel PCF and PCA policy, pursued consistently until 1958, that PCF support for Mollet in the winter and spring of 1956 must be viewed. The Communists wished to give Mollet the strength to translate electoral promises into acts. The PCF coupled its support for Mollet with carefully timed gestures toward the FLN. On the eve of Mollet's assumption of power Léon Feix called for recognition of the "Algerian national reality" (*fait national algérien*), indicating that the party now viewed Thorez's "nation in formation" as an accomplished reality. The Socialist André Le Troquer was again elected President of the National Assembly with Communist support. The PCF supported the Mollet government on February 1; shortly thereafter, Léon Feix specified that France could only negotiate a cease-fire with those who were doing the fighting and named the National Liberation Front.[44] Simultaneously, the Algerian Communists placed their miniscule insurrectionary force under control of the Algerian National Liberation Army and accepted a political role subordinate to the FLN.

The PCF voted in favor of plenary powers for Mollet on March 12, 1956. Duclos, explaining the vote, endorsed the Socialist leader's plan of social reform for Algeria and repudiated any use of the special powers for military repression.[45] Mollet's capitulation before the settler riots of February 6 offered little hope for a settlement, but the alternative was to force him to rely on conservative support in the Assembly, foreclosing the precarious option of peace that still existed. Mollet informed Duclos about secret negotiations with FLN representatives in Yugoslavia.[46] The vote for Mollet was a desperate gamble for peace and an effort to spur the Socialist government's program of social reform and détente with the USSR. Mollet left for a week's sojourn in Moscow on May 14.

Nevertheless, many in the party leadership questioned the vote, and the PCF became infamous in New-Left circles.[47] The PCF began an orchestrated program of popular pressure designed to force Mollet to rely on the leftist elements within his coalition of support. Joint Communist-Socialist meetings, delegations, demonstrations, and work stoppages, were reported regularly in the pages of *L'Humanité* through the spring of 1956. On May 3, 1956, a protest demonstration of draftees coincided with another PCF vote supporting Mollet; the party defended the manifestation as legitimate, normal, and necessary, a means of insisting upon respect for promises by those in power.[48] *L'Humanité* endured the indignity of seizure by Mollet two days before the latter's May departure for Moscow.

On June 5, 1956, the Communists abstained for the first time on a vote of confidence in the Mollet government. Thorez, troubled by criticism of PCF policy and the Khrushchev revelations, opened the vote for discussion in the Central Committee: twenty-six favored abstention and twenty-five were opposed, Thorez noting the same devotion to the working class on both sides.[49] The Communists were still unwilling to break with Mollet in the desperate hope he might be persuaded to negotiate. Characteristically, the announcement of oil discoveries in the Sahara on June 16, 1956, convinced the party that Mollet's government had become a prisoner of the monopolies. The Communists now sought to encourage disaffection with Mollet within the Socialist party and achieve a government with PCF participation reflecting the January 2, 1956, majority in favor of peace.[50] The Algerian Communists continued efforts to ingratiate themselves with the FLN and inflect its policies toward a negotiated end to the war. Communism remained, in the party's view, the best hope to provide a link between the French government and the rebels. The party alone could accomplish the ideal of "a fraternal union freely negotiated."

The tactical desire to retain contacts with Mollet motivated the party to de-emphasize the issue of torture during the battle of Algiers. The leadership of the anti-torture campaign fell by default to the intellectuals of the non-Communist left.[51] Still, the PCF was not insensitive to the humanitarian aspect of the anti-war struggle. It provided some of the early martyrs, Maurice Audin, a mathematics student at the University of Algiers, and Henri Alleg, editor of *Alger Républicain*. Alleg's account of his torment caused a sensation upon its publication in 1957.[52] The Communist sub-culture provided the first cases of soldiers like Alban Liechti, who went to the stockade rather than carry out their assignment in Algeria. Communists were ubiquitous among those condemned to execution by French military authorities for aiding the rebels.[53] The most notorious case involved the candidate-officer Henri Maillot who deserted to the FLN in July 1956 with a truckload of arms to become leader of a band of rebels in a *maquis*.

Duclos protested the torture and the permanent brutalization of French youth it entailed, and Communist Deputies demanded an inquiry into the fate of Maurice Audin. The issue of torture gave the Communists grounds for pause because of the party's unwillingness to accept the Kantian moral premise of those who protested or the one-sided way their premise was applied. Protesters tended to overlook or justify FLN terrorism to which the torture often was a response. The party was severely critical of the military tactics adopted by the rebels in the Battle of Algiers. The PCF and the PCA condemned urban terrorism as left-adventurist and self-defeating and warned against terrorist acts in metropolitan France.[54]

In October 1957 Thorez announced he was ready to support the Socialists on any platform calculated to bring peace. France would lose nothing through peace; a free Algeria would offer French industry a greater market than an Algeria impoverished by colonial exploitation ever had been able to do. But the PCF did not insist on complete acceptance of its views; the aim was compromise, for "we have never been advocates of all or nothing."[55] The Algerian Communists simultaneously recognized the preeminence of the FLN leaders. Algerian Communists would settle for nothing more than a supporting role in the struggle, as long as they had an opportunity "to go with the masses."[56] It was all to no avail. Both parties remained isolated and impotent through the May 13, 1958, crisis, the PCF pathetic in its pleas for a new birth of the instinct of republican defense, inability to mobilize the masses, and squandered vote of emergency powers on behalf of a timid Pierre Pflimlin.

The Fourth Republic at its moment of agony was not the victim of Communist "ambiguity" toward the democratic system. At the moment of truth the other parties proved more ambiguous. The advent of de Gaulle appeared to foreclose any possibility that the party could escape isolation and contribute to the achievement of a negotiated peace. To the extent that it blocked this scenario the Fifth Republic vindicated Thorez's resistance to de-Stalinization after the Twentieth Congress of the CPSU. For Thorez, a proto-fascist regime had taken power in France as a consequence of the threatened integration of the PCF and democratization of French politics. Not only was continuation of the war in Algeria now likely, but also the end of détente and a reactionary internal social policy, which would make a mockery of the idea of a peaceful, parliamentary road to Socialism. Condemnation of the Gaullist regime as a vehicle for the direct rule of monopoly capitalism, a regime of personal power which "opened the way to fascism," followed logically.[57] Gaullism was illegitimate, the fruit of violence, sponsored by reactionaries, colonialists, colonels, and large industrialists, whose intentions were to pillage Algeria. The only possible PCF policy was to oppose de Gaulle while cautiously refraining from any illegality. But this policy also appeared, as the devastating results of the party's campaign against the constitution of the Fifth Republic indicated, a recipe for continued isolation and impotence.

As early as October 1958, the party's student organization, Sorbonne-lettres, influenced by New-Left theorists, criticized the PCF's negativism and pursuit of a coalition with the Mollet Socialists. The students echoed a new analysis of Gaullism by Serge Mallet, which was becoming increasingly fashionable on the non-Communist left. Mallet argued that de Gaulle represented the monopolies and technocrats of French finance capital impatient with parliament and its susceptibility to archaic pressure groups representing the interests of backward sectors of the economy opposed to modernization and industrial concentration.[58] The PCF, ever since the Popular Front of the 1930's, had championed the cause of the petty bourgeoisie threatened by monopoly power and failed to grasp its dependence on imperialism. The ideology of the petty bourgeoisie was "national-Molletism"; by defending these strata, the PCF competed for the natural constituency of fascist Pierre Poujade. The exploitation of the Sahara in a neo-imperialist world required the sacrifice of the Algerian settlers or *colons*; the struggle of Gaullist technocracy against these archaic elements was the new basis of French politics. Hence the parliamentary option enabling the PCF to choose between factions of the bourgeoisie was now foreclosed. The "no" vote on de Gaulle's referendum had not been the left's struggle, said Mallet, since the monopolies were, paradoxically, the best hope to force negotiations with the FLN.

A similar analysis developed within PCF intellectual circles where it occasioned one of the most far-reaching internal debates the party ever experienced. The party's theoretical review, *Economie et Politique,* under Jean Pronteau and Maurice Kriegel-Valrimont, and even *France Nouvelle,* discovered still new contradictions within the monopoly-finance constituency of Gaullism. The traditional program of the monopolies was a junior partnership of France in the system of American capitalist hegemony, but a nationalist current had developed seeking to limit American domination of French industry and preserve the exploitation of Algerian oil for itself.[59] Hence the chauvinistic complexion of the regime and its flirtation with neutralism. These views were echoed within the PCF's Political Bureau, where Marcel Servin and Laurent Casanova championed them and tried to persuade Thorez to adopt their point of view. Thorez appeared tempted for a brief period, although he must have immediately recognized the similarity of Casanova's ideas with Duclos' opportunistic national front of 1952. In May 1959 Thorez suggested it would be in the interest of a capitalist France to deal with an autonomous Algerian people, master of their own petroleum resources and escaping from German and American domination.[60]

When de Gaulle announced his readiness to accept self-determination on September 16, 1959, Thorez's initial reaction was to suspect a trap. The regime was incapable of negotiating peace; de Gaulle's offer was a maneuver to mask as a negotiated peace what were really terms of surrender. But the party was forced to repudiate this view. Khrushchev reacted positively to the de Gaulle declaration, rudely undercutting Thorez and implicitly supporting the views of the Servin-Casanova group. The Russians were clearly prepared to encourage the nationalist tendencies within Gaullism, hoping to lure France out of the American orbit. With unusual frankness, the PCF condemned its initial reaction to de Gaulle's statement as hasty and ill-conceived.[61] Once self-determination had been made the basis of policy, the party announced, the regime would find it impossible to retreat; self-determination was inevitable in Algeria's future. The monopolies were ready to sacrifice certain interests of the colonialist ultras in the hope of remaining masters of Algeria's oil.

The PCF made a gesture to de Gaulle; the Algerian Communists undertook a new effort toward the FLN as well. The PCF had misjudged Gaullism; so had the PCA underestimated Algerian nationalism. The coup of May 13, 1958, revealed that the *colons* were not likely to accept a bi-national Algeria. The PCA, in a demonstration of self-criticism, declared Thorez's 1939 formula of a "nation in formation" had been interpreted "dogmatically"; emergence of an Algerian nation had been prevented by the colonialist presence and the *colons* won over to a chauvinist, racist ideology while the Algerian Muslim nation was being forged in the independence struggle.[62] The Algerian nation was now a historical reality. This did not mean that the *colons* were to be abandoned; the Communists would never accept Sartre's conclusion that the Europeans of Algeria were "condemned by history." The Algerian Provisional Government declared its willingness to recognize the rights of its minority citizens of European extraction.

As the war moved toward its sixth year, public opinion in France was clearly turning toward peace. The Gaullist regime opened preliminary negotiations with the FLN at Melun in June 1960. The party claimed that these developments reflected its efforts of propaganda and pressure on the public authorities. The party appeared ready to resume the path of integration interrupted in May 1958, but it was prevented from so doing by a challenge from a new quarter, the movement of students and intellectuals whose anti-war perspective rejected the possibility of working within the political system. The party could not react positively to the students nor could it fully believe in the peaceful intentions of de Gaulle after the Melun negotiations collapsed. Rather than continue to pursue a policy predicated on the internal contradictions of Gaullism, the PCF retreated into isolation and sectarianism, aggravated by a severe internal conflict over policies and future party leadership.

The problem of defining a PCF position vis-à-vis the New Left became entangled with the PCF's internal struggle over de-Stalinization. Servin and Casanova emerged as advocates of the Khrushchev line; pushing de-Stalinization to its limits, they began talk of Stalin's "crimes," Casanova earning the gratitude of the Russians and the Lenin Peace prize. Casanova advocated a PCF alliance with the anti-war movement in France. At the May 1960 meeting of the PCF Central Committee, he delivered a radical analysis of the capitalist technocracy that Gaullism represented, citing new forms of protest emerging among youth and urging the party to cooperate with New-Left students and intellectuals. Casanova was applauded vigorously and spontaneously by the assembled delegates to the visible irritation of Thorez.[63]

Thorez was outraged by the anti-patriotic tendencies among anti-war activists apparent in the exposure of the Jeanson network in February 1960. François Jeanson had for some years been giving clandestine aid to the National Liberation Front; his efforts were of no great quantitative significance nor might they have become an issue without the heavy-handed attempt by the French government to smear the anti-war movement with the charge of treason.[64] The attendant publicity of a formal prosecution and trial obliged the anti-war movement to take a position on aid to the FLN and the associated questions of refusal of the draft (*insoumission*) and desertion. Implicit in New-Left tactics was a direct challenge to the premise of the nation-state, although some of the accused claimed to be acting in the name of a higher conception of French values and patriotism.[65] It was not simply outraged Jacobinism that conditioned the PCF's response to this reasoning; no political party that aspired to influence in a modern national setting could afford to reject the national idea. For the PCF to do so could only mean rejection of any hope of escape from isolation. The New-Left protesters further claimed that their methods were the only alternative for effective action; refusal of military service, desertion, and aid to the FLN became the only valid methods of struggle against a criminal war and the only real means of struggle on behalf of the cause of socialist revolution as well. Whatever its specific ideology, the FLN's struggle would ineluctably lead it to Socialism. An FLN victory offered the best hope for Socialism in France.

The sixth year of the war brought challenge and confrontation to the PCF on a number of fronts simultaneously. Reeling under the impact of de-Stalinization, which Thorez was trying to oppose in the International Communist Movement, the party was asked to adapt to the "progressive" aspects of Gaullism, enter an alliance with the New Left and condone new forms of struggle predicated on a rejection of the national idea. The PCF refused to identify the cause of socialist revolution with the armed struggle of the FLN. Yet a growing number of militants within its own ranks, particularly among its student and youth groups but also on the Central Committee and the Political Bureau, advocated an alliance with the New Left's revolutionary romanticism. To complicate matters further, the Servin-Casanova group had the support of the Russians.

The French Communist party responded to this challenge with refusal on all fronts. Thorez warned against exaggerating the contradictions of capitalism; they were secondary to the struggle of the laboring masses and the Socialist block against imperialism.[66] The proletariat must act distinctively as a class. The only segment of the bourgeoisie with which it could ally was the petty bourgeoisie, toward whom the party had correctly oriented its appeal. The so-called nationalist content of Gaullism was purely rhetorical: U.S. investment in France had increased since the advent of de Gaulle at a faster rate than under the Fourth Republic. On desertion the party refused to depart from good Leninist principle: Communists leave for all wars for which they are mobilized. The PCF expressed sympathy for front-line soldiers who rejected military missions in Algeria, but it refused to advise others to follow their example.[67] After the April 1961 Algiers uprising the PCF claimed its position was vindicated. Communist soldiers were instrumental in defusing the crisis, refusing to obey their insurgent officers and remaining loyal to the Republic.

The PCF also rejected New-Left assumptions concerning the FLN. By 1960 the Algerian Communists had made one concession after another to the rebel leadership while the French Communists endorsed the negotiating position of the FLN. But the rebel leaders made no concessions to the Algerian Communists, who were still excluded from participation in the Provisional Government. It was ludicrous to argue under these conditions that the FLN was the incarnation of hopes for socialist revolution in France. Larbi Bouhali, Secretary of the Algerian Communist party, chose the forbidding pages of the Soviet theoretical review *Kommunist* to detail the PCA's (and by implication the PCF's) dissatisfaction with the FLN.[68] Bouhali praised the Algerian Army of National Liberation and pledged PCA support to the Algerian provisional government. But he regretted that the essential unity of all rebel forces had not been achieved; the legitimate desire of the Algerian Communists to participate in the Provisional Government of the new Algeria had been frustrated by the FLN, and several officials within the rebel leadership made no secret of their anti-Communist convictions. The FLN was worthy of tactical support as a movement of the nationalist bourgeoisie, Bouhali said, but it had displayed hesitation, compromise, and error during the course of the struggle. Crucial political work was neglected in favor of over-emphasis on the military, and "dirty individuals" (terrorists) had been allowed to defame the revolutionary cause. The isolation of the Algerian Communists must be ended, Bouhali insisted; a correct understanding of the problem of unity was essential.

In the meantime, the PCF condemned those who advocated subordinating the struggle in France to helping the FLN. *L'Humanité* quickly pointed out at the time of the uncovering of the *reseau Jeanson* that Communists were not among its members.[69] The trial and declaration of 121 intellectuals condoning the actions of the accused forced a more subtle statement of the party's position. The declaration was welcome as a testimony to the evolution of mass opinion, and the PCF protested against government persecution of those courageous enough to sign.[70] But the conceptions of the signers were not those of the Communists, and Thorez was disturbed that some party members associated with so flagrant a repudiation of Leninist doctrine. Draft refusal was a gesture of despair; Sartre and his followers placed themselves at the disposition of the rebel leadership. Thorez was clear on this point: "We are not obliged to base our policies, or the forms of our action, on those of the FLN."[71]

The October 27, 1960, *journée* of protest was instructive as an example of the party's fear of being outflanked on the left, a foretaste of May 1968. The party reacted with hostility to the initiative, which was accompanied by charges that PCF behavior in the anti-war movement had been inadequate.[72] The Communists distrusted initiatives emanating from others and feared that the working class would be used as an auxiliary force in a struggle for goals not its own. When organizers of the demonstration announced their intention to defy a police ban, the party legitimately feared that the regime would use the occasion for repression of which the PCF was certain to be the primary victim. Thorez, in summing up his objections, defined what he saw as the strength of party policy and what his critics took to be its confining weakness: "Measuring at each step the temperature of the masses, neither overestimating nor underestimating the possibilities": again the golden mean. Despite the claims of its organizers, the day of action was not a success. Negotiations between the government and demonstration leaders permitted a mass meeting to occur at the Mutualité, but the Communist party was excluded.

The party's willingness to engage in more serious forms of mass action as the war drew to a close was more a reaction to the threat of fascism as represented by the Secret Army Organization (OAS) than a concession to New-Left "adventurism." Until the war's end, the Communists continued to deny that the Gaullist regime could or would sign a peace. The PCF blamed OAS outrages on the complicity of Gaullist authorities. Major demonstrations were held in reply to the insurgencies in Algiers of January 1960 and April 1961, and the party was proud of the role of its recruits in refusing to follow rebel officers. It saw its warnings against adventurism justified by the tragic fate of nine demonstrators, suffocated on February 8, 1962, as a result of police charges at the entrance to Metro Charonne. The martyrdom of the nine, eight of whom were Communists, became the symbol of a new left-wing unity growing out of the final days of the war.

Ironically the party felt it necessary to defend itself against the charge that it was discomforted or embarrassed by the conclusion of peace. The Communists claimed that they were sincere in their appreciation of the signing of accords; they had more reason than anyone to wish for an end to the hostilities.[73] By bringing de Gaulle to power, the war interrupted progress toward integration into the democratic structure of French politics. During the early years of the Fifth Republic, the party continued efforts to inflect the policies of the regime toward peace, at the same time as the PCA tried to influence the FLN. In 1960 both efforts ended in mutual recrimination. Further integration had to await the war's end and the establishment of the regime's anti-fascist credentials with the definitive suppression of the OAS and the discovery of the "progressive" aspects of de Gaulle's foreign policy. But the basis of integration under the Fifth Republic had been established. Despite its bitter hostility to the regime the party never made its slogan of the "renovation" of French democracy a precondition for ending the war and called for organized action for peace "within the framework of personal power."

Most importantly, the party firmly rejected the "harmful" attitudes of *gauchistes*. Their irresponsible actions, the party argued in 1962 and again in 1968, served to assist the policies of the Gaullist regime and the ultras.[74] The PCF restricted its efforts to modes of activity its constituency and potential allied groups were prepared to accept. The party carefully sensed the attitudes of the masses and tried to educate them to the need for peace. By carefully adjusting its activity to mass sentiment, the party pursued its goal of integration into the political system and the national, mass context of French life. Any gesture in the direction of the New Left would have interfered with that goal. As under the Fourth Republic, the PCF's integration under Gaullism depended upon alliance with the traditional forces of the political left.

NOTES

1. Alfred Grosser, *La IVᵉ République et sa politique extérieure* (Paris, 1961), 398.

2. Forcefully argued by Tony Smith, "The French Colonial Consensus and People's War, 1946–58," *Journal of Contemporary History,* IX, 4 (December 1974), 217–47. Smith argues that the Communists were outside the consensus, however. See also his *The French Stake in Algeria* (Ithaca, N.Y., 1978).

3. See J. Moneta, ed., *Le Parti Communiste français et la question coloniale, 1920–1965* (Paris, 1971) for a collection of documents. Monographs include G. Madjarian, *La question colonial et la politique du Parti communiste français* (Paris, 1977) and F. Joucelain, *Le PCF et la première guerre d'Indochine* (Paris, 1973). The excellent dissertation by E. Rice-Maximin, "The French Left and Indochina, 1945–1954" (University of Wisconsin, 1974) also slips into this perspective. For the PCF's point of view see Monique Lafon, ed., *Le Parti Communiste français dans la lutte contre le colonialisme* (Paris, 1962).

4. See D. Bruce Marshall, *The French Colonial Myth and Constitution-Making in the Fourth Republic* (New Haven, Conn., 1973), 243–45.

5. Maurice Thorez, *La France du Front populaire et les peuples coloniaux* (Paris, 1937); also *Textes choisis sur l'Algérie* (Paris, n.d.), 12–14.

6. Paul Sorum, *Intellectuals and Decolonization in France* (Chapel Hill, N.C., 1977), 104; Tony Smith, *The French Stake in Algeria,* 41.

7. *Cours de Formation Marxiste-Leniniste,* in Archives André Marty (AAM), microfilm collection, especially Reel 9. See also Etienne Fajon, "Les Problèmes de l'Union française," reprinted in Parti Communiste français, *Questions du Moment* (Paris, 1947).

8. Jean Guillon, "A propos du Viet Nam: la question nationale et coloniale," *Cahiers du Communisme,* 3–4 (March-April 1947), 217–45.

9. On the Algerian Communists see Emmanuel Sivan, *Communisme et Nationalisme en Algérie, 1920–62* (Paris, 1976).

10. Léon Feix, "Pour une veritable Union Française," *Cahiers du Communisme,* 1, 2 (January-February 1956), 30–47.

11. Madjarian, *La Question coloniale,* 173–97; Rice-Maximin, "The French Left," 124. On the Russians see J. Frankel, "Soviet Policy in South East Asia," in Max Beloff, ed., *Soviet Policy in the Far East 1944–1951* (London, 1953), 222. Also Charles B. McLane, *Soviet Strategies in Southeast Asia* (Princeton, N.J., 1966), 266–68.

12. Harold Isaacs, *No Peace For Asia* (New York, 1947), 173.

13. The Yugoslavs criticized the Vietnamese for dissolving their party in February 1948. McLane, *Soviet Strategies,* 432–33. The Yugoslavs were shortly to receive the same critique from the Russians.

14. Leo Figuères, *Jeunesse Militante* (Paris, 1971), 225–29.

15. On the Bollaert mission see Vincent Auriol, *Mon Septennat 1947* (Paris, 1970), 124–28, 160.

16. Figuères, *Jeunesse militante,* 228–29.

17. Vermeersch's speech is in Lafon, ed., *Le PCF dans la lutte,* 61. André Marty

complained of the practice of blaming atrocities on legionnaires: *L'Affaire Marty* (Paris, 1954), 37.

18. *Cahiers du Communisme,* 3–4 (March-April 1947), 217–45, 9 (September 1949).

19. See AAM, Reel 12, *Dossier de la campagne pour Henri Martin*; Hélène Parmelin, *Liberez les Communistes* (Paris, 1979) is invaluable; Parmelin covered the campaign for *L'Humanité.*

20. *Cahiers du Communisme,* 6 (June 1952), 593–607, 3 (March 1952).

21. *L'Humanité,* August 22, 1953, May 13, 1954, July 2, 6, 23, 1954.

22. *Cahiers du Communisme,* 8–9 (August-September 1954), 982–95.

23. See Ruth Morgenthau, *Political Parties in French Speaking West Africa* (Oxford, 1964), 22–27; Jean Suret-Canale, *Afrique Noire, De la colonisation aux indépendances* (Paris, 1972), III, part 1, 16.

24. See the frank admission by Felix Houphouet-Boigny, "Le Continent Africain en marche," *Democratie Nouvelle* (July 1947), 74–80.

25. See the report of the congress in *Cahiers du Communisme* by Raymond Barbé (February 1949), 231–35.

26. *Cahiers du Communisme,* 5 (May 1951), 565–75.

27. *Afrique Noire* (Organ of the RDA) No. 27, June 24, 1952, July 3, 1952.

28. See Lafon, ed. *Le PCF et la question coloniale,* 160. *Cahiers du Communisme,* 1, 2 (January-February, 1956).

29. *Cahiers du Communisme,* 3 (March 1958), 357–76.

30. Aimé Césaire, *Letter to Maurice Thorez* (Paris, 1954).

31. *Cahiers du Communisme,* 11 (November 1957), 1709–38.

32. *Cahiers du Communisme,* 9 (September 1947), 857–69; also André Marty, "La Théorie Leniniste de la question nationale et coloniale" (February 1948) in AAM, Reel 9.

33. Thorez, *Textes choisis sur l'Algérie* (Paris, n.d.), 17–21. Also *Cahiers du Communisme,* 2 (February 1955), 147–48.

34. This view of Abbas was, so far as I have been able to determine, only circulated privately, however. Elie Mignot, "Les Problèmes de l'Algérie," typed ms. dated February 1948 in Archives André Marty, Microfilm collection, Reel 10.

35. *Cahiers du Communisme,* 6 (July 1948), 703–21.

36. Larbi Bouhali, "L'Algérie veut un statut démocratique," *La Démocratie Nouvelle* (July 1947), 357–61.

37. Emmanuel Sivan, *Communisme et Nationalisme,* 142, 166–70, 206, 216, 228.

38. Jean-Paul Sartre, "Le Fantôme de Staline," *Les Temps Modernes,* Nos. 129–31 (January 1957), 690–92.

39. *L'Humanité,* July 31, August 4, 1954.

40. Ibid., November 9, 1954.

41. Ibid., October 4, 12, November 24, 1955.

42. Sivan, *Communisme et Nationalisme,* says the two parties broke definitively at this point: 242–54. Etienne Fajon says the PCF understood the necessity of the PCA position: personal interview, April 10, 1978.

43. Roland Gaucher, *Histoire secrète du PCF* (Paris, 1974), 548–68, and Richard and Joan Brace, *Ordeal in Algeria* (Princeton, N.J., 1960), 104–06.

44. *L'Humanité,* January 16, February 1, 2, 14, 1956.

45. Ibid., March 13, 1956.

46. For a criticism of the secret negotiations as sapping the French war effort, see Philippe Tripier, *Autopsie de la guerre d'Algérie* (Paris, 1972), 151–53.

47. Etienne Fajon concluded in retrospect that the vote was an error. See *Ma Vie s'appelle liberté* (Paris, 1976), 223. For a defense from a Soviet source: V. Schirovsky, *Borba frantsuzskoy Kommunistichiskoy Parti protiv voyny v Alzhire* (Moscow, 1962), 33–36.

48. *L'Humanité*, April 14, 26, May 3, 4, 1956.

49. Jean Pronteau, personal interview, April 25, 1978. Also in Philippe Robrieux, *Histoire intérieure du PCF* (Paris, 1981), II, 462.

50. Schirovsky, *Borba*, 39. *Cahiers du Communisme*, 8–9 (August-September 1956), 832.

51. Michel Crouzet, "La Bataille des intellectuels français," *La Nef*, XIX, 12–13 (October 1962-January 1963), 47–66.

52. *La Question* (Paris, 1957), English edition (New York, 1958).

53. Maurice Maschino, *L'Engagement [le dossier des réfractaires]* (Paris, 1961), 11–21.

54. See the remarks by Algerian Communist leader Bachr Hadj Ali, in *Cahiers du Communisme*, 2 (February 1961), 397.

55. Thorez, *Textes choisis*, 59–61.

56. Larbi Bouhali, "La révolution socialiste d'Octobre et le mouvement national algérien," *Cahiers du Communisme*, 11 (November 1957), 1709–38.

57. Thorez speech of June 9, 1958, to the Central Committee of the PCF, in *La Politique communiste: vers le XVIᵉ Congrès du parti* (Paris, 1960), 88–89.

58. Serge Mallet, "Pour un programme de l'opposition," *Les Temps Modernes*, No. 149 (July 1958), 174–88, Nos. 150–51 (August-September 1958), 466–77.

59. Michel Hincker, "La bourgeoisie en quête de son pouvoir," *Economie et Politique* (March 1960), 6–21.

60. *La Politique communiste*, Thorez speech of May 31, 1959, 144.

61. *L'Humanité*, October 26, 1959, cited in *La Politique communiste*, 173–74.

62. "Essai sur la nation algérienne," supplement to *Cahiers du Communisme*, 8 (August 1958), 3–32.

63. Philippe Robrieux, *Maurice Thorez, vie secrète et vie publique* (Paris, 1975), 550. Also *Notre génération communiste* (Paris, 1977), 211. A book within a book on Servin-Casanova is contained in *Histoire intérieure*, II.

64. See Marcel Peju, *Le Procès du Reseau Jeanson* (Paris, 1961), also François Jeanson, *Notre guerre* (Paris, 1961), and *Le Droit à l'insoumission: le dossier des 121* (Paris, 1961).

65. Simone Signoret said she signed the declaration out of national pride; Natalie Sarraute wished to preserve the "identity of France and freedom." *Le Droit à l'insoumission*, 94–95. Maurice Maschino, *L'Engagement*, was unafraid of the charge of treason: 86–91.

66. *La Politique communiste*, 194–288.

67. *L'Humanité*, November 1, 1960; *La Politique communiste*, 124. *Cahiers du Communisme*, 6 (June 1961), 19.

68. Larbi Bouhali, "Alzhirski narod v borbe za nazional'nuyu nezavisimost," *Kommunist* (November 1960), 76–87. ("The Algerian People in their Struggle for National Independence.") This article provoked a stinging reply by a spokesman for Islamic socialism: see Amar Ouzegane (Ammar Uzighan), *Le Meilleur Combat* (Paris, 1962).

69. *L'Humanité,* March 9, 1960.

70. See the editorial by Pierre Vigier, *L'Humanité,* October 3, 1960, reprinted in *Le Droit à l'insoumission,* 128–29.

71. Thorez speech to the Central Committee, October 14, 1960, in *La Politique communiste,* 224.

72. Claude Bourdet, in *France Observateur,* October 27, 1960. Louis Couturier, *Les "grandes affaires" du P.C.F.* (Paris, 1972), 64–73.

73. *Cahiers du Communisme,* 5 (May 1961), 869–76; 3 (March 1962), 1–20.

74. Declaration of the Central Committee of the PCF, Ibid. (May 1962), 183–88.

10
THE PCF AND DE-STALINIZATION, 1956–1962

The PCF's continuing crisis over de-Stalinization provided an opportunity for a historian to make history. In January 1977, in response to the publication of Philippe Robrieux's biography of Maurice Thorez, the PCF Political Bureau requested Georges Cogniot to clarify how the contents of Khrushchev's secret speech at the Twentieth Congress of the CPSU became known in France.[1] Cogniot, who with Thorez, Duclos, and Pierre Doize represented the PCF, confirmed the French were shown a copy of the speech just before its delivery on February 25, 1956. Thorez immediately decided to conceal it from the PCF and swore the others to secrecy. When the "report attributed to Khrushchev" was published by the world press in June 1956, the PCF leadership affected total surprise and refused to admit its authenticity. The PCF's vain effort to block the process of de-Stalinization flowed logically from Thorez's initial act. In 1978 the PCF acknowledged the Thorezian leadership was "late" in its response to the Twentieth Congress causing serious political consequences, among them failure to recognize the anti-capitalist aspects of the student revolt of May 1968. The last years of Thorez's leadership, 1956–64, came under increasing criticism by party members and dissidents after 1978 when most of the principal figures involved were safely dead.

The intellectuals commissioned in 1978 to re-evaluate the PCF's relationship to the USSR concluded that Thorez reacted as he did because of the changed international climate. True, Thorez lacked confidence in the new Soviet leadership and saw a threat to Marxism-Leninism in any repudiation of the Stalinist past. But his primary concerns were the campaign against the Algerian war and op-position to Anglo-French imperialism during the Suez crisis.[2] Thorez's con-cealment of Khrushchev's speech also coincided with the PCF's support for Guy Mollet and maximum effort to escape political isolation. In March 1956 the PCF voted plenary powers; in May it endorsed warmly Mollet's visit to the USSR. A positive response to de-Stalinization would have helped the party's effort to achieve acceptance, but instead the PCF showed it was more Stalinist than the Russians. The peculiar PCF dialectic, authoritarian internal organization, and Moscow-centered internationalism as conditions of democratic participation in French politics were exemplified in the February-to-June timetable. Thorez was not improvising; he had been resisting trends toward de-Stalinization evident in the USSR since 1953, all the while pursuing a Popular Front, the only policy he knew. Thorez was mesmerized by his "glorious" past. He wished again to participate in the French government while cutting a figure of influence and prestige in world Communism. He did not seem aware of any contradiction between these ambitions.

At a secret Moscow meeting of the Cominform in July 1953 after the Beria affair the French and the Italian Communists were both informed of the coming de-Stalinization in the USSR.[3] Thorez was encouraged in his natural impulse to resist de-Stalinization by the Malenkov-Molotov group, who assured him they would win the internal struggle for power in the USSR. Lecoeur was cashiered for urging adoption of the Khrushchev line. The Thirteenth Party Congress provided consolidation of Thorez's hold and a declaration of his opposition to de-Stalinization. In February 1954, in an introduction to a pamphlet on the life of a little known Communist militant, Georges Levy, Thorez idolized Stalin and warned against an attack on the Communist past.[4] At the Thirteenth Congress Duclos quoted Thorez thirty-four times, Stalin twenty-nine, Malenkov six, and Molotov twice; Khrushchev, although Secretary of the CPSU, was not quoted at all. This pattern continued through the Twentieth Party Congress of the CPSU. Thorez's ties to Molotov led him to oppose Khrushchev's commitment to détente and peaceful coexistence, despite his own "historic" initiatives for peace and France's central role in the Peace Movement. The Communist press gave the widest possible publicity to Frederic Joliot-Curie's declaration of January 13, 1955, that peaceful coexistence was the only possible policy; atomic war meant the "annihilation of the human race." Yet in April Thorez repeated the Molotov position later made famous by the Chinese, criticizing "exaggeration" of the dangers of atomic war.[5] If war occurred, Thorez wrote, it would only cause the death of capitalism; the Socialist camp would survive to rebuild. Apocalyptic visions of atomic destruction were propagated by the Americans to disarm the masses and encourage a belief in fatalism.

The PCF turned to a new round of sectarian policies after the failure of its romance with Pierre Mendès-France. Algeria provided a first source of disagreement; when after defeat of the EDC Mendès-France negotiated new international agreements allowing for West German rearmament, the Communists returned to the opposition with renewed fervor. Ratification of the accords was "a betrayal of France and a crime against peace."[6] Mendès-France was not a progressive but a wiley politician dedicated to serving the capitalist class. His chief collaborator, François Mitterrand, manipulated an unsavory mixture of police connections and political trickery for the benefit of capitalism and war. The Socialists supported the German rearmament agreements; Guy Mollet again became a zealous advocate of German revanchism and Social-Democracy an agency of American Imperialism. New attacks on Social-Democracy reached a level of invective probably unequaled in Communist propaganda before or since. Roger Garaudy attacked Léon Blum for "deliberately falsifying" Marxism at the Congress of Tours in 1920, "ignominiously slandering" the USSR in 1937 by defending the traitor Tukhachevsky whom Blum knew to be guilty, rescuing the bourgeoisie during the Popular Front, and zealously defending American imperialism.[7] Even Zhdanovian socialist-realism received new support: *Cahiers du Communisme* praised the theories of Communist physicist J. P. Vigier as a reaffirmation of dialectical materialism and a setback for "bourgeois idealism" in the probabilistic views of Heisenberg and Bohr. The journal's editors wrote a self-critical editorial regretting their insufficient attention to German rearmament, mass organizations, party organization, and unity with colonial peoples. New tributes appeared to Stalin's genius and role as an original Marxist theorist.

In the context of this renewed sectarianism Thorez launched the third of his "historic" theoretical initiatives, the campaign to uphold the vulgar-Marxist theory of relative and absolute pauperization of the working class under capitalism. Thorez tried to claim the mantle of succession to Lenin and Stalin by presenting himself as defender of the orthodox faith against revisionism in the USSR.[8] With Stalin dead, Thorez might assume for Western Marxism the role Mao Tse-Tung enjoyed in the East. Mao experienced a wave of officially sponsored prestige in the French party lasting from 1955 until the outbreak of the Sino-Soviet split in 1961. Thorez was afflicted with some megalomania in the entertainment of these ambitions. He adopted a monarchical life-style, permitting his party to purchase a chateau for him amid the Mediterranean playground of the world's decadent capitalist elite. His work habits came to reflect his new imperial isolation. He relied exclusively on his secretary, Georges Cogniot, made decisions privately, keeping his own counsel, and allowed an extraordinary role and influence to Jeannette Vermeersch.[9]

Thorez's peace initiative of 1950 had meant subordination of internal politics to international considerations. The pauperization campaign signalled a return to internal economic issues and a greater role for the CGT. Previously attacked by critics for subordinating working-class demands to the Peace Movement, the party ironically was now criticized for giving wages higher priority than the Algerian war. But in 1955 it was not yet clear that Algeria would become the central issue of French politics. PCF propaganda focused on the pauperization campaign, attributing every manifestation of working-class discontent and combativeness to Thorez's penetrating insight. The campaign was not as absurd as Thorez's critics alleged. The "myth" of prosperity, Thorez said, resulted from a superficial veneer of increased consumption in France. "Impartial" observers, impressed by the number of workers owning scooters, failed to ask if they reflected an underlying decline in popular living standards due to longer commuting distances to work.[10] Thorez's bleak picture of the economy did not seem inaccurate to many workers who had not yet shared in the new prosperity. France was producing more than it had in 1929, Thorez admitted, but still lagged far behind Germany. There had been little investment in fixed capital because of the military drain in Indochina and Algeria. Increased industrial concentration and the subordination of nationalized enterprises to private interests resulted in a system best described as "State Monopoly Capitalism." Wages, adjusted for inflation, were still at only 50 percent of prewar levels, industrial fatigue and accidents had increased, and workers' health worsened. Employment was down, and the industrial reserve army growing. Alcoholism was on the rise, encouraged by state subsidies to wine producers in Algeria while local needs in wheat grains there were unmet: "Thus those who despoiled the people of Algeria were the same who poisoned the people of France." Thorez singled out Mendès-France, characterizing his economic policies as little better than those of Pinay.

When Mendès-France accepted Thorez's challenge and criticized pauperization as archaic and in conflict with the facts, Thorez made yet another major theoretical statement of Stalinist orthodoxy, emphasizing the non-material aspects of pauperization.[11] Physiological exhaustion was also a form of worker impoverishment. The growth of "parasitic social elements" in the army, police, bureaucracy, and among cadres placed a heavier pyramidal burden on productive workers. Tied to a pale imitation of the grand bourgeoisie's life-style, these groups were tempted easily by opportunism, political reaction, or fascism.

Thorez's analysis remained an enduring theme of PCF political analysis and tactics. The PCF always appealed to other social groups but refused to concede them any authentic political role. The middle class had no ideology and had to ally with either capitalism or the workers while the PCF defined the working class in the narrowest terms and insisted on the existence of misery in the face of prosperity. Georges Marchais' 1978 election campaign was widely criticized by Communist dissidents for its narrow, sectarian appeal to the poorest workers, excluding everyone else.[12] The party complicated efforts to forge alliances by these tactics, inappropriate even to the Communist electorate among whom skilled and higher-paid workers were as numerous as the very poor. The Soviets were not overjoyed with Thorez's neo-Stalinist analysis in 1955. Jean Baby, an editor of *Economie et Politique,* was criticized for his heterodox views on pauperization, eventually leaving the PCF to write a scathing critique of Thorez's sectarianism on the issue. Yet in October, *Cahiers du Communisme* republished a Soviet article on French "progressive" economic thought, which singled out Baby for praise.[13] E. Pletniev faintly congratulated Thorez for exploding the "myth" of French prosperity but also condemned the work of orthodox PCF economists who mechanically and incorrectly predicted capitalist economic crisis must inevitably lead to war. Pletniev analysed the work of Charles Bettelheim and Alfred Sauvy, congratulating them on their critique of neo-Keynesianism and noting approvingly that certain bourgeois economists were capable of coming over to the positions of the working class. Thorez's critics noted the discrepancy between Soviet and French Communist views in their polemics.

The Soviet rapprochement with Yugoslavia further troubled relations between the CPSU and the PCF in 1955. *L'Humanité* reported the news without comment on May 16. Many Communists in France were shocked; for intellectuals like Domenique Desanti, who had been made to compromise their integrity in the anti-Tito campaign, the rapprochement was the turning point in their romance with Stalinism.[14] Thorez was not pleased. The enmity between the French and

Yugoslav parties was personal as well as ideological, dating from the founding Congress of the Cominform in September 1947. Khrushchev referred to the Yugoslavs as a "Marxist-Leninist" party while they in turn warmly praised Social-Democracy as an authentic expression of the working class.[15] The PCF stuck to its characterization of Social-Democracy as "principal support of the bourgeoisie." Both these positions could not be Marxist-Leninist, or a simple matter of disagreement between fraternal parties. In July 1955, at the Central Committee meeting of the PCF at Gentilly, Laurent Casanova insisted that despite "sectarian errors" in application the criticisms of the Yugoslav party's actions formulated by the Cominforn in 1948 were correct.[16] PCF-Yugoslav relations remained troubled thereafter. Casanova did not stop there: The USSR was not infallible, Casanova warned, and while it was certainly superior in principle to other countries because of its socialist system, solidarity with the USSR by the French was always subject to verification that "the actions of Soviet power are in conformity with [Marxist-Leninist] principles." Thorez repeated the same warning a year later when he repudiated the formula of "unconditional attachment" of French Communists to the USSR. Already in 1955, however, the PCF warned the USSR not to go too far in the de-Stalinization process.

The PCF's internal strategy was not determined by the International Movement. The November 1955 *tournant* vis-à-vis the Socialists was accompanied by no softening of resistance to de-Stalinization; it was precipitated by the prospect of elections resulting from Premier Edgar Faure's dissolution of the National Assembly. Thorez had been mechanically applying class-against-class tactics to that point in the hope of forcing a change in Socialist attitudes but the Communists made repeated overtures for common action as well. The PCF offered cooperation in the National Assembly and on the local level to block the construction of atomic weapons in France, and Communists offered to withdraw on the second ballot of cantonal elections in favor of any Socialist candidate who would accept a joint minimum program. On September 1 the PCF Political Bureau wrote the Socialist Directing Committee to offer common action in the struggle against colonialism and in favor of a negotiated peace in Algeria.[17] In October 1955, however, a "profound gap" was still said to separate French Communists and Socialists; only the elections brought a definitive change. On November 8, 1955, Thorez told the Central Committee that the two parties agreed on lay education, salaries, protection of the peasantry, the French Union, disarmament and détente. This was an impressive list. "For our part, we solemnly declare that we are ready to come to an agreement with the Socialists immediately after the elections for a policy conforming to the will of the people, and to give to France the government that she expects."[18] The PCF was ready "to assume its responsibilities" in the government; a "stable and productive left-wing policy is now possible in France."

Jeannette Vermeersch tried to give the policy change an image somewhat more palatable than blatant opportunism. True, Jeannette Vermeersch wrote, Zhdanov had demonstrated the treason of the right-wing Socialists in 1947. But changes in the international and national situations had occurred; far-sighted Socialists like Jules Moch opposed German rearmament, and mass pressure was making the SFIO leadership move toward the left.[19] The election campaign stressed the prospect of revived Socialist-Communist unity of action; the PCF called upon its supporters to vote Communist "to prepare the victory of a new Popular Front."[20] The PCF wanted to believe that Guy Mollet would bring peace to Algeria. The campaign also had its discordant notes. On December 12 *L'Humanité* allotted one-quarter page to the seventy-sixth anniversary of the birth of Stalin. Jean Freville characterized the dead Soviet leader as a loyal disciple of Lenin and a genius, whose historical stature was "*gigantesque.*" On December 30 Guy Mollet, in explaining why the Socialists could not unite with the PCF, branded the Communists with an epithet they would never live down: ". . . their elected officials are neither to the right nor the left, but to the East, and their only preoccupation is to further the interests of Soviet foreign policy."[21]

The party chose to ignore Mollet's attack as it had done with Mendès-France's refusal to count its votes in 1954. In the aftermath of the elections, Duclos noted the Socialists had augmented the number of their votes. But the PCF had gained 500,000 votes and fifty-four parliamentary seats over its 1951 totals, restoring the Communist political presence in the National Assembly to full strength.[22] The elements of a renewed Popular Front were in place, and the PCF placed great hopes on Mollet's promises for peace in Algeria; Duclos, consulted by President Coty, advised the latter to call upon a Socialist as Premier.[23] The party continued to regard Mendès-France phenomenon with suspicion. Duclos called for the formation of unity-of-action committees throughout France. But on February 15, 1956, the PCF again tarnished its image by excluding one of its most prominent intellectuals, Pierre Hervé, on the charge of "vulgar opportunism." Hervé had written a scathing indictment of the party's dogmatic application of crude canons of socialist realism in its cultural policies. More importantly, Hervé sensed the moderate evolution under way in the USSR and criticized the PCF for failing to adapt to what was clearly becoming the new reality of Soviet Communism.[24] As the Twentieth Congress of the CPSU unfolded, moreover, it appeared the PCF was preoccupied with the East to the detriment of its hopes for integration into French politics.

In February 1956, prior to the Twentieth Congress, Thorez published an article in *Pravda* that pointedly ignored the themes of the Congress and twice cited Stalin, thus sharing honors with the Chinese as the only foreign delegations to mention Stalin with approval. Thorez renounced the theory of the inevitability of war and referred to his London *Times* interview in his speech, but he affirmed the pauperization theory, condemned opportunism, and proclaimed his fidelity to the heritage of Marx, Engels, Lenin, and Stalin.[25] Khrushchev's secret speech was discussed only privately; the agonized reaction of Thorez's son Jean, "we are all assassins," only firmed up Thorez's resolve to maintain secrecy. Within the PCF, however, there were already three categories of persons: those who knew the contents of the report, those who knew of it, and those who knew nothing, and the first two categories were rapidly growing.[26] Domenique Desanti gained access to the report through the Poles, who also released it to Jean Pronteau and the CIA. Pronteau just back from a trip to Eastern Europe, confronted Thorez with his knowledge of the report, explaining that he had a copy in his briefcase. Thorez was caustic: "we must act as if it did not exist." If the report were published, Thorez elaborated, it would be denounced as a forgery.[27]

On March 5, 1956, *L'Humanité* published a photo of Stalin in commemoration of the third anniversary of his death, noted his "eminent" role at the head of the CPSU and linked his name to the great victories of World War II. Jacques Duclos summarized the "achievements" of the Twentieth Soviet Party Congress on March 9.[28] The Congress had been a clarion call for left-wing unity and peaceful coexistence, and it affirmed the doctrine of different and parliamentary paths to Socialism as in Thorez's London *Times* interview of 1946. But the transition from capitalism to socialism still meant revolution, not reformism, Duclos warned; whether or not the process was peaceful depended upon the bourgeoisie. Having qualified the notion of the peaceful transition to Socialism, Duclos clarified the limits of de-Stalinization in France. The Congress had affirmed the necessity of collective leadership and repudiated the cult of personality. The name of Stalin, however, could not be forgotten or erased from history. He was the defender of the 1917 Revolution, builder of Socialism, victor in the war against Hitler, and a key figure in the development of Communist parties everywhere. "The merits of Comrade Stalin are inscribed in history," Duclos announced to partial but thunderous applause, "they are part of the patrimony of the international workers' movements." Duclos concluded by promising to protect the purity of Marxist-Leninist doctrine and defending the exclusion of Pierre Hervé, accused of revisionism.

Thorez absented himself from the Central Committee meeting of March 22, leaving Duclos to repeat the same message to the assembled delegates, but it was becoming difficult for the leadership to prevent reverberations of the Twentieth Congress. The vote in favor of plenary powers for Mollet did not have universal approbation in the party either. From March 18 through 20 *L'Humanité* reported further disquieting moves in the de-Stalinization campaign in the USSR. Florimond Bonte caused a sensation by revealing criticism of Stalin by Walter Ulbricht. A group favorable to de-Stalinization made its presence felt and the resolution reflected a compromise authored by Waldeck Rochet, who appeared from that time forward to favor "change without risk."[29] Thorez preferred to legislate from a distance. On March 27 he published an article in *L'Humanité* endorsing the major themes of the Twentieth Congress of the CPSU, specifically peaceful coexistence and the peaceful transition to socialism. He also noted approvingly Mollet's plans to go to Moscow, correctly noting that this was a shift in the Socialist position but misunderstanding that the Socialists were responding to the Khrushchev line, not his own.[30] The basic PCF position, Thorez emphasized, would not change. The cult of personality had not affected the correctness of the historic CPSU line nor did criticism of Stalin detract from his great stature. Thorez criticized Stalin for the "erroneous" thesis of the intensification of the class struggle under Socialism, which became a justification for "violations of Socialist legality" in the USSR. But the French Communist leader would go no further, rather hurrying off to Italy to enlist Togliatti in the struggle against de-Stalinization. Upon his arrival in Rome, Thorez complained to his confidant in the PCI, Giulio Ceretti, that Khrushchev had "dragged through the mud a brilliant and heroic past."[31]

The meeting with Togliatti ended in an impasse; the Italian leader was disposed to push for more thorough de-Stalinization. Thorez's absence at his party's Central Committee meeting and unhappiness in the PCF over the resolution passed had meanwhile leaked to the French press. *Le Monde* reported that Jeannette Vermeersch and Waldeck Rochet had openly contradicted each other while the major party figures, Billoux, Guyot, Mauvais, and Servin, sat in silence. The PCF's lack of enthusiasm for the de-Stalinization campaign was widely noted in the press and a flurry of speculative reports appeared on Thorez's imminent replacement by Frachon or Billoux.[32] The French Socialists meanwhile warned the PCF that Communist resistance to de-Stalinization was inconsistent with affirmations of a possible parliamentary road to Socialism.[33] Hopes for a new Popular Front in France were clearly premature.

Thorez addressed the PCF parliamentary group on April 14 but did not discuss de-Stalinization in greater depth. Stalin's errors did not detract from his historic achievements; Thorez deplored the susceptibility of so many comrades to the uproar created in the non-Communist press.[34] The Twentieth Congress of the CPSU had opened new perspectives; it had not given license for questions about party organization, principles, and the pauperization doctrine or for *gauchiste* critiques of PCF tactics. Defending Communist support for Mollet, Thorez also launched a vicious attack on birth control. Was this a diversion, as was frequently charged? The attack on "Neo-Malthusianism" as blaming the poor for their own misery and perpetuating the domination of the bourgeoisie was hardly new. It fit in with pauperization and was consistent with Thorez's nostalgia for the Popular Front: the same themes were articulated at the party congress of Villeurbanne in 1936.[35] Thorez's new outburst reacted to the publication of a book advocating birth control by a French Communist doctor, Derogy. But Thorez was undoubtedly more concerned about internal party discipline; he was unable openly to silence advocates of de-Stalinization in the PCF because of his knowledge of the secret speech, awareness that Togliatti and others were advocates of de-Stalinization, and fear the Soviets might use pro-Khrushchev sentiment in the PCF to undermine his leadership. Birth control became a handy issue with which to reassert Thorez's control over Communist intellectuals and warn dissidents there were limits they would not be allowed to transgress.

Thorez's motive was evident in his speech to the PCF's May 9–10 Central Committee meeting, in which he linked birth control and party discipline.[36] The theses for the PCF Fourteenth Congress were already under discussion Thorez noted. The PCF was the most democratic party in France, and criticism was to be encouraged on condition it strengthened Communism. Nobody had the right to introduce bourgeois ideology or neo-Malthusianism in the PCF: there was no discussion possible on the issue. The advocacy of birth control was contrary to Marxism. Had not Lenin warned against treating sex like a "glass of water"?

There was "no right to error" in the party. Discipline reaffirmed, Thorez turned to de-Stalinization. Some further concessions were necessary, but he would permit no weakening of the general party line. Whatever Stalin's faults, the historic achievements remained. Had the errors persisted, Thorez conceded, catastrophes might have occurred, but the mistakes had been corrected in time. Stalin, who had taught the necessity of criticism and self-criticism, had himself ceased to practice it, and instead fallen victim to self-satisfaction and presumption. Hence, the violations of Socialist legality. Stalin had ceased to be a Stalinist; that was his main fault. The PCF, however, had remained ideologically pure and had no need to reexamine its past. Thorez then criticized the formula of "unconditional attachment to the USSR" as unfortunate: loyalty to the USSR had always remained conditional upon the Soviet Union continuing in the correct path of Socialism. Thorez thus again warned the group in power in the USSR not to carry their revisionism too far. To emphasize his independence further, Thorez again insisted the Cominform had been correct to criticize Yugoslav revisionism in 1948. Only intervention in Yugoslav internal affairs, the effort to overthrow the Yugoslav leaders, had been unjustified. Thorez was warning the Soviets not to try the same thing in France.

With the Stalin cult repudiated Thorez could no longer evade the question of his own personality. The formula "party of Maurice Thorez" was to be condemned, Thorez declared, but he refused to ask why it emerged. Somewhat incredulously, Thorez said that he had protested use of the slogan to the Political Bureau and *L'Humanité,* but without effect. Thorez said he now regretted that his complaints had not been brought to the attention of the Central Committee earlier. In appearance it was an absurd claim. The implication remained, however, that Thorez had been unable to bring other matters to the Central Committee because of resistance in the Political Bureau, particularly in the period after his return in 1953. Thorez insisted personal autocracy had not been the problem in the French party, rather its absence. His inability to make his will prevail from 1950 to 1954 was the cause of the PCF's problems. The party must share in the blame for the personality cult; there had been too much birthday celebration, quotation in the press and adulation of individuals at all echelons. But collective leadership always existed; it was not perfect, but "the Political Bureau is a collective organism, this despite certain problems connected with the (past) illness of the Secretary General." The cult of personality was not to be confused with normal manifestations of affection toward leadership.

Thorez's balancing act had the desired effect; the PCF absorbed publication of the "report attributed to Khrushchev" with minimum shock. *Le Monde* carried the report on June 4; the PCF remained silent until its authenticity could not be denied. On June 18 the Political Bureau made the following official declaration:[37]

The bourgeois press has published a report attributed to Comrade Khrushchev. This report, which adds to the already known errors of Stalin the enumeration of very serious faults committed by him, gives rise to legitimate emotion among members of the PCF.

The French Communists, the same as Communists in all countries, condemn the arbitrary acts, contrary to the principles of Marxism-Leninism, with which Stalin is reproached. . . .

The Political Bureau regrets however that because of the conditions in which the report of Comrade Khrushchev was presented and divulged, the bourgeois press has been in a position to publish facts of which the French Communists had no knowledge. Such conditions are not favorable to the normal discussion of these problems in the party. They facilitate, on the contrary, the speculations and maneuvers of the enemies of Communism.

The explanations given thus far of the mistakes of Stalin, their origin, the conditions under which they took place, are unsatisfactory. A thorough Marxist analysis is indispensible in order to determine the ensemble of circumstances in which the personal power of Stalin was able to be exercised.

The declaration conceded the authenticity of the report and reproached Khrushchev for the manner in which it was divulged which aided the cause of anti-Communists. The "Marxist analysis" of the conditions in which Stalin's errors occurred was prejudged in the remainder of the declaration, which stated that "Stalin played a positive role for an entire historical period." His errors arose because of the "iron discipline" necessarily imposed on the Soviet people due to the encirclement of the USSR by its enemies. The Political Bureau further requested an official copy of the report so French Communists could discuss it in preparations under way for their Fourteenth Party Congress. This request was never honored.[38]

In the meantime, Palmiro Togliatti authenticated the report, admitted prior knowledge, and called for a Marxist analysis of the causes of personality cult within the Soviet system.[39] Togliatti came perilously close to Trotskyist modes of analysis of Soviet bureaucratic degeneration. Thorez reacted with alarm. A delegation of French Communists consisting of Waldeck Rochet, Marcel Servin, and Etienne Fajon was dispatched to the USSR to demand explanations from Khrushchev. According to Fajon, the purpose was to obtain an authenticated copy of the secret speech and insist the Soviets undertake analysis of the Stalinist past.[40] But the PCF was trying to limit the harm already done and mitigate the impact of Khrushchev's revelations. The joint declaration of the PCF and CPSU published on July 6 asserted the personality cult arose as a result of historic circumstances and the peculiarity of Stalin. Its causes could not be found in the structure of the Soviet system; any such interpretation stood condemned as "idealism."[41] Togliatti's "interesting" views were erroneous. There had been no degeneration of Soviet society at any time in the past. The declaration simply elaborated upon the Political Bureau analysis of June 18. The causes of the personality cult were capitalist encirclement, the struggle against Trotskyism, the need for discipline, Stalin's "rudeness," and the activities of Beria. The PCF accepted the declaration as the "profound and satisfying" Marxist analysis the party had been seeking.[42] Thorez had won his concessions: Khrushchev retreated from the analysis in the secret speech and Togliatti was repudiated. From this point on the PCF leader regarded the issue closed.

The PCF's Fourteenth Congress demonstrated, paradoxically, that the peculiar way in which Khrushchev's secret speech became known in France was less harmful than any method the leadership might have devised. Prominent intellectuals like Pierre Daix, Domenique Desanti, Pierre Noirot, and Annie Kriegel heard rumors of Stalin's crimes and received partial information at various stages of the de-Stalinization process. For some, internal personal crisis led to a break with the party; for others, adherence to the party continued on a new basis. The differences appeared to reduce themselves to questions of temperament. The apparatus proved more docile. Those who owed a livelihood to the counter-society were least likely to leave no matter how they were affected by the revelations. At the base, where commitment to the Stalin cult was less intense, the revelations made less impact. Finally, many Communists retained a measure of disbelief with regard to the most serious charges against Stalin. Khrushchev did not enjoy generalized admiration in the PCF; many, like Thorez, regarded the new Soviet leadership with suspicion. The secret speech was never published by the Communist press and as a "report attributed to Khrushchev," from bourgeois sources, it could be more easily managed. The report's content strained the credibility of devoted Communists. In 1978 Etienne Fajon still remained skeptical that Stalin, as presented by Khrushchev, planned Soviet military strategy during the Second World War on a globe.[43]

Thorez took the necessary precautions to maintain discipline. Party officials were brought to headquarters for discussions; where persuasion was inadequate, the Secretary General could cajole and threaten.[44] Many had previously done things they did not want revealed. Thorez combined inducement with blandishment. At the Fourteenth Congress in Le Havre none were eliminated from leadership positions; both the Political Bureau and the Central Committee were enlarged in size to accommodate the promotions of all alternate members to regular status.[45] Central Committee membership rose from 75 to 102. Frederic Joliot-Curie was appointed to the Central Committee without having been an alternate. Thorez appeared to promise some democratization in party functioning. The Secretariat was demoted in importance to accentuate the new emphasis on collective leadership; Fajon told the Congress it had usurped too many functions that belonged to the Political Bureau. To insure against a recurrence, it was expanded to seven members, three of whom were not to sit on the Political Bureau.

Thorez's speech at the Fourteenth Congress was a personal triumph. Superficially the PCF continued to demonstrate unity, vitality, and enthusiasm. The Communist leader's major themes were the same. The aim was still unity with the Socialists, who, regrettably, had slid to the right since June 1956. The Popular Front was not an occasional tactic but one of the basic principles of Marxism-Leninism. The PCF was the dynamic party of the future with 5,500,000 votes, 144 Deputies, and 46,000 new members. There were disquieting notes: the usual dangers of sectarianism and opportunism were present. Sectarians criticized the March 28 vote in support of Guy Mollet and the June 5 abstention; opportunists resisted the pauperization and anti-neo-Malthusian campaigns. Thorez criticized insufficient effort at recruitment in party youth organizations and announced the replacement of the old "Union of Republican youth of France," whose Communist ties, despite the name, were well known, with the new "Union of Communist Youth." The PCF remained a workers' party, and proletarians would continue to lead it; factions were not allowed. Intellectuals must stay within the confines of Marxism-Leninism. The speech was vintage Thorez, opportunist in parliamentary tactics, sectarian on internal party organization and pretending to the correct middle ground. Thorez never seemed to grasp that the mean between extremes could mean immobility.

Thorez regarded the de-Stalinization episode ended. The Soviets, he noted, had done self-criticism without parallel among the bourgeoisie. Which capitalist politicians were prepared to admit to the errors of Spain, Munich, and Dien Bien Phu? Stalin had demonstrated "exceptional merit"; his personality cult in no way reflected upon the Soviet system and was a Russian problem in any case. There had been no personality cult in the PCF, only some "traces," which had been eliminated. The Twentieth Congress of the CPSU had highlighted the PCF's original contributions to Marxist theory: the Popular Front, peaceful road to Socialism and non-inevitability of war.

Thorez's success in maintaining party cohesiveness became apparent during the crisis over Hungary. Although he regarded the Hungarian uprising as the consequence of de-Stalinization, Thorez saw no alternative to supporting the Soviet leadership in an effort to bolster the International Communist Movement, its future in doubt since the dissolution of the Cominform in April 1956. People's power had been restored in Hungary, the Communist press declared; the timely intervention of Soviet troops averted a fascist restoration of capitalism.[46] The PCF was vulnerable on the issue: polls showed much of the Communist electorate shared the general French feelings of hostility to the Soviet move.[47] Yet the party weathered the crisis with ease. The PCF was again assisted by the French right: the Anglo-French invasion of Suez seemed to validate the PCF's claim that imperialism was the danger to peace. A violent attack on the headquarters of *L'Humanité* on the night of November 5 gave militants a chance to rally around the popular themes of antifascism and republican defense.[48]

The Hungarian invasion had damaging effects of a deeper kind. Jean Paul Sartre discovered the PCF's sclerosis and pronounced "a plague on both houses." Ten Communist intellectuals published a protest in the non-Communist press, the first action of its kind.[49] Thorez promised during the Fourteenth Congress to recognize Communists' freedom to disagree as long as they submitted to discipline. Comrades in error would be re-educated like the Chinese rather than excluded; the protest of the ten provided an opportunity for a show of such magnanimity. The real casualty of the Hungary-Suez crisis was the hope of Socialist-Communist unity for peace in Algeria. The crisis thus helped destroy the Fourth Republic, although a different PCF reaction toward de-Stalinization or Hungary could not in themselves have saved the regime.

Thorez pursued contradictory policies until the fall of the Republic. In his internal policy the line remained a Popular Front. The PCF regretted it had been "constrained" to cease supporting Mollet, but it could no longer support a war that was, in the words of the Socialist leader himself, *"imbécile."*[50] In October 1957 the PCF made personal appeals to Socialist leaders. The Popular Front was a basic principle of Leninism; the PCF wanted unity, and Communists would not interfere in Socialist affairs or challenge the SFIO leadership. The PCF would do anything to facilitate negotiations (October 6, 1957), support any government taking steps to end the war (October 23). In March 1958 the party warned that continued alliance of the Socialists with the right would lead to fascism. In April, following the bombardment of Sakiet, Tunisia, by French warplanes, the PCF again appealed for a government of the left. In May 1958 the PCF fully supported legality against the fascist-style putsch from Algiers. The Republic fell, the party said, because the Socialist leaders since February 6, 1956 had engaged in treasonous complicity with the bourgeoisie.[51]

But the PCF bore its own historic responsibility for May 1958 through its zealous defense of Stalinism. By championing the sectarian line in the International Movement, Thorez reinforced opposition among non-Communists to unity with the PCF at home. The disintegration of the world Communist monolith was under way; instead of using it creatively, Thorez joined in a vain effort to prevent liberalization. Thorez supported the Molotov-Kaganovich group against Khrushchev; Jean Pronteau carried a message from Thorez to the "anti-party" group early in 1957, but failed to deliver it.[52] Pronteau instead joined the Khrushchevites on the PCF Central Committee who, led by Servin and Casanova, struggled against Thorez's line until they were ousted in 1961.

Thorez hoped to see Khrushchev overthrown while Togliatti and Tito tried to strengthen the Soviet leader, hence the PCF's attacks on Italian and Yugoslav "revisionism" in 1957. Roger Garaudy criticized the Italian Communists for tolerating the revisionist Giolitti faction and accepting the pluralism of political parties under Socialism. The Italian constitution was a typical bourgeois republic; to count on it to provide the framework for a peaceful transition to socialism was to foster illusions; no historical example of a successful peaceful transition to Socialism yet existed.[53] Togliatti's notion of "multiple centers" of the International Communist Movement, Pierre Villon wrote, was a departure from Marxism-Leninism. The USSR remained the decisive center of the international working class. Thorez saw Togliatti in Moscow shortly after Garaudy's article appeared. "Togliatti has not yet swallowed your article on the PCI's Eighth Congress," Thorez wrote Garaudy by way of congratulation.[54]

The PCF criticized the Yugoslavs with a vigor reminiscent of the days of Tito's alleged fascist clique. Duclos eagerly resumed the role of ideological policeman as in the condemnation of Browderism in 1945. The unity of the Communist world was essential; "national Communism" aided the bourgeoisie by dividing the Socialist camp.[55] The Yugoslavs used the term "Stalinism" as if it were a doctrine in and of itself. This was a total repudiation of the principles of Marxism-Leninism. The French echoed Soviet criticisms of the Yugoslav system. The Yugoslav experiment was totally unsuitable as a model; it restored a market economy, neglected the dictatorship of the proletariat and won the praise of Wall Street and the *New York Times*.

Thorez became the spokesman of Communist orthodoxy and the self-appointed savior of the International Movement. While upholding Moscow's central role, he was still more Stalinist than the Russians. The PCF denounced all "liquidationist and opportunist" interpretations of the Twentieth Congress of the CPSU, condemned preoccupation with the peaceful transition to socialism and neglect of the class struggle, repudiated "polycentrism," and warned against the spread of revisionist delusions.[56] Thorez returned to the pauperization theme, carrying his arguments to the point of absurdity. Consumer goods were no substitute for earlier times when spacious workers' housing had gardens and women were able to stay home. Three-week paid vacations were a necessary response to industrial cadences and psychological stress. Thorez warned his *Times* interview of November 1946 implied no denigration of the importance of the Russian Revolution, and he condemned the efforts of leftists like Sartre and Claude Bourdet, who sought to open the PCF to the ideology of the bourgeoisie.[57] Troubled by the absence of formal international Communist ties, Thorez launched another "historic initiative"; bi-lateral discussions with fraternal Communist parties. Delegations were dispatched to Moscow, Rome, Belgrade, Prague, and Sofia. With the Cominform in dissolution since April 1956, Thorez's rejection of Togliatti's doctrine of multiple centers of the International Movement amounted to recognition that the world Communist monolith was splitting apart. The joint declarations of the PCF with East-European parties condemned revisionism; those with the Yugoslavs and Italians frankly recognized differences.[58] Thorez's introduction of "new forms of proletarian internationalism" had no visible effect.

Thorez's hopes were dashed by Khrushchev's liquidation of the so-called anti-party group in July 1957. The PCF could do little else now but solidarize with the triumphant Khrushchev faction though its support contained a warning. "We approve [the line of] the 20th Congress," Thorez said, "because sometimes we ourselves have not always seen our initiatives appreciated, because certain of our ideas and theses have also been misunderstood and combatted."[59] Thorez cited his London *Times* interview and his peace initiative of 1950, neither of which had received the support in the Cominform they deserved: "We have suffered from that. It has weighed heavily on our party, and it has not favorized a political line taking into account the needs and the particular aspirations of our country." Thorez was making a declaration of PCF autonomy. In international affairs, the PCF still intended to support the CPSU against Khrushchev if necessary, as it had been more Stalinist than Stalin. In internal affairs the PCF maintained its tight party structure while pursuing alliance with Mollet's Socialists and excluding the new left.

Thorez had to settle matters with the French Khrushchevites, whose attachment to the USSR, like that of the Duclos-Fajon-Lecoeur group, constituted a potential threat to his authority. The Servin-Casanova group, despite Khrushchev's support, never exercised more influence than Thorez allowed them. It was ironic that the advocates of a more subtle analysis of capitalism in France and an opening to the New Left were also unconditional advocates of loyalty to the USSR.[60] There were about fifteen members of the Central Committee involved, but they did not constitute an organized faction.[61] After the condemnation of the anti-party group in 1957 Thorez gave them free reign. They were responsible for a genuine airing of differences inside the PCF and Thorez seemed on occasion seduced by their analyses. In the Political Bureau Vermeersch, Guyot, Billoux, Fajon, and Duclos expressed varying degrees of hostility to Servin and Casanova while Frachon and Waldeck Rochet tendered cautious support. Thorez tolerated the divergence. Servin and Casanova were strengthened not only by Khrushchev's support but also by the catastrophic defeat the PCF suffered in the November 1958 elections: only 3,822,204 votes or 18.9 percent, a loss of 1,650,427 votes since 1956. Thorez reversed his reaction to de Gaulle's statement on Algerian independence in 1959 under Casanova's urging and agreed that the PCF must adjust its policies to profit from the internal contradictions of the bourgeoisie. He allowed the group to articulate the view that parliament was a genuine instrument through which the workers might achieve the transition to socialism without civil war, even when it directly contradicted his favorite, Roger Garaudy. In March 1958 Maurice Kriegel-Valrimont wrote in reply to Garaudy that bourgeois democracy was the "most favorable terrain of the class struggle," and that Czechoslovakia had indeed provided a historical example of a totally peaceful transition to Socialism.[62] In January 1957 Garaudy had written that no successful historical example of a peaceful transition to Socialism existed.

Despite the Servin-Casanova group, the PCF remained rigidly sectarian internationally. Duclos expressed the party's satisfaction at the declaration of the twelve ruling Communist parties at their Moscow meeting of November 1957: there could be no "absolutely new" ways to Socialism, nor could any transition dispense with the Soviet example. The PCF remained steadfast through the 1960's in trying to preserve the Communist monolith. The eruption of the Sino-Soviet split in 1961 left Thorez no choice but to rally to the Soviet leadership, despite his personal attraction to Mao's views. The other alternative was to follow the revisionist path of Togliatti, a course which, temperamentally, Thorez regarded with horror.[63] Thorez's Jacobin-style nationalism still impelled him toward Moscow, and he acted instinctively to support the USSR when he perceived Soviet security to be threatened. In the spring of 1958 a new Soviet-inspired campaign for peace, focusing on opposition to the installation of American missile-launching sites in France, occupied the PCF's and the Peace Movement's energies. Finally, democratic centralism, continued power for the co-opted working-class elite that ruled the PCF, militated against any concession to the prejudices of bourgeois intellectuals. The choice of Casanova to articulate the PCF position of refusal to compromise on intellectual matters was not fortuitous. In April 1958 Casanova denounced opportunist and revisionist tendencies, as exemplified by Lecoeur and Hervé, whose approaches ultimately became anti-Sovietism.[64] There was great irony in Casanova's remarks, for Lecoeur and Hervé had both, in their own ways, championed de-Stalinization and thereby fallen afoul of the PCF's neo-Stalinist orthodoxy. Casanova and Servin committed the same errors.

Neither Servin nor Casanova was excluded from the PCF. Casanova's main reproach to Thorez remained that the PCF leader had never digested or properly understood the general line of Khrushchev or the meaning of the CPSU Twentieth Congress. For Casanova, Thorez was the opportunist: his un-Leninist suspicion of mass action prevented him from appreciating the importance of auxiliary organizations such as the Peace Movement, which needed to pursue an independent line in order to be effective.[65] With these views Casanova placed himself in the tradition of PCF dissidents; Charles Tillon argued in 1951 for the autonomy of mass organizations, losing his job as head of the Peace Movement to Casanova in 1951 over that issue. Casanova's wish to unite with the emerging New Left against the Algerian war, abandon the Socialists, and play upon the internal contradictions of the bourgeoisie followed from his concerns as head of the Peace Movement. Despite or because of his difficulties with Thorez, Casanova retained Soviet support and received the Lenin Peace prize in 1960 just before his demotion from the PCF leadership. Several analysts hypothesized that Thorez bargained his support for the Soviet position against China in 1961 for Khrushchev's agreement to the dismissal of Casanova.[66] There is no need for such elaborate explanations. Thorez rallied to the Soviet side in the Sino-Soviet dispute and dumped Casanova for his own reasons. Neither action required Soviet assent. Casanova supported the Soviet invasion of Czechoslovakia in 1968, and until his death he hoped he would be restored to a position of authority in the party. Servin was a convert to the Khrushchev position from the time of his mission to Moscow following publication of the secret speech in 1956. He was the first Communist leader in France to speak of Stalin's "crimes" in 1960. He identified with Casanova's views on technology, peaceful coexistence, and the importance of generational conflict, and he advocated cooperation with *gauchistes*. He joined Casanova in the house cleaning of January 1961, which also signalled the end for other noted militants such as Maurice Kriegel-Valrimont, Jean-Paul Vigier, André Souquières, and Philippe Robrieux. Those promoted shortly after lead the party today: Roland Leroy, Paul Laurent, and Georges Marchais.[67] Waldeck Rochet received the job of delivering the *coup de grace* to the two dissidents at the January 1961 meeting of the Central Committee despite and because of his prior defense of their positions. They were removed from their positions at the Sixteenth Congress in May.

The putsch of May 1958 removed the immediate possibility of a left-wing coalition governing France and thus made unity easier. It is impossible to gauge to what extent considerations of blocking the PCF from participating again in the government of the Fourth Republic contributed to the regime's overthrow. Since PCF participation also would have meant a negotiated peace in Algeria and the regime fell because it was suspected of seeking peace, the question in part answers itself. Since 1954 PCF participation had appeared a possibility. In

July 1955 Michel Debré, a lieutenant of de Gaulle, speculated that Moscow wanted the PCF to share power in France and noted that the constitution of the Fourth Republic made it possible. But Moscow dealt readily with regimes that suppressed Communists; return of the PCF to power would cause a grave internal crisis while bringing no better relations with the USSR.[68] In May 1958 the PCF declared that the goal of Communist participation had progressed and was now entertained by all elements in the French political spectrum. Politicians like François Mitterrand declined to exclude PCF participation.[69] May 1958 did it for them. Guy Mollet's collaboration with de Gaulle and Vincent Auriol's role in bringing the General to power precipitated a new round of PCF anti-Socialist invective. A definitive turn in PCF-Socialist relations had to await the end of the Algerian war and a significant modification of Socialist attitudes. The two parties only began cooperating in 1962, with Communist support on the second ballot for the election of Guy Mollet.

Accounts of a historic turn in PCF policy occurring in 1962 are exaggerated. Objective circumstances helped the development of left-wing unity; the Twenty-second Congress of the CPSU in 1961, which forced the PCF to adopt a rhetoric admitting to Stalin's "crimes," contributed to the Socialist change of view. But the PCF dated its call for a Common Program with the Socialists to its Fifteenth Congress in 1959, and its desire to restore the Popular Front was present virtually since the collapse of tripartism in 1947. It had always been a question of when the Socialists would adjust their policies sufficiently to the PCF's point of view. Gaullism created the circumstances for left-wing unity and alliance of the left remained the dynamic of French opposition politics at least until 1978, carrying the two parties almost despite themselves to victory in 1981.

NOTES

1. *L'Humanité,* January 16, 1977.
2. Alexandre Adler et al., *L'URSS et nous* (Paris, 1978), 21–22.
3. Philippe Robrieux, *Maurice Thorez, vie secrète et vie publique* (Paris, 1975), 421. Lilly Marcou, *Le Kominform* (Paris, 1977), 120–21. Donald L. M. Blackmer, *Unity in Diversity: Italian Communism and the Communist World* (Cambridge, Mass., 1968), 19–25.
4. Robrieux, *Maurice Thorez,* 425. *Histoire intérieure du PCF* (Paris, 1981), II, 363.
5. *L'Humanité,* March 3, 1955.
6. See the Editorial, *Cahiers du Communisme,* 2 (February 1955).
7. Ibid., 4 (April 1955).
8. See Pierre Daix, *La Crise du PCF* (Paris, 1978), 28–35.
9. Robrieux, *Maurice Thorez,* 490–91.
10. *Cahiers du Communisme,* 3 (March 1955).
11. Maurice Thorez, "Nouvelles donées sur la pauperisation," *Cahiers du Communisme,* 7–8 (July-August 1955).
12. See Jean Elleinstein in *Le Monde,* April 18, 1978.
13. *Cahiers du Communisme,* 10 (October 1955). Jean Baby, *Critique de Base* (Paris, 1961).

14. Domenique Desanti, *Les Staliniens* (Paris, 1975), 283–85.

15. See Richard Lowenthal, *World Communism, The Disintegration of a Secular Faith* (New York, 1966), 13.

16. *L'Humanité,* July 8, 1955.

17. *Cahiers du Communisme,* 4 (April 1955), 9 (September 1955), 10 (October 1955).

18. *L'Humanité,* November 11, 1955.

19. In *Cahiers du Communisme,* 12 (December 1955).

20. See Duclos' speech in *L'Humanité,* December 30, 1955.

21. *Le Populaire,* December 30, 1955.

22. Editorial, *Cahiers du Communisme,* 1–2 (January-February 1956).

23. *L'Humanité,* January 26, 1956.

24. Pierre Hervé, *La Révolution et ses fétiches* (Paris, 1956).

25. Robrieux, *Maurice Thorez,* 449. *Histoire Intérieure,* II, 431.

26. Etienne Fajon, personal interview, April 10, 1978.

27. Jean Pronteau, personal interview, April 25, 1978.

28. *L'Humanité,* March 10, 1956.

29. Branko Lazitch, *Le Rapport Khrouchtchev et son histoire* (Paris, 1976), 14–16. *Le Monde,* March 23, 1956. Robrieux, *Histoire Intérieure,* II, 443–44.

30. *L'Humanité,* March 27, 1956. Robrieux, *Maurice Thorez,* 460.

31. Giulio Ceretti, *A L'Ombre des Deux T: 40 ans avec Palmiro Togliatti et Maurice Thorez* (Paris, 1973), 343.

32. *Le Monde,* April 4, 1956. Also *Journal de Genève,* April 21, 1956, and *L'Express,* April 13, 1956.

33. *Le Populaire,* March 27, 1956.

34. *L'Humanité,* April 15, 1956.

35. Robrieux, *Maurice Thorez,* 465. Also François Fejto, *The French Communist Party and the Crisis of International Communism* (Cambridge, Mass., 1967), 46–63.

36. See text in *L'Humanité,* May 11, 1956.

37. Published in *L'Humanité,* June 19, 1956.

38. A. Adler, et al., *L'URSS et nous,* 27.

39. Blackmer, *Unity in Diversity,* 56–61.

40. Etienne Fajon, *Ma vie s'appelle liberté* (Paris, 1976), 229–31.

41. *Documents: Comment a été surmonté en URSS le culte de la personalité de Staline* (Paris, July 6, 1956). PCF Brochure.

42. *L'Humanité,* June 22, 1956.

43. Fajon, interview, April 10, 1978.

44. Robrieux, *Maurice Thorez,* 471; *Histoire Intérieure,* II, 460.

45. See *L'Humanité,* July 19, 1956.

46. *Cahiers du Communisme,* 11 (November 1956).

47. See Hadley Cantril, *The Politics of Despair* (New York, 1958), 186–93.

48. Robrieux, *Maurice Thorez,* 484–85.

49. Helene Parmelin, *Liberez les Communistes* (Paris 1979), 311–13. Also David Caute, *Communism and the French Intellectuals* (London, 1964), 220–30.

50. The relevant texts here are conveniently reprinted in Parti Communiste français, *Du XIVᵉ au XVᵉ Congrès, Trois années de lutte pour l'unité ouvrière et l'union des républicains* (Paris, 1959).

51. *Cahiers du Communisme,* 5 (May 1958).

52. Pronteau, interview, April 25, 1978. Cited in Robrieux, *Maurice Thorez*, 487. *Histoire Intérieure,* II, 483.

53. In *Cahiers du Communisme,* 1 (January 1957), also cited in Blackmer, *Unity and Diversity,* 124–27.

54. *Cahiers du Communisme,* 2 (February 1957) for Villon's article. Roger Garaudy was kind enough to provide me with the text of Thorez's note.

55. *Cahiers du Communisme,* 2 (February 1957).

56. Ibid., 3 (March 1957).

57. Ibid., 5 (May 1957).

58. Ibid. Thorez announced his initiative on February 14, 1957. For the texts of the joint declarations see *Cahiers du Communisme, Documents,* March through May 1957.

59. Ibid., 7 (July 1957).

60. Casanova's loyalty to the USSR comes through clearly in his memoir in the Robrieux archive.

61. See Paul Noirot, *La Memoire ouverte,* 238–46, and the exhaustive account in Robrieux, *Histoire Intérieure,* Il, 510–80.

62. *Cahiers du Communisme,* 3 (March 1958).

63. Casanova memoir, in Robrieux archive.

64. *Cahiers du Communisme,* 4 (April 1958).

65. Casanova memoir.

66. Andre Laurens and Thierry Pfister, *Les Nouveaux Communistes* (Paris, 1973), 48–60. Louis Couturier, *Les "grands affairs" du PCF* (Paris, 1972), 64–73.

67. Robrieux, *Histoire Intérieure,* 565–70.

68. *Combat,* July 5, 1955.

69. *Cahiers du Communisme,* 5 (May 1958).

EPILOGUE

With the end of the Algerian war in 1962, the conditions for a new Popular Front were quickly restored. The Socialists left de Gaulle's government and returned to the opposition; diatribes against SFIO leaders ceased in the Communist press. The PCF voted with 80 percent of the French population for the referendum on peace in Algeria and alongside the Socialists against election of the President of the Republic by universal suffrage. Support of Socialists on the second ballot of the November 1962 elections followed logically; Guy Mollet won thanks to Communist backing. In 1963 the PCF made a Common Program with the SFIO first in priority and in 1965 supported François Mitterrand for President of the Republic, declining to put forward a candidate of its own. The miners' strike of March 1963 forged a new syndical unity that, consecrated by victory, proved lasting.

The evolution of the party during the lengthy phase of left-wing unity from 1962 to 1977 engendered lengthy controversy over whether the PCF had "changed." The PCF adapted its strategy to altered circumstances, while holding inviolate its ideological commitment to Socialism and democratic-centralist organization. Changes in PCF ideology were based on precedent and fundamentals retained. Even abandonment of the term "dictatorship of the proletariat" had precedent in 1946 and was a semantical alteration at best. Strategically the options of Front populaire versus Front national continued to dominate. Front national, raising international commitments to priority, again became the policy from 1977 to 1981, to the dismay of members and sympathizers who believed that the policies in effect from 1962 to 1977 were definitive. The legislative elections of 1981, by returning a homogeneous Socialist majority, created an unprecedented situation, leaving the party impotent whether it joined the majority or the opposition. Nobody believed such a result possible between 1978 and 1980, when a renewed period of sectarian behavior reinforced the authority of the party's working-class elites, isolated intellectuals, and renewed ties to the USSR. While the USSR preferred Front national for the PCF, consistently favoring conservatives over moderate Socialists, it by no means followed that the party adopted that policy because of Soviet pressure. The PCF rejected the "Soviet model" of Socialism, while insisting the Soviet experience was "globally positive" and agreeing with major elements of Russian foreign policy.

Once committed to the line of the Twenty-second Congress of the CPSU in 1961, Thorez lost no time in demarcating his own traditional spheres of influence: cultural policy and religious issues. Thorez's "Critique of the philosophical errors of Stalin" was articulated by Roger Garaudy in a June 14, 1962, meeting.[1] Present were Billoux, Guyot, Waldeck Rochet, and Paul Laurent, a new member of the Political Bureau who rapidly became known as a liberal. Staunchly pro-Soviet Duclos and Fajon, and Georges Marchais, the new Secretary for Organization, were absent, perhaps unwilling to be associated with ideological deviation. Garaudy severely criticized the Zhdanovian period of cultural repression in PCF history, identifying its roots in Stalin's errors: the cult of personality, schematization of Marxism-Leninism, and severing of Dialectical Materialism from its rich Hegelian heritage, leading to dogmatism and scientism. The Hegelian basis of Marxian theory had been neglected by Stalin, leading to a "mutilation" of Marxism. A step toward the New-Left interpretation of Marxism, Garaudy's rediscovery of the "young Marx" helped give the PCF a new progressive image. A year later Garaudy published a warm appreciation of Pope John XXIII's encyclical *Pacem in Terris,* foreseeing a fruitful collaboration between Catholics and Communists. Garaudy criticized the Soviet insistence that religion must disappear under Communism. The Political Bureau, angered by this departure, moved to reprimand Garaudy, but Thorez refused to permit it.[2]

By the time of his death in 1964, Thorez had moved the PCF toward acceptance of the Gaullist political system. In 1963 the PCF declared the building of Socialism must be the joint effort of several parties. This declaration was later expanded into the principle of political pluralism under Socialism and a promise to respect "alternance," that is, relinquish power in the event of an election defeat. The PCF was reluctant to state these positions formally because it was unwilling to admit it had ever advocated procedures contrary to standard democratic practice. The party's record was liberally sprinkled with statements endorsing democratic freedoms and the PCF interpreted the dictatorship of the proletariat to mean forceful rule by a majority. Violence would occur only in the event of illegal obstruction of working-class rule by the bourgeoisie. But the PCF insisted that a workers' government must be prepared to deal with violent opposition; hence the famous *"petite phrase"* in the joint declaration of the PCF and Socialists in 1967, which committed the two parties to devise policies to deal with illegal obstruction of a socialist transformation. Although critics noted the contradiction between the party's commitment to democratic practice and endorsement of the Soviet model, the party refused to concede until the mid–1960's that the USSR was not democratic.

The decision to support François Mitterrand on the first ballot of the 1965 presidential election was not a transformation in PCF policy.[3] The party elected Vincent Auriol in 1947 and supported Marcel Naegelan in 1953. The 1965 election was unique only because it was the first held under universal suffrage. A more substantial shift in PCF policy came in February 1966 with Aragon's criticism in *L'Humanité* of the trial of Soviet dissidents Siniavsky and Daniel. Aragon's statement was personal but reflected Waldeck Rochet's recognition that the PCF's commitment to the democratic process was not likely to be taken seriously unless the party acknowledged repression in Soviet society. The Political Bureau divided over Waldeck Rochet's policies, which unequivocally put internal politics above Soviet strategy. According to Philippe Robrieux, resistance to Waldeck Rochet was led by Duclos and Fajon who won over Jeannette Vermeersch and Georges Marchais. Waldeck Rochet was supported by Frachon, Georges Seguy, Paul Laurent, and René Picquet, with Billoux and Guyot wavering between the two positions. Political Bureau debate was now real, and Waldeck Rochet opened up the Central Committee meeting of Argenteuil in March 1966 as well. Zhdanovian socialist realism was buried there, Garaudy referring to "30 years of sclerosis under Stalin" over the objections of Fajon and the old guard.[4]

The March 1967 legislative elections were a narrow defeat for the left; subsequent Socialist-Communist cooperation in the National Assembly heralded the emergence of a united and loyal opposition. But unity foundered on the crises of May and August 1968. The PCF signed a common platform with Mitterrand's Federation of the Democratic Left in February 1968; the party hoped agreement on a Common Program would follow. The foreign policy differences between the two parties following the Arab-Israeli war of 1967 were successfully overcome. But the student-worker upheaval of May 1968 and Soviet invasion of Czechoslovakia in August constituted new setbacks to unity. The PCF's hostile reaction to the students was consistent with the Servin-Casanova affair. The party would have no dealings with the infantile revolutionary romanticism of the students, regarded as the spoiled offspring of a privileged and decadent bourgeoisie.[5] This attitude was caricatured rather than articulated by Georges Marchais' May 3, 1968, article in *L'Humanité,* which denounced Daniel Cohn-Bendit, hero to thousands of students, as a "German anarchist."[6] Marchais attacked the students as Gaullist provocateurs. Waldeck Rochet believed they expressed genuine issues, but were exploited by irresponsible *gauchiste* troublemakers. These differences did not affect the party's orientation during the May events but did presage further conflict, since Marchais appeared heir apparent to Waldeck Rochet.

The PCF's hostility to the students stood in stark contrast to the warm reception accorded them by Mitterrand and Pierre Mendès-France. While the PCF was forced to cope with the spread of unrest to the working class after May 13, Mendès-France was lionized by the students at Charléty stadium. Following the disappearance of de Gaulle, Mitterrand announced his readiness to form a government whose legitimacy could only come from the streets. The PCF's reaction was much more in keeping with its historical traditions. The CGT assumed a central role in the spread of the strikes after May 16 in an attempt to bring the movement under its control.[7] An angry confrontation occurred in the Political Bureau between Marchais and CGT leader Georges Seguy, Marchais demanding that Seguy restrain the strike movement.[8] Seguy angrily refused, warning that any attempt to do so would cause the union to lose its following among the workers. The CGT denied any political aims to the strike movement and negotiated a settlement with Premier Georges Pompidou. The PCF meanwhile repudiated Mendès-France, citing his ties with the students and 1954 rejection of Communist support, and spurned Mitterrand's attempt to form a left-wing government, arguing that no Socialist-Communist cooperation was possible in the absence of a common program. The collapse of left-wing unity allowed no alternative except elections. De Gaulle emerged triumphant, 8 million strikers returned to work, and a divided left suffered humiliation.

For Roger Garaudy, May 1968 marked a fundamental break with the PCF's past and the definitive conversion of the party to the status quo. Garaudy called upon the party to modernize its approach to politics, update its class analysis to include students, intellectuals, and the new technical intelligentsia, and declare an end to Stalinist-bureaucratic centralism.[9] These were the same demands made by Servin and Casanova in 1961, and the PCF responded with the same refusal. In its eagerness to reject Garaudy's advice the PCF showed insensitivity to its own role in the May events. By defining the events as non-revolutionary, the PCF helped make them so; possibilities for change in 1968 depended upon what the PCF would do.[10] Virtually all the student leaders, moreover, were ex-Communists and products of the PCF's political and educational sub-culture. The students' anti-Communism in May 1968 assumed some of the characteristics of a neurotic son-versus-father psychodrama.

The Soviet invasion of Czechoslovakia was the precipitant of a new PCF lapse into sectarianism. That effect was not apparent at the outset of the crisis. While not endorsing all the reforms of the Prague Spring, the PCF defended the right of the Czechs to carry out their experiment. Waldeck Rochet tried to negotiate a modus vivendi in July 1968, warning the Russians the PCF would disapprove military intervention while admonishing the Czechs against a revival of anti-Socialist elements. When the invasion came, Waldeck Rochet led the Political Bureau in an expression of "surprise and reprobation" at the action, marking the first open disagreement between the PCF and the CPSU on a major foreign-policy issue. But the PCF backtracked quickly. Within a week the leadership condemned an interview granted by Roger Garaudy to the Czech news agency CTK in which Garaudy termed the invasion a relapse into Stalinism and a blow to the International Communist Movement.[11] The PCF actively pursued a policy of "normalization" in the Czech crisis thereafter.

Waldeck Rochet's unhappiness over the Soviet invasion was not shared by the old guard on the Political Bureau, who approved the statement for different motives. Georges Marchais was conspicuously absent in the aftermath of the Czech affair reappearing later to play a prominent role in "normalization." A circular by Gaston Plissonnier, widely recognized as Duclos' successor in the role of Moscow's advocate in the PCF Political Bureau, stated the following:[12]

. . . it is necessary to stress the context in which the leading organisms [of the party] have been called upon to adopt resolutions capable of shocking many comrades. The strategy of our party, notably with regard to the quest for a programmatic agreement of the left, obliged us to take a certain distance vis-à-vis our Soviet comrades—whose imperatives, on another level, we understand—and the favorable reaction of the leaders of the FGDS [Fédération de la Gauche Democrate et Socialiste] or of the SFIO, notably of Guy Mollet, show the wisdom of this tactical position of our party . . . the Soviet comrades understand our problems perfectly.

The circular warned that elements in the party supporting the Garaudy declaration on Czechoslovakia "must be immediately pointed out to the party's central commission of political control" and isolated. The tactical motive for the PCF's critical stand on Czechoslovakia was not the sole consideration in the decision, but neither can it be dismissed. Dissension in the Political Bureau continued through the Czech crisis. Whether it played a role in the passage of power from Waldeck Rochet to Georges Marchais remains a subject of speculation. Waldeck Rochet's lapse into a debilitating illness while in Moscow in February 1969 has intrigued some observers.[13]

Waldeck Rochet's legacy to the PCF was summed up in the December 1968 Manifesto of Champigny, in which the PCF declared its goal to be an advanced democracy as an intermediate stage between capitalism and socialism. The party forswore violence, reaffirmed its commitment to democratic liberties, and vowed to protect private property. These commitments affected the outcome of the Garaudy affair. Garaudy was permitted to defend his positions in *L'Humanité* and in a public speech to the Nineteenth Party Congress in February 1970. His disagreements were fundamental, and he was joined by other well-known Communists; Charles Tillon ended a seventeen-year silence to break with the party over the Czech question. But the PCF again survived the disillusionment among intellectuals without effect on its rank-and-file support. The PCF patiently waited for the Socialist party to rebuild itself following the disastrous Presidential elections of 1969, in which Jacques Duclos received 21 percent of the vote to Socialist candidate Gaston Defferre's 5 percent. The lesson seemed clear. The PCF was still hegemonic on the left, and the Socialists had no future in France except in an alliance of the left. The Common Program was duly signed in June 1972 amid widespread hopes that a new era in France had opened.[14]

In 1975 Etienne Fajon appended the text of Georges Marchais' June 1972 report to the PCF's Central Committee to a small volume entitled *L'Union est un combat*.[15] The secrecy in which the report was kept for three years was as indicative of continuity in Stalinist practice as its content. Amid the euphoria surrounding the signing of the Common Program, Marchais emphasized some eternal verities of left-wing unity. Continuous pressure must be exerted at all times on the Socialists lest they revert to their past bad habit of allying with center parties, the tactic of which "all the Socialists' past history was made." No illusions must be entertained concerning their sincerity. The Common Program represented no ideological rapprochement between the two parties, nor did the PCF wish for any. The new Parti Socialiste (PS) was "fundamentally reformist"; the mass movement behind the Common Program was the only guarantee of success. Most importantly, success depended upon the PCF remaining hegemonic on the left.

Notwithstanding Marchais' warning, the PCF clearly wanted Mitterrand to win the presidential elections of May 1974. The Socialist leader made minimal reference to the Common Program during the campaign, but Marchais did not protest. Marchais joined his voice to the chorus of moderation and reiterated the party's commitment to political pluralism, alternance, and the expansion of democracy. He also promised to guarantee inheritance and reassured owners of apartments and homes against expropriation. The Communists forswore any interest in running the "key" ministries, Interior, Foreign Affairs, or Defense. Marchais' appetite for power brought him into conflict with the Russians, who preferred Giscard d'Estaing to Mitterrand. The PCF protested the Soviet ambassador's visit to Giscard d'Estaing between ballots as interference in French internal affairs, and Marchais' break with Brezhnev may have dated from that incident.

At every step in the process of political integration the PCF demonstrated a corresponding unwillingness to compromise its ideology or organization. In 1965, while supporting Mitterrand for President, the PCF took disciplinary action against its student group, among whom sympathies with the Italian Communists' moderate policies vied with Trotskyist and Maoist tendencies. In 1968 the Manifesto of Champigny was accompanied by the Garaudy affair. In 1972 the signing of the Common Program was the occasion of Marchais' sectarian secret speech. So it was in 1974. Following the presidential elections, observers expected a bold and liberal step forward at the extraordinary party congress scheduled for the fall. Instead, the party's *ouvrieriste* tendency reasserted itself. Attacks on the Socialists predominated and the new slogan "Union of the French People" appeared a return to a national front. The PCF declared its support of the Stalinist Portuguese Communist party whose tactics were condemned by the Italian and Spanish Communists.[16] It is doubtful that a fundamental sectarian shift was occurring although observers thought a faction of hard-liners headed by Leroy and Plissonnier was briefly in control.[17] Renewed attacks on the Socialists were rather a response to the dramatic change in fortunes of the PS since the signing of the Common Program in 1972. Defferre had received 5 percent as the Socialist candidate on the first ballot in 1969, and Mitterrand got 49 percent on the second ballot in 1974. The PCF vote remained static. Within the context of left-wing unity the PCF felt constrained to undertake a bitter struggle to preserve its hegemony.

But the PCF remained committed to left unity until 1977, coming into conflict with the USSR, which preferred Front national and the foreign policy of Giscard d'Estaing. Adoption of the "Eurocommunist" label appeared a natural consequence of the party's alliance strategy. Yet there is irony in the PCF's Eurocommunism. On the one hand, the PCF characterization of itself as Eurocommunist conferred upon that term a concrete historical significance. On the other hand, the party's nationalist conception of Eurocommunism brought the movement to an ignominious demise.

Analysts were unhappy with the term "Eurocommunism" for good reason.[18] Attempts to give it a doctrinal, strategic, or regional definition, divorced from its historical context, were unsatisfactory. Rejection of the Soviet model, commitment to democratic freedoms, and a peaceful transition to socialism were characteristic of such widely diverse and scattered non-ruling parties as the Mexican, Australian, and Japanese and rejected by some key European parties, including the Portuguese. Least of all could Eurocommunism denote a common strategy of the PCF, PCI, and Spanish Communist party (PCE) on European issues: the PCF disagreed with the Spanish and Italian Communists on admission of Spain, Portugal, and Greece to the Common Market, remained more hostile than they to NATO, and opposed attempts to strengthen the supranational institutions of the European Community. The PCF also rejected the doctrine of the "third way" accepted by the Italian and Spanish parties. Carrillo's notion of a separate Communist pole of attraction which, while reforming Western capitalism, would also spur democratic and liberal tendencies in Eastern Europe, was regarded by Georges Marchais as completely unacceptable.

Eurocommunism acquired historical significance in 1975 when it began to appear that although the French and Italian parties were pursuing diverse strategies (historic compromise in Italy, unity of the left in France), both had a realistic opportunity to exercise power in their respective countries in the near future. The Spanish Communists, though weaker, hoped to come to power as well, once democratic legitimacy was conferred upon Eurocommunism by the satisfactory performance of the PCI and PCF. With the Italian party's substantial improvement at the polls in 1976, the barriers to its participation in a coalition with the Christian Democrats seemed likely to disappear. Widespread fear existed, however, that an isolated Italian experience with Communists in power would fail because of economic policies that might be imposed by her anti-Communist trading partners, specifically Germany and the USA. When in the municipal elections of March 1977, the coalition of the left demonstrated that it was a majority in France, the 1978 legislative elections loomed as the central focus of Eurocommunist aspirations. A victory of the left followed by a period of shared PCF power could provide the impetus necessary to overcome the barriers to Communist participation in Italy and protection against the hazards of Communist participation attempted in isolation. Eurocommunism might then achieve its culmination and the Western Communist parties be definitively integrated into a newly stabilized and reformed Western democratic order.

Lost in the general euphoria was any genuine appreciation of the reasons for the PCF's divergence from the USSR. Long considered with justification the most Stalinist of the West-European parties, the PCF manifested the most serious breech with Moscow after Marchais' heart attack in January 1975.[19] Marchais refused even to set foot in the USSR while Carrillo and Berlinguer felt no such compunctions. Contacts between the PCF and the CPSU appeared to have been suspended for a time in 1977, although cynics pointed to the continued existence of economic relations and the importance of Jean Jerôme, Jean-Baptiste Doumeng, and Gaston Plissonnier, all of whom retained close ties to Moscow. The PCF reverted to historic form in its break with Moscow; its continued Stalinist perspective remained the basis of its action, and it remained more sectarian than the Russians. The basis of the Marchais-Brezhnev divergence was the PCF's perception of Soviet strategy as opportunist. As Marchais declared in December 1974 "Peaceful coexistence . . . does not at all mean the maintenance of the political and social status quo."[20] In March 1976 a Central Committee report by Jean Kanapa, Marchais' chief adviser on foreign affairs, criticized Moscow for abandoning the struggle against NATO and failing to appreciate the global dimensions of the current crisis of capitalism.[21] Because the Soviets believed that the capitalist depression was temporary, they courted Giscard d'Estaing and discouraged the adoption of political strategies that might make it possible for Communists to share power and carry out structural reforms.

The PCF made two important changes in ideology and strategy in 1976 and 1977, both undertaken with the perspective in mind of soon sharing power. The abandonment of the historic phrase "dictatorship of the proletariat" at the Twenty-second Congress was justified on pragmatic grounds; it was symbolically important even if a semantic change. The PCF had never meant by the term anything other than forceful majority rule, and the word "dictatorship" induced fears in some who might otherwise vote for the left.[22] More significant was the way the change was made: Marchais announced it on television before it became a subject for discussion in the party. Marchais may well have acted in anticipation of opposition from the party's *ouvrieriste* and traditionalist component, but the authoritarian aspects of democratic centralism were demonstrated nonetheless. The same was true of the decision to support nuclear weapons announced in a declaration of the Central Committee on May 12, 1977. In arguing for a military strategy of multi-directional targeting, *"tous azimuts,"* along the lines of the Gaullists, the PCF meant to deter Bonn and Washington from interfering with an experiment of left-wing government in France. The step was taken immediately after the PCF made its proposals to the Socialists and Radicals to renegotiate the Common Program. The timing appeared adequate demonstration that the Communists expected the negotiations to succeed.[23] But PCF publication of an extravagant "costing" of the Common Program on the eve of a Mitterrand television debate with Premier Barre led to the suspicion that hard-liners in the Political Bureau were seeking to sabotage unity.

All the traditional stereotypes of the left were in evidence during the 1977 negotiations contributing to their failure. In following so closely the April-through-September timetable of the left-wing split thirty years before, the left politicians seemed determined to relive a traumatic experience of their youth. The PCF accompanied its proposals for "updating" the Common Program with an appeal for mass mobilization of workers to pressure the Socialists into concessions. Workers held meetings to demand the nationalization of their enterprises; fact sheets explaining the justice of PCF positions were distributed in millions of copies; and petitions, telegrams, messages, and worker delegations arrived at Socialist party headquarters in such numbers that Mitterrand at one point was unable to enter.[24] The PS, for its part, continued to regard the PCF as undemocratic. Mitterrand's 1972 speech, in which he said he hoped that 3 million Communist voters would desert their party and vote Socialist, was given wide publicity by the PCF. Mitterrand's belief that Communist strategy was predetermined made him less attentive to details of the negotiations: hence, his September 26 comment that it was "useless to capitulate. . . . In any case the PCF has made its decision a long time ago. If it wishes to break [negotiations,] it will break, no matter what we do." When the Radicals showed interest in Communist proposals for restructuring the cabinet, Mitterrand was caustic: "Do you know [who] Fierlinger [was]?" he asked, adding for their edification that Fierlinger was a Czech socialist leader who, as a cabinet minister in 1948, had "betrayed to the profit of the Communists."[25]

The proposal to update the Common Program was reasonable which explains the Socialists' rapid agreement to negotiations. The economic crisis had deepened since 1972, and inflation had rendered the levels of social benefits included in the Common Program obsolete. The Socialists had accepted Communist proposals twice before, in agreeing to the Common Program and establishing common lists for the 1977 municipal elections. There is no evidence that the Communists were aware that a different understanding of the Common Program existed in the two parties over nationalization of subsidiaries as well as parent concerns. The Communists proposed extending the 1972 list of nationalizations to include the ailing steel industry, Peugeot-Citroen, and the oil company Total, basing their position on increased state subsidies granted those corporations since 1972. The misunderstanding over the subsidiaries emerged during discussions held by the negotiating committee of the two parties in July. It swiftly became the dominant issue during the final summit meetings in September, causing first a dramatic walk-out from the sessions by Radical leader Robert Fabre and then the breakdown of the negotiations.[26]

The difference over the subsidiaries was not the major obstacle to successful conclusion of the negotiations, although both parties appeared to prefer that the public believe it was. The Communist list of nationalizations included some 1400 enterprises. The Socialist list was slightly in excess of 100. Final Communist concessions brought their list down to 729, and the last Socialist offer included 227 enterprises. Negotiations then collapsed. The reduced PCF list involved a total of 503,000 workers, while the augmented Socialist list included 350,000 workers, hardly a substantial difference in terms of the total effect on the economy.[27] Moreover, the remaining subsidiaries were already 50 percent or more owned by the major industrial groups, and the Socialists agreed to include subsidiaries under statutes governing nationalized enterprises. But it was over internal governance that the two parties were unable to agree. Communist ideas had not changed since the Liberation; they wanted administrative councils composed of an equal number of worker, consumer, and government representatives with a preponderant role for the CGT. The Communists wanted the heads of nationalized enterprises selected by the administrative councils; the Socialists insisted directors be named by the government. Communist proposals to divide the ministries of interior and finance were also designed to further party positions. The struggles experienced by the two parties in 1947 and 1948 thus reappeared with brutal effect; the PCF wanted its Liberation positions of power restored. The Socialists, responsible for the elimination of Communists in 1947 and 1948, would not undo that historic achievement. Mitterrand defined the issue clearly at the Socialist party conference after the 1978 elections: "the taking of control [by the PCF] of 729 new nationalizations," he asked rhetorically, "don't you believe that preoccupation dominated all the others?"[28] Thirty years after the beginning of the Cold War the French political class, Socialists included, was still unwilling to accept integration of the PCF on the party's terms.

In the absence of the required guarantees, Marchais, during the election campaign, made restoration of the PCF's hegemony on the left the condition for renewed Communist-Socialist cooperation. Unless the PCF received 25 percent of the vote on the first ballot, support of better-placed Socialist candidates on the second round could not be guaranteed.[29] The PCF refused to promise alliance with the PS following the elections either. The Communist barrage of criticism of the Socialists undoubtedly contributed to the PCF's relative defeat at the polls in March 1978. The PCF received 21.3 percent of the vote on the first ballot, a slight decline. But the PS received only 22.5 percent, far less than the 26 to 28 percent forecast by the polls. Analysts insisted that reducing the power and influence of the PS had been the major aim of the PCF when it broke negotiations; in this sense the Communists had won a victory of sorts, restoring equilibrium on the left. But the cost was dear—defeat of the left as a whole. The rapid patching up of differences between the two parties between rounds of the election struck observers as the makeshift affair that it was. With the victory of Giscard's majority on the second ballot, the PCF leadership appeared to opt for retrenchment, political isolation, and restored ties with the USSR as after such defeats in the past.

The PCF did not expect the explosion of dissidence that the election defeat caused within its ranks. Moreover, since Italian and Spanish Eurocommunism's strategies depended upon the results of the 1978 French elections, French Communist dissidents found support in the leaderships of those two parties. Marchais consequently found it much more difficult to deal with internal PCF protesters. The dissidents blundered, however, by failing to coordinate their attacks: Louis Althusser and Jean Elleinstein criticized the PCF leadership for opportunism and sectarianism respectively, permitting Marchais to argue that he was following the correct path between traditionally dangerous pitfalls.[30] But Marchais' Stalinist argument ignored that Althusser and Elleinstein both criticized the practice of democratic centralism in the PCF and accused the leadership of secretly following one policy while openly supporting another. Both violated democratic centralism by publishing their critiques in the prestigious *Le Monde*. Of the two, Elleinstein's criticism was more broadly based.

Elleinstein had been for a brief period the PCF's favored intellectual, playing a role for Marchais analogous to Garaudy for Waldeck Rochet. Elleinstein made his reputation on a history of the USSR which, unique among Communist-sponsored publications, dealt honestly and forthrightly with the Stalinist era.[31] He was a leading force behind the increasingly vocal criticism of Russian political repression expressed in *L'Humanité*. Elleinstein saw that a turn by the PCF back toward a sectarian mode would jeopardize his position and feared it would consign the party to a permanent future of sterility and impotence. In *Le Monde* he noted the decline in PCF support and the serious erosion of party influence, averaging from 3 to 5 percent, in Paris' red belt. Elleinstein criticized the sectarian *ouvrieriste* campaign which stressed misery in a society of plenty and failed to appeal to non-proletarian segments of the population. But most seriously, Elleinstein focused on the PCF's relationship with the USSR. He aired publicly the embarrassing affair of the electoral brochure *Vivre*. Prepared to dramatize the PCF's commitment to human rights, the brochure included a photo of Communist intellectuals at a meeting in support of Soviet dissidents. Gaston Plissonnier ordered 2 million copies of the brochure destroyed. Elleinstein warned that the PCF must deepen its critique of Soviet society: the USSR was "neither a model nor an example" of Socialism. In terms of what the PCF hoped to achieve for France, "it rather constitutes an anti-model."[32]

Following Marchais' reply to the PCF dissidents a period of detente ensued. Elleinstein, despite vicious attacks in the Soviet press, was greeted by Marchais at the fête of *L'Humanité*. Publication of the joint work *L'URSS et Nous* by Alexandre Adler, Francis Cohen, and others seemed to presage a continuation of the PCF's critical line vis-à-vis the USSR.[33] But news accounts detailed a rift in the Political Bureau between liberals, led by Paul Laurent, and sectarians led by Gaston Plissonnier.[34] Dissidents saw some development in their favor at the party's Twenty-third Congress in March 1979 when Leroy was dropped from the Secretariat. But Marchais announced that despite differences with the USSR over democracy, the PCF considered the historical experience of the USSR and the People's Democracies "globally positive." Marchais' ability to isolate dissident intellectuals and control the party apparatus was apparent, and dissenting opinion, though freely expressed in the party cells, rarely percolated any higher.[35] The persistence of ugly Stalinist practices, moreover, was evident in the Fiszbin affair.

Henri Fiszbin's clash with the party leadership had several revealing aspects. The affair could have been considered a harbinger of the inevitable decline of Stalinism as well as its persistence. As Secretary of the Paris federation and leader of the Communist group in the Hôtel de Ville, Fiszbin was a leader in the new liberalism symbolized by the Twenty-second Congress. The Paris federation did not follow the party leadership in the sectarian turn after the elections, and in January 1979 Fiszbin found himself charged with opportunism.[36] As a career official for thirty years, Fiszbin was expected to submit meekly and offer self-criticism; instead, he delivered a spirited defense of his policies and accused the leadership of abandoning the line of the Twenty-second Congress. Embarrassed, the Political Bureau allowed the matter to lapse, but Fiszbin enjoyed strong support in his federation and the equivocation could not continue. Fiszbin was forced to resign after agreeing to plead ill health. The Central Committee took up the affair in November 1979, by which time the Paris federation was subordinated to the party. Fiszbin defended his policies forcefully, but the Central Committee unanimously endorsed the Political Bureau's version of the affair, insisting there had never been any criticism of Fiszbin intended or a change in the party line since the Twenty-second Congress. The whole affair was declared to be a product of Fiszbin's imagination. Fiszbin had defied the Political Bureau, but the Paris federation was successfully disciplined, and the Central Committee, including Fiszbin's friends, endorsed a fabricated version of the the truth. Fiszbin defended his liberal policies in Paris by arguing that the social composition of the city was changing as the working class was pushed to the suburbs. Liberal policies were more appropriate to the city's large numbers of intellectuals and *cadres*. No more convincing demonstration could be given of the perceived functional relationship between democratic centralism and the working class.

Marchais' endorsement of the Soviet invasion of Afghanistan on Moscow television in January 1980 dramatized the PCF's policy turn. With a renewed rhetoric of unity at the base, attacks on the Socialist leadership, and internal Stalinist practice, the PCF was accused of class-against-class tactics. Soviet pressure, financial and other, may well have been at work; as pleased as Brezhnev was with Marchais' reaction to Afghanistan, he had more reason to appreciate Giscard's.[37] But the realignment represented the PCF's independent judgment that Moscow, again showing aggressiveness in world affairs, was worthy of renewed support, while the Socialists had shifted to the right and were unworthy of PCF backing. The notion of a Socialist shift was not challenged by the party's dissident intellectuals, but the new PCF policies were costly in terms of popular support. During the period of the Common Program, party membership rose regularly, reaching an estimated 700,000 in 1978. After 1978 membership stagnated or declined and by-elections showed the party slipping in electoral support. In November 1980 the average fall-off was 3 to 4 percent and the Communist electorate supported Socialists and Radicals on the second ballot despite contrary signals from the leadership.[38] The Communist rank and file still aspired to unity of the left.

Georges Marchais' independent candidacy for the May 1981 presidential elections was a bold gamble given internal dissatisfaction and the unknown effect of personal attacks on Marchais' past. Whether or not Marchais went to work in Germany voluntarily in 1942, it was clear that he did not flee to join the Resistance. The date of his return from Germany and activities until he joined the Communist party in 1947 became active subjects for speculation in the press.[39]

But the real issue was not the alleged mistakes of Marchais' youth but how, despite his cloudy past and self-criticism of 1954, he managed to rise to the position of supreme leadership.

Whether the PCF's defeat in 1981 was a temporary setback or a historically significant decline was unclear. Nor was it evident that Marchais' personal defeat would affect his leadership: since Thorez's day no precedent existed for removing a PCF General-Secretary from office except by death or debilitating illness. Even before the elections analysts with a sense of humor were extrapolating from the PCF failure in 1978 to predict future decline. Emmanuel Todd described Communism as a therapy for mass schizophrenia and saw the afflicted generation dying out as the Communist vote declined to 15 percent by the year 2000 and zero by 2050. Todd's projection of 15 percent materialized early but it would be foolhardy to assume the rest of his forecast must follow. Guy Konopnicki, a Communist dissident, depicted a ludicrous tableau of the PCF celebrating its centenary in the year 2020 with the same stale and outworn rhetoric of the 1980's.[40] Such predictions assumed too lightly the untroubled continuity of French modernization, prosperity, and political stability. A more serious view of Communism's decline focuses on the party's inability to adapt its political line to face new kinds of social problems, including ecological questions, emancipation of women, and self-management in industry.[41] But Communists have not revealed any less capacity to face these problems than other French parties. A broad consensus of which the PCF is part exists in France on the use of nuclear power.

Marchais' tactics from 1977 to 1981 turned out to be an unmitigated disaster. Having engineered defeat for the left when it was united, he permitted the Socialists to win on their own and achieve an unprecedented hegemony on the left. One-quarter of the PCF electorate deserted Marchais, who blamed the PCF electorate's habit of supporting Mitterrand since 1965 and fear that Mitterrand might not survive the first round leaving a choice between Giscard and Chirac on the second. But Communist voters were clearly reacting to their party's endorsement of the Soviet invasion of Afghanistan and position on Poland, as well as the PCF role in the demise of Eurocommunism and left-wing unity. The PCF leadership recognized this by unconditionally supporting Mitterrand on the second ballot and entering into an agreement on Socialist terms for the legislative elections following his victory. The PCF was now following its voters; but its support for Mitterrand was still ambiguous. Communist voters who deserted Marchais on the first ballot did not necessarily vote for Mitterrand, and the PCF may well have really been trying to engineer Mitterrand's defeat by privately encouraging followers to vote for Giscard on the second ballot.[42] Only 1 percent returned to the fold in the legislative elections of June, while the electorate as a whole gave the Socialists a majority without needing Communist support. Marchais had indeed achieved the worst of all possible scenarios.

The PCF's post-election dilemma was to accept a share of power in a position of total subjection to the Socialists or continue the sectarian policy, hoping eventually to regain popularity as the Socialist government inevitably disillusioned its supporters. There were pitfalls in either approach. To follow tamely wherever the Socialists led without the strength to influence them risked the charge of opportunism in exchange for the legitimacy conferred by a few minor ministerial posts. On the other hand a sectarian policy of conditional support for Mitterrand coupled with criticism of his policies held the danger of reduction to a negligible force. France may be in for an extended period of Social-Democratic rule into the twenty-first century.

Whichever choice the PCF made (the leadership was divided on the options and may yet pursue them both alternatively), its goal remained to retain its autocratic internal structure and Soviet ties while exercising a measure of genuine political power. The PCF in 1981 was neither a force for revolution nor a source of social unrest. It was a deeply nationalistic party whose constituency shared the goals of most Frenchmen and whose leadership aspired for little more than equal acceptance by the French political class. As long as the PCF's co-opted working-class elite was denied acceptance at home, it was likely to seek recognition of its legitimacy abroad. What Giscard and Mitterrand refused Georges Marchais was granted him willingly by Leonid Brezhnev. Mitterrand's gamble on including the Communists within his coalition revealed the party's dialectic: internal Stalinist practice combined with loyal participation in a democratic framework. The party gave ample evidence of both during its first year in office. In an unprecedented outpouring of books, analysts with diverse perspectives bemoaned the PCF's peculiarities. At the same time, they paid tribute to the party's ability to provide French politics with its unending interest and fascination.

NOTES

1. *Cahiers du Communisme,* supplement, 7–8, (July-August 1962).

2. *Cahiers du Communisme,* supplement, 7–8 (July-August 1963). Roger Garaudy, personal interview, September 11, 1980.

3. Jacques Fauvet exaggerates in comparing 1964 to 1934 and 1939. *Histoire du Parti Communiste Français,* 2nd ed. (Paris, 1976), 511–17.

4. Philippe Robrieux, *Histoire Intérieure du PCF* (Paris, 1981), II, 630–35. The liberal heritage of Waldeck Rochet is also emphasized by François Hincker, *Le Parti communiste au carrefour* (Paris, 1981), 52–80.

5. See Waldeck Rochet, *Les enseignements de mai-juin 1968* (Paris, 1968). Also René Andrieu, *Les Communistes et la révolution* (Paris, 1968).

6. Roger Garaudy reprinted Marchais' article in *Toute la verité* (Paris, 1970).

7. Georges Seguy, *Le Mai de la CGT* (Paris, 1968). George Ross, *Workers and Communists in France* (Berkeley, Calif., 1982).

8. Interview with Roger Garaudy in the Trotskyist organ *Rouge,* May 25, 1978. Cited by Auguste Lecoeur, *La Stratégie du mensonge* (Paris, 1980), 176.

9. *Toute la verité.* Garaudy expanded on these views in *Le Grand tournant du socialisme* (Paris, 1969).

10. See Marc Goldstein, "Le Parti communiste du 3 Mai au 6 Juin 1968," *Les Temps Modernes,* No. 269, 827–94.

11. Garaudy, *Toute la Verité*.

12. Robrieux archive. See also the documents from the Garaudy archive published by Robrieux in the *Histoire Intérieure,* II, Annex. Hincker says majority sentiment in the party opposed Waldeck Rochet's action. *Le Parti communiste au carrefour,* 80–81.

13. Branko Lazitch speculated that the Russians liquidated Waldeck Rochet physically: "La vraie vie de Georges Marchais," *l'Express,* July 24–30, 1978.

14. Writing in 1976 Jean Elleinstein saw the signing of the Common Program in this light. See his *Le P.C.* (Paris, 1976).

15. Paris, 1975, Editions Sociales.

16. See the interview with Alexandre Adler in *Critique Communiste,* No. 33 (October 1980), 50–78. Also Richard Johnson, *The Long March of the French Left* (New York, 1981), 171.

17. Philippe Robrieux maintains the myth of Leroy as hard-liner and and Marchais as the good king surrounded by bad ministers dates from the Twenty-first Congress, during which Leroy actually suffered a demotion. *Histoire intérieure du PCF* (Paris, 1982), III, 225.

18. The literature on Eurocommunism is enormous. See Rudolf L. Tökés, ed., *Eurocommunism and Détente* (New York, 1978), Morton A. Kaplan, ed., *The Many Faces of Communism* (New York, 1978), Carl Boggs and David Plotke, *The Politics of Eurocommunism* (Boston, 1980) and George Schwab, ed., *Eurocommunism, the Ideological and Political-Theoretical Foundations* (Westport, Conn., 1981) for representative samples.

19. Robrieux follows Branko Lazitch in arguing Marchais feared the Russians would attempt to unseat him because of his illness. *Histoire Intérieure,* III, 233–36, and note 13 above.

20. Cited by Annie Kriegel, *Le Communisme au jour le jour* (Paris, 1979), 62–63.

21. Cited by Auguste Lecoeur, *La Stratégie du mensonge,* 182–83. The report appeared in *Rouge* and *Le Matin de Paris,* April 9, 13, 1979.

22. See the critique by the Althusserian rear guard in Etienne Balibar, *Sur la dictature du prolétariat* (Paris, 1977), which reprints Marchais' justification as well. Also Bernard Brown in George Schwab, ed., *Eurocommunism,* 123–28. I cannot agree with Brown that the PCF revived classical Leninism at the Twenty-second Congress. But he is correct to emphasize the party's sectarianism.

23. See François Loncle, *Autopsie d'une rupture: la désunion de la gauche* (Paris, 1979), 60. For the PCF justification see *Cahiers du Communisme,* 5 (May 1977).

24. See *L'Humanité,* May 19, September 5, 10, 1977. *Le Monde,* September 25, 1977.

25. *Le Nouvel Observateur,* September 26, 1977.

26. See the stenographic account of the negotiations: Pierre Juquin, *A Dossiers ouverts* (Paris, 1977).

27. See Gilbert Mathieu's analysis in *Le Monde,* September 23, 1977.

28. Cited by Branko Lazitch, *L'Echec permanent,* 253. For these reasons I cannot agree with Robrieux, who sees Marchais capitulating to Russian pressure and sabotaging the negotiations after his vacation in August. *Histoire intérieure,* III, 276–94.

29. See my analysis of the elections in "France," *Yearbook on International Communist Affairs* (Stanford, Calif., 1979).

30. Jean Elleinstein's criticism appeared in *Le Monde* from April 14 to 18, 1978. Althusser's followed from April 25 to 28. Marchais implicitly charged both intellectuals with "liquidationism," *L'Humanité,* April 21, 1978.

31. See Jean Elleinstein's *The Stalin Phenomenon* (London, 1976).

32. *Le Monde,* April 14, 1978. See also Jean Elleinstein, *Ils vous trompent camarades* (Paris, 1981).

33. Alexandre Adler et al., *L'URSS et nous* (Paris, 1978). The preface appeared in *L'Humanité,* September 6, 1978.

34. See Thierry Pfister's analysis in *Le Monde,* October 17, 1978.

35. See the article by Jane Jenson and George Ross, "The Uncharted Waters of De-Stalinization: The Uneven Evolution of the Parti Communiste Français," *Politics and Society,* IX, 3 (1980), 263–99. Jenson and Ross assume a connection between the PCF's internal democratization and its integration into the French political system.

36. Henri Fiszbin, *Les Boûches s'ouvrent* (Paris, 1980) has his account of the affair and the relevant documentation.

37. Robrieux notes four means by which the USSR pressures the PCF: The revelation of "secrets," finances, the threat of a split in the PCF, and geopolitics. But each of the first three is as potentially harmful to Moscow as the PCF, and the Russians have never made foreign policy with the interests of Communists abroad in mind. Robrieux says the PCF exercises as much autonomy as Kadar's Hungary. Ceausescu's Rumania is a better analogy. But the PCF is best understood as uniquely French. See the *Histoire intérieure,* Vol. III.

38. See *Le Monde,* issues of November 1980, for continuing coverage of the by-elections.

39. For good examples of the adhominum literature on Marchais, Auguste Lecoeur, *Stratégie du mensonge,* and Nicolas Tandler, *L'impossible biographie de Georges Marchais* (Paris, 1980).

40. Emmanuel Todd, *Le Fou et le proletaire* (Paris, 1979). Guy Konopnicki, *Vive le centenaire du PCF* (Paris, 1979).

41. Alain Touraine, *Mort d'une gauche* (Paris, 1979). Also Jean Chesneaux, *Le P.C.F., un art de vivre* (Paris, 1980).

42. On first ballot shifts see my "The Elections of 1981" in *Proceedings of the Ninth Annual Meeting of the Western Society for French History* (Lawrence, Kans., 1982), 454–66. On the party's second-ballot tactics see Robrieux, *Histoire intérieure,* III, 502–20.

CONCLUSION

Sixty years after the Congress of Tours, André Laurens observed in 1980, we still do not understand the PCF. The same remark could be applied to the human condition. Laurens expressed the understandable frustration of a journalist covering a political party that concealed its decision-making process to preserve the appearance of unity. The PCF may be more difficult to understand than other parties, but it is not incomprehensible. The burgeoning literature on the party, to which Laurens has significantly contributed, is eloquent testimony. Surely it cannot all be wrong.

Preoccupation with the hidden motives of PCF policies frequently dominates historical writing with the result that the party's actions are distorted or ignored. The continuing appeal of Communism derives from its successful articulation of social justice in the midst of a society characterized by disparities of income and frequent abuse of power. In the face of an entrenched political conservatism the PCF was allowed by default to articulate the only meaningful political opposition. The Fourth Republic carried on an unprecedented effort of economic reconstruction. Desperately needing the cooperation of labor when wages had to be depressed, the regime spurned Communist cooperation and met protest with force. Simultaneously, the regime embarked upon a futile attempt at colonial reconquest, which rendered its appeals for mass sacrifice unworthy of support. To many, the PCF alone, despite its compromised past, offered a reasoned and humane political alternative. Communists complained that workers bore a disproportionate burden of economic sacrifice and pleaded for a liberal approach to the shared aim of maintaining France's relationship with her former colonial empire. Communists destroyed much of their effectiveness by uncritically supporting Soviet foreign policy and worshipping Stalin. The PCF remains proud of its role as an opposition whose policies were justified, but its Stalinist legacy jeopardizes its political effectiveness.

Stalinism was a mechanism of bureaucratic control by which a co-opted working-class elite maintained itself in power. It must be understood in historical perspective. The Popular Front, Resistance, and Liberation presented the possibility of the PCF's definitive integration into French national life and the emergence of a species of French national Communism. The politics of the postwar era required the party to reward its Resistance heroes and insurrectionaries even when they had challenged the party line. Communists who had challenged Soviet policies were vindicated in November 1946 when Thorez rejected the Soviet model and insisted upon the necessity of an independent French road to Socialism.

The PCF's vision of integration extended to the socio-economic as well as the political spheres. Ministerial posts became meaningful in relation to a quasi-autonomous sphere of Communist power that extended to the nationalized enterprises and the welfare state. When the party was ousted from the cabinet in May 1947, it misunderstood the crisis because its socio-economic positions remained intact. In time it became clear that the French political elite also intended to dismantle the infrastructure of Communist socio-economic power. The PCF did not choose isolation in 1947. Isolation was forced upon it. Communists were eliminated from their positions in nationalized enterprises, the social security system, and the bureaucracy. The strikes of 1947, often interpreted as internationally mandated and insurrectionary, were economic in motive. The CGT defended workers' purchasing power eroded by a deliberate government policy of inflation, while Communists fought to preserve their entrenched positions throughout the French economy. The issue of CGT power in the coalfields turned labor unrest into violent confrontation. Despite the founding of the Cominform and Russian criticism of PCF "opportunism," the strikes remained part of a fundamentally internal political drama which was resolved at the end of 1948 with brutal suppression.

When the PCF was deprived of its political influence and isolated, its focus shifted to the International Movement. The Peace Movement originated in France, but was quickly internationalized and subordinated to the needs of Soviet foreign policy. A seemingly unending series of signature campaigns consumed a virtual monopoly of the party's attention and energies. The Vietnam war and the perennial struggle for working-class interests assumed subsidiary positions. With the Socialists dismissed as "principal support for the bourgeoisie," the PCF's aspiration to be part of a Popular Front coalition for internal political reform could not be realized. The creation of a national front against American hegemony in Western Europe became the primary aim of PCF policy. The party appeared a well-disciplined section of the CPSU.

Even under Stalin the Communist world had its politics. The monolithic façade created by democratic centralism masked conflict but did not eliminate it. Within the PCF, Jacques Duclos held responsibility for the implementation of Soviet policy. Maurice Thorez remained a partisan of the Popular Front, which represented his original contribution to the theory and practice of the International Communist Movement. Thorez based his power on use of Stalinist techniques, recognizing their consonance with aspects of French revolutionary tradition. The Stalinization of the PCF is not to be confused with its domestication to Russian interests. At every stage in PCF history some tension was inherent between the party's aspirations for internal political influence and its desire to create a diplomatic climate conducive to the security, prosperity, even expansion of the

USSR. This was no less true in the Stalinist era, even if it only became fully apparent in the 1960's and 1970's.

The purge of Resistance heroes at the Twelfth Party Congress in 1950 opened a prolonged period of internal upheaval in the PCF. Thorez resisted the party's subordination of its policies to Russian interests. Duclos masterminded the purge, which was part of the generalized witch hunt of Titoists in the International Communist Movement. Forced to take part in the proceedings, the purge was a personal defeat for Thorez, who had been associated with several of the victims. The purge victims were also advocates of the Popular Front and critics of Duclos' uninhibited opportunism in pursuing Front national. Thorez's position was weakened and collapsed when he fell ill and was removed to the USSR for a combined cure and imprisonment.

Thorez's absence opened the most confused and absurd period in the PCF's history. To Thorez and his sectarian stalwarts of the Barbé-Celor era, Billoux and Guyot, Duclos' policies, implemented with the aid of Fajon and Lecoeur, appeared to be leading the party to its ruin. Thorez's group briefly resumed control of the party in February 1952 and implemented a shift to a more sectarian line. Class against class was adopted as the necessary prerequisite to Front populaire; Thorez thought he could recreate his fictionalized version of the 1930's. The policy failed and Duclos resumed control of the party with Fajon and Lecoeur. But Thorez was gradually able to reassert his authority in the PCF, aided by rivalries in the Soviet Political Bureau and the circumstances surrounding Stalin's death. After his return to France Thorez removed Lecoeur from power and forced Duclos to suffer self-criticism and a diminution of authority. As the "party of Maurice Thorez" became a reality, Thorez turned his efforts to the struggle against de-Stalinization in the International Communist Movement.

It is the peculiar nature of the PCF's internal dialectic that systemic Stalinism in internal organization translates into Social-Democratism in political practice. The PCF is a Stalinist party, not a Leninist one. It is a mass organization, multi-faceted bureaucracy, tribune of the oppressed, and intermediary between the working class and the political system. It is not a revolutionary force. The PCF's major political campaigns in the Stalinist era, other than the meaningless signatures for peace, were against the European Defense Community and the Indochinese and Algerian wars. In its opposition to colonial war, the PCF demonstrated its liberalism and moderation, arguing that autonomy and social reform were the best means to bind former colonial peoples to France. The PCF tried to recreate a Popular Front around the issue of anti-colonialism. The Communists supported Mendès-France because he settled the Vietnam war and Guy Mollet because he promised to negotiate an end to the Algerian conflict. Recognizing the danger to democracy in the persistence of colonial conflict, the party acted in 1958 to defend the Fourth Republic. The May 1958 crisis was a severe setback for PCF hopes to return to a governing majority. But the PCF, like other French parties, eventually accepted the constitutional system of the Fifth Republic.

At the same time, the PCF became a major force in the International Communist Movement in opposition to the process of de-Stalinization. Accusing Khrushchev of slandering a "glorious past" in 1956, Thorez schemed to overthrow him with the so-called anti-party group and supported the Chinese. Critical of Soviet rapprochement with the Yugoslavs, the PCF attacked Togliatti and polycentrism. The PCF held firm to democratic centralism as the means of preserving its leadership for a working-class elite and refused to follow the Russians in repudiating the Stalinist past. Despite the party's commitment to a renewed Popular Front policy from 1962 to 1977, the PCF was still a Stalinist party. Throughout the negotiations prior to, and the period immediately following, the signing of the Common Program, the PCF remained fundamentally ambiguous in its attitude toward the Socialists, recognizing them as necessary allies yet distrusting them. The PCF's commitment to Eurocommunism from 1976 to 1979 was based upon the party's fear that the Soviets had lapsed into opportunism. The failure of Socialist-Communist negotiations to modernize the Common Program in 1977 and the 1978 election defeat stemmed from the PCF's need to reestablish its hegemony on the left. In the absence of guarantees spelling out the party's expected powers in the socio-economic as well as political domains, the PCF refused to experiment again with political power. The French Left's election defeat in 1978 destroyed the Eurocommunist movement, and the PCF supported the 1980 Soviet invasion of Afghanistan, restoring close relations with the USSR.

Despite widespread perception of a fundamental sectarian shift in PCF policy, the party insisted upon its formal commitment to the restoration of left-wing unity in France. Coalition politics still presented the PCF's only realistic policy option. The PCF never perceived a contradiction between its internal organizational practices, role in the International Communist Movement, and ambitions for political integration in France. The contradiction existed, however, for the PCF's prospective allies until François Mitterrand's historic experiment of May 1981. But a share in power came in the wake of unprecedented defeat and appearance of decline. To remain an effective political force the PCF may yet be made to face the legacy of its Stalinist past.

Biographies of French Communist Leaders

The leaders profiled in this section are arranged roughly in order of importance: Maurice Thorez, Jacques Duclos, André Marty, Etienne Fajon, Raymond Guyot, François Billoux, Auguste Lecoeur, Charles Tillon, Benoît Frachon, Jeannette Vermeersch, Laurent Casanova.

MAURICE THOREZ (1900–1964)

Thorez's career shows how the counter-society functioned as an alternative path for social mobility. Born in 1900 to a poor coal-mining family, he was a good student and received a patriotic education. His aptitude and docility motivated teachers to seek a clerical position for him, but this project was interrupted by World War I. His village under German occupation, Thorez was sent to his grandfather's farm in the Creuse. Returning to the Pas-de-Calais after the war, Thorez was refused a white-collar job, but his clerical skills found an outlet in the union and Socialist party which Thorez joined in March 1919, adhering to the faction favorable to the Russian revolution. Thorez was drafted into the army in March 1920 where he also gravitated to a clerical post: his abilities and generous, outgoing, jovial yet appropriately serious nature made him popular with fellow officers. Upon his release the same qualities brought Thorez to the attention of PCF officials in Paris, alone seeking these attributes among persons of working-class origins. Thorez's rise in the party was meteoric; party leaders overlooked his flirtation with Trotskyism and sent him to Moscow for training. Thorez led the the party's campaign against the Rif war, during which he proved a brilliant organizer and exponent of party policy, but revealed distaste for illegal action. In 1929 he submitted to arrest while Duclos and the others escaped when police surrounded a clandestine party meeting. Thorez's insistence on paying his fine, thereby recognizing "bourgeois legality" to secure his release, remained a characteristic act for France's leading spokesman of social revolution.

Thorez formed a lasting association with the left-sectarian Barbé-Celor group, in particular Raymond Guyot and François Billoux, who with Jeannette Vermeersch and Georges Cogniot remained his closest counselors. The Comintern figure Eugen Fried also played a role in Thorez's development. From the time he became Secretary General of the PCF Thorez's career became synonymous with party history except during his stays in the USSR, from 1939 to 1944 and 1950 to 1953, when the party was led by Jacques Duclos. Thorez's departure from the front lines in 1939 was widely construed as desertion; together with his 1948 declaration that French workers would never wage war on the USSR and death on a Black Sea cruise in 1964, it helped solidify views of him as a pliant functionary of Moscow. But Thorez acted independently of the Russians repeatedly during his career. He guarded party autonomy on cultural questions. While promoting his personality cult and enforcing democratic centralism, he exercised independent judgment on strategic issues, coming into conflict with Duclos and Moscow from 1950 to 1954. Frequently hampered by factional disputes in his party, Thorez remained an independent-minded Communist of unbounded ambition, aspiring to the highest posts in the French government and a position of influence in the International Communist Movement. The contradictory nature of these two ambitions prevented Thorez from fulfilling either to his satisfaction.

JACQUES DUCLOS (1896–1975)

Jacques Duclos, like Thorez, found in Communism the means through which humble origins were transcended and a career as journalist, party leader, and parliamentarian achieved. Duclos was born on October 2, 1896, in the Pyrenees. Trained as a pastry cook, he was drafted into the army in 1914, served with distinction, and became president of the Communist war veterans' association. Duclos joined the Socialist party in 1919 and was a founder of the PCF at Tours in 1920. Trained at party schools in Moscow in 1924 and 1925, he entered the Central Committee in 1926. He joined the Political Bureau and secretariat in 1931, participating in the liquidation of the Barbé-Celor group, and in 1935 joined the Comintern executive. Duclos was elected to the Chamber of Deputies in 1926 and served as its Vice-President during the Popular Front, demonstrating his exceptional talents as a propagandist and a parliamentarian. After the war Duclos assumed the presidency of the PCF's parliamentary group. He was brilliant in debate, bitingly sarcastic, and his knowledge of French politics was unexcelled.

Duclos also became one of the most important figures in the International Communist Movement. Unconditionally pro-Soviet, he approached the Germans in 1940 to request the legal publication of *L'Humanité,* and created the OS used to liquidate Communists who rejected discipline from 1939 to 1941. During the war years, Duclos lead a troika leadership with Frachon and Tillon, with whom he occasionally was in conflict. He was the leading international Communist to condemn the heresy of Browderism and was present at the founding congress of the Cominform, where he represented the PCF thereafter. Duclos again became party leader in 1950 following Thorez's removal to the USSR, leading the party through one of its most confused periods. He presided over a divided Political Bureau and was unable to prevent the party from slipping back and forth between sectarian policies and the opportunistic line he favored. In 1952 he was arrested while in possession of secret Political Bureau meeting notes subsequently published by the French government. With Lecoeur he implemented the most extreme version of the Zhdanovian socialist-realist line in PCF cultural policy.

With Thorez back in control in 1954, Stalin dead, and Lecoeur eliminated, Duclos went into decline, devoting himself to propaganda. Duclos became a Senator in 1958 and was the PCF's presidential candidate in 1969, by which time his grandfatherly image overshadowed his pro-Soviet past. Duclos perhaps harbored ambitions of displacing Thorez but was destined to a secondary role by his meridional accent, short stature, and corpulence, revealing a continued taste for the pastries he once made. Duclos' relationship to Moscow remains to be clarified. French police called him the "principal Soviet spy in France." It is clear that he more than anyone held the key to a resolution of the cloudier points in party history. There is no telling how many secrets he took to the grave in 1975. His memoirs reveal nothing. He awaits a biographer.

ANDRÉ MARTY (1886–1959)

One of the legendary founding heroes of the PCF, André Marty became a leading Comintern official and party secretary. His expulsion in 1952 was part of an upheaval in the leadership, and his rehabilitation remains an aim of PCF dissidents. Marty was a Communist before the fact, organizing a mutiny among French sailors in the Black Sea in April 1919. He was born on November 6, 1886, in Perpignan; a good student, he became a naval mechanic and petty officer, serving through World War I. He identified with the Russian revolution while in Odessa with French naval forces in 1919, mutinied, and received a twenty-year sentence to hard labor. Pardoned in 1923, he joined the Communist party, which had been campaigning for his release. Socialists later charged Marty repented his role in the mutiny to win his pardon and the Communists made the same accusation in 1952–53. Nevertheless, Marty's rise in party ranks was spectacular; he was elected to the Chamber in 1924 and entered the Central Committee in 1925. Marty entered the Political Bureau in March 1931 and was an accuser and inquisitor in the liquidation of the Barbé-Celor affair.

Marty was appointed to the Comintern executive in 1933 and its Secretariat in 1935. In 1936 he took charge of the International Brigades in Spain, where he acquired a reputation for ruthlessness that dogged him for the remainder of his career. In Moscow from 1939 to 1943 Marty seemed to take precedence over Thorez by virtue of his Comintern functions. He went to Algiers in 1943 as a delegate to the CFLN and after the war became a member of the PCF Secretariat, third in command behind Thorez and Duclos. Isolated from Political Bureau factions, Marty occupied himself with education and the campaign against the Indochina war while promoting a mini-cult around his role in the Black Sea mutiny. Marty was self-assured and aggressive, freely distributed insults and won the enmity of many of his colleagues. Yet he lived entirely within the confines of the counter-society and found contacts with bourgeois politicians repugnant. His behavior won him an undeserved reputation as a hard-liner. He did not advocate insurrection in 1944, supported the experience in government (although he later criticized certain aspects of it) and was as unprepared as anyone for the turn of 1947.

Marty was thoroughly disliked by Thorez and Duclos, but his removal in 1952 worked to the advantage of Duclos, Lecoeur, and Fajon, whose control of the Secretariat during Thorez's absence was thereby unimpeded. Marty challenged Moscow in 1951, protesting the purges of his former colleagues in the International Brigades. At his exclusion Marty was sixty-six years old and a diabetic. He was stung by accusations that he was a police agent and hurt when his wife turned against him. He died in 1959 an embittered and broken man.

ETIENNE FAJON (1906–   )

A schoolteacher by training, Fajon became head of the PCF's educational division, director of *L'Humanité,* and a PCF ideologue. He was born in Herault on September 11, 1906; his father was a small winegrower and his mother a schoolteacher. Fajon joined the PCF in 1926. He was dismissed from his job, arrested and imprisoned for anti-war activities in 1929 and turned to full-time party work, becoming a regional secretary in 1931 and joining the Central Committee in 1932. French intelligence sources placed him at the Marx-Lenin advanced school in Moscow during this period. Fajon formed a close, early friendship with Jacques Duclos, whom he found seductive by his "culture and eloquence," and polemicized against Thorez during the Barbé-Celor affair; his relationship with the PCF Secretary General remained problematical thereafter. Fajon was elected to the Chamber in 1936 and remained a Deputy, with one interruption until 1978. On January 16, 1940, while on leave from the army, he defended the PCF anti-war position in the Chamber with courage amid the indignant protests of Deputies who ejected him from the hall. Arrested shortly thereafter, Fajon was tranferred to Algiers where he was released in 1942.

By his association with the so-called Algiers group Fajon gained a reputation as a sectarian, but he remained close to Duclos, with whom he attended the founding conference of the Cominform in 1947. Fajon enjoyed the confidence of the Soviets, attending further meetings of the Information Bureau and making up part of the 1956 delegation sent to Moscow to question Khrushchev about the secret speech. Fajon served two terms in the party secretariat, one in 1952, during which time he became the principal spokesman for Duclos' leadership of the party, and again from 1954 to 1956. A talented journalist, Fajon became editor of *L'Humanité* in 1958. Aloof and professional in his bearing, Fajon radiated a certain charm which belied the U.S. intelligence characterization of him as "the outstanding Stalinist member of the Politburo." His importance in the PCF continued into the Georges Marchais era.

RAYMOND GUYOT (1903–   )

Raymond Guyot was a member of the PCF Political Bureau, a high Comintern official, and a PCF Deputy, parliamentarian, and propagandist for a period spanning forty years. Although he never served on the Secretariat, Guyot was a close associate of Maurice Thorez and a principal in all key decisions. Guyot was born on November 7, 1903, in Auxerre where he became Secretary of the Communist youth in 1922. Trained as an accountant, he worked at the Magasins du Louvre in Paris. Like Thorez, he was attracted by the Trotskyists but corrected himself in time to become a member of the Central Committees of the Communist youth in 1927 and the party in 1928. He served a short term in prison for anti-military propaganda during his army service. Promoted to the Political Bureau along with the Barbé-Celor group, he was first to repudiate their activities by means of a self-critique in July 1931, probably at Comintern urging. Guyot was quickly rewarded by promotion to high Comintern functions, simultaneously taking charge of the International Communist youth and joining the Comintern executive in 1935. He was elected to the Chamber in 1937. Guyot organized Communist youth for the Spanish Republic. Mobilized in 1939, he made an anti-war speech in the Chamber for which he was ejected by irate Deputies. He allegedly played a role in Stalin's 1939 purge of the Polish Communist party.

Guyot was the Central Committee delegate to the Resistance for the Southern zone and participated in the insurrection at Lyon. After the war, he again became a Deputy, president of the Communist youth front, the Union de la Jeunesse Républicaine de France (UJRF), and a member of the party's important control and purge commission. He was a regular on the Political Bureau and attended several Cominform meetings. Despite his involvement in Spain and the Resistance, Guyot escaped the purges, all the more remarkable since his wife was the sister of the wife of Arthur London, Czech foreign minister and victim of the Slansky purge in Czechoslovakia in 1952. Guyot remained close to Thorez and Billoux, with whom he shared a similar sectarian outlook from Barbé-Celor days. He was a prominent spokesman in denouncing the "opportunism" of the Duclos-Fajon-Lecoeur current from 1952 to 1954. In resisting de-Stalinization, he remained a firm ally of Thorez, and assumed responsibility for critical PCF relations with other Communist parties in 1956. Guyot was removed from the Political Bureau in 1972 when Georges Marchais became the PCF's Secretary General.

FRANÇOIS BILLOUX (1903–1976)

François Billoux was a leading PCF ideologue, Deputy, and member of the Political Bureau throughout the Stalinist era. Born in May 1903 in Roanne, Billoux became the employee of a textile firm in 1918, a member of the Socialist youth in 1920, and a founding member of the Communist party at Tours in 1920. He became Secretary General of Communist youth in 1926 and entered the Central Committee and the Political Bureau in the same year. French intelligence sources placed Billoux at the Marx-Lenin school in Moscow between 1929 and 1932. He was a member of the Barbé-Celor group and like Guyot, repudiated his activities and was received back into the good graces of the leadership. In 1934 he became secretary of the Marseille federation and was elected to the Chamber in 1936. Arrested in 1939, Billoux was an outspoken representative of the pacifist line, distinguishing himself by a letter to Petain in which he offered to testify at the infamous Riom trial against Blum, Daladier, and Reynaud. After a period in prison, Billoux was released in Algiers in 1942 and became a member of the Consultive Assembly and a Minister of State in the Provisional Government of 1944. Billoux was a symbol of the PCF's reintegration as Minister of Defense from January to May 1947 although the post had been shorn of most of its powers. He was remembered for ostentatiously sitting during a tribute by the National Assembly to French armies fighting in Indochina.

A rigid sectarian and a close ally of Thorez, Billoux was spokesman of the critique of the opportunist line of Duclos and Lecoeur and leader in the struggles from 1952 to 1954, frequently clashing with Duclos and helping Thorez to reestablish control. With Thorez's success in 1954 Billoux entered the Secretariat, in which he served until 1956. Billoux took responsibility for ideological questions and the PCF's often tortured relations with its intellectuals. In 1957 he became editor of *France Nouvelle,* which he guided on a firm line of resistance, behind Thorez, to Soviet plans for de-Stalinization. Billoux, along with Guyot, was removed from the Political Bureau in 1972 by Georges Marchais. He died in 1976.

AUGUSTE LECOEUR (1911–   )

Auguste Lecoeur's rise to the position of presumed successor to Maurice Thorez, followed by his exclusion from the party, poses one of the most difficult problems of PCF history. Lecoeur was born on September 4, 1911 to a family of miners in Lille and worked as a miner from 1924 to 1935. In 1927, under the impact of the Sacco-Vanzetti executions, he joined the Communist party. A volunteer in Spain, Lecoeur became a battalion leader under Marty, and returned to France as secretary of the Pas-de-Calais federation in which capacity he served until the outbreak of the war. Lecoeur accepted the Nazi-Soviet pact without hesitation. He was drafted, saw action at the front in 1940, was a war prisoner, and escaped to rejoin the clandestine PCF. He organized the miners' strike of May-June 1941, which assumed a hallowed place in PCF mythology. Lecoeur was called by Duclos to take charge of the clandestine organization of the Communist party and continued in this capacity throughout the war. His career remained closely linked to Duclos until his removal from the leadership in 1953.

Following the war, Lecoeur was elected mayor of Lens and a Deputy from the Pas-de-Calais, and he joined to the PCF's Central Committee. He was reprimanded by Thorez for protesting the PCF's lack of zeal in purging former Vichy personnel from the mines, yet became Under-Secretary in charge of coal production in the Felix Gouin government of February 1946. In 1950 he joined the Political Bureau and Secretariat, taking responsibility for organization. Despite his past in Spain and the Resistance, Lecoeur escaped the purges of 1950 and the Marty-Tillon affair and was widely regarded as Thorez's most likely heir, the third most powerful Communist in France. With Thorez in Russia and Duclos in prison, Lecoeur functioned briefly as PCF leader, trying, with the help of Fajon, to keep the party on the opportunist line charted by Duclos, but running afoul of Billoux and Guyot, who were pushing a more activist policy under the urging of Thorez. Lecoeur's attempt to enforce the Zhdanovian socialist-realist line on intellectuals appeared a naked grasp at personal power. Nor did Lecoeur display any of the charm and seductiveness that made these policies more tolerable when they were articulated by Duclos. Lecoeur was an effective, if humorless, party spokesman in the National Assembly, however.

Lecoeur's importance slipped with Thorez's return, and the self-criticism endured by Duclos in 1953 spelled his doom. His innovations in organizational matters failed to arrest the PCF's membership decline, and Thorez suspected him of using his organizational base to acquire personal power. Lecoeur was counting on Soviet support in his campaign for party leadership; when he sensed the changes in the USSR after Stalin's death and sought to bring the French party into line, Lecoeur ran further afoul of Thorez, who resisted de-Stalinization. Lecoeur was ousted from the PCF leadership in 1954 and made to bear responsibility for all the "errors" committed in Thorez's absence. He refused to cooperate in any of the proceedings brought against him and left the party in 1955. He joined the Socialists, then migrated to the right of the political spectrum. He authored several books on the PCF, revealing some key points of the party's past in which he was involved but declining to clarify the exact nature of PCF rapports with the USSR. Lecoeur was said to have an understanding with the PCF, but he charged the leadership with beating and trying to kill him in 1956. Lecoeur was a leading figure in the campaign to discredit Georges Marchais' past, the details of which were known to Lecoeur while he was organizational secretary.

CHARLES TILLON (1897–   )

Charles Tillon's career embodied a deep current of independent-minded nationalism within the PCF. His removal from the leadership in 1952 and exclusion in 1970 continue to disturb PCF dissidents. Tillon was born on July 3, 1897, in Rennes and trained as a mechanic. In 1916 he was drafted into the French navy. In 1919 he was one of the leaders of the naval mutinies protesting French anti-Bolshevik intervention in the Black Sea, along with André Marty with whom his career remained subsequently linked. When Tillon was sentenced to five years of hard labor, the party championed him while he was in prison, and he joined the Communist party upon his release, becoming prominent as a union organizer. A regional secretary of the CGTU in Rennes, he was brought to Paris in 1930 to take charge of the national union of chemical workers. He abandoned union work in 1936 when his skills were co-opted by the party. On the Central Committee since 1932, he entered the Political Bureau in 1936, became Secretary of the federation of Paris-Nord and was elected to the Chamber of Deputies.

Tillon was an international coordinator of aid to Republican Spain and was especially active in organizing the evacuation of Republicans in 1939. He became an early advocate of resistance after the fall of France, issuing proclamations to resist from the Southern zone. Tillon there organized the first armed groups of the PCF, local units of the OS (Organisation Speciale) which became the basis of the PCF's military arm during the war, the Francs-tireurs et partisans français (FTPF). As commander of the FTPF and part of a troika leadership with Duclos and Frachon, Tillon frequently clashed with them over strategy. He issued the call for the August 1944 Paris insurrection and emerged from the war as one of the PCF's most popular leaders, serving as Minister of Aviation, Armaments and Industrial Reconstruction. After the 1947 turn Tillon became an organizer of the Peace Movement, to which he largely devoted his talents until his demotion in 1952.

Never an ideologue, Tillon understood the Russian revolution and Communism as emanations of the glorious French past. Tillon took independent initiatives in policy which angered the party leadership, yet he gained public popularity and advanced his career. He established a mini-personality cult in the armaments ministry and resisted budget cuts his party supported. He took the initiative in establishing the Peace Movement, running into the opposition of the Russians. Accused of using the Peace Movement for personal power, he was removed from his official functions in 1952 with Marty, in the clearest demonstration of the PCF's allergy to its Resisters and subservience to the anti-Titoist line of the Cominform. Tillon bore his disgrace in silence, eventually earning partial rehabilitation in 1957. His exclusion came in 1970 following his criticism of the party's stand on the Soviet invasion of Czechoslovakia and accusation of Georges Marchais for doing voluntary labor in Germany during World War II. A talented prose stylist, Tillon wrote several books on the PCF. He remained an engaging public figure of charisma and charm and made frequent television appearances. His treatment by the PCF, in view of his heroic past, remained a source of embarrassment to the leadership.

BENOÎT FRACHON (1893–   )

Benoît Frachon's parallel careers in the PCF-controlled trade unions and the party gave him an independent power base and made him, with Thorez and Duclos, one of the most important Communists in France. Frachon was born in 1893 in the Loire, where he was trained as a metalworker. Following his World War I military service, Frachon became a trade union activist and joined the Socialists in 1919 and the Communist party at its founding in 1920. By 1924 he was secretary of the Communist unions in the Loire. In 1926 he became a member of the PCF Central Committee, joining the Political Bureau in 1928. Frachon's forte, however, remained trade-union work, to which he was singularly devoted. He became Secretary of the CGTU in 1933 and conducted the unity negotiations with the parent CGT in 1935, becoming a Co-secretary of the reunified union movement alongside Léon Jouhaux from 1936 to 1939. In this capacity Frachon gave up his post in the PCF Political Bureau, to which he did not return officially until 1956. But Frachon continued to rank highly in the party and attended Political Bureau meetings, preserving thereby the party's tight control over the CGT.

Frachon served on the Comintern Executive from 1928 to 1935. As trade-union leader he exercised sober reflection, independence, intelligence, and a genuine concern for working-class interests. He excelled in the management of strikes, continuing in that capacity through the events of May 1968.

Frachon was part of the leadership during the war, maintaining the PCF's liaisons with the trade unions and coming into conflict with Duclos. He was rumored to have resented the Nazi-Soviet pact and the PCF line from 1939 to 1941, and he very likely aided the independent line pursued by Tillon. Frachon was never as self-assertive as Tillon and Marty, however, and submission to discipline remained characteristic. His major concern remained working-class unity and a Popular Front, which brought him on occasion into conflict with Duclos, ever the partisan of Soviet-sponsored National Fronts, and more often with Thorez, firm believer in the efficacy, for limited periods, of class-against-class tactics. Arguments erupted between Frachon and the leadership during the strike movement of 1947, when he criticized the extreme party tactics, and 1952, when he resented Thorez and Billoux's attempts to foment strikes for political purposes. In 1954, he again resisted the politicization of strikes and was forced to undergo self-criticism at the Thirteenth Party Congress in June 1954. Frachon was a brilliant and effective trade union leader who had more to do than any other Communist with the successful implantation of the PCF in French life.

JEANNETTE VERMEERSCH (1910–   )

As Thorez's wife and most trusted adviser during a critical period of PCF history, Jeannette Vermeersch left a lasting imprint on PCF history. She was born on November 26, 1910, to a working-class family in Lille. Vermeersch was a servant girl from age ten and later apprenticed as a textile worker, joining the Communist party young women's group in 1925, and becoming an official of the textile-workers' union from 1925 to 1930. Her successful service as an administrator of the PCF women's auxiliary brought her to the attention of Thorez in 1932. Two years later, following the dissolution of his marriage, she became his companion and eventually his second wife. Although their marriage was based on affection, politics remained an integral part of the Thorez household, and Vermeersch incurred the resentment of other members of the party leadership. Before the war her official role was confined to women's work. She was instrumental in organizing the shipment of foodstuffs to Republican Spain and accompanied Thorez to Moscow in 1939.

After the war her rise in party ranks was rapid: member of the Central Committee in 1945 and the Political Bureau in 1950, the only woman to rise that high in the Stalinist era. She was also prominent in international women's organizations and a leading figure in the Peace Movement. Vermeersch was a sectarian, continually pushing Thorez toward the extremes and working with Billoux and Guyot. She clashed openly with Marty, Tillon, and Lecoeur and played a role in the elimination of each of them. Her importance was greatly magnified at the time of Thorez's illness, when she became the conduit for his directives in France. Vermeersch joined Billoux on the adoption of the new, harder line in 1952, and she was obliged to undergo self-criticism alongside him when that line was reversed by Duclos. With Thorez's return, however, she was vindicated. It is not an exaggeration to say that she was virtually second-in-command of the PCF until Thorez's death, especially after the eclipse of Duclos in 1956. Vermeersch staunchly backed Thorez in his opposition to de-Stalinization and returned to full approval of the Soviet position in the Brezhnev era. After Thorez's death, however, her role was diminished and she broke with the leadership over its criticism of the Soviet invasion of Czechoslovakia in 1968. After 1968 Vermeersch sought to remain a symbol of the PCF's Stalinist past.

LAURENT CASANOVA (1906–1972)

Laurent Casanova embodied the spirit of unconditional attachment to the USSR as the incarnation of world proletarian revolution. Born in Algeria on October 9, 1906, he studied law and joined the Communist party in 1928. By 1934 he was Secretary of the Communist students taking responsibility for anti-militarist activities within the army until 1936. In 1937 Casanova became personal secretary to Thorez, beginning a close relationship between the two men, which lasted until 1956 and extended to their wives as well. Casanova accepted the Nazi-Soviet pact; mobilized in 1939, he became a German prisoner in 1940 and escaped in 1942 to join the Resistance. He was a national commander of the FTP and a key figure in the insurrection of 1944.

With the war's end, Casanova became a member of the Central Committee and was elected Deputy from the Paris region. He was Minister of War Veterans in 1946, joining the Political Bureau in 1947. His major responsibilities embraced the Peace Movement, which he took over from Tillon and converted into an instrument of Soviet foreign policy. Casanova also supervised PCF intellectuals and prosecuted ideological deviants. He played a role in the Marty-Tillon affair but straddled the Political Bureau's rift of 1952. He visited Thorez in the USSR and accompanied him to France in 1953, emerging with Marcel Servin as firmly in the Secretary General's good graces in 1954.

In 1956 Casanova rallied strongly to de-Stalinization and tried to convince Thorez to do so; Casanova also sought to open the PCF up to the New Left in the struggle against the Algerian war, emerging as principal spokesman for the Khrushchevite current. Thorez liquidated the group in 1961, and Casanova was demoted. He remained in the PCF, however; his rift with Thorez stemmed from pro-Soviet sentiment as well as disagreement over policies. In 1968 Casanova approved the Soviet intervention in Czechoslovakia and hoped to be received back into the leadership's fold. He died disillusioned in 1972, but achieved a final wish when top party dignitaries, including Georges Marchais, appeared at his funeral.

BIBLIOGRAPHICAL ESSAY

The literature in English on the PCF is now impressive. Robert Wohl's *French Communism in the Making* (Stanford, Calif., 1967) covers the formative years and Daniel Brower, *The New Jacobins: The French Communist Party and the Popular Front* (Ithaca, N.Y., 1969) the 1930's. Angelo Tasca (A. Rossi), *A Communist Party in Action: An Account of the Organization and Operations in France* (New York, 1949) is tendencious but still useful. Alfred J. Rieber, *Stalin and the French Communist Party, 1941–1947*, touches on the period covered here as does Ronald Tiersky, *French Communism, 1920–72* (New York, 1974). Two important interpretive French works of political science are now available in English: Georges Lavau, "The PCF, the State and the Revolution," in D. Blackmer and S. Tarrow, eds., *Communists in Italy and France* (Princeton, N.J., 1975) and Annie Kriegel, *The French Communists: Profile of a People* (Chicago, 1972). For the period since 1956 see François Fejto, *The French Communist Party and the Crisis of International Communism* (Cambridge, Mass., 1967), Annette Eisenberg Stiefbold, *The French Communist Party in Transition: PCF-CPSU Relations and the Challenge to Soviet Authority* (New York, 1977), Richard Johnson, *The French Communist Party Versus the Students: Revolutionary Politics in May-June, 1968* (New Haven, Conn., 1972), R. W. Johnson, *The Long March of the French Left* (New York, 1981) and George Ross, *Workers and Communists in France: From Popular Front to Eurocommunism* (Berkeley, Calif., 1982). David Caute, *Communism and the French Intellectuals* (London, 1964) is unsurpassed on its subject. The articles of Thomas H. Greene, "The Electorates of Non-ruling Communist Parties" and "Non-ruling Communist Parties and Political Adaptation," *Studies in Comparative Communism*, IV (Fall 1971) and VI (Winter 1973) deserve mention.

The literature in French is of enormous wealth and diversity; all works listed were published in Paris. The works of Annie Kriegel have been pathbreaking: *Aux Origines du Communisme français, 1914–1920*, 2 Vols. (1964), *Communismes au miroir français* (1974), *Les Grands procès dans les systèmes communistes* (1972), *Le Pain et les roses: jalons pour une histoire des socialismes* (1968), and with Michelle Perrot, *Le Socialisme français et le pouvoir* (1966). Philippe Robrieux has now surpassed Kriegel as the leading authority on the PCF and advocate of *Histoire événementielle*: see his *Maurice Thorez, Vie secrète et vie publique* (Paris, 1975) and *Histoire intérieure du parti communiste*, of which the third volume has now appeared (1980–82). Georges Lavau's *A Quoi sert le Parti communiste français?* (1982) contains the latest views of the founder of the functionalist school. In a similar vein see Bertrand Badie, *Stratégie de la grève: pour une approche fonctionnaliste du PCF* (1976), Pierre Gaborit, "Contribution à la théorie générale des partis politiques: L'exemple du PCF pendant la cinquième République" (Thesis,

University of Paris, 1976), the Colloquium, *Le Communisme en France* (1969) and Domenique Labbé, *Le Discours communiste* (1977).

Other very important works include Jean-Paul Brunet, ed., *L'Enfance du Parti communiste 1920–38* (1972) and *Saint-Denis la ville rouge 1890–1939* (1980), Stephane Courtois, *Le PCF et la guerre: De Gaulle, la Résistance, Staline* (1980), Pierre Daix, *La Crise du PCF* (1978) and *Les Hérétiques du PCF* (1980), Jean Elleinstein, *Le P.C.* (1976), Jacques Fauvet, *Histoire du Parti communiste français* (1976), Jacques Girault, *Sur l'implantation du PCF dans l'entre-deux-guerres* (1977), André Laurens et Thierry Pfister, *Les Nouveaux communistes aux portes du pouvoir* (1977), Yves Le Braz, *Les Rejetés: l'affaire Marty-Tillon* (1974), Jacob Moneta, ed., *Le PCF et la question coloniale* (1971), Nicole Racine et Louis Bodin, *Le Parti communiste français pendant l'entre-deux-guerres* (1972), Emmanuel Sivan, *Communisme et nationalisme en Algérie* (1976), Nicolas Tandler, *L'Impossible biographie de Georges Marchais* (1980) and Alain Touraine, *Mort d'une gauche*.

For the Stalin era there is no substitute for the extensive memoirs that have appeared. Most useful by Communists are François Billoux, *Quand nous étions ministres* (1972), Giulio Ceretti, *A l'ombre des deux T: 40 ans avec Palmiro Togliatti et Maurice Thorez* (1973), Georges Cogniot, *Parti Pris*, 2 Vols. (1976), Jacques Duclos, *Memoires*, 6 Vols. (1968–72), Pierre Durand, *Vingt Ans: Chronique, 1945–1965* (1965), Etienne Fajon, *Ma vie s'appelle liberté* (1976), Léo Figuères, *Jeunesse militante* (1971), Robert Francotte, *Une vie de militante communiste* (1973), Lucien Midol, *La Voie que j'ai suivi* (1973) and André Wurmser, *Fidèlement Votre* (1979). In a separate category are works by dissident Communists which tend to be more critical and hence revealing: Jean Baby, *Critique de Base* (1960), Jean Coin, *J'en appelle à cent mille hommes* (1969), Henri Fiszbin, *Les Boûches s'ouvrent* (1980), Roger Garaudy, *Toute la verité* (1970), Maurice Goldring, *L'Accident: un intellectuel communiste dans le débat du printemps, 1978* (1978), Jean Rony, *Trente ans du parti: un communiste s'interroge* (1978), Antoine Spire, *Profession permanent* (1980) and Helene Parmelin, *Liberez les communistes* (1979).

The work by ex-Communists, many of whom have given extraordinarily objective and detailed accounts of their experiences, include Pierre Daix, *J'ai cru au matin* (1976), Domenique Desanti, *Les Staliniens: une experience poltique, 1944–56* (1975), Edgar Morin, *Autocritique* (1970), Emmanuel Le Roy Ladurie, *Paris-Montpellier: P.C.-P.S.U. 1945–63* (1982), Paul Noirot, *La Memoire ouverte* (1976), Roger Pannequin, *Les années sans suite*, 2 Vols. (1976–77), Marcel Prenant, *Toute une vie à gauche* (1980), Jean Récanati, *Un gentil stalinien* (1980) and extraordinary for their literary power Charles Tillon, *On chantait rouge* (1977) and *Un procès de Moscou à Paris* (1970). Much more tendencious but equally useful with care are Pierre Hervé, *Dieu et César, sont-ils communistes?* (1956), *Lettre à Sartre* (1956), and *La Revolution et les Fétiches* (1956), Auguste Lecoeur, *L'Autocritique attendue* (1955) and *Le Partisan* (1963), and André Marty, *L'Affaire Marty* (1955). Finally some works by Socialists were especially valuable, including Vincent Auriol's *Journal du septennat*, 6 Vols. (1970–78), Léon Blum, *L'Oeuvre de Léon Blum*, 7 Vols. (1954–65), Edouard Depreux, *Souvenirs d'un Militant* (1972), and Jules Moch, *Une si longue vie* (1976).

The study of Communism requires detailed scrutiny of the press. *L'Humanité*, as the central organ, always expressed the party line. With the weekly, *France Nouvelle* and the monthly *Cahiers du Communisme* a fairly complete picture emerges, especially as one learns to read between the lines. Other useful party sources are *For a Lasting Peace, For a People's Democracy* (the Comintern organ), *Les Lettres françaises, La Vie du parti, La Vie Ouvrière* (CGT organ), and *La Nouvelle Critique*. Among the non-Communist press *Le Monde, L'Express, Le Populaire, Unir,* and *Est et Ouest* are usually most rewarding. An invaluable research tool is the *Dossiers de la Presse* maintained in the Fondation Nationale des Sciences Politiques, where one also finds an up-to-date listing of all articles published on political subjects including the PCF.

PCF archives are closed except to certain party historians. A complete holding of the voluminous published record, including all propaganda pamphlets, is held at the Centre d'Etudes et de Recherches Marxistes, formerly the Institut Maurice Thorez. The Archives of the Hoover Institution, Stanford, California, are rich, as are the Archives André Marty, conveniently available in microfilm at several U.S. research libraries, and the *Fonde Angelo Tasca* in the Fondazione Giangiacomo Feltrinelli, Milan. The National Archives of the United States, Record Group 226, Office of Strategic Services, and Diplomatic Branch, Decimal File 851.00 and 851.00B reward the researcher. I was privileged to have access to the personal archives of Philippe Robrieux.

The era of Stalin is still within the living memory of many participants. Among these the following shared their experiences with me in personal interviews: Corentin Boerveau (April 7, 1978), Jean Chaintron (April 7, 1978), Roger Codou (July 19, 1978), Pierre Daix (May 5, 1978), Pierre Durand (April 6, 1978), Etienne Fajon (April 10, 1978), Roger Garaudy (September 11, 1980), Blanchette Gillet (April 11, 1978), Dr. Pierre Klotz (September 18, 1980), Auguste Lecoeur (July 12, 1978), Roger Pannequin (May 2, 1978), Marcel Paul (May 30, 1978), Jean Pronteau (April 25, 1978), and Charles Tillon (May 29, 1978).

INDEX

Beure-Marie, Hubert, 110
Bevin, Ernest, 95
Beyer, Georges, 106, 145
Bidault, Georges, 23, 33, 34, 38, 39, 54, 67, 178
Billoux, François: Algiers group and, 31; article in *Cahiers du Communisme* by, 136, 161, 164, 169; Barbé-Celor group and, 14, 108; biography of, 247; class against class and, 13, 32; criticism of Blum by, 83; criticism of Duclos by, 169-71, 174; criticism of Fajon by, 153; demotion of, 173; de-Stalinization and, 210, 224; historic stature of, 131; loyalty to Thorez of, 111, 135, 140, 141, 142, 148-49, 151, 241; Mendés-France and, 178; as minister, 24, 33, 36, 37, 39, 45, 47, 53, 54; peace movement and, 185; promotion to secretariat of, 175-76; prosecution of, 154; Rosenbergs and, 162; sectarianism of, 142-43, 150, 152, 155, 165; Servin-Casanova and, 217; Thorez succession and, 210
Black Sea mutiny, 32, 144, 154
Bloch-Dassault, Marcel, 44
Blum, Léon: Bolshevism and, 10; Communist criticism of, 83, 204-05; government of 1936, 16-17, 41; government of 1946, 47, 53, 55, 58; Marie government and, 83-84; national front and, 18; 1948 strikes and, 86-87; PCF and, 15, 33-34, 67, 83; Rhineland and, 38; Saar and, 54; Stalin's genius and, 34; Vietnam war and, 184. *See also* Socialists
Bodin, Louis, 13
Bogomolov, Ambassador, 78
Bohr, Niels, 205
Bollaert, Emile, 54, 184
Bolshevism, 9, 10, 13, 46, 99, 119, 123
Bonte, Florimond, 19, 33, 141, 175, 209
Bordeaux, 21-22
Bossus, Raymond, 106
Bouches-du-Rhône, 115, 126
Bouhali, Larbi, 196
Bourbonnais, 124
Bourdet, Claude, 177, 216
Bradley, Omar, 97
Brayance, Alain, 122, 129
Brezhnev, Leonid, 228, 230, 234, 236
Brittany, 21, 44, 69, 105
Browder, Earl, 31
Browderism, 31, 104, 137, 147, 183, 215
Brussels, 20
Buber-Neumann, Margrete, 95
Buchenwald, 37, 42, 44
Budapest, 119

Bukharin, N. I., 10-11
Bulgaria, 154
Bureaucratic degeneration, 212

Cachin, Marcel, 10, 13, 46, 78, 81, 131, 189
Caffery, Jefferson, 33, 38, 55, 69, 70, 83
Cahiers du Communisme, 136-37, 140, 142, 148-50, 153, 161, 205-06
Calas, Raoul, 66, 68, 118
Camphin, René, 21, 68, 106, 171
Carlini, Michel, 63
Carn, Albert, 106
Carrel, André, 84
Carrillo, Santiago, 229
Casanova, Laurent, 32, 39, 78, 97, 110, 137, 165, 193, 194-95, 207, 215-18, 225-26; biography of, 251
Catholics: counter-society and, 116, 118; outstretched hand to, 14, 18, 82, 102; PCF dialogue with, 99, 224; schools and, 138
Catroux, Georges, 31
Celor, Pierre, 11, 13-14
Center of Marxist Research, 173
Central Intelligence Agency (CIA), 209
Ceretti, Giulio, 210
Césaire, Aimé, 187
Ce Soir, 163
Chaintron, Jean, 34, 36, 67, 101, 105-07
Charbonnages de France: CGT control of, 43; government subvention and, 65; purges in, 58, 87; strikes in, 69, 75, 80-82, 85-87, 89
Chaumeil, Jean, 105, 106
Cherbourg, 98
China, 88, 136, 184
Chirac, Jacques, 235
Cinema industry, 79
Clamamus, Jean Marie, 20
Class against class, 11, 12-13, 32, 63, 86, 141; Thorez and, 93, 96, 103, 108, 143, 161, 207, 234. *See also* Parti Communiste Français, Stalinism of; Sectarianism; Stalinism
Clement. *See* Fried, Eugen
Clermont-Ferrand, 83
Coal industry. *See* Charbonnages de France
Codou, Roger, 130
Cogniot, Georges, 46, 70, 107, 140, 153, 155, 203, 205
Cohen, Francis, 233
Cohen, Stephen, 101
Cohn-Bendit, Daniel, 225
Cold War, 25, 53, 135, 147, 154, 161, 163, 232
Collective leadership, 169, 171-72, 209, 211, 213

About the Author

IRWIN M. WALL is Professor of History at the University of California, Riverside. His articles on French history, communism, and socialism have appeared in the *Journal of Contemporary History, French Historical Studies, Journal of European Studies, International Review of Social History,* and *Contemporary French Civilization.*